A HISTORY OF
SEXUAL CUSTOMS

BOOKS BY RICHARD LEWINSOHN

A History of Sexual Customs

Animals, Men and Myths

A History of
SEXUAL
CUSTOMS

RICHARD LEWINSOHN

TRANSLATED BY ALEXANDER MAYCE

HARPER & BROTHERS
NEW YORK

CONTENTS

ILLUSTRATIONS

PLATES

IN THE TEXT

ACKNOWLEDGMENTS

We are indebted to the following for permission to reproduce
illustrations:

Alinari for Plate 16 (top); Archives Photographiques, Paris, for
Plate 16 (bottom); Historia Photo, Berlin, for Plates 4 (bottom),
6 (top), 7 (top), 8, 9 (top), 11 (top), 13, 22 (top right), 24 (top)
and 32 (top left) and pages 146, 160 and 241; Historisches
Bildarchiv Hanke Berneck for Plates 11 (bottom), 17, 18,
19 (bottom left), 20 (bottom), 23 (bottom), 24 (bottom) and
27 (bottom) and pages 143, 149 and 169; Hulton Picture Library
for Plates 28 (top), 28 (bottom left and right), 29 (top), 30 (top)

and 31; Messrs. Macmillan & Co. Ltd. for Plate 5 (bottom) from
Evans: *The Palace of Minos*, Vol. 4; Marcellin Boule & Henri
V. Valois 'Les hommes Fossiles', Paris, 1952, for Plates 1 and 2,
and page 7; Mansell Collection for Plate 19 (top right and bottom
left and right); Museo Correr, Venedig, for Plate 15; Petit Palais,
Paris, for Plate 25; Photo Kleinhempel, Hamburg, for pages
141, 150 and 183; Planet News Ltd. for Plate 32 (bottom right);
Southern Region British Railways for Plate 30 (bottom);
Sterling Studios for Plate 29 (bottom); Ullstein, Berlin, for
Plates 3, 4 (top), 5 (top), 9 (bottom), 10, 12, 14 (top), 19 (top
left), 20 (top), 22 (top left), 22 (bottom), 23 (top), 26, 27 (top),
32 (bottom left and top right) and pages 36, 129, 132, 134
and 339.

A HISTORY OF
SEXUAL CUSTOMS

I

IN THE BEGINNING WAS THE WOMAN

THE sex-instinct is the most animal of human instincts. If we choose these words to open what is primarily a study of the cultural and social aspects of human sex-life throughout history, it is with no intention of branding man's sex-life in advance as something degrading and 'animal'. The sentence simply expresses the fact that animals have carried the forms and habits of their sex-life to a relatively advanced stage of evolution, to which human beings have added little.

A simple and familiar comparison will make our meaning clear. The only natural instinct comparable in intensity with the sexual is that of hunger. Now man is, indeed, a less fastidious feeder than many animals; he is, within certain limits, omnivorous, like the dog and the swine. Nevertheless, there is this clearly-marked difference: that no animal has got beyond the crudest way of preparing its food: tearing it up, and perhaps further softening it. Man, on the other hand, even the most primitive, cooks his meals over a fire—a landmark hardly less important than that of articulate speech.

In the field of sex there is no difference so important as this. The sex-life of animals is by no means 'wild'; in many respects it is more orderly than that of human beings, and fully up to their moral standards. Many animals are monogamous, and model family spouses and parents. There are, of course, neglectful mothers in the animal world, and there are even more unnatural fathers; but, generally speaking, care for the offspring is highly developed—often so marked as to reduce the apparent role of the sex-instinct to that of a preliminary to the reproduction and preservation of the species.

The male animal is usually more aggressive than the female in the sex relationship, but ravishing, rape, mating against the will of the female partner is a physiological impossibility: only a single species of spider shares with mankind this questionable privilege,[1] which has exercised legislators and courts of justice so painfully throughout history. Precisely for this reason, mating in the animal world is usually preceded by a love-game, an approach, courtship or flirtation, in the course of which animals display the brightest and most attractive colours with which nature has endowed them. We now know that in the case of many birds this love-game follows an exact ritual.[2]

The courtship is often accompanied by scenes of jealousy. The conquest of the female is preceded by duels with rivals, or, at least, threatening scenes. In this field, too, man has contributed little that is new. Similarly, sexual anomalies corresponding to almost all forms of human perversion occur in the animal world. In brief, the sex-life of *homo sapiens* has nothing distinctive about it. If it is true that he, of all living creatures, is the latest arrival on the globe, then we must admit that Nature reserved for him hardly anything which she had denied to other species. Only in one respect has the 'paragon of animals' excelled: he unites in himself many attributes otherwise peculiar to a single species of animal.

Eve rises out of the Earth

How much of this variety was bestowed on man in his cradle? Which of his good and bad qualities were his innately, and which did he develop and acquire later? The question is difficult to answer, because we really know nothing whatever about man's sex-life in the first stages of his evolution. It is even often very hard to say, when some fragment of a skeleton comes to light in Europe, Africa, Java or China, whether it was male or female.

The first prehistoric 'woman' to rise out of the earth, the famous Red Lady of Paviland—a skeleton smeared with red ochre, which was found in Wales in 1823—proved later to be a man; in any case, the 'Red Lady' is now no longer regarded as very old.

How men and women lived together in prehistoric times—whether in pairs or in larger groups, in unrestricted sexual promiscuity or under some horde-law, whether the woman was held in high or low esteem—the answers to all these questions, so far as they relate to the 'homonides' of perhaps half a million years back, must remain a matter of hypothesis or, rather, pure guess-work.

If one wants firm ground under one's feet, it is unsafe to go back farther than 20,000 years or so. Our first certain knowledge of human sex-life is derived not from bones but from representations of the human form, usually of women. Our knowledge of these is comparatively recent. It was only towards the end of the nineteenth century that certain statuettes, obviously meant to represent human beings, were discovered in the South of France. Artistically and technically, these were much cruder than the representations of animals which had already been discovered in the caves of southern France and in northern Spain; but they were unquestionably meant to represent human figures, and usually females.

The statuettes are mostly about the size and bulk of a hand, though many are even smaller. In this narrow space the pre-historic sculptors fashioned entire female bodies; women with large, pendulous breasts, disproportionately broad hips, protuberant bellies and prominently figured sexual organs, thus betraying a patent pleasure in emphasizing the sexual *motif*. The face is hardly indicated, except in one case, a graceful girl's head in ivory, which was discovered on the very first site, the 'Pope's Grotto' at Brassempouy, near Bayonne.[3] The peculiar opulence of the lower parts of the body was even more marked in the second important find, that made in the Grimaldi Grottoes near Mentone, and consequently anatomists at first supposed women of that age to have suffered from steatopygy, or excessive fattiness of the buttocks.

The French *savants*, in gentle irony, gave these statuettes the generic name of 'Venus', after the Venus of Milo, although not the smallest proof has been found that they represented goddesses of love, or fertility goddesses. But the name soon caught on, and was in regular use among archaeologists by the summer of 1908, when the most impressive of all such finds was made.

At a small place called Willendorf, on the banks of the Danube, some thirty miles up-stream from Vienna, a workman employed on the construction of a railway found a small figure in reddish stone. He thought it merely a freak of nature, a fortuitous formation which happened to look human, and was going to toss it aside; but, fortunately, three archaeologists on the scene rescued it. Although the figure had been lying only a bare yard or so under the surface, the formation of the rocks, and remains of prehistoric animals found in the same stratum, showed conclusively that this was a piece of palaeolithic sculpture, dating from the same age as the finds in France or, possibly, according to some experts, still earlier. In many specialist works, and in even more guide-books, the 'Venus of Willendorf' still figures as the oldest extant representation of a human being. Today the curious have to content themselves with the sight of a plaster cast of this sculptured Eve, for the original is locked away, safe from light and weather, in the Natural History Museum in Vienna.

This oldest (to date) of all female portraits is a figure in porous sandstone, eleven cm. high. It had been smeared with red ochre, traces of which are still visible, but is otherwise much as it must have been when its author fashioned it, some 20,000 years ago, with a stone scraper and chisel. Like the French statuettes, the Austrian Eve is naked; she conceals nothing. It is impossible to improve on the description given in his first report by one of its discoverers:

It represents a fat, over-blown woman, with large lactatory glands, a prominent belly, and full hips and thighs, but not actually steatopygous. These are very much the dimensions of the Venus of Brassempouy. As in that figure, the labia minora are clearly indicated. The presumption of steatopygy, which the heavy thighs of the French figure (which is very badly damaged) led experts to form, is not confirmed. The hair is represented by a raised spiral strip running round the skull; the sculptor has not troubled about the face at all; the features—eyes, nose, mouth, chin, ears—are not so much as indicated. The arms are disproportionately small, the fore-arms and hands being expressed only by shallow strips of relief above the breasts. The knees are very highly developed; the shins are given calves, but are greatly foreshortened, the feet omitted altogether. The whole figure shows that the artist possessed an excellent artistic command of the human form, but that he deliberately over-emphasized those parts concerned with the reproductive function, and the adjacent parts, while under-emphasizing the rest by the technique still used by caricaturists today.[4]

It is not surprising that, though they named her Venus, men regarded this ancestress with consternation. Up to that date people had pictured prehistoric Eve as a fascinating beauty. Each age depicted her according to its own taste. The Eve of the early Middle Ages, which were still influenced by the Roman ideal of beauty, was rather broad and heavy. In the Gothic period she was over-slender, with seductive eyes and theatrical poses. In the Renaissance she was a generously-built, high-bosomed, symmetrically-proportioned woman, almost too noble to perform her mission. But never had any form of art, realistic or stylized, produced a woman so monstrous as the Venus of Willendorf. Whether created for the purpose of a religious cult or not, she was the work of an artist who was capable of observation, though concerned not with a portrait but with a female type. If this type bore even the remotest resemblance to her contemporaries' ideal of beauty, sex-life in the palaeolithic age must have been quite unerotic, for this Venus was no more than a lump of fat, and surely far from attractive to any man; no fertility symbol, but a matron deformed by child-bearing. This authentic prehistoric relic was sexually repulsive, even by comparison with the anthropologists' repellent reconstructions of Neanderthal woman, or other imaginary 'missing links'.

On closer inspection, however, even this representation

suggests that palaeolithic man did not regard woman as purely a child-bearing machine; that even this woman had attempted to make herself attractive. She wears bracelets on both arms, and certain marks on the head seem meant to represent some adornment—possibly, some archaeologists think, a hood trimmed with mussels, such as has been found on similar pictures from eastern Europe. It is probable, too, that the Venus of Willendorf represented only a particularly unprepossessing local type—and not necessarily an 'Austrian' one. It is conceivable that this fat-bodied Danubian Venus may have been imported from the East. Some of the representations of the female form which have been found since in other parts of Europe are much more attractive, and this is probably due not only to the artist, but also to the women who served him as models, and above all to a male taste which preferred proportion and grace to corpulence. Two French ladies exploring the *Roc aux Sourciers* at Aigle-sur-l'Anglin, in the French Department of Vienne, recently discovered a bas relief of three women whose classical lines would not be out of place in a Renoir painting or a Maillol statue.[5]

The Cult of the Woman

Only one feature is common to almost all palaeolithic representations: all the woman's sexual characteristics—not only the secondary features such as the breasts, the broad hips, and the curved pelvis, but also the primary organs are displayed on many sculptures and bas reliefs, and with complete anatomic fidelity, although sometimes more clearly than in nature. In any case, the Mount of Venus is emphasized. In the stylized representations—and some of the palaeological female pictures, such as the Venus of Lespugue, are highly stylized—this becomes a triangle, formed by the fold of the belly and the contours of the thighs. It is this triangle, not the long trapezoid which adolescents of today scribble on walls, that is the popular female sex-characteristic, the cunnus, of Stone Age man.

One reason for the pleasure which men obviously found in these sexual pictures may have been a lack of opportunity to see the organs in real life. For the men and women of the Aurignacian age, in which most of these works were produced, were no nudists. Cold winds, if not prudery, forced them to clothe themselves. The inclement climate allowed them to leave their twilit caves only during a few months in the year, when they went hunting; the women most likely showed themselves abroad more rarely still. The sight of a woman naked was therefore an unusual experience for a man.

It does not follow from the fact that men were curious about women's sexual peculiarities that sex-life was coarse and licentious. The oldest known representation of a love-scene, a relief in the cave of Laussel (this was formerly thought, erroneously, to depict a birth) shows a man and a woman mating in amity. A later picture, scratched on a bone, discovered in the grotto of Isturitz, in the extreme south-west of France, shows an erotic caricature which also indicates that love-life in the Stone Age was completely respectable. It shows a man with hands lifted in supplication and yearning eyes, gazing up at a naked woman who is no paragon of beauty. To make the meaning perfectly clear, an arrow is engraved on the woman's thigh. Here is no violence, no licentiousness—rather a comically exaggerated adoration of the female form, which is, indeed, represented in much more robust terms than that of her adorer, whose face displays a super-abundance of stupidity, anxiety and desire. The man, in short, is 'taken off'. It is the prototype of the erotic cartoon: the woman is the victor, the man the eternal fool.

These pictorial reports of sex life in the Stone Age are undoubtedly one-sided; their

Erotic scene. Engraved on a bone from the cave of Isturitz, S. France. Palaeolithic.

authors, clearly, are men. If the women had transmitted to us their experiences and views on their sex-life, the picture might look very different. This one-sided nature of the sources is indubitably a drawback which makes itself apparent not only in prehistoric ages but up to the most modern times. A history of sex-life which is founded, as far as possible, on contemporary documentation is inevitably a history of women as seen through men's eyes. Men idealize woman and distort her; they always tend to represent themselves as the weaker partner in the sex relationship, precisely because they are the more desirous; they seek and claim, while the woman consents and gives. They record the heroic deeds performed by themselves for woman and for the community, but it is much more rarely that they set down the work which, at all stages of civilization, woman has performed for man. This gives even humanity's earliest artistic manifestations the aspect of a woman-cult.

It would, however, probably be quite erroneous to attribute any religious significance to the word 'cult'. A reaction against the materialist outlook of the nineteenth century led to an attempt, headed by Reinach[6] and Frazer,[7] to invest all early representations into which sex entered with a magical-religious significance. Even marks as unambiguous as the cunnus triangle or the arrow in the Isturitz love-scene were interpreted as magic symbols. Any female picture that one hung round one's neck had to be an amulet. The stout Venus statuettes had to be religious fertility cult-symbols,[8] or possibly goddesses of family life, simply because some statuettes of this kind had been discovered in front of a hearth in south Russia.

But the striking feature about the palaeolithic pictures of women is precisely their complete concentration on the sex aspect as distinct from the reproductive. Many of the women, indeed, look as though they were pregnant, but no single representation of a mother and child, no 'Madonna', has survived from this epoch. The artists of the Stone Age were not interested in the idea of reproduction—which is natural enough, for the men of that age were hunters, and hunters usually attach no great importance to large families. The hunting-grounds were, it is true, rich in the later Aurignacian Age; great herds of wild horses abounded, and horse-flesh probably constituted the main article of men's diet.[9] Yet none of the many pictorial representations dating from that age suggests any special interest in children.

The next age, the Magdalenian, was one of cultural brilliance. It is the age of the great cave-paintings. Materially, however, it was a hard time for humankind. The climate had grown colder, the vegetation was scantier, big-game hunting less rewarding. Men huddled in their caves and dugouts, closer than ever, and ventured less into the open air. There is nothing to suggest, however, that any decisive change took place in the man-woman relationship; neither does the social position of women seem to have altered perceptibly. After man had discovered the spear and—a little (that is, some thousand years) later—the bow and arrow, and was thus able to go hunting big game, the economic role of woman became secondary. She was responsible for the vegetable diet which was still necessary to supplement the meat brought home by the man. These duties, especially as they had to be combined with those of bringing up a family, were as strenuous as the hunt, and not without danger from beasts of the forest, but they lacked heroic interest and dramatic action. The artists of the Magdalenian period, who set down so many minutely observed hunting-scenes, have bequeathed us no single picture of women at work.

The earliest picture which may possibly represent a woman not as a sexual being but working, dates from the age known to archaeologists as the mesolithic or Middle Stone Age, *circa* 16,000 B.C. Northern Europe was by then covered with ice and men had moved south, and it is from the south that this curious document comes: it was discovered in an artificial cave in the province of Valencia, in south-eastern Spain. It shows a human figure standing on an ingeniously constructed rope ladder and collecting honey out of a bees' nest into a basket. The figure is unnaturally slim, the style quite African. Most likely it is a female figure; but opinions on the point differ.

Semen and Fruit

A great social change, which brought with it far-reaching effects on sexual life, set in when the climate altered and Europe gradually became ice-free. Geologists put the end of the last Ice Age at about 12,000 B.C., but this was followed by a period of great drought, and it was probably another 6,000 years before human beings were able to maintain themselves in the valleys of the larger rivers of the Mediterranean area. The age of the huntsman was over. The big beasts had perished in the cold, or migrated elsewhere. Gradually, however, men came to realize that they could keep themselves fed without shooting or stabbing every beast that came within range. Stock-breeding replaced hunting. Now stock-breeders have to observe how much time elapses between fertilization and birth.

As stock-breeding itself was insufficient to maintain life in most districts, men had to set to work to extract other edible fruits from the earth. We do not know what people it was that discovered the device of putting the grains of wild plants in the ground, to produce more grains. It is believed that rice was first cultivated in south-west Asia, and that, soon after, barley was being grown in the Nile valley. The sowing of the earth drew attention to the process of reproduction. It was now that man became fully conscious of the conception of fertility, which is usually strange to hunter-peoples. They realized that fertility was not something automatic; that nature, the sky and the earth must help, but that first there must be a grain of seed. Man is able to promote, and up to a point, to regulate fertilization. As this was the case with plants and animals, human reproduction was probably something similar. It needed no great learning to reach this conclusion. All the same, if one wanted to have a child, it was well to see that the weather was right, to take account of the celestial signs and the influences of the moon and the stars. A large family was counted a heavenly blessing, and was much desired, for agriculture required many hands.

It is fairly clear that women from the first took a very large part in this novel work on the land. Even if prehistoric peoples did not leave agriculture entirely to the women, as the backward tribes of our own age do, yet women had to do most of the work of sowing; the cutting of the ripe ears may have been the man's job.

On top of this heavy labour in the fields, women soon had another function to fulfil. As there were no longer enough animals—and in the warmer climate furs were, in any case, disagreeably hot—man had to devise another type of clothing for himself. At first clothes were probably produced by an adaptation of the basket-weaving process, which was already highly developed. Hairs, sheep's wool and flax were used as material. Even after the discovery of the spindle, which produced a more even thread, it must have been a very heavy labour; and it fell exclusively on the women.

Jus Maternum *and* Patria Potestas

The extraordinarily important economic role played by woman in the foundation of our civilization was partly responsible for one of the boldest and most controversial sex-theories of the past century: the doctrine of *jus maternum*. According to this theory, human beings originally lived in complete promiscuity, and since no one knew who was the father of any child, the one certain physical relationship was that between the child and its mother. Consequently, mothers, and women in general, were highly regarded. They were also the politically dominant class. Gynaecocracy was the original political form among all peoples of antiquity. It was only gradually, after a prolonged struggle, that a new form of human co-existence was evolved, that of the monogamous family. Now it was known to which father the children belonged, and thereby the man became the dominant partner in the sexual partnership, the family, the tribe, the State. *Jus paternum* replaced *jus maternum*.

Theories of this sort had been advanced before, notably by the French Jesuit missionary Lafitau[10], who found a form of *jus maternum* in practice among the North American Indians at the beginning of the eighteenth century. These theories had, however, gained few disciples, so that when, in 1861, the Swiss jurist, Johann Jakob Bachofen, published his fundamental work on *Das Mutterrecht* (*jus maternum*) his views passed for a new, highly-important discovery. The book came at a fortunate moment. It was an age in which the numerous discoveries had awakened a very keen interest in everything connected with pre-history, and a general determination to re-cast all theories on the past development of nature and of mankind. It was two years after the publication of Darwin's *Origin of Species*, and of Marx's first great critical analysis of society; everywhere, in physics, in chemistry, in medicine, the foundations of established authority were tottering.

Bachofen seemed the more reliable as an authority because he was personally anything but a revolutionary. Nevertheless, the theory produced by him was of a nature to shatter one of the pillars of the existing social order, the belief in the natural superiority of man over woman.

Bachofen denied that nature had in any way ordained man to figure as ruler over the family. The natural right was woman's, and she had proved in the past that she knew how to exercise it. Man was a usurper. Bachofen did not deplore this development; on the contrary, he regarded it as an advance. Nevertheless, he thought it necessary to give man a history lesson, to show him that he had not always been the master, and was not even master everywhere today. Where men were still near to nature, the body ruled, and the body was woman. Only when the spirit conquered did man succeed to the rule.

Basically, the theory was very flattering to the male sex, but it did not enhance its prestige, for a ruler who has not always been ruler can be evicted again one day. Bachofen had first been led to formulate his theory by reading a passage in Herodotus, who writes that among the Lycians men took their mothers' family names, not their fathers'. Bachofen collected some further data from antiquity, and from certain 'primitive' peoples of modern times among whom nomenclature and inheritance pass through the maternal line. But in general, his views were based on philosophical and general cultural-historical considerations. Once the question had been thrown open, however, his theories received powerful reinforcement from British and American writers. The richest material was contributed by an American ethnologist, Lewis N. Morgan, who had watched the transition from a system based on *jus maternum* to one of *jus paternum* taking place among the Iroquois Indians.[11]

Fortified by Bachofen's ideas, Morgan evolved a system of the sex and family 'law' of primitive peoples[12] which appeared to solve all riddles in this field, and established a gradation of sex-relationships, both for prehistoric man and for the surviving 'savage' peoples. It was only in the primitive horde that complete promiscuity had been the rule; in the organized hunter tribes sex-life was already strictly regulated. Each tribe was divided into groups, and the men of any group could marry only a woman out of another group; but the marriage was collective, not individual. As it was not known who the father was, the mother remained the decisive factor in all questions of family relationships and of inheritance. Only when production had so far developed that two human beings, man and woman, could maintain themselves economically, by stock-breeding and agriculture, without the constant need of help from their fellow-tribesmen, did the family split off and become a monogamous unit. Monogamy thus went hand in hand with the evolution of private property.

As the man became economically the more active and stronger partner, so the woman fell under his domination, sexually and otherwise. She became 'his' woman, with all the servitudes which a ruler may impose on his subjects. She now exists only for him. Unfaithfulness on the part of the woman is visited with the harshest penalties, repudiation or even death, while the man reserves to himself the right to have intercourse with other women and, in many countries, to keep several women as permanent possessions, to the extent permitted by his means. The natural superiority of the woman—natural because she is more closely connected with the offspring—is succeeded by the artificial, unnatural primacy of the man.

Bachofen's and Morgan's theories of evolution were especially welcomed in 'progressive' learned circles. The Socialists made the *jus maternum* part of their catechism. Marx read Morgan with enthusiasm; Engels[13] and his pupil Bebel[14] popularized the American ethnologist's theories and used them as a weapon in their campaign for the emancipation of women, although conditions among primitive peoples gave only weak support to the case for equality of rights in modern society or, *a fortiori*, in the socialist state of the future.

But while these theories became the commonplaces of 'educated' society, the specialists brought up ever heavier artillery, and made one breach after another in this artificial doctrinal structure. That traces of *jus maternum* are to be found among many primitive peoples, and also among peoples of antiquity, especially in Greece and Rome, is undeniable. But one must distinguish between 'matrilinear' and 'matriarchal'. That origin is traced through the mother is no proof that the woman was the ruler of the family, and still less of the tribe. If one surveys the mass of archaeological and ethnological material, pure matriarchy seems to be the exception rather than the rule. Where women were really recognized as rulers, there was generally a man behind them who exercised the effective power; if not the woman's husband, then her brother.

But even less certain appeared the suggestion that men originally lived in sexual promiscuity. No one knows what the position was in prehistoric times, but analogies from among the surviving primitive peoples show monogamy to be the practice precisely in the most primitive hordes, which possess only vestiges of tribal organization.[15] This is not surprising; monogamy is usual among the anthropoid apes—although it might be said that the forms of social existence among these, man's nearest presumptive relatives, are so multifarious and so mutually contradictory that the only safe generalization is to say that generalizations are impossible.[16]

So it is today with our views on primitive human society. The Tables of the Law which science thought it had erected a hundred years ago have been broken, and so far there is nothing to put in their place. Research into the particular has destroyed the universal picture. After centuries of laborious inquiry, scholars are more disunited, more sceptical than ever. One of the leading contemporary specialists on sex questions, Bronislaw Malinowski of London, once summed up the position in these words: 'As a member of the "inner ring", I may say that whenever I meet Mrs. Seligman or Dr. Lowie, or discuss matters with Radcliffe-Brown or Kroeber [all specialists of high standing], I become at once aware that my partner does not understand anything in the matter, and I end usually with the feeling that this also applies to myself. This refers to all our writings on kinship, and is fully reciprocal.'[17]

2

THE HUSBAND IS THY LORD AND MASTER

PREHISTORIC men are for us the anonymous representatives of a species. In order to distinguish them, we name them after the places in which the traces of their existence were first discovered. We use the geological stratification of these places, the anatomical characteristics of the fossil bones, the degree of perfection of the implements, and the style of the paintings, as our guides to reconstruct a rough chronology, which cannot be accurate to within a few thousand years. Anything more exact must be based on bold hypotheses. But the human beings whom we fit into these chronological tables remain spectral outlines; they have always something abstract about them.

History begins only when names appear which oral or written tradition attaches to specific individuals. Even though the names may be less authentic than the fossil skeleton of some pre-historic man, they yet invest their bearers with a breath of individual reality which the anonymous lacks. He who has a name has a father and a mother, and often the name itself gives some indications of who they were. He who has a name belongs to a stock, a tribe, a people, whose existence does not need to be proved by craniometry. In this sense, even legendary names possess more reality than the nameless Unknowns of pre-history.

Hard as archaeologists and historians have striven to bridge the two ages, a great gulf still yawns between the nameless era of pre-history and the beginnings of the historic period, with its names. All of a sudden our eyes behold great empires ruled by mighty monarchs, courtiers, priestly castes who prescribe to men what to do, and what to leave undone. Instead of a few poor

villages acquainted at the most with one craft—the potter's—
besides that of agriculture, vast cities and a wealth of callings;
buildings the construction of which called for complex mathematical calculations; masters and slaves, overseers and merchants.

Whence came all this activity? Who created this new world?
Probably it was men: we know something of a few. This is not,
however, quite certain; it is in any case noteworthy that as soon
as names appear we hear tell of women, and women in very
high places: queens ruling as well as kings, high priestesses as well
as high priests serving temples and men. Often women appear
to take precedence—not as dominant partners in the sex-
relationship (although this may sometimes have been a factor), but
because woman ranks as the natural link between the generations. If one traces the family tree farther back, this ceases to
apply: man appears to have been on the better footing with the
gods, but for the last and the penultimate generation the mother
unquestionably offers a better guarantee of the legitimacy of the
offspring than the father. Nature has so ordained it. Men may
invent laws to disguise this fact, but they cannot do away with it
altogether.

Class Morality

Then was the original form of society matriarchal? Put in such
general terms, the thesis is untenable, for it presupposes a pansexualism for the existence of which there is no proof at any stage
of social development. Sex is always important—more so in some
ages, less in others—but never all-important. Man has never
been governed exclusively by his loins. Other instincts and needs
have always demanded their rights: in the oldest organized states
known to history we already find precedence between the sexes
following a tripartite class-stratification, many traces of which
are recognizable in our own day.

The upper class thinks in terms of the line. It invokes descent
either from a god or from some great ancestor. All descendants
of this august forefather, without distinction of sex, are in
principle regarded as equal in rank. They may not all be entitled

to wear the crown or to receive an equal portion of the inheritance, for power cannot be shared *ad libitum*, nor property subdivided *ad infinitum*, or the power would vanish. The inheritance
has therefore to be regulated by special laws, which vary from
country to country and from age to age. If it can be physiologically justified, so much the better. The so-called 'natural law' of
primogeniture was certainly in origin devised in obedience to
pragmatic considerations of this kind. The seed grows weak with
age: therefore the first to bear fruit is the best. Yet even those
members whom nature has blessed less, enjoy the social privileges
due to them by virtue of their descent.

These privileges are enjoyed by woman and man alike. The
consequence in many ages is that upper-class women, like their
brothers, enjoy considerable sexual freedom—provided they do
not adulterate the blood by intercourse with base-born men. For
begetting and conceiving are not the same thing. The man who
bestows his princely virility on a woman of the people ennobles
her, but a princess who gives herself to a man of lower rank
debases her own race.

In the middle class, later known as the bourgeoisie, woman's
social position is from the first far less advantageous. Her inferiority is dictated by economic factors. The man alone practises
a trade, as merchant, artisan or civil servant, and thus earns the
family livelihood, while the woman does work which is unpaid
and therefore—as in our own day—is not counted as income. She
consumes and spends, and is consequently regarded, from the
material point of view, as a debit. It depends on the man's income whether he makes do with one such burden or whether he
can treat himself to several wives; but in either case the woman
must be faithful to him, for even if, legally speaking, she is not
purely his chattel, she yet belongs to him; he has acquired her in
order that she should conceive and bring up his children, not
those of some other man.

In the lower classes poverty makes the sexes equal. Polygamy
is too expensive, even brothels are beyond the means of many.
Vocational activity, too, brings the sexes together. In the fields

young men and girls work together in a highly unrestricted atmosphere. The hayrick and the green meadow-grass were the most convenient of bridal beds long before the pastoral poets sang their praises; mankind would have been far less numerous without them. In ancient China, conditions in the fields approached promiscuity. The idylls were, however, not long-lived. When the girls reached the age of twenty, the youths that of thirty, they had to contract themselves. Even this, however, was no marriage in civil law, no *huen*; the peasant derived only from a *pen*, an association.[18]

In the Near East, too, marriage sealed by a contract was a privilege of the higher classes. In Egypt the plebs acquired this right only in the great social revolution which took place about the year 2,000 B.C.[19] It now not only advanced its social status, but became entitled to dispose of land and houses. To exercise these rights, however, a man had first to possess some property. The only real gain achieved by the poor was that they were now granted a burying-place on which the family could perform the cult of the dead, thus obtaining entry into the next world, which had previously been denied to them. In Babylon marriage did not bring them even this advantage. The Babylonian family law, with its elaborate regulations for inheritance, and its classification of the positions and duties of junior wives and concubines, is framed exclusively to meet the requirements of the wealthy classes: it is meaningless to the proletariat. Indeed, the many marriage contracts from Mesopotamia which have come down to us relate exclusively to marriages involving considerable dispositions of property.

The lower classes usually lived in monogamy, but since they had nothing to lose and nothing to gain, it was the man's and the woman's own affair how they got on together. The State only concerned itself with the issue, this because the rulers of Babylon aimed at the maximum increase of population. They needed man-power to till the fields, build the temples and palaces, fight the wars and extend the frontiers of the realm. The progeny of all classes had therefore to be protected. A woman attempting to destroy the child in her womb by any means whatsoever—and several such methods were known in antiquity—was bound to a pillory and whipped. If she died before the punishment had been inflicted, she was refused ritual burial. A person who accidentally brought about a miscarriage by striking or pushing a pregnant woman had to pay a fine and do a month's forced labour for the king. It is true that the penalties were carefully graded according to the victim's status: the fruit of a bourgeois' daughter's womb was five times as costly as that of a slave-girl, three times that of a prostitute. In all cases, however, the somewhat enigmatic rule applied that the culprit had to replace the woman's 'living creature'.

Incest in Egypt

Among the rulers of Mesopotamia there is only one woman's name, and that the name of a woman who most probably never existed: the legendary Semiramis, the reputed foundress of Babylon and architect of its hanging gardens. In Egypt no woman before Cleopatra achieved fame so lasting; nevertheless, Egyptian history is filled from the beginning with women who ruled *de facto* and were often more powerful than any male Pharaoh. The first queens, Neit-Hetep, wife of Menes, and Mert-Neit, wife of Usaphais, were princesses from the Delta and brought their husbands dowries of fertile land—an asset almost more important to rulers of all ages than physical fruitfulness itself. Egypt set the example of the political marriage, the union of individuals which automatically results in the forced unification of whole peoples.

Sexually, these earliest Pharaohs appear to have been completely normal. It was only many centuries later that marriages between brother and sister came into fashion. In some dynasties it was absolutely compulsory for the heir to the throne to marry his sister: otherwise he would not be recognized as legitimate ruler. Later the tradition died out, and kings looked for their consorts in other princely families, but it was revived from time to time: for the last time in the Hellenistic age. Alexander the Great's successors, the Ptolemies (a Greek dynasty), practised marriage between brother and sister for three hundred years without noticeably bad physical effects.

This practice has been derived from religious roots, in particular from the cult of the divine pair, Isis and Osiris, whose generative power survived death. But many religions know precedents of this kind, and they have not given birth to political institutions. Any family tree, divine or human, that traces its origin back to a pair of first ancestors, must assume incest between parents and children or between brothers and sisters. Cain and Abel had no other way of reproducing their kind.

A rationalist explanation seeks to link up this Pharaonic practice with the law of inheritance. Under Egyptian law the man was the owner of the family property, but on death it passed to the blood-relations of the wife. A Pharaoh who wished to keep together the family property—which often amounted to the entire country—and to prevent it from falling into the wrong hands, was therefore forced to marry his own sister.[20] This sounds plausible enough, but it still only takes the question one step farther back without solving it. If marriages between brother and sister were considered unnatural, why was the family law not altered? Sexual union between brother and sister was obviously not regarded as a perversion, at least in the highest circles. In Egyptian love-poetry,[21] which is very sophisticated and uninhibited, lovers address one another as 'brother' and 'sister' precisely when they are conversing on the most intimate subjects, and that was, in fact, often their relationship.

The attitude towards incest varied very widely, both among primitive peoples and in the nations of antiquity. The Jews of the pre-Mosaic era allowed marriage between children of the same father, but not of the same mother. Abraham was free to marry Sarah, who was his step-sister. Later the rule became stricter. The detailed legislation on sex in Leviticus absolutely forbids not only marriage between brothers and sisters but any sexual relationship between near blood-relatives. In Old Persia there existed a 'holy' marriage between close relatives, whereas in India Gautama Buddha forbade marriage within the sixth degree of affinity. Babylon ignored the question, while in Egypt, as we have seen, marriage between brothers and sisters was at times a State institution and was never prohibited. It is true that when the Pharaohs took their sisters to be their legitimate consorts, they kept enough concubines to save their marital lives from excess of monotony. Rameses the Second is said to have been the father of 160 children. Nor do the women who sat on the throne of the Pharaohs seem always to have contented themselves with their brothers' attentions. Cleopatra, the last of the Ptolemaic line, was assuredly not the first occasionally to bestow her royal favours elsewhere.

It is well attested that wives of the Pharaohs, whether their sisters or not, played an important part in all ages of Egyptian history, and often completely dominated their husbands. In the disturbed times around the middle of the second millennium the women came to occupy so dominant a position that their husbands often ranked simply as prince-consorts. The balance was restored by an anti-feminist movement originating in the army, and the name of the great Queen Hatshepsut was erased from all public buildings. But in the end the women proved the victors after all. If they could not rule the country from the palace, they managed it through the temple. Under the XXIII Dynasty, in the eighth century B.C., a princess became High Priestess of the temple of Ammon in Thebes, an institution which fulfilled approximately the same role as Delphi in Greece, enshrining oracles which had to be consulted before any important political decision was taken. Here, therefore, high politics were decided. The High Priestess could, indeed, take no husband except her god, but she was allowed to adopt a young girl, who ultimately became her successor. So the temple of Ammon became the seat of a kind of female unofficial government, which lasted over two hundred years, down to the conquest of Egypt by Persia.

The Law of Hammurabi

While Egypt presents itself to the later world, in story and in picture, as a feminist land, a land of ambitious, clever, beautiful, gracious and intriguing women, in Babylon, the other great State of the Near East, the male element was obviously dominant. Even here certain institutions existed which might be interpreted as survivals of an earlier matriarchy, but in historical times public affairs were in the hands of men. Woman's role was to bear children, to attend to the household, and, not least, to minister to man's pleasure. This still did not mean that man sought, as in later days, to reduce woman to complete subjection. She was his partner, a human being to be treated as such, not a head of cattle with which he could do what he would. She had her duties, but also her rights, and in many respects she was in practice his equal before the law.

Babylon was the true forerunner of Rome. The Babylonian State was a State ordered by law: written codes informed the citizens what they might do, what not, and what penalties awaited those who transgressed. At the beginning of the second millennium before Christ, King Hammurabi codified the existing legislation and the most important judicial decisions in a single document which then remained in force for many centuries. Hammurabi's legislation contains a larger social element than most codes of antiquity. It protects the weak, including women. Its chief interest, however, is in the maintenance of property. The Babylonians were practical-minded men, and their legislators skimmed lightly over principles; their object was to clarify and decide typical problems of day-to-day life.

It is true that Babylon's religious legends say that man was created to give the gods pleasure. In this world, however, the thoughts of the Babylonians centred on money. There was, as yet, no minted money, but bars of silver and measures of barley performed its function. Most of the family law in Hammurabi's codification dealt with money, real and personal property, sales, loans and mortgages; but it also attached importance to the regulation of human relationships within the family, between man and wife and their relatives. Family law, in the strict sense, is the subject of no fewer than sixty-four of the 252 articles of the Code.

The basis of the family was the First Marriage, which was confirmed by a marriage contract. The husband might, in addition, keep one or more concubines, whom he might even take into his house, especially if his wife was ailing or barren. If a man had no children, even by his concubines, and insisted on having issue, he might, in exceptional cases, while retaining his legitimate spouse, also take a second wife. The second wife, however, occupied only a subordinate position, in token whereof she had to wash the first wife's feet.

Under the older legislation, a young man who had seduced an innocent girl was obliged to ask her parents for her hand. To refuse to marry her could cost him his head. This severity was afterwards relaxed. Hammurabi's code no longer mentioned pre-marital intercourse. The State only began to interest itself in its subjects' affairs of the heart at the point when a man himself decided to marry. As marriage entailed extensive financial obligations, all details had to be carefully regulated in advance.

The commercial side was accomplished in two stages: first the man bestowed wedding-gifts on the bride, then he received from the girl's parents a dowry, which was not, however, a purchase price, but only a contribution towards the cost of maintaining the wife. If, as happened not infrequently, the wife remained in her parents' home after marriage, the husband had to pay the parents a sum towards her upkeep. The dowry remained the wife's property in law, and it was at her disposal if her husband put her away to take another wife.

The grounds for divorce were numerous and fairly loosely defined. The principal ground was childlessness: naturally, since the purpose of marriage was to give the man children. A husband could, however, also divorce his wife if she became incapacitated by ill-health from carrying out her domestic duties, or if for any other reason she proved a bad housewife. In all such cases a unilateral declaration by the husband sufficed to dissolve the marriage: the wife then took her dowry with her—or what was left of it. If there were children, the husband was responsible for their upkeep, but he had no other obligations. If he wanted to be magnanimous, and if the judge agreed, he could keep the wife on in his house as a slave without formally putting her away.

All this sounds very cruel, but it was mitigated by the provision that the wife, in her turn, could divorce her husband if he behaved badly and neglected his conjugal duties too crassly; she, however, needed the consent of the Court. If successful, she recovered her dowry, and also received indemnification, and was entitled to marry again. Thus, the divorce laws of ancient Babylon were not, fundamentally, very different from those of the modern world, except that under them divorce was easier for men than for women.

The differences in respect of fidelity were larger. If the husband neglected his wife too much, she could leave him; she had no further redress. Infidelity on the part of the man entailed no punishment except a possible indemnification to the wife. An unfaithful wife, on the other hand, risked being thrown into the water to drown. If she was caught *in flagranti* with her lover, both were bound and thrown into the water; where the guilt was not proved, the god was made judge: the suspected couple were thrown into the water unbound, and the god of the river decided whether they were guilty. Throwing into water was a favourite penalty in Babylonian justice. A Don Juan or a loose woman needed to be a good swimmer to escape a premature end in the Tigris or the Euphrates.

Another very harsh provision allowed a husband, subject to the consent of the Courts, to lodge not only his wife but also his children with a creditor as security for debts: he was thus quit not only of his debts but also, if he chose, of his wife.

To prevent this device from being used as a cheap substitute for divorce, the law limited to three years the period for which the wife could be pledged. It is improbable that many husbands took advantage of this right. Later, however, the period was lengthened, and in the Neo-Babylonian Empire the business of pledging wives and children developed into what amounted to a specialized branch of slave-trading.

After the Assyrian Conquest the law became even more

drastic. Besides the ordeal by water, an unfaithful wife might lose her nose, while her lover could be castrated. Bawds who procured married women had their ears cut off. Assyrian morals, then, were capable of anatomical differentiations.

Temple Prostitution

The stricter the provisions of family law, the greater is the urge felt by men for a free zone in which they can satisfy their sexual desires without incurring subsequent obligations, The woman must be paid for her services, but has no further claim on her visitor. If he pleases, he may come again, but even frequent or regular visits create no legal obligation. The complicated man-wife relationship produced by marriage and concubinage is replaced by a simple transaction. The need to worry over moral and material consequences (although not necessarily physiological ones) is eliminated. There remains only the sexual act, the sole and undisguised purpose, without either a long prologue or an epilogue.

This extreme convenience, from the man's point of view, is the foundation of prostitution. It exists among very primitive peoples; it appears as a firmly-rooted institution in the oldest historical times. In the third millennium B.C. it was in full swing in the oriental empires, which at that time embodied the most advanced civilizations yet achieved by man. Everywhere it was a public institution, and connected with the temples, which derived part of their revenues from it; and everywhere it was bi-sexual: both males and females were engaged in the trade. The fact that prostitutes acted as servants of the gods and that contemporary reports call them 'holy' does not alter the realistic nature of their business.

It is certainly no accident that our sources for this branch of sexual economy are particularly abundant for Babylon, the most practical of all the eastern States. Temple prostitution was once believed to have been a speciality of the Semitic peoples; in fact, however, the earliest recorded temple brothel was in the State of a non-Semitic people, the Sumerians, in the sanctuary of Anu, the supreme deity, in Uruk. The prostitutes were dedicated to the cult of Anu's lustful daughter, Ishtar. The female prostitutes lived in a special house, the Gagum, under the supervision of a manageress. There were three categories of prostitutes, the Kizrete, the Senhate and the Harimàte. The last-named enjoyed a particularly evil reputation: the man who fell into their hands, said an old text, was lost.[22]

Much the same reproaches were levelled against the Harimàte as against prostitutes in later ages: 'Wed no Harimàte who possesses countless men. In thy ill-fortune she will not succour thee. Before the judge she will speak against thee. Respect and subjection she knoweth not. She will assuredly bring thy house down. Therefore cast her out whose eye follows the steps of strange men. Every house into which she cometh is brought low. He who marries her will find neither happiness nor prosperity.'

This warning, which is obviously addressed to a young man, suggests that the women did not confine the practice of their profession exclusively to the precincts of the goddess, but moved outside it, and sometimes tried to enter bourgeois society by the gate of marriage. They were, however, ranked as outcasts, in contrast to the real priestesses, who enjoyed high esteem. Temple prostitutes were not allowed to bring up their own children: these were entrusted to foster-parents and it was forbidden under pain of death to inquire who was the father. A woman who had once belonged to the caste of prostitutes was held to be lost for ever.

This contemptuous attitude towards prostitution is hard to reconcile with Herodotus' statement that in Mesopotamia every woman, before marrying, had to give herself once to a stranger in a temple. This may be a survival from a very early age, but the report dates from the middle of the fifth century A.D., after the Persian conquest. And by this time the temple brothels had long ceased to be the only places in which pleasure could be bought. Documents have been found, dating from the reign of Nebuchadnezzar II, the last great Chaldaean king, and thus hundreds of years before Herodotus, which show that some rich

citizens of Babylon derived substantial incomes from the prostitution of their female slaves. One of these, a certain Nabu-Aki-
Iddin, made his servants work in a brothel owned by one Kalba,
and drew seventy-five per cent. of the profits. The clay tablets
of Babylon are assuredly better evidence than the romantic
stories of the Greek historians that the good burghers' daughters
had to visit the temple and there give themselves once to whom-
soever cast a piece into their laps (once, but not in any circumstances whatsoever a second time).[23]

Herodotus' explanation of this obligatory prostitution, which
has been generally accepted by modern scholars,[24] is that it was a
purely religious act, a sacrifice to the goddess, to whom every
woman must belong for a night or at least an hour. The goddess
selected a lover for her. It was a completely anonymous union,
a mystical juncture with divinity that took a girl's maidenhead
before she entered into marriage. We do know of pre-nuptial
customs of this sort among primitive peoples; but it is surprising
to find them practised in Babylon, where the sex-life of the middle
classes was most strictly regulated, if only because of the problems
of inheritance. If Herodotus' story is true, there must have been
innumerable pre-nuptial births, particularly since abortion was
forbidden. What was the social position of these pre-nuptial
children, conceived in the service of the goddess Ishtar, and did
they inherit? None of the Babylonian sources enlightens us on
this point, or even mentions it.

Herodotus also describes another form of temple prostitution.
High up in the famous Tower of Babylon, the Etemenanki,
which King Nabopalassar restored,[25] stood a shrine which contained a great bed, richly adorned, and beside it a table of gold.
Every night this mysterious room was occupied by a woman,
chosen from among the daughters of the land by her god—
presumably the great Marduk—to be his companion. Whether
it was only in her dreams that this woman enjoyed the embraces
of the god, or whether his part was taken by some mortal, the
king or a high priest, we do not know.

Homosexuality was widely practised in Mesopotamia, as in all

Eastern countries, and a special class of prostitutes served its needs. In the greater temples, including that of Ishtar in Babylon, the male prostitutes occupied a special brothel, under religious supervision, of course. A senior priest, the *Ukkurum*, was in charge.

Gradually, particularly in the Assyrian period, the Court assumed the forms familiar to us from the later Sultanates of the Ottoman Empire. The palace was equipped with an extensive harem, under an inspector and a chief eunuch. Generally speaking, however, Babylon does not appear ever to have been that hotbed of indiscriminate vice which the authors of the Bible, who were hostile to it on political grounds, would have us believe. The legislators of Babylon created a system of family law which was the exemplar for the whole Western world: indeed, traces of its influence can be discerned today, after four thousand years. The system was at pains to strengthen the individual family, to protect the interests of the issue, to strike a balance in sex-life between liberty and obligation; and it accorded to women rights for which they are still fighting today in many countries. In brief, in spite of certain aberrations, Babylon did good service in this field, as in many others, and moralists have reason to pay homage to this maligned city.

Onanism and Circumcision

Since men learned to decipher hieroglyphics and cuneiform writing, it has been discovered that the sex-life of the ancient Hebrews did not differ greatly from that of their neighbours. Their morals and vices, their commandments and prohibitions, agree in essentials with what we find in Babylon, Assyria, and Egypt. The Hebraic attitude to the relationship between man and wife in marriage is almost identical with that laid down in the code of Hammurabi,[26] except that the patriarchal note is struck even more strongly. The head of the family has an almost unlimited right of disposal over wife and children.

The purpose of marriage is reproduction. If it does not fulfil this purpose it can be dissolved. Celibacy is not expressly forbidden, but it is regarded as unnatural. In one special case a man is bound to marry: if an elder brother dies without leaving male issue his younger brother must marry the widow. This form of compulsory marriage, the *levirate*,★ is known among many primitive peoples. The Jews enforced it very strictly. It was not always, however, a pleasure to the man in question, particularly since sons born of such a marriage ranked as the legitimate issue of the dead brother. The younger brother had thus only to take over the physiological role of the begetter, and he was sometimes recalcitrant.

The Old Testament records the strange story of Onan and Thamar.[27] Er, son of Judah, was smitten by God with death on account of some sin, and his brother Onan had now to marry his widow, Thamar, but he rebelled. When he went in to Thamar he defiled himself and the family honour by spilling his seed on the ground instead of giving it to continue his brother's line. The anger of the Lord descended on him too for his iniquity, and he died. The biblical narrative does not make it clear whether his offence was masturbation or *coitus interruptus*, but later generations adopted the former hypothesis, and masturbation, in either sex, is known to this day as onanism.

The commandments of the Decalogue, 'Thou shalt not commit adultery' and 'Thou shalt not covet thy neighbour's wife', were applied exceedingly strictly even before Moses' day; only the ordeal by water was rather less rigorous than in Babylon. A woman suspected of adultery was not at once thrown into the water: first she was forced to drink a certain kind of water, prepared in a not particularly savoury fashion. If her belly swelled, she was guilty. As in Babylon, however, she was protected against evil speech by a provision that a false accusation, too, was punishable by death. The two elders who unsuccessfully attempted Susannah's virtue in the bath and then bore false witness against her paid for their lubricity with their lives. The story thus had graver consequences than are suggested in the paintings of Tintoretto, Rubens, Rembrandt, and others.

The Jews prized intelligence even above beauty and virtue. It

★ From the Latin *levir*, husband's brother.

was no male prerogative. The Jews were a masculine society, yet
intellectually gifted women could reach the highest positions in
it. The best-known example is that of Deborah the Prophetess,
the Jewish Joan of Arc, who encouraged the doubters in the
fighting for Canaan and brought about the victory over Sisera,
King of the Canaanites. Deborah was recognized by her countrymen as a judge, the equivalent of a member of the government.

Deborah was a prophetess by calling and standing. This was the
highest position that a woman could occupy in ancient Jewish
society. The Jewish religion, unlike that of other peoples of
Eastern antiquity, had no priestesses except, perhaps, priestesses of
love. In spite of the general ban on paederasty[28] and despite all
the thunders of the prophets, temple prostitution was never
altogether rooted out in Israel. As in Babylon, there were male
and female 'saints'—Gedesim and Gedesot. But as demands on
their services were apparently fewer in the Temple of Yahveh
than in the shrines of Ishtar, the prostitutes practised their trade in
villages also, for the benefit of travellers. They were despised
socially: the people called the male prostitutes 'dogs'.

Other elements in Jewish sex-life were of Egyptian origin.
These include the practice of circumcision, for two thousand
years counted as a reproach against the Jews but originally (and
now again today in some places) regarded as a sign of progress.
Scholars are still not agreed on the original meaning of this
operation. Some hold the removal of the foreskin to be a survival
from the days of human sacrifice. In this case the operation would
be, as St. Augustine supposed, a way of purging the infant, who
had come into the world laden with the sin of his forefathers.
Others see in it a test of courage, which every young man had
to undergo before he could be admitted as a full member of his
tribe or people. Only one explanation seems impossible, and that
the common one, that the Jews introduced circumcision to distinguish them from other peoples.

Circumcision could not constitute a distinctive mark in biblical
times, for the good reason that most of the peoples with whom
the Jews came into contact were themselves circumcised. During

their sojourn in Egypt the Jews found their uncircumcised condition a disadvantage. Circumcision was not an Egyptian invention: it is practised throughout Africa—from the northern tribes down to the Hottentots—and especially in the tropical areas. The Egyptian priest-doctors made this custom a hygienic-ritual obligation which no self-respecting man could evade. He who retained his foreskin was a barbarian—worse than a man who wore his hair and beard long. Moses, who, as a protégé of the Court, had the entry into educated circles—according to Egyptian sources he was even for a time a priest in Heliopolis—was obviously not very deeply convinced of the utility and necessity of circumcision. The Bible expressly states that he never allowed himself to be circumcised. His son was circumcised, but the operation was performed not by Moses himself but by his wife Zipporah, daughter of a priest of Midian.

It was only after Moses' death that Joshua issued a general order for all Jews to be circumcised. To secure obedience he had to appeal to ancestral example. He declared that Abraham had introduced the practice, but that it had fallen into desuetude and must be 'renewed'. Modern higher criticism believes these words, which do not figure in the oldest texts, to be a later interpolation,[29] but even without the philologians' help, it is obvious that circumcision derived from Egyptian practice. Abraham was a native of Ur, a provincial town south of Babylon, and circumcision was not generally practised in the Babylonian Empire; but he had been in Egypt, and it was only after this visit that he and all the males of his house underwent the operation. Even in the age of the Patriarchs it was neither a national, nor, strictly, a religious commandment, but only a social obligation, to which slaves of other races and even friends enjoying Abraham's hospitality had also to submit. It was a requirement of cleanliness, and consequently of ritual, for what was unclean was an abomination to the Lord.

This was still the point of view in Joshua's day. The Jews were now proud of being circumcised, and despised the Philistines for being uncircumcised, as they themselves had formerly been despised by the Egyptians for the same reason. Gradually, however, many Eastern peoples, beginning, it appears, with the Phoenicians, gave up the practice. The Jews retained it even in the diaspora, and thus a measure which had begun precisely as a sign of assimilation and adaptation to more civilized peoples became a racial characteristic, derided by the uncircumcised as a barbaric atavism. But even this idea did not last for ever. Just at the moment when Hitler's followers were directing their mockery against the circumcised, medical authorities in other Western countries recognized the great hygienic value of circumcision, and today eighty-five per cent of all male children born in clinics in the United States, without distinction of religion or race, are circumcised shortly after birth.[30]

Suttee and the Art of Love

The cruellest of all the sexual practices known in antiquity comes from India, the land of patience and non-resistance. Suttee, the Indian practice of self-immolation by widows (the word means literally 'the virtuous woman') represents the attachment of the woman to the man, carried to its last logical extreme. A woman who has been pledged to a man must remain with him for ever, in the next world as in this, uninterruptedly. Mourning, adoration of the dead, even celibacy are not enough. A woman who has been truly devoted to her husband may not part from him, even physically. If death calls him to another world, she must go with him and mingle her ashes with his on the day on which his body is cremated. This sounds both poetical and heroic —a sort of affirmation of the mystery of wedlock and of marital fidelity stronger than the fear of death. The gesture loses something of its grandeur, however, when we reflect that it is the consequence of an unparalleled sexual slavery imposed on women by men and by society. It becomes even more distasteful when we consider the circumstances in which the practice originated and maintained itself up to modern times.

Suttee goes back to at least the second millennium before Christ. It can never have extended over all India. It originated among the Aryan-speaking peoples of northern India: the

Dravidian tribes of the south never adopted it extensively. It would be natural to seek its origin in a sacrament of human sacrifice, but the oldest Indian religious books, the Veda, fail to bear out this interpretation. At the most they tolerate suttee, and they strongly recommend various methods of escaping it. If a woman lays herself on the pyre by her dead husband's side, and another man takes her by the hand at the last moment, she is bidden to recognize him as her second husband and to return into the land of the living.[31] This good advice does not appear to have been followed often, for the man had to make up his mind as quickly as the woman—unless, indeed, they had agreed before-hand on this curious form of marriage—which may sometimes have happened, for, prisoner though she was, the Indian wife was not always a pattern of fidelity.

If religious dogma is not to blame for suttee, the more heinous is the guilt of the priests who stoked the fires. The Brahmans were especially insistent in advising wealthy widows to perish with their husbands; it was usually they who were the benefici-aries of the widow's estate.[32] They were obviously less interested in the *auto-da-fé*s of poor women, who, having nothing to leave behind, were not required to be so virtuous. The priests did not even interfere if they lived in polyandry with several husbands at once. Thus suttee remained primarily a privilege of the higher castes. In circles where polygamy was practised, several wives sometimes committed themselves together to the flames which consumed their lord and master, in the expectation of being new-born with him after death. Cases of this occurred as recently as the nineteenth century, even after 1829, when Lord William Bentinck, Governor-General of India, forbade suttee, in the face of strong protests from the priests.

One redeeming feature of this grotesque tale of cruelty mingled with legacy-snatching was that suttee was at least confined to adults. It was fashionable among the highest castes to marry little girls almost in infancy to husbands of the same age. Daughters in India were always regarded as a burden on their parents; the sooner they could be provided for, the better. This gave rise to the most absurd situations. If a three-year-old 'husband' died of measles or whooping-cough, his wedded wife became a widow at the same ripe age, and remained one for the rest of her days.[33]

It is true that the position of women varied in the different phases of India's colourful history. They enjoyed periods of relative liberty, especially under the influence of Buddhism, and others of extreme oppression. Under the Gupta dynasty, in the fourth and fifth centuries A.D.—a period of prosperity and high cultural development—women are found occupying high administrative positions, though this did not prevent the same period from witnessing an extension of polygamy, strict insistence on the celibacy of widows, and general prevalence of suttee.[34] It was considered disgraceful for a high-caste wife to survive her husband.

Yet precisely this age, during which women perished in their thousands on the funeral pyre, saw the composition of India's most famous, and presumably oldest, breviary of love, the *Kâmasûtra*. The composer of this work, Mallaniga Vàtsyâyana, was no light-hearted Don Juan; his repute was that of an exceptionally sage and pious man, and this is entirely borne out by the pedantic accuracy with which he introduces his readers to the secrets of eroticism, *Kâmasûtra* means, literally, 'love-precepts', and Vàtsyâyana is a very thorough teacher. His work does not differ greatly in structure from the old Indian treatises on the arts of war, statecraft, dramatic art, etc. Even sexual intercourse, for all the excitement attendant on it, is an art which must be studied scientifically to get the full pleasure out of it. It is the exact opposite of the Buddhist nirvana: man must live for the pleasure of his senses, and enjoy it to the uttermost. It is noteworthy, however, that the art of love is not designed solely to give pleasure to the man: the woman, too, must get the maximum of enjoyment. Vàtsyâyana even maintains that a woman is capable of attaining greater delights than a man, for yielding herself means to her 'the bliss of self-consciousness'. Her role is, however, by no means passive: she is encouraged to launch attacks of the most various kinds, to bring her full satisfaction.

The Indians are men of numbers. They like exact numerical lists of everything. Numbers facilitate, and sometimes replace, system. In the *Kâmasûtra*, accordingly, all conceivable processes of love-life, both psychological and physiological, are listed in

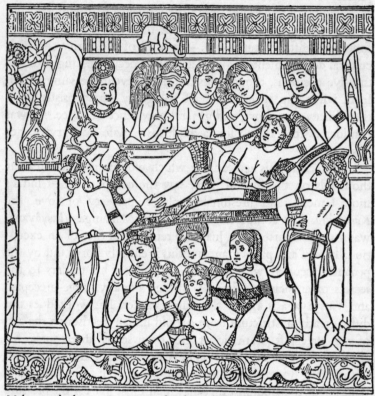

Mahamaya's dream. Drawing of a bas-relief in the Temple of Amaravati, India.

numerical tables. There are three basic types of love-couples, which Vàtsyâyana distinguishes by means of zoological analogies: hare and gazelle; bull and mare; stallion and cow elephant. There are four ways in which a man making a woman's acquaintance can come into physical contact with her. When the courtship has progressed farther, there are ten possible kinds of kiss, ranging from the symbolical kiss bestowed on the woman's reflection in the water to the most elaborate exploration with the tongue. The technique of the possible embrace is treated in equal detail. The higher school of Indian erotism distinguishes four varieties, described by poetic names: the liana embrace, climbing the tree, the sesame-rice embrace, and the milk-and-water embrace. Ingenious combinations of kisses and embraces give sixty-four possible variants of the caresses preceding coitus. The sexual act itself is given multiple special rules and variants. All in all, however, it must be said that Indian love-technique adds nothing to what young people in other countries find out for themselves without scientific instruction.

The sage Vàtsyâyana himself seems to have felt that his ordinary doctrine offered his readers too little. He therefore appended a 'secret doctrine', treating chiefly of drugs to strengthen male virility, overcome coldness in women, equalize temperaments, or prevent unfaithfulness in women. The *Kâmasûtra* medicine-chest is extremely extensive: it ranges from drugs still used today as aphrodisiacs, to monkeys' excrement.

As usual with such literature, Vàtsyâyana claims to write not only as a scientist but also as a moralist. His whole purpose, he says, is to strengthen married life by perfecting its technique and thus to make men more virtuous. As a pious man, he strongly recommends lovers always to pray for the Brahmans' blessing, even in love, but never to practise it in their neighbourhood, still less in a temple. For the religion of India, unlike that of the Near East, did not tolerate temple prostitution. In this respect the Hindu priests drew strong distinctions between faith, business, and sex-life, contenting themselves with drawing their profit from the terrors of virtuous women.

3

BELIEF IN BEAUTY

A MODERN historian has coined the phrase: 'Democracy banished woman from the street to the house.'[35] Absurd as this aphorism sounds, applied to modern times—and it is far from being generally true even of antiquity, for women had been banished to the home long before the first traces of democracy appeared—it possesses a measure of justification in respect of Greece, the cradle of democracy. In earlier days the sex-life of the Greeks had been as exuberant and as motley as that of the Eastern peoples. The myths of the gods and heroes revolve round women; wars are fought for love and to avenge infidelity; no earthly force seems stronger than the sex-urge. Where, as in Sparta, authoritarian régimes prevail, the position of women was, even later, still one of dignity. But in democratic Athens sex seems to have become side-tracked. Politics was exclusive to men, and women disappeared from public life. Even in the home, woman no longer held men in demoniac thrall as in the East. She became so respectable and uninteresting that Greek literature, satire excepted, hardly concerned itself with her existence.

Husbands seemed to take less interest in their wives than in the least of their slaves. The picture which emerges from contemporary evidence of husbands' relations with their wives is less one of contempt than of indifference. The sexual atmosphere which attracts men of any intellectual interests is that of the world of *hetairae* and *ephebi*. The Greek world at its cultural zenith appears to us today—probably far more than the facts justify—dominated by the demi-monde and the practice of paederasty.

It is true that later ages saw Hellas, as it were, across the foot-lights. We commonly look at Greek antiquity through the spectacles of the poets and the artists, who preferred the extra-ordinary to the ordinary. But after all allowances have been made for exaggeration, for love of the grotesque, the penchant for tragic complications, and the play of fantasy and imagination, the strange and undeniable fact remains that the sex-life of the Greeks of the classical age clearly differed in essential respects from that of earlier and later periods and from that of their contemporaries in neighbouring lands.

What had happened? What had wrought this difference? Did Nature accidentally create a people with entirely abnormal physiological reactions? Or was it the Greeks' spiritual outlook that determined their sex-life? Was it religious ideas that carried the sex-impulse away from its normal course and down a side-track? Were wars the reason—or economic circumstances? The very fact that it is possible to put forward so many possibilities suggests that it is too easy and convenient to saddle the political institution of democracy with the sole responsibility for the low position occupied by Greek women.

The Amazons

Although the Greeks of all ages peopled their Elysia with goddesses to whom they erected temples and prayed in time of need, they never submitted easily to women's rule on earth. A British scholar of our time has attempted to prove the existence of a true matriarchate in the Aegean area,[36] but his results have been somewhat meagre. The showpiece of such attempts remains the legend of the Amazons, which the Greeks certainly did not regard as a fairy tale, but as an episode of their early history. It is true that Herodotus maintained that these war-like women (of whom, in general, he has little good to say) were no Greeks; they were defeated and taken prisoner by the Greeks, but eventu-ally escaped by sea to the Crimea, where they became friendly with the Scythians. The Aegean islands and the Ionian coast, however, retained a more flattering tradition of them. Many cities ascribed their foundation to the Amazons; the oldest temple of Artemis in Ephesus was also credited to them. They were by no means regarded as a wild degenerate horde, but as a civilized people with perfectly presentable ancestors.

It is characteristic, however, that before admitting the Amazons to respectability the Greeks found it necessary to de-feminize them thoroughly. Being a logical people, they began by correcting their physical shapes. A woman might conceivably be capable of riding on horseback across the world—but could she handle the necessary implements of war—lance, bow, and arrow? Obviously not! Consequently the Amazons were made to burn their breasts off in early childhood—hence the name (*amazone*, breastless). That they had to abstain from intercourse with men when campaigning was clear. If, however, the Amazons had copied their patroness, the chaste huntress Artemis, and remained virgins all their lives, their stock would have died out. After their military service they had accordingly to perform a second service, that of producing the new generation. For that purpose they were allowed to have intercourse with men. This did not mean that they then became housewives subject to their husbands, for their third duty was to occupy themselves with public affairs. The Amazons were not merely subject to a queen; they administered their own State. If they were to fulfil this duty, someone had to relieve them of the burden of looking after the children and the house, and this duty devolved on their husbands.

Thus in the world of the Amazons all relationships of the normal world were reversed (the Greeks were fond of this kind of *jeu d'esprit*). They were not, like the fauns and centaurs, physically different from human beings. They were human beings, living in a differently ordered social world. The Greeks did not regard the Amazon State as an ideal or as a State of the future, but neither did they see it as anything monstrous: it was an experiment. They imagined what would happen if men did women's work and vice-versa, and the answer showed what the Amazon State was like. The question was by no means regarded as mere food for an Aristophanic burlesque: historians treated it in all seriousness. In the Emperor Augustus's own day the geographer Diodorus wrote a detailed description of the Amazons' migrations and campaigns.

It was obvious that the Amazons' mode of life, with its enforced repression of the sex-impulse in the years of puberty, must give rise to conflicts, and the poets describe these. This gave, however, no reason simply to deny that the women could be soldiers and administrators. There are always conflicts: man cannot escape his destiny. The military-political experts argued as follows: if women, too, bear arms, it will be less convenient for us in many respects, but the State will be the stronger. Women are not naturally a weak sex; they only need to be properly drilled, and their physical capacities developed. Education in Sparta made these its objectives: it aimed from earliest youth at reducing, not emphasizing, the differences between the sexes, so that men and women could take one another's places at need.

In practice, not much came of this effort. Even in Greece women took a hand at moments of supreme danger in a siege or repelling a hostile attack, but the Greek armies were still always composed of men. Greek history, unlike Jewish or Roman, does not even record any national heroines. Woman was the prize of victory, the booty of war, and the warrior's recreation (to use Nietzsche's formula). It was not only outside Troy's walls that the generals brought their mistresses, their favourite slave-girls, their dancing girls and flute-players with them into the camp and took their pleasure with them in hours of relaxation. The lower ranks had to make do with the daughters of whatever country they happened to be fighting in.

Aesthetics and Sex

Yet the Amazonian concept of the interchangeability of the sexes lies at the root of Greek aesthetics. It did not, indeed, exercise a decisive formative influence on the Greek ideal of beauty, for that ideal was not born in Greece; it came from the southern coasts of the Mediterranean. The Greeks, including even the immigrants from Ionia, early emancipated themselves from the Asiatic female type. The corpulent women of the Near East were not to their taste. Fruitfulness of the womb may be praiseworthy, but it is not beautiful. All the features so treasured by the Orientals—the full breasts, dangling like clusters of grapes, the big belly, the spreading hips, the exaggerated fatty cushions of the buttocks, were repulsive to the Greeks. They admired a different line, less full and more youthful: a lighter, more agile, more graceful body.

The Egyptian dancing-girl was the model. The ideal of Grecian dreams was the gracious female type bred by the Nile, with broad shoulders, delicate bud-breasts, a straight, over-slender body springing from the cup of the thighs, without bulges or protuberances, like a half-opened blossom. This type became Hellenized in Crete, midway between Africa and Europe. The advanced culture which flourished in Cretan Knossos in the middle of the second millennium B.C. fixed the ideal of beauty which the Greeks continued to cherish up to Praxiteles' day.

The sexual characteristics were even less pronounced than in Egypt. It was an a-sexual type, a general ideal of human beauty, which owed more to the spirit than to the desires of the flesh. It is difficult to say at a glance whether the dancers depicted on the frescoes of the royal palace at Knossos are male or female. Even in the archaic sculptures created eight hundred years later on the Greek mainland, the sex is not always easy to distinguish unless the hair or the clothes give guidance. Whether the inscription styles the figure Hermes or Aphrodite, the face wears the same sexually undifferentiated expression, the body is boyishly slim, the arms girlishly fine. Even in the classical period, when art was aiming at grandeur and pathos, the sexual element is neutralized to vanishing-point. Apollo with his lyre, the robed god leading the chorus of the Muses, is so little more masculine than his female train that archaeology has to help out biology.

The decisive motive here was undoubtedly not prudery. The representations of human beings, or of gods in human form, are not purposefully de-sexualized, as in the Middle Ages, to save the beholder from lascivious thoughts. All pictures of antiquity, even the virginal Artemis and the severe Athene, are sexualized after a fashion, but it is a neutral fashion which does not seek to excite the other sex. Sex is a sphere of its own, rooted in aesthetics, as aesthetics, in its turn, cannot exist without a sexual element. Within this sphere there is no difference of principle between man and woman, no absolute dividing line, nothing to attract one sex exclusively and repel the other.

So it is in art, and so also in nature. The two together form what we call reality, the content of our lives. There are no aesthetic laws which are valid exclusively for works of art and inapplicable to human beings of flesh and blood. Even here sex forms a sphere of its own, inseparable from the aesthetic. It would be absurd to say this young man is handsome, but only to girls, or that girl is beautiful, but only to men.

As attractiveness cannot be confined to one sex, so there can be no dividing line between heterosexual and homosexual attraction. The distinction which seems so obvious and so fundamental to other ages and peoples is meaningless to the Greek mind, since the attraction exercised by one human being on another is not based on difference of the sex organs, but rather on the secret laws of aesthetics, which indubitably exist, for all that our knowledge of them is only fragmentary; it is based on pleasure in certain proportions, in the rhythm of movement, the tone of words, in harmony and even in contrast between thoughts and feelings of the most various kinds. The need for nearer approach, which is born of these things, is above sex. The object can be male as easily as female. It is neuter of its nature, as is the cause which excited it.

It was only the Hellenistic age, when Asiatic influences again began to penetrate the Greek spirit, that sought to dismember this neutrality in a coarsely sensual fashion by making Eros into a hermaphrodite, a lustful, exhausted hybrid, possessing both male and female genitals and displaying both. The Orientals conceived this bisexual Eros in the form of a monstrous man-woman, i.e. a woman with a beard and male generative organ. This anatomical abortion was too unaesthetic for the Greeks, who bestowed on it at least a breath of poetry and charm. They invented a fable which satisfied logic and dealt with the natural paradox in a gently allusive fashion. A beautiful youth once bathed in a well, and the sight of him so entranced the nymph of the well that she implored the gods to fuse her body together with his. Thus was born Hermaphroditus, the son of Hermes and Aphrodite. This was the legend perpetuated by the sculptor Polycles, in the second century B.C., in his dreaming, reposeful nymph-youth. Polycles' prototype was imitated many times in Alexandria, being adapted to the taste of the age, which liked its erotica comfortable. The later Renaissance added a further touch: the Hermaphrodite was bedded on voluptuous marble pillows, inviting and promising, like a *bonne à tout faire*. He still sprawls in this posture in the Paris Louvre, the Termi Museum in Rome, and other art galleries of the modern world.

Population Policy

The great objection traditionally raised against Greek sex-life is—What happens to the family if sex is thus sealed off and set to form its own world? In fact, sex-life in Greece became a purely economic business activity for the preservation of private property, the maintenance of women and the service of men. By and large, it fulfilled these three functions, while its fourth function, the most important of all for the State, the provision of the next generation, operated very uncertainly.

Greece had its good and its bad periods in respect of population policy. The good ones were, indeed, very early. Homer in the *Iliad* lauds the Trojans' wealth of children. Priam, King of Troy, had no fewer than fifty sons and twelve daughters. The Achaeans from the west coast of the Aegean could not compete with such figures; nevertheless, Nestor, the oldest of the Greek princes, had six sons and numerous grandchildren. Aeolus had twelve married children. Alcinous, the father of Odysseus' friendly hostess, Nausicaa, had five sons. These are demographic figures familiar to this day among well-to-do members of ruling classes. We do not, indeed, know whether they reflect the conditions of the twelfth century B.C., in which the sacred towers of Ilium fell, or of Homer's own ninth century. It is certain, however, that already in Homer's day, and still more so a century later, it was difficult for a poor man to bring up more than one son. The problem was a lack of arable land. Great lords had their flocks and herds from which they could live comfortably. The poor man had a single plough-ox; if a second son arrived, he had to take service as labourer on one of the big estates, or as a casual worker in the town, for the family plot could no longer be subdivided.[37]

In Sparta, whose fertile soil made it one of the richest parts of Greece, the poverty was so abject that several brothers shared a single wife, as among the most primitive peoples. But even polyandry brought no solution. Hunger compelled the limitation of families to a single child. If another was conceived, every device was used to interrupt the pregnancy.[38] If, however, the child did arrive and proved to be male, the parents were not, as in most other Greek States, free either to bring it up or expose it or otherwise get rid of it, as they chose. In theory, the child belonged to the State, and now that process began which has caused many eugenists to describe Sparta as a model State. The father was obliged to take the new-born child to a health-commission, which examined it to see whether it was likely to grow up into a good soldier. If so, the State took charge of its upbringing; if not, it was thrown on the infants' graveyard in the gorge of Taygetus. The constant diminution of the Spartan population suggests that relatively few children passed the test.

Athens, the easy-going, troubled less about eugenics, but had more social sense. The poor who were unable to earn their own bread received two obols daily from the State; there were times when more than 4,000 families were thus being supported by the State. With this backing even the poorest ventured to bring up a second or third child. After the Persian wars the population rose sharply—more, it is true, through immigration than through natural increase. Around the middle of the fifth century B.C.

Athens had a population of some 200,000, not including the outlying districts. This was a figure far below those of Memphis, Babylon or Rome in their prime, but it made Athens one of the most populous cities of the world; too populous, its prudent statesmen thought.

The Foundation of Marriage: the Dowry

The growth of the population and the intermingling of the classes alarmed men of property. Their sons married late, rarely before thirty. Conversely, their daughters found it increasingly difficult to marry, because well-to-do young men found themselves companions in the lower classes of the population and were often reluctant to part from them when the time for marrying came. Misalliances between rich and poor became frequent. That was all wrong; it was pushing democracy too far. When fatherly warnings ceased to be effectual, the patricians set the machinery of State in motion. In 451 B.C. a law was enacted that the marriages of citizens' sons were recognized as valid only if the wife also was daughter of a full citizen. If she was the daughter of a 'metic', still more, of a slave, the union was only a concubinage and its issue were not entitled to inherit. On the other hand, the law, in its anxiety to prevent subdivision of family property, was extremely tolerant towards marriage between near relatives: as in the East, even marriages between children of the same father were permitted, provided the mothers were different.[39]

The man who carried this law through was Pericles, an aristocrat of unblemished repute. He was between forty and fifty years of age, married to the daughter of a great house, father of two legitimate sons. No one could suspect such a man of contempt for the law. Yet not long afterwards Pericles put away his lawful wife and took up with Aspasia, a woman of a notoriously chequered past. She was beautiful and witty, but admittedly a courtesan. Furthermore, she came from Miletus and her father was not an Athenian citizen. She was therefore many times disqualified under the law; yet Pericles took her into his house, and the two lived together for years as man and wife, as though the law did not apply to them.

Since Pericles was the most powerful man in the State, even the most respected citizens accepted his non-conformist views on marriage. His colleagues brought their lawful wives with them when they called on him, and ladies of good society paid court to Aspasia. When Pericles' star waned, however, people remembered that Aspasia was, after all, only his concubine, and a woman with a dubious past. When marriages broke up, she was blamed: it was said that she had set citizens' wives the bad example; she was the evil genius corrupting civil life, and must be rooted out. She was brought before the Courts on a trumped-up charge of secret procuring. Pericles, by impassioned oratory, obtained her acquittal, but the trial spelt, morally, the end of his career and the heaviest defeat of his life. Respectable society had triumphed over the outsider.

It was the victory of the family over the sex-impulse. A man might have as many women as he could pay for, but he must not do it Eastern-fashion. The home itself must be 'pure'—that is to say, monogamous. The property system demanded this, because marriage was founded on the dowry. The dowry remained the wife's property; there was no joint ownership. Respect for money imposed respect for its owner. This was a sacrifice to which the husband had to submit. On the other hand, he was unlimited master in the house in all questions concerning the children. His rights began even before their birth. If his wife interrupted her pregnancy without his consent she could be prosecuted for murder, but the husband could order an abortion. The wife had hardly any other resort than to expose the child secretly, for after the birth the husband, again, decided whether he wanted children or not. The marriage contract did not even automatically legitimize the issue, as in the East, with its large families. The recognition of the child by the father was effected, on the tenth day after birth at the latest, by solemn ceremony, the *amphidromia*. It was only after this that the father ceased to have unrestricted disposal of life or death over the child.

Far-reaching as the father's rights were, the position of women in democratic Athens was not entirely subordinate.[39a] By comparison with the East, Greece was the cradle of freedom in this respect also. A woman's life was retired, but not shut off from the world. We know more about what was forbidden them, or regarded as unbecoming, than what was allowed, and this in itself shows that the prohibitions constituted the exceptions. If the wife of a respected citizen did not herself go to the market, but sent her servants, this was a token of class-consciousness. The reason why married women might not attend the Olympic games was certainly not because the athletes performing there were stark naked, for young girls were allowed to be present. The fact was that the Olympic games was a popular festival, and rowdy; moreover, the road to it from most of Greece passed through Corinth, the city of extra-marital pleasures; even married men wanted a change once every four years.

At Delphi, and above all, at the Pan-Athenian festivals in Athens itself, women made up a large part of the audiences, as they did at the plays in the theatre of Dionysus at the foot of the Acropolis.[39b] As the highly moral tragedies were regularly followed here by the scabrous satiric plays, and as the plays of Aristophanes, and even lewder performances, were regularly enacted, women had ample opportunity of learning what went on outside their homes; nor was any objection raised to their casting a look at the Dionysiac carnival, which centred round the phallic cult. Many Athenians, women as well as men, went every September to attend the Eleusinian Mysteries, where the sombre festivities in the sanctuary of Demeter were succeeded at night by orgiastic dances. It cannot, therefore, be said that Greek wives were strictly confined to their homes, or led a dreary seraglio-life from their wedding-day.

What they lacked was the other side of the seraglio: the domination over the man when he entered the bed-chamber. There were, it is true, few nominal, unconsummated marriages. Custom demanded that the families of both man and wife should be informed, the very day after the marriage, that the union had really been consummated. Yet many marriages remained hollow. Owing to their extra-marital connections, Greek husbands were rarely passionate lovers in the home, and often not even very gallant. They were bored, and showed it to their wives, who reacted in their own way. At first, perhaps, they were awkward, stupid geese—they were often married at fifteen—but later they became stubborn, shrewish she-asses, who embittered their husbands' lives. Socrates, who spent his nights with his pupils, and was probably no model husband in certain other respects also, was not the only possessor of a Xantippe. Ancient Greek literature is full of complaints about intolerable wives, and usually the writers take the man's side.

The Emancipation of Women in Athens

Things appear to have changed towards the end of the fifth century B.C. The first impulse was given by the long war between Athens and Sparta. The men were in the field and the women were left to their own devices. Some moaned and waited, others consoled themselves. Many marriages broke up. Were the women to blame? Euripides, the most popular poet of the day, who exercised a great influence on public opinion but also possessed a keen nose for what his public wanted, defended the women. In his early plays he had written many hard things about them, but now he was the first man to take their side openly. Men, he wrote, should not presume too much on the fact that they were called to risk their lives for their country; 'bearing a child is worse than fighting three battles' he makes Medea say caustically. Nor is this all. Medea's appeal to conscience leads on to a battle-slogan: 'The hour of woman's honour draws nigh.'

Aristophanes showed the Athenians what might happen if women were encouraged to rebel. In his *Lysistrata* they forced the conclusion of peace by locking their bedroom doors against their husbands when the latter came home on leave. Aristophanes was in favour of peace, and in favour of women; but the *Lysistrata* is, after all, only a *jeu d'esprit*. Meanwhile, however, a serious thinker was warning Greek husbands to take the matter seriously. If women had been guilty of excesses during the war, this did not mean that they were bad: they were sick. The physical condition of sex-starvation destroyed a woman's spiritual balance.

The propounder of this doctrine was a certain Hippocrates, a physician from the island of Cos, who had done good service in fighting an outbreak of plague in Athens. The idea was not new, but Hippocrates was the first to describe the symptoms of the sickness in detail or to offer an anatomical and physiological explanation of it. The most important female sex-organ was the hystera, the womb. If the womb was not regularly excited by the man's semen, the blood moved upward, clouding the woman's mind and sometimes even affecting her breathing. The restlessness and nervousness prevalent among women was therefore a disease of the womb, a hysteria. Fortunately, the trouble, if taken in time, was easily cured. Women must be allowed to satisfy their normal sexual instincts, thereby automatically keeping the circulation in order. *Nubat illa—et morbus effugiet* ('let her marry and the sickness will then disappear'); this for two thousand years was the Hippocratic school's regular prescription for all cases of hysterical phenomena.

In Athens, however, the roots of the evil seemed to lie deeper still. When the war ended at last, the women were greedier for men than ever, but the men showed small inclination to settle down in marriage. The war had been lost, business was bad and the future uncertain: why also tie oneself up with a wife who will probably cuckold one? Divorces multiplied, young men did not marry: it was a veritable crisis. What was the remedy? Still closer restraint on the women, still more liberty for the men? Or should one distract women's minds from their hysteria by improving their legal standing, giving them a better, more liberal education and, if possible, admitting them to a place in public life?

The Sophists, who were quick to pronounce their verdict on most problems of daily life, were silent; they made their livelihood in the Courts and were reluctant to offend their masculine clientele. The nobler spirits, however, took the women's side.

Socrates advocated making the mother's rights over the children equal to the father's. His pupil, Plato, would have based the relationship between husband and wife on complete equality of rights.[40] As he was himself a bachelor, and his relations with women were something less than platonic, it was easier for him as a disinterested party to be radical—and impartial. He advocated a law forbidding a married citizen to have sexual intercourse with any woman except his lawful wife. All adultery with hetairae and slave-girls, and still more with the lawful wives of other citizens, should be forbidden. When this demand fell on completely deaf ears, Plato beat a retreat: in his ideal State free love was to prevail, with complete sexual and social equality between men and women. In the work of his old age, the *Laws*, he takes the view that where the institution of marriage is in force, extra-legal connections may be allowed, provided the necessary discretion is preserved and scandal avoided.[41] This is not a very consistent attitude for the philosophic champion of the True, the Good and the Beautiful; but it shows that a breath of genuine realism sometimes blew through the groves of Academe, where Plato conducted his lofty thinking.

Aristotle on the Inferiority of Women

Plato's pupil, Aristotle, turned the wheel still farther back. He brought up heavy guns of learning to defend man's privileged position. Before pronouncing on a moral question, he wrote, man must consult the voice of nature; and nature is quite unequivocal on male superiority. Everywhere in the animal world the males of the species are demonstrably more advanced than the females—larger, stronger, more agile. So is it also with man, and this is clearly nature's will. Ought this to be challenged in the name of an imagined principle of equality? No, this was contrary to the interests both of the individual and of the community.[42]

But Aristotle's proof of the superiority of man was not based on external characteristics alone. He was not only a zoologist, he was primarily a philosopher and, as such, he worked out a system of the nature and development of the sexes into which his individual observations, true or false, had to be fitted. The organic is matter given form. The formation is the essential, the true creative force, and this force is masculine in character. Male and female are to one another as sun and earth, as energy and matter. Man is, so to speak, the carpenter, while woman provides the wood. The semen of the man contains the life-giving formative element. Unlike the older biologists, who saw in the female organism only a receptacle, or at best a seed-bed for the male germ, Aristotle allowed women a share in the generative process of which the child is made. Women emitted a sexual substance of their own, the menstrual blood, which was 'half-cooked semen'.

It was precisely in this point, according to Aristotle, that the inferiority of the woman was manifest. Heat is energy, and woman is colder than man. There are, indeed, differences—largely dependent on age—among men. Young men are stronger and hotter than old; consequently they beget more boys, while older men (Aristotle sets the upper limit of generative power at the seventy-first year of life) are usually only able to father daughters. Physical constitution and age are not, however, the only factors. External temperatures also exercise an influence. When a cold north wind is blowing, more girls are conceived; in warm weather, more boys.

Biologically speaking, the Aristotelian doctrine of reproduction, for all its errors, constituted a great advance on all its predecessors,[43] for it showed for the first time that the mother is more than a pre-natal nurse. She does not only carry the child and bring it into the world, but she gives it something of herself: it is stuff of her stuff. It is not only the father's issue, but biologically related also to the mother. But Aristotle qualified the importance of his own discovery by insisting, far more strongly than any of his predecessors, on the essential unity of the sex-principle.

For all his fine similes of sun and earth (which derive from platonic imagery) he regards the difference between man and woman as one only of degree, not of kind. Both possess energy and heat, but the woman's are less. Both emit a substance which is fundamentally the same, only the woman's is less developed and therefore less effective. If men and women were entirely different they might be called equals, in their respective categories. This, however, was not the case. The generative process itself proved the existence of a natural hierarchy which even the most unprejudiced social philosopher must needs accept.

The Greek movement for female emancipation and equal rights for women ended by petering out. No important changes were made in the law. Women remained excluded from the franchise and from public office. The marriage tie was relaxed still further, but in so far as it survived, man was still the ruler. A husband could still put away his lawful wife at will. A father could sell his unmarried daughter into slavery if she lost her virtue. It was, perhaps, rare for a father to make use of this right, but its existence showed that virginity still possessed a value in the citizen world. But the real victor in the battle for the liberation of the wife from the fetters of the old family law was not the husband, nor the father, but the hetaira. Sex had won the battle over the family.

The Hetaira: Fact and Fiction

The hetaira is as integral a figure of Athenian life as is the maiden goddess Athene on the Acropolis. She has been greatly celebrated in all ages. In antiquity itself an extensive literature in verse and prose was devoted to her, with the result that we know the names of more great courtesans than of respectable wives. It is true that the chief sources which have come down to us, Athenaeus' historical excerpts, Lucian's *Hetairic Dialogues* and Meleager's anthology, are of much later date, and it is reasonable to suppose that in the interval fiction and fact had become more intermingled still. The golden age of the great courtesans was the fourth century B.C., when Phryne sat as model for Praxiteles' statues of Aphrodite, when Plato's disciple, the sage Aristippus, kept company with the hetaira Lais, when the comedian Menander chose Glyka the well-beloved to be his muse, when the philosopher Epicurus tasted the pleasures of life with the hetaira Leontion.

Besides these who achieved the slopes of Parnassus, there were others who devoted themselves rather to power and wealth and enjoyed even more spectacular renown. As early as the Persian wars, according to Plutarch,[44] a courtesan achieved a crown—not, indeed, through her charms alone. The hetaira Thargelia, like Aspasia a native of Milos, carried out propaganda and espionage for the Persian King and died Queen of Thessaly. In the age of Alexander the Great, charming and beautiful women could spare themselves political service of this kind.

The Macedonian kings and generals were open-handed lovers and not too particular about ancestry and reputation. Alexander's mistress, Thais, an Athenian hetaira, was passed on to his favourite general, Ptolomaeus, by whose side she mounted the throne of Egypt, thus becoming foundress of the Ptolomaic line, ancestress and prototype of Cleopatra. Her fellow-countrywoman and fellow-courtesan Lamia achieved even higher honour in her own home. She became the lover of General Demetrios Poliorketes, who set up a princely court in the Parthenon on the Acropolis and required the Athenians to pay divine honours to himself and his mistress. The citizens of Athens, cowed and humbled, submitted and erected an altar to 'Aphrodite Lamia'.

The Grecian hetairae are reputed to have bewitched men not by their beauty alone, but also by their wit. This may have been true of some of them. It is reasonable to suppose that the women with whom men like Pericles, Menander and Epicurus passed long years of their lives must have been of intelligence above the average, interested in things of the spirit and receptive to ideas. In Epicurus's day, at the turn of the fourth and third centuries, it was the fashion among ambitious hetairae to attend courses at the schools of philosophy. Epicurus's lover, Leontion, is said herself to have composed a philosophic treatise, spiced with more Attic wit than the works of her teacher.

But the women who were capable of combining wit with

charm formed, after all, only a small *élite*. They were the exception, even in Athens. The great majority of Greek hetairae were no different in spirit, speech, manners or ambitions from those of their profession in other lands and other ages. The prostitute's life is a hard and heavy one which ages prematurely those who lead it, blunts the spirit even of the gifted, concentrates their minds on a very restricted sphere of interests, and soon forces them to devote themselves unremittingly to the requirements of their business—the care of their over-wrought bodies, their make-up, their little seductive tricks, and the eternal struggle with poverty. There is no time to cultivate the mind, and as a rule, no need, for the customer does not ask it. Even in Greece, most men did not expect intellectual diversion from a hetaira. This emerges clearly, not only from Lucian's more or less imaginary *Hetairic Dialogues* and from the numerous scenes in Greek comedy in which hetairae figure, but also from the love-letters from and to hetairae which have come down to us. The higher-class representatives of the guild were able to make a little conversation, but their visitors rarely bothered with long preliminaries.[45]

Only a minority of the hetairae worked on their own account. Besides the great courtesans who held sumptuous state and set their price accordingly, there was middle-class prostitution in which the customers found the bourgeois atmosphere which was what they sought outside marriage. An epigram by Antipater, which could well be taken for a political verse of today, but was actually addressed to an Athenian woman named Europa, describes the pleasures of venal love as follows:

Six obols will buy you Europa, the beauty of Athens;
  never reluctant or cross, nothing whatever to fear;
Bed as clean as can be, and properly heated in winter;
  This one won't ask you, Zeus, to turn yourself into a bull!

Most of the hetairae lived in brothels, of which Athens offered a large assortment. There were *maisons de rendezvous* in which gallant ladies kept their lovers dangling a little before yielding themselves; establishments disguised as hotels or restaurants; night-clubs in which the female dancers, flute-players and acrobats performed their professional turns and others beside; brothels whose owners sometimes hired out their tenants for long periods to wealthy clients and even carried on a slave-trade in women. The prices were high, but a girl could be bought outright for twenty to forty pieces of silver. This was the dream of many prostitutes, for they were usually then emancipated and promoted to the rank of *pallakae*, or concubines.

Prostitution for the lower classes was carried on in special streets of brothels. From as early as the days of Solon, the great legislator of the sixth century, it was, on grounds of security, confined to licensed houses and strictly controlled. In these houses the price was only one obol, so that it was genuinely no profit motive that made the Athenian Republic maintain the houses of ill-fame in the potters' quarter and the streets round Piraeus harbour. The State had no scruples, however, in making a financial profit out of better-class prostitution. The Council of Athens imposed a regular annual tax on hetairae and periodical censuses were taken, to enable the State to estimate its revenue. The Athenian hetaira-tax was widely copied. A similar tax was later introduced in Rome, and levied up to modern times; in the Renaissance age it was one of the Curia's principal sources of revenue.

Temple prostitution was early introduced into Greece from the East, but most Greek cities regarded it as beneath their dignity to combine the cult of Aphrodite with brothel-keeping. Only Corinth adopted it, and became thereby an international attraction. Strabo, writing at the time of Augustus, says that over ten thousand hetairae were employed in the Temple of Aphrodite in Corinth.[46] This number is quite unbelievable, for rich and gay as Corinth was, and the largest port in Greece after Athens, there can never have been half this number of visitors in it, except at the season of the Athenian and Olympic games. The travel season in Greece was short; as soon as the autumn storms set in, no ship ventured to put out to sea. To whom, then, should the priestesses of Aphrodite sell their favours? Yet the fame of their charm and their piety was great: no less a man than Pindar dedicated one of his finest odes to them.

Paederasty

Besides female prostitution, male prostitution also was extensively practised in Greece, particularly in Athens. It was lawful for adult males to prostitute themselves, and even to hire themselves out at a fixed rate, if the customer was a foreigner. If youths or boys engaged in the trade, and it was proved that their fathers or uncles had incited them to it, the latter could be punished; but we may be sure that only a small proportion of such offenders came before the Courts.

It was, in fact, much harder for men than for women to draw the line between free and venal love. Unpaid love-relationships with young girls were rare in Greece, whereas love-affairs with *ephebi* (young men) were commonplace. It is true that Solon's Code laid down that citizens practising this form of love should confine their attentions to youths of the citizen class, the purpose being partly to preserve class dignity, partly to prevent the transactions from becoming pecuniary ones. But this rule was never strictly observed, nor were boys of the citizen class always indifferent to pecuniary inducements. If not money, they were given other presents, often very valuable ones: rich garments, or whole outfits of armour. More often still, lovers took their young protégés into their homes and paid for their schooling and upkeep. Thus the ephebi's parents profited and yet could not be charged with procuring.

As we have already remarked, homosexual love was widely practised in antiquity in all countries of the eastern Mediterranean, as it is today, even more than in the West. No physiological explanation has, however, been found for the special prevalence of it in Greece. There is nothing to suggest that the physical constitution of the Greeks differed from that of other peoples. The explanation must therefore be sought in some sociological factor, in the development of a definite ideal of beauty most nearly realized in the slim body of a youth. Even so, it remains remarkable that youths of the age, usually prone to attraction to human beings of their own age, but the opposite sex, were able to endure without disgust the embraces of much older persons of their own sex.

This last perversion of what is usually regarded as the normal form of sex-life was obviously the result of a compulsion imposed on the young people under the mask of education and sweetened for them by material benefits, gifts, a life more easeful than that of their own homes, and the promise of a brilliant career. If a youth had once got over the objectionable element in the situation, vanity did the rest. He was flattered at being treated as an equal by men older and more influential than himself; at being handled not as a graceless urchin, as his father or his schoolmaster treated him, but as the equal member of a circle of friends. In such circumstances young men found it in them to embrace tenderly a man physically so repulsive as Socrates and to complain that he fondled them too little.

Men of high lineage fostered a youth's ambition and complaisance further by telling him that love between men was the truly aristocratic and knightly form of eroticism. It was 'Doric'. This was a word of power. Crete was 'Doric', Sparta was 'Doric'; Doric meant 'blue-blooded', and this was a lure even in democratic Athens. Whether there was any historic truth behind this is extremely doubtful. The Dorians had come to Greece long before the Ionians, but we hear nothing of homosexuality in the earliest ages. Homer's poems, in which sex figures so largely, record no specifically erotic relationship between men. Achilles, whom Aeschylus represents as the lover and Plato as the beloved of Patroclus, hazards the whole Greek army when robbed of his favourite slave-girl, Briseis. The leaders of the Achaean army, the princes of Lacedaemon, are no paederasts; they have wives for whom they do battle. Even Hesiod's great divine epic, the *Theogony*, written a hundred years after the *Iliad*, hardly hints at the existence of homosexuality. Hesiod's Olympus is heterosexual, as were, in all probability, the Greeks of his day.

It is only in the sixth century that signs of a change appear. The sons of Peisistratus were involved in a homosexual affair, while Harmodius and Aristogeiton, the murderers of the Tyrants, were confessedly lovers. Solon's remarks on 'paedophily'—love of boys—are definitely friendly. A century later we find two statesmen, the virtuous Aristides and the bold Themistocles, estranged out of jealousy over a handsome youth named Stesilaos. It is nevertheless a great exaggeration when Plato, in that homosexuals' bible, *The Symposium*, makes Aristophanes say that only those young men who are devoted body and soul to homosexual love develop into statesmen.[47] Even the heyday of paederasty can show numerous statesmen who lived completely normal, heterosexual lives.

Platonic and Lesbian Love

Plato's *Symposium*, which is set not in Plato's own house but in that of the tragic dramatist Agathon, a notorious homosexual, and at a date when Plato was still a child, is in many respects untrustworthy as an historic source. It is a typical product of homosexual literature. It sees the world distorted through the glasses of a paederast. Half-tipsy men, alleged to represent the *élite* of Greece, wrangle lengthily about who should sleep next to whom, the object of the propinquity being left in no doubt. Nevertheless it is precisely to this work that Plato owes his repute as the apostle of the pure 'platonic' love, cleansed of all lusts of the flesh, and to this day women defending their reputations boast that their relations with men, their later husbands excepted, have been purely 'platonic'.

The whole lexicon of eroticism knows no odder misunderstanding. Plato—or rather, Pausanias, into whose mouth Plato puts the words—draws a distinction between 'sacred love', which is based on spiritual harmony and intellectual attraction, and 'profane love', which aims only at physical satisfaction. But he adds at once that sacred love can exist only between men:

Aphrodite Urania, the divinity of heavenly love, has no part in love between man and woman. This falls into the natural sphere of Aphrodite Pandemos, the love-goddess of the whole people, of Krethi and Plethi. Woman is thus debarred *a principio* from 'platonic' love, which belongs exclusively to the 'Uranians', as the homosexuals were afterwards nicknamed in derision.

We have no exact information on Plato's own sex-life. His greatest admirers have been forced to admit that his views inclined towards homosexuality.[48] The antique world, which was at less pains to canonize him, took it for granted that his relations with men were not always purely 'platonic' and wrote verses to him, of which the following is an example:

> When I kissed Amathio, my soul hung on my lips.
> Poor Psyche, she was ready to pass over.[49]

Plato undoubtedly admitted that even in a country such as Hellas, in which society sanctioned homosexual love, conflicts might arise against which the State must guard. He took a very definite stand against paederasts in the strict sense of the word, that is to say men who sought their lovers among boys and 'beardless youths'. The abuses of homosexual love should be forbidden by law. The demand that youths should be protected from seducers and insistent lovers was no new one. Long before Plato, Aeschylus had treated the subject in his play *Laios*. But Greece never got as far as making paedophily and paederasty legal offences, unless accompanied by procuring.

How far women kept pace with men in this field is not clear. One of the earliest Greek lyric poets is the tragic Sappho, who kept a humanist school for girls, a modest forerunner of the Platonic Academy, on the island of Lesbos. In Lesbos, as in Athens, admiration of beauty could not be divorced from sex, and many women took delight in one another. Sappho herself fell in love with one of her pupils, but her love remained unanswered, as did her passion for her mysterious friend, Phaon. In the end she cast herself into the sea in despair. This was probably

at the beginning of the sixth century B.C., the time when paederasty was taking root in Athens.

This is the only famous case of such love known to us from
Lesbos or elsewhere in Greece. The Greeks bestowed on women
who indulged in this practice the contemptuous name of *tribades*,
from *tribein*—to rub one's body against that of another. Sappho
and Lesbos remained, however, the symbols of female homosexuality. Lucian says that tribades are Lesbians, who are indifferent to men and behave together as though they were man and
wife. Both Lucian and the Roman poets Juvenal and Martial
have more to say on Lesbian love, which seems to have been
more widely practised in Imperial Rome than in ancient Greece.
'Lesbian' has become a universal generic term, but the practice
was not characteristic of Greek sex-life.

4

THE PSEUDO-FAMILY

IT was the Romans who invented the word 'sex'. Its origin has greatly puzzled the philologists. Some derive it from the Greek word *hexis*, which means a man's physical and moral state, especially his temperament, but not precisely what the Romans understood under *sexus*, the natural differences between man and woman. Most philologists who have attacked the problem incline to emphasize the element of differentiation, even in the etymology. They derive the word from the Latin verb *secare*, to cut or sever; particularly since the form *secus* also occurs in poetry.

The term may originally only have been a joke, or an allusion to the old Greek fable that human beings were originally bisexual and possessed all the sexual organs, both male and female, until Zeus punished them by severing them. It is certain that the word appears relatively late, towards the end of the Republic. The first instance of it in literature is in Cicero, who in his treatise on the art of oratory makes the somewhat banal remark that human beings are reckoned as male or female according to their sex (*hominum genus et in sexu consideratur, virile an muliebre*).[50] In another passage Cicero speaks of freemen of both sexes (*liberi utriusque sexus*), meaning male and female citizens. A hundred years later, however, Pliny tells the Romans that there are also hermaphrodites (*homines utriusque sexus*). Pliny is probably also the author of the expression 'the weaker sex' (*sexus infirmus*).

The Romans were not particularly interested in sexual half-shades. They made jokes about hermaphrodites, but all sexual abnormality was repellent to them. Homosexuality was called 'the Greek practice'. It was not penalized, but was regarded as unworthy of a true Roman. The Romans knew only two sexes, man and woman, and wanted both to lead full and active sex-lives, as their natures demanded. This was so, not only in the reputedly decadent Imperial age, but from the first. Views on morality and the forms of sex-life obviously underwent modification in the course of a history which lasted over a thousand years, but the basic features remained unaltered. The Romans regarded the sex-instinct as a natural force, not to be restricted even by the State except under extreme necessity. The enjoyment of it was mankind's natural right, woman's no less than man's. Rome was therefore not very punctilious about either virginity or marital fidelity. If man and wife proved ill-assorted, or could not satisfy one another, let them change partners. Even if complications occasionally arose, that was still better than letting sex starve.

The Country of Divorces

Modern historians of Rome assume that the prehistoric society of Italy was promiscuous, and that traces of this lingered on into the days of the kings.[51] The obscene ceremonies in honour of the god Tutunus Mutuus suggest that marriage was originally by no means a monogamous institution. It was an act of initiation. Sexual activity began very early; at twelve with girls and at fourteen with boys. Considerations of demography may have been a factor here, for until the Romans felt themselves a match for their neighbours they were always extremely anxious to see the population grow. The urge, however, came from the sex-instinct, not from politics. In Rome, as in Greece, the interruption of pregnancy was always legal.

In the oldest times marriage usually took the form of wife-purchase. If, however, a man was able to acquire a wife without her father's consent and to live with her for a year, the union became a legal marriage through *usus*; only if it could be proved that the wife had spent three nights away from home was her father entitled to retrieve her.

She may well have had reason to regret this for, in early Rome, the *pater familias*, the head of the family, had absolute power over his children, sons and daughters alike. He could kill them, or sell them into slavery. This terrible *patria potestas* went far beyond anything known in Greece; it reminds one rather of Babylon. In practice it was, however, soon limited by a rule that a father must not act on his first impulse. He must first consult a family council, composed of friends, as well as relatives. He gradually lost his power to dispose of his sons altogether, and his interest in his daughters was reduced to a pecuniary one. A daughter's marriage brought in something to her father, so that even girls had a value.

But about the same time as in Athens, and for the same reasons, the question of marriages between rich and poor became acute. The first written record of Roman law, the Twelve Tables (457-449 B.C.) forbade marriages between patricians and plebeians. In Rome, however, sex proved too strong. Only a few years after this law had been eternalized in bronze, it was repealed. In Rome, as in Greece, a love-affair in high society was the immediate occasion of this. The Roman counterpart of Pericles was a certain Appius Claudius, a haughty patrician, one of those very Decemviri who had just banned marriage between patricians and plebeians. Then he himself became madly enamoured of a young plebeian girl, whom he wanted to make his mistress. But the girl, who had the appropriate name of Virginia, was no Aspasia. She was an officer's daughter and betrothed to a Tribune of the People. To save the family honour, her father stabbed the girl to death in the Forum. The incident led to an army revolt, which forced the patricians to give way and to sanction mixed marriages with plebeian girls.

The story of the virtuous Virginia and of her cruel but high-principled father seems to correspond unusually closely to the picture which is still often drawn today of old Roman family life: an inexorable *pater familias*, a noble maiden, the innocent victim of a class war, and at her side an equally noble paladin of liberty and justice. All that is missing is the dignified matron pacing the hall in long, purple-fringed *stola*, or seated on a stool weaving garments for her husband.[52] Wives were indubitably better off in Rome than in Greece, although in the oldest period the husband's rights over them were as extensive as over his children. He could kill them, or sell them. Presumably, however, the power of life and death was seldom exercised. Later, husbands lost it in law, except if they caught their wives in *flagrante delicto*: under the Emperors even this survival of domestic lynch-law vanished.

The causes of the change were economic. Rome had ceased to be an overgrown village whose women-folk helped in the fields or pastured the cattle. Men earned the family income, while women had only to look after the housekeeping. Their economic value sank accordingly. The price formerly paid by the bride-groom to his father-in-law on marriage gave place to the dowry. This was at first, apparently, a form of compensation to the husband for undertaking the expense of the wife's upkeep. As husbands did not always handle it very prudently, however, fathers-in-law preferred to settle the dowry on the wife, and since the partition of property gave rise to not infrequent quarrels, fathers-in-law went a step farther and reserved paternal authority over their daughters, even after marriage.

This made the wife very independent of her husband. If she carried out her wifely duties her husband could do nothing against her, and even a certain laxity in respect of the marriage tie did not at once lead to bloody tragedy—with few exceptions the Romans were no raging Othellos. When it became obvious that a marriage would not work, it was dissolved. After the Second Punic War divorces increased. Women could now sue for divorce if sufficient grounds were forthcoming. Judges became less strict in deciding what constituted such grounds. If the husband was long away campaigning, the wife could find herself another husband. In the end the calling up of the husband for military service was made sufficient grounds for divorce. Under the Emperors a simple declaration by either party sufficed to dissolve a marriage.

Often, matters did not get even so far; a more amicable arrangement yet was reached. It was a common practice in society for a man to hand his wife over to a friend, his own or the woman's. Even such a pattern of Roman civic virtue as Cato the

Younger ceded his wife, the equally respectable Marcia, to Hortensius, because Hortensius wanted to have children by her.[53] Octavian's own first wife, Livia, had been passed on to him by Claudius, her former husband; this did not prevent her becoming Rome's first Empress and enjoying all the honours attendant on that rank.

The word 'cession' seems to echo the primeval view which regarded the Roman wife as a chattel at her husband's free disposal, like a cow or a piece of furniture; but in fact, things had changed. It is certain that under the late Republic a wife could not be passed on to another man against her will. It was no arbitrary act, sale or procuration; simply a friendly arrangement between the three parties of a marriage that had proved unsatisfactory, on physical or other grounds. In most cases the marriage had already broken up and the 'cession' only sanctioned the wife's adultery. Instead of resorting to the barbarous measures allowed him by the old Roman law—and again required of husbands, in later ages, by their code of chivalry—a man simply passed his wife on to her lover. There were no more family vendettas over women; Roman citizens were too prosaic for that.

Lucretia and the Sabine Women

Decorum had, however, to be preserved. The violation of a woman was a crime in Rome too, and had to be expiated. The rape of Lucretia, to which legend ascribed the fall of the Monarchy, became a national myth and a warning: Rome protected the honour of its women, and even a prince's son might not venture to lay hands on a virtuous citizeness of Rome. Looked at soberly, however, the issue of this romance was an unhappy one for the participants. It was not as in the *Iliad*, in which the cuckolded husband's side won and the seducer's side lost. Here all alike, the attackers of the woman's honour and its defenders, fared ill. The Tarquinians who had fought so doughtily over Lucretia fell, and the State system fell with them. The only moral one could possibly draw from this would be that it is not worth while fighting over a woman.

The practical-minded Romans—and the great majority of Romans were practical-minded—were able to appeal to another precedent from the heroic days of old. The first and greatest sexual adventure recorded in Roman annals is the legend of the rape of the Sabine women. The Romans, under their King Romulus, invited their neighbours, the Sabines, to a feast in honour of the god Consus. The Sabines appeared, with their wives and children. In the midst of the feast Romulus gave a sign and the Romans fell on the Sabine women and chased away their male guests. War ensued between the two States and looked like ending badly for Rome when, at the last moment, the women threw themselves between the combatants and persuaded the men to be reconciled and to make their two countries one.

The first part of this story does Rome no particular credit. The Roman historians have explained the mass-rape by a shortage of women in Rome—although it is not clear why there should have been such a surplus of males. But even if we grant the Romans' motives to have been demographic, or simply expansionist, it was nevertheless an act of common felony, treachery to guests at a religious festival; about the most serious offence possible, by the moral standards of antiquity.

The rape of the Sabine women is a violation of human and divine law: the very contrary of what a national myth ought to be. The Romans themselves are indubitably the villains of the story, their opponents its heroes.

The denouement of the legend, however, makes one forget its unfortunate opening and points the moral of the story: women, even if wrongfully acquired, constitute the cohesive, reconciling element between men and peoples. Sex creates relationships which are more potent than all ties of friendship and comradeship. He who would conquer, he who would enlarge his sphere of influence, must make use of women. So it is in high politics, and also in private life. Woman is the bridge leading from one *gens* or family group to another; she prevents a city from splitting up into self-contained cliques. She smooths out class differences, helps to conclude alliances between political opponents and uncertain friends. In the last century of the Republic this was systematized. There was hardly a pact between leading statesmen or generals that was not sealed by a marriage, one of the contracting parties taking the sister or the daughter of the other to wife.

Sons without Mothers

There is no need to see in this either a survival of an old matriarchy or the germ of a new. An intelligent and ambitious woman is often able to exercise an important influence on her husband, and through him, on policy. Brutus, the murderer of Caesar, was completely under the thumb of his wife, Portia. In general, however, it was the man who wore the breeches in Rome. Even in politics, woman was a bargaining counter, a bait, a means to an end. Under the Empire a few women succeeded for short periods in getting real authority into their hands, as regents or the mothers or wives of weak and incompetent rulers; but these were exceptional cases, and always unpopular. There was never any true matriarchate in Rome. In historic times women were better respected than in the East or in Greece, but they were not allowed to rule.

An important point was that in the Roman monarchy—kingdom and empire alike—the succession was never regulated strictly on the dynastic principle. Monarchs usually desired to be succeeded by one of their sons, if possible the eldest; but they knew this to be a chancy business—no father can guarantee that his sons are capable. They therefore preferred to bequeath the throne to a non-relative in whom they had confidence rather than to an incapable or unreliable member of their own family. They took their nominee into their family as adopted son or son-in-law; this sufficed to legitimize his succession. Of the six kings after Romulus, two were not related in any way to their predecessors and two were their sons-in-law. One, Servius Tullius, was the son of a slave-girl. This may all be legend, but such legends could not have grown up in a country which set much store by the ancestry of its monarchs.

Under the Empire the succession was more irregular still. The text-books write of the Julian-Claudian house, the Flavians, or the Antonines: this is misleading. In fact, the Empire in Rome was always elective. At first the Emperor himself designated his successor; later, the soldiers did it. But even in the period when the Emperors still decided the succession, they seldom chose the sons of their body. Although their statues depict them as virile enough to have peopled all Rome, most of them were not very fertile; or else their wives were barren, or their sons died early deaths, natural or violent. The great rulers of the first two centuries of the Christian era, Augustus, Trajan, Hadrian, and Marcus Aurelius, were all adopted sons.

Adoption was by no means a privilege reserved for Emperors. Any Roman citizen could acquire a legitimate 'son' and lawful heir by adoption. Adoption was known even in Greece, but in Rome it became a pillar of society. The only limitation was that the adopted sons had to be Roman citizens in their own right; it was unlawful to smuggle aliens and slaves into society by this channel. There was no other restriction whatsoever. The 'father' could be unmarried; he need not ever have known a woman. A man could become a grandfather at a single leap, by adopting someone as his grandson. The adopted son could be older than his 'father'.

It was only under the later Emperors that society became sensitive to some of these absurdities, and a law was enacted that the adopted son must be at least eighteen years younger than his 'father'. Later still the lawyers laid down that a eunuch might not adopt children;[54] but a man impotent from any other cause was free, so far as the law of inheritance went, to fill the gap by adoption.

Women, on the other hand, were, save in quite exceptional individual cases, not allowed to adopt children. Thus a woman who wanted to have children had to have a husband, whereas a man desirous of becoming a father need not have a wife. This distinction shows that, benign as Rome's attitude was towards women, it was not prepared to admit the sexes to complete legal

equality, and another indication of this is that no decisive importance was attached to the mother's role in the upbringing of the
children. A child could grow up without a mother, but he had
to have a father. The basis of the family community in Rome
was the father, not the mother, for the family was not a natural,
physiological unit, but a legal institution for the preservation of
property and the satisfaction of certain religious obligations.
The domestic gods, the *penates*, accepted prayers and sacrifices
equally from adopted children who were not the issue of the
pater familias. There was no absolute need for a matron to be
sitting before the hearth. On close scrutiny, the far-famed Roman
family reveals itself as a fable with not so much historic truth in
it as the legends of Romulus and Remus.

The Mysteries of Pompeii

As a wife's importance from the point of view of the next
generation was less in Rome than in the East, or even in Greece,
her relations with her husband depended even more on her
ability to give him sexual pleasure. If she failed to do this he had
to be provided with satisfaction elsewhere. If for this purpose
alone, prostitution was tolerated. The great moralists, Cato the
Censor, Cicero, and Seneca regarded prostitution as an institution
directly serving to protect marriage, since it kept men from
breaking up the marriages of others. In Rome, however, venal
love was regarded more realistically than in Greece. It was not
swathed in a religious cloak, as in Corinth; prostitutes were not
known by the affectionate names bestowed on them in Athens,
or later, in France (*hetaira* means, literally, lady friend, or companion, and a *courtisane* is a lady to whom her adorer pays court).
For the Romans, prostitution was a trade—perhaps a necessary
one and, at any rate, demonstrably one for which there was a
lively demand; but the women practising this trade were never
allowed to pose as priestesses of love or ladies bountiful. The
Roman jurists defined a prostitute accurately as a woman who
earns her livelihood with her body (*quae corpore meret*). The
official word for her was *meretrix*—earner.

Rome was richer than Athens, but we seldom hear of *meretrices* making big fortunes, like some of their Greek sisters. Most of them were employed by brothel-keepers. Every Roman provincial city had one house of public resort, a *lupanar*. Garrison towns were, of course, better provided, and in Rome, as in Athens, there were whole brothel quarters; the most notorious was the *Subura*. Most brothels were simple and unappetizing. The very name 'lupanar', which means literally 'the she-wolf's den' is, to say the least, unflattering. There were, however, also elegant establishments for the rich.

One of these luxury-brothels, the famous House of the Vettii, in Pompeii, was preserved intact under the lava of Vesuvius. It must clearly have been one of the finest and most sumptuous houses of the town, of which it is one of the architectural glories. The frescoes of *amoretti* in the great reception-room, the decorations of the side-chambers, the delicate work of the columns round the inner court, are still a delight to the beholder. The luxury of the main rooms is in sharp contrast with the minute ill-lit *cellae* in which the more intimate part of the love-drama was enacted. There is only just room in each for a low stone bed. Even here, however, the *leno* (brothel-keeper) gave his guests something to look at. On the walls are displayed by a skilful hand the various postures which lead to erotic bliss, while to put customers in the proper mood as soon as they entered the house, they were greeted in the door by a picture of a bearded man in a Phrygian cap laying his vast penis on a money changer's scales with a self-satisfied smile.

Pictures of this kind are to be found also in the private villas of the rich Roman merchants who passed the summer months in Pompeii. In the Villa of the Mysteries, which was owned by the Julian-Claudian family, but dates from the Republican era, the principal decoration consists of a Roman version of the cult of Dionysus. A noble Roman lady is stripped half naked and flagellated with a priapus until all her inhibitions disappear and she dances nude. The Dionysian orgies had gone out of use by the time Pompeii reached the zenith of its prosperity, but pictures of this sort were still a pleasant seasoning to a jovial banquet. The Romans made no concealment of their sex-instinct, and representational art and poetry were called in to serve its needs. The mythological wrappings and sublimation of the sensual which the Greeks never entirely outgrew did not appeal to the Romans. Sex was a reality: why should it not be represented realistically? Plautus's and Terence's knock-about farces, so popular in the older Rome, were no longer to the taste of the age. Upper-class Romans were no hooligans, scrapping in the street. They were men of the world and required the poets who lived from the rich men's tables to recognize the fact.

Ovid on Free Love

For the sculptors and painters who worked to order, it was relatively easy. They knew the rule: everything can be shown inside the house, but discretion outside it! For the poets it was harder to harmonize what they had to say with what their readers wanted to hear. The Maecenases could, indeed, be flattered into satisfaction, and the poets did not spare their flattery. Still, they wanted to be praised and read by others besides their patrons, and they did not know into whose hands their books might fall. Poetry was a public profession long before the invention of printing.

Then what did the public want? To hear more about sex and the sex-life of the time: that seems certain. In the first years of the Empire a whole pleiad of poets flung themselves on this theme. Almost all of them were free-thinkers on the subject of love and extolled free love; it was only on the method that opinions varied. Propertius and Horace stuck to their Greek models and sang the praises of the demi-monde. Women who lived by love were so experienced, so charming, so gay that there was no need to go seducing citizens' wives and daughters. Propertius puts it most plainly in one of his elegies: 'How I love this quite uninhibited She, who walks with gown thrown half back, unabashed by curious and desirous looks, who loiters in her dusty shoes on the pavement of the Via Sacra and does not hang back when you beckon to her. She will never refuse you, nor clean you out of all your fortune.' This tickled the fancy and yet it could offend no one, for it was in exact accordance with the old-fashioned views on morality. The poets who confined themselves to such counsels might wander unmolested on the heights of Parnassus, and if they served their odes to the *meretrices* with a good draught of wine, as Horace does, they can be presented to schoolboys two thousand years later as guides to the joys of living.

Ovid, the youngest and most gifted of this generation of poets, had another recipe for earthly bliss. The true delight of love lies in the conquest of the woman, and one loses this pleasure if one contents oneself with women whom anyone can buy. The harder the conquest, the greater the pleasure when the fortress falls. The supreme pleasure is thus that of a love-affair with a married woman who is closely guarded by her husband. Ovid describes delicate situations with a charm and wit unequalled by any writer after him until Boccaccio. He has invited his beloved, Corinna, to his home with her husband. Secretly he wishes the husband only ill—'would, O gods, this were the man's last meal' —but he is a properly brought up young man, and will not be guilty of a rude word. But how is he to endure the caresses which her husband bestows on Corinna before his very eyes? So he gives elaborate advice how to behave so that the husband sees nothing and he still achieves his purpose.

When he lies down on the cushions, go to him with modest demeanour.
Lay yourself down by his side, but see that your foot presses mine.[55]

The last warning which Ovid addresses to his love is that she shall never admit to him that she submits to her husband of nights.

What you give him in secret, you give of duty, and because you must;
But, whatever the fate the night may have for you
Deny to me stubbornly the next day that you were his.

The roles are reversed: the lover is the jealous one, whom the husband betrays in taking a pleasure that is no longer rightly his. The night spent in the marriage bed is the hour of betrayal, of dishonourable love. The true love is that of the daytime, when the married woman visits her lover and the shutters are closed against the sun's glare. Ovid is the bard of the snatched hour, the twilight in which two lovers unite. He paints his meetings with Corinna in the tenderest of shades—how hesitantly she yields herself, how she still defends her diaphanous petticoat, how she stands before him at last in radiant beauty. It is descriptive lyricism, appealing exclusively to the senses, but so subtle, so finely wrought that it never reads like pornography.

Ovid's love-elegies to Corinna, his *Amores*, brought him instant fame. He was still in the early twenties. A provincial of good family, he had studied in Athens and travelled in Asia. He may even have heard some reports of India; in any case, he brought back from the East something which gives his verses a special aroma. His second work, of which only a fragment has survived, the *De Medicamine Faciei*, a didactic poem on make-up, is quite oriental in tone. His beloved, Corinna, has spoiled her wonderful gold hair by using a bad wash, and many other women have fared no better. The Roman women had learnt much from the Greeks, but were still no artists in this field. They still trusted too much in what nature had given them. But beauty is not a gift from the gods alone: man must help. Ovid, who had been educated in the law, sat down now to study cosmetics, and gives women most exact advice, with weights and measures, on how to embellish their looks without spoiling their health.

This excursion into the chemistry of eroticism led Ovid on to his great work on the art of love—the *Ars Amatoria*. This, too, is a didactic poem in form, but it is no dry systematic treatise with lessons on the gymnastics of the bed, like the *Kâmasûtra*. It shows how young people may find one another without burdensome thoughts of dowries, children and inheritances. It is a glorification of sex and, withal, one of the most charming books of love-lyrics ever written.

The art of love, as Ovid understands it, is the art of approaching a married woman who is prepared to carry on an affair. To conquer her, strategy is necessary. The first question is, where is she to be found? The Roman citizen's home offered few opportunities in this respect. Sometimes a woman could be met at a banquet, but the more convenient way was via her maid; Ovid himself had tried this method to approach Corinna. The recipe has remained in use, at least in literature, up to modern times. In French, Italian, and Spanish comedy romantic ladies always possess accomplices in the persons of their maids. Gallants know this; the maid must be won first, then the mistress.

This detour is not, indeed, always necessary. Young Roman ladies showed themselves in public often enough at the theatre or the arena. These were the best places to form tender connections. The essential is for the wooer to have self-confidence. He must not, indeed, be importunate. Ovid himself was no tempestuous lover, and warns other men against trying to take ladies by storm. This only cuts the pleasure short and is, moreover, beneath a man's dignity. Stallions and bulls do not behave so foolishly, for animals know that their females are at bottom as hot as themselves. Patience, good manners, and small attentions will bring anyone to his goal.

It is harder to keep the lady's love, for *la donna è mobile*; it is not only clumsy husbands who are betrayed. A man who loves a woman must keep his body fresh, not neglecting his spirit either, for the attraction of the spirit is the only lasting one. He must avoid quarrelling, look after his beloved, and stand by her in sickness. He must make her presents which give her pleasure without awakening her cupidity, for true love must not be founded on material advantage. After giving his male readers these sage counsels, Ovid gives women equally sensible advice, leading them in their turn through the whole labyrinth of love, from the selection of a lover to the satisfaction of desire and to the difficult art of retaining the man's love.

The moralizing tone of the work did not save Ovid from a public scandal. His *Ars Amatoria* went too far even for Roman society of the Augustan age. The manifold little ironical touches, the keen observation of private and public life, the glimpses into their homes, the drawing-room and the bedroom, the side-glance at their servants—all this made them uncomfortable. If Ovid had put it in satirical form, as Juvenal did after him, they would have taken it; but the *Art of Love* did not purport to be a caricature of Roman society, but a faithful portrait, as it probably was. The likeness was too speaking.

To appease his critics, Ovid wrote a fourth book on love—the *Remedia Amoris*, a somewhat melancholy treatise on how to rid oneself of an unhappy love. The unlucky lover in search of consolation must shun his former love, avoid the places where they used to meet, abstain from thinking of her. The echo of the poem was as flat as the work itself. It read like the poet's farewell to his own youth. In fact, Ovid soon turned to other fields and won fresh fame with a work on the Roman feast-days, and with the *Metamorphoses*, an imaginative reconstruction of old Greek mythology. He had become a mature man of over fifty and his youthful sins seemed to have been forgotten and forgiven.

Then sentence of banishment suddenly descended on him. He was on holiday in Elba when an Imperial edict suddenly banished him to Tomi, on the Black Sea, the remotest corner of the Roman Empire. No reason was given, no appeal allowed. No source tells us what his offence had been. As his banishment fell in the same year (8 A.D.) as that of the Emperor's grand-daughter, it is thought that he may have been involved in a Court scandal, but this is pure guess-work. What alone seems certain is that Augustus thought his influence demoralizing and had never forgiven him the *Ars Amatoria*.[56]

The Sex Tragedy of the Emperor Augustus

The banishment from Rome of its most popular and esteemed author was obviously meant as a warning to all those who took the morality of marriage too lightly; yet no one was less well fitted to fill the role of avenger and judge than the man on whom his fellow-citizens had bestowed the name Augustus. Ovid had painted a delicate picture of things as they were; Augustus was one of those who had made them so. No Consul or Tribune of the People had set Rome so evil a moral example as he. He was very strongly sexed, but had probably been a sufferer from venereal disease since early manhood. It is possible that in youth he had contracted a gonorrhoea which affected his powers and produced sterility in the women with whom he had intercourse. Although he was greatly desirous of continuing his name, only one of his three wives bore him a child.

His own married life was the very pattern of what he condemned in his old age. He had deserted Clodia, his first wife. He had had a liaison with her successor, Scribonia, while she was still the wife of another; the divorce took place only just before Scribonia was delivered. Augustus parted from her on the ground of her loose morals—it was always the women who were to blame for his matrimonial misadventures—and married a third time, again another man's wife. The lady, Livia, brought him two children of her previous marriage, but her union with him was unblessed. To retain his favour, she used to procure for him quite young girls from the lower classes. They had to be virgins; the doctors believed that this would strengthen his generative power, but the recipe did not work with Augustus. He had to resort to adoption.

Julia, his daughter by Scribonia, was married at fourteen, but twice widowed. The third time, Augustus mated her against her will with Tiberius, one of Livia's sons; but Julia preferred other men to her own husband. To punish her, her father banished her to the island of Pandataria, where she was treated as an ordinary prisoner. Of her five children, only one daughter survived. This was another Julia, and as over-sexed as her mother. Her adulteries became the talk of the town, and Augustus banished her also; a son whom she had borne to one of her lovers was exposed as a bastard on the Emperor's orders. She died in exile, like her mother and Ovid.

This was what the second Roman monarchy looked like from outside in its first years. It was natural that Augustus should be none too confident in its stability. He was fundamentally a sceptic, but the older he grew the more he came to feel himself the *pater familias* of the Roman people. He might have failed to break the tyranny of sex in his own home, but he could at least protect his subjects against its dangerous power. When already over sixty he became an apostle of morals and introduced a corpus of legislation for the protection of the family. He knew that he could not go very far in this field, or the Romans would rebel; there could be no question of restoring the unlimited paternal authority of the old family law. But experienced politician as he was, Augustus thought up ways and means to repopularize marriage by striking at the insubordinate in their weakest point.

Poets can be banished; prosperous citizens must be taken by the purse. The *Lex Julia de maritandis ordinibus* laid down that no one but their nearest relatives might make bachelors of marriageable age their heirs, or leave them legacies. Under the *Lex Julia de adulteriis*, women found guilty of adultery lost their dowries, half of which went to the wronged husband, the other half to the State. Intercourse between married men and unmarried women, except prostitutes, was made an offence punishable on both parties. Divorce was made more difficult: seven witnesses were required. Freed slave-girls who married their previous owners might not sue them for divorce: that would be too easy a way of achieving freedom. In general, Augustus's legislation bore harder on women than on men, but it took social considerations and population policy into account: in the making of State appointments the fathers of large families were to be preferred, and testamentary law discriminated against childless married couples, as against bachelors.

All this had clearly been very carefully thought out. In practice, however, the old Emperor's legislation proved totally ineffective. The laws long remained on the statute-book, but they were universally disregarded. Their effect might have been greater if the Imperial House had set a better example, but conditions in it were disgusting. Augustus's successor, Tiberius, passed for a morose eccentric; after his painful experiences with Julia he refused to have any more truck with women. Very many of the later Emperors were paederasts. Vitellius sold one of his boys who had been faithless to him into slavery to a fencing-master. Elogabalus, a young Syrian whom his grandmother had manœuvred on to the throne, used to show himself in the streets of Rome dressed as a woman. The Romans had a short way with perverts like this. Vitellius, the bull-necked, was killed by Vespasian's soldiers, and Elogabalus, at eighteen years of age, by his own.

Only one homosexual Emperor, Hadrian, was tolerated by his Roman subjects. He brought Rome peace again after long years of war; moreover, he spent most of his time in Greece. He was a convinced Grecophile and grew a Greek philosopher's beard, so the Greek practice of paederasty was tolerated in him. The friend of his bosom, the Bithynian Antinous, was an athletic young man with girlish looks, sultry eyes and sensual lips. He was drowned in the Nile. The Emperor had numerous marble busts of him made, so that he might enjoy his features even after death.

The Adventures of Messalina

Unexpectedly, the most notorious monsters among the Roman Emperors were comparatively normal sexually. Caligula, Nero, Domitian and Commodus were neither indifferent to female charms, nor insatiable woman-hunters. They divorced their wives when they got tired of them and ran amok only when their lives or their thrones were threatened. It would be difficult to explain their sadism by their sex-lives. The sadism of the dictator, the lust of absolute power, is a primary instinct which only occasionally strays into the sphere of sex.

The true sex-monsters on the imperial throne of Rome were not men, but women. One of them, Valeria Messalina, ranks as the prototype of the man-mad, man-destructive nymphomaniac. Many authorities also believe her to have been a sadist,[57] but this is not strictly true. She was cruel, like many rulers of her day, but her central interest was in sexual adventure. The man who satisfied her—obviously no easy feat—became her protégé; the man who did not at once give way to her desires forfeited his life.

The old sources describe her as a pretty, rather heavily-built brunette. On a cameo of her which has survived she looks like any country lady, while her marble statue in the Louvre shows her the complete matron in dress and bearing, virtuous and dignified, an unapproachable *grande dame*. In any case she was not one of Rome's numerous beauties and it cannot have been to her external charms that she owed her career. When she became the third wife of the Emperor Claudius she was no longer in her first youth, while he was in his fifties. When he unexpectedly came to the throne, her first care was to establish her own authority. She roused the aristocracy against her by basing this on two freedmen of Greek extraction. She waded to power through the blood of the Roman nobility; she had one man executed because he had once rejected her favours, another because she coveted his garden.

Once she was the real ruler of Rome she threw aside all restraint in her choice of lovers. She had an actor fetched from the stage into her bed. She spent nights in a brothel to learn what the pleasures of venal love were like. She made the brothel-keeper give her a cell, hung up a plate, as was customary in the lupanars, with the name Lysisca, and satiated herself on customers from the street. All Rome was talking of her doings, but as Claudius appeared not to notice them, she became bolder yet. When Claudius was in Ostia, she commanded her youthful lover, Gaius Silius, to divorce his wife, and married him in all form, clearly with the intention of raising him to the throne. Only when this was reported to the Emperor did his pride revolt, and he had Messalina put to death.

Yet even this experience did not put Claudius off women. To rehabilitate himself, he married, when over sixty, a member of the Imperial family, his own niece Julia Agrippina, a lady of a chequered past whom her brother Caligula had banished after living in incest with her. Agrippina was only in the early thirties, but lived in constant fear of being superseded by younger and more beautiful women. Court ladies in whom she saw possible rivals were deported or murdered. She got Claudius's true son excluded from the succession to secure the crown to her own son by a previous marriage, Nero. As Claudius lived too long, she had him poisoned. Her hope of dominating Nero as she had Claudius proved, however, ill-founded. When she became troublesome, and even conspired with Messalina's son, Nero had her killed.

The moving spirit on this occasion was a very seductive young woman named Poppaea Sabina, the vamp among the Roman empresses. She, too, had not a few amorous campaigns behind her when she ascended the throne of Rome. When Nero's eye fell on her, she was the wife of the Commander of the Pretorian Guard. The young Emperor had certain qualms before he took this woman to him. He passed her to a friend, the later Emperor Otho, who was to be the nominal husband, while in reality Poppaea was Nero's mistress. This attempted *ménage à trois* did not come off. Otho objected to sharing his wife with Nero, and was accordingly sent off to govern Lusitania (Portugal). But still less was the ambitious Poppaea content with the role of an Emperor's mistress; she wanted to be Empress.

Meanwhile, the Empress-Mother, Agrippina, opposed this union with a woman of lower rank. When scheming for the succession to the throne, she had married Nero to Octavia, the daughter of Claudius and Messalina. Octavia did not take after her mother; she was submissive and long-suffering. Yet she was in the way, so Nero divorced her and banished her, and when his behaviour evoked criticism in Rome he had her executed. Now Poppaea's way was quite free, and she could become rightful Empress.

Nero entirely capitulated before this woman. When she presented him with a daughter, he was wild with joy; he promoted Poppaea to be 'Augusta', and when the child died a few months after birth, had her sanctified. But after the fire of Rome, Nero became less and less controllable. When Poppaea became pregnant again, there was a scene. Nero gave her a push of which she ultimately died. To show all the world how greatly he loved her, he paid her the highest honour ever accorded to a

Roman Empress. She was apotheosized, i.e. raised to divine rank, and the pious ladies of Rome hastened to erect a temple in her honour. Thus the fifteen years' era of woman-rule and sexual crime which had been opened by Messalina's violence ended with a grandiose farce of marital love.

5

THE SINFUL FLESH

THE Roman habit was to legislate for the world. Now, however, itinerant preachers came out of the East, proclaiming a moral law which purported to be valid for all mankind, including the Romans. Men were bidden to think less of their temporal welfare and their life in this world, more of their souls and their life in the next world after death. In the sphere of sex, too, the foreign preachers invited the Romans to follow an unwonted code of behaviour. Marriage was to be for life, divorce was sinful, and re-marriage during the lifetime of the former partner was adultery.

Had such maxims been proclaimed in the age when Augustus was introducing his moral reforms, they might have been accepted at the Court with satisfaction. Now, however, Nero and Poppaea were ruling in Rome. The moral teaching of the Christian missionaries sounded like a criticism of the private life of the Imperial family, an attack on Roman law and on the morals of Roman society. The upper classes did not, indeed, let it worry them, but since this foreign sect won certain adherents among the proletariat, the police smelt a rat. Persons propagating and accepting such doctrines were capable of anything, even of deliberate subversion of the Roman Empire. The inquisition set on foot against the Christians after the burning of Rome in July A.D. 64 yielded no evidence that they had been responsible for the fire, but they were, as Tacitus reports,[58] found guilty of 'hatred against human-kind'. This was ground enough for organizing a massacre of them. The Romans wanted to live in their own way. They loved life and wanted to enjoy it. Men who cared more for promises of the next world than for the entertainments in the circus offered by the Emperor to his subjects could not be tolerated. Man-haters like this were enemies of the State.

In the homeland of the new faith it was not possible to form such a picture of the Christian communities. The older generation still remembered the miraculous healings with which the faithful credited the Founder of the religion. Men who devoted them-selves to alleviating pain, to helping the sick and the poor, as the Christians did, could not be regarded as man-haters. Jesus's followers were no fanatics seeking in death refuge or release from a burdensome life. They lamented their own deaths and the deaths of those they loved, just like other men. Even the promise of a better life beyond the grave could not tempt them to pre-mature renunciation of life on earth, for resurrection did not follow immediately on physical death, but only in the distant future: there was no short cut. A man who tried to shorten the road by voluntarily ending his life shut the doors of paradise in his own face. The Christians, no less than the Jews, considered self-destruction a grievous sin, an infringement of God's right to call man to him when it pleased him.

As it was unlawful for a man to take away with intent his own life, so also was it to destroy life in the womb. The gospels never mention this question, and the natural deduction is that the first Christians simply accepted the old Mosaic law, which forbade abortion. Much more remarkable is the absence of any discussion of this point in the succeeding generations, when the Christian doctrine was being propagated in the Greco-Roman world. In both Greece and Rome the interruption of pregnancy was sanctioned by law, advocated by the leading philosophers and moralists, and generally practised by the people. Acute differences were bound to arise if the question were raised. Yet even Paul, who devoted so much attention to the problems of sex-life, found it prudent not to endanger the success of his missionary work by broaching this delicate question. It was only much later and in quite different circumstances that St. Augustine expressly renewed the old Jewish ban on abortion and con-demned all forms of contraception.

It was certainly no lack of courage that deterred the first apostles of Christianity from raising their voices against birth-control. One aspect of the question was moral, and here there could be no two answers. But it had also a social aspect, and one of population-politics, and the latter was all-important among the peoples of the East, and particularly the Jews. The children of Israel had been commanded to multiply. Even in Christ's day the strictly orthodox Jews obeyed this law, although its effects had been by no means advantageous to the Jewish people, or the Jewish State. It had not saved Palestine from losing its freedom for five hundred years, during which it had passed successively under Persian, Egyptian, Syrian, and Roman rule. The little country was over-populated; it could no longer support the rising genera-tion. Continuous emigration had already produced the result that far more Jews were living outside Palestine than in the country itself.[59]

These were considerations which would-be reformers of human relationships could not leave out of account. The nationalist point of view, which determined the Mosaic population-policy, was irrelevant for the adherents of the new, universalist doctrine, and vanished altogether when the two faiths had finally separated. The social aspect, on the other hand, became increasingly promin-ent. Could the leaders of what in its basis and its appeal was essentially a movement of the poor man, say to its adherents: 'Multiply, then it shall be well with you'? If they did not openly advise their followers to limit the growth of population, they yet gave them good counsels conducive to that result.

Since contraception and interruption of pregnancy were considered immoral, continence was the only solution left. The apostles of the new faith were far too wise and practical to try to impose this as a law on would-be converts. Nor did they want mankind to die out; least of all did they want precisely the faithful to be childless. Christianity was radical only in matters of faith; in questions of sex-life and of social relationships it sought a compromise between the ideal and reality. It respected the sex-instinct as a natural one; only men must not yield themselves entirely into bondage to the 'sinful flesh', for that was bad for them—detrimental both to their physical and to their spiritual welfare.

This tolerant attitude appears most clearly in the most fiery of all crusaders for the faith, the Apostle Paul. He does not tell every man to marry as soon as he reaches puberty, for multiplicity of children is for him no end in itself. But neither does he follow his contemporaries, the Jewish sect of Essenes, in opposing marriage. The basic principle of his sexual morality is simple and clear: if a man finds sexual abstinence easy, let him remain unmarried; but if his sexual impulses are so strong that he cannot live in continence, let him marry. This rule applies alike to bachelors and widowers, to men and to women. It is a thoroughly liberal doctrine which allows ample freedom to individual proclivities and aversions. For the rest, Paul does not tamper with the old tradition. It is still for parents to determine their children's future, but they must take account of the sex-instinct. No one who wishes to live in virginity is to be forced to marry, and no one unable to restrain himself sexually is to be debarred from marrying.

The New Dogma of Marriage

Nevertheless, the marriage-tie seemed to need strengthening. It was not the apostles who first undertook this task: Jesus himself laid the foundation-stone in a fashion which had lasting consequences for the world. He proclaimed the indissolubility of the marriage-tie.

After his successes in Galilee the young wonder-working rabbi had gone to Judaea, followed by a great throng of disciples. A group of Pharisees, representatives of the official body of rabbis, came to him to 'tempt' him, as St. Matthew puts it. But the first question which they put to him had nothing inquisitorial about it, and the discussion which followed[60] was more of a debate than an examination. It was a free discussion between experts in the law on a burning social question: is it lawful for a man to put away his wife for any cause whatsoever?

The Pharisees were interested to know Jesus's views on this question, for there were serious differences of opinion on it in their own ranks. There were two schools of thought among the rabbis: the one held with Rabbi Shammai, who allowed divorce only for proven adultery; the other and more conservative school, backed by the authority of Rabbi Hillel,[61] defended the current Mosaic law of divorce. The Mosaic law was, in fact, a modification in the wife's favour of the very similar Babylonian law of the age of Abraham. A man could not simply put away his wife: there must be a bill of divorcement, giving the woman the right to marry again. But in Christ's day the right of divorce was practised very laxly. A husband wanting to be rid of his wife could make out the bill of divorcement himself: no official check or confirmation of the document by the authorities was necessary. Divorce was thus even easier in Palestine than in Rome after the Augustan reform. It bore exceedingly hard on wives whose parents were dead and had no home to which to return.

This was what Jesus meant when he told the Pharisees that the Mosaic law was a concession to 'hardness of heart'. Everyone possessed of any social sense saw that some reform was necessary; the only question was how far it should go. Jesus raised the question from the plane of little reforms into the sphere of great principles. Against the one extreme of unilateral and arbitrary dissolution of marriage he propounded the opposite extreme of a lifelong tie binding equally on man and wife.

This demand was no complete novelty in the history of law. The old Roman law knew one form of wedlock, the *confarreatio*, which was sacramental in character and imposed very strict ties. The union was contracted in the presence of the Pontifex Maximus and of ten witnesses, following a ritual somewhat similar to that of the Christian communion. The bridegroom and bride ate together of a sacramental loaf of unleavened bread, the *panis farreus*; in doing this they were eating the body of the god and were bound together in the god so long as they both lived.[62] Divorce for persons who had contracted together in this form was exceedingly difficult; it was impossible for patrician priests, who could not marry in any other form. It was still practised under the Empire and certainly known to legal experts in Palestine.

Nevertheless, there was an enormous difference between confining the indissolubility of marriage to a limited circle of persons who submitted to the *confarreatio*, and propounding, as Jesus did, a universally valid principle. Not only the law of Moses but the codes of all peoples of antiquity legalized divorce. Now it was branded as a sin. This was more than reform; it was revolution, and the effect was extraordinary, even among Jesus's closest friends. The disciples, accustomed as they were to hear so many new ideas from the Master's mouth and to accept them reverently, were taken aback. They thought that if divorce were abolished, and the husband thereby deprived of the right to put away his wife, marriage would become too hard for him, and many men would prefer not to marry at all. The result might be not a strengthening of the marriage tie but a flight from marriage.

Jesus did not examine this objection: he only answered the disciples that not all men were capable of marriage. Some men were born eunuchs, some were made eunuchs, and finally there were some who voluntarily abstained from marriage because their eyes were fixed on heaven. If, then, anyone regarded a lifelong and irrevocable connection with a woman as too heavy a burden, let him renounce marrying. For marriage was not a legal institution created by man: it was a law of nature laid down in God's plan of creation. Husband and wife were 'one flesh': once joined together no man could put them asunder.

Adultery and Childlessness

Did Jesus mean, then, to forbid divorce altogether, or did he allow exceptions? The various Christian Churches have debated this question endlessly without reaching an agreed answer. The Catholic Church interprets Jesus's words to mean that no exception is allowed, while nearly all the Protestant Churches take the opposite view. The texts allow either interpretation, since they do not agree. After the two passages in which the Gospel according to St. Matthew speaks of the prohibition of divorce, it adds the words: 'Whoever shall put away his wife except for fornication [in the Greek text, παρεκτὸς λόγον πορνείας, in the Latin *nisi ob fornicationem*] and shall marry another, committeth adultery.' The parallel passages in Mark[63] and Luke,[64] however, omit this reservation, as does Paul,[65] who also lays down the unqualified prohibition of divorce.

Nor is this all. The words πορνεία and *fornicatio* are strong expressions, commonly used to describe the life of a harlot, not a lapse by an otherwise respectable woman. How are they to be interpreted in this connotation? If one adopts St. Matthew's version, is a single act of adultery sufficient to justify divorce before God, or must there be persistent unfaithfulness? Only a few years ago the Church of England rejected the former interpretation and pronounced a single act of adultery to constitute insufficient ground for divorce.[66]

Important as these problems may be for the lives of thousands of families, they still do not touch the real heart of the Christian teaching on marriage. No legal code has yet succeeded in preventing adultery. In the oldest historical times a woman committing adultery hazarded her life. About the sixth century B.C. civilized countries abandoned this draconian punishment and devised milder penalties. In most countries, too, the crass disproportion in the penalties incurred for adultery by the two sexes was gradually reduced. In Rome it was in practice equally easy for either partner to divorce the other for infidelity. The absolute prohibition of divorce goes farther still. In a way it overshoots the mark, for it can lead to the guilty party's escaping scot free while the injured husband or wife is forced to continue living in wedlock with the unfaithful partner. Canon law has found a way out of this dilemma by allowing separation from bed and board in lieu of divorce, but even the innocent party is unable to contract a new marriage. He must accept his fate, as must a man who has lost a leg in an accident.

While in modern discussions on the right of divorce the central question is that of adultery—or was so until recently, for in modern America quite other considerations now hold the field— it was only of secondary importance in Christ's day, especially in Eastern countries. In all countries of antiquity marriage was primarily an association for reproducing the species. This was its ultimate end and purpose, and if in any case that purpose was not achieved, the marriage could and should be dissolved. Not adultery but childlessness was by far the most important ground for divorce. If a marriage proved unfruitful, it was the man's right, and in many countries his duty, to put away his wife and take another, in the hope that she would give him children. If the cause of the unfruitfulness clearly lay with the man, the woman, too, had the right to divorce him, for she, too, should not be left childless. Variations of population-policy, poverty, and the search for comfort, the chase of the dowry and the subterfuge of adoption might from time to time obscure this main purpose of marriage, but it always remained perceptible, even in Rome. No legislator ever dared simply ignore it.

The new and revolutionary element in the Christian dogma lay in its breach with this ancient tradition. Even childless marriages might not now be dissolved, for reproduction was not the exclusive object of marriage. If children came, well and good: they must be brought up lovingly and carefully. But marriage had no need of this seal. Childlessness was no ground for married couples to part and seek more fruitful associations. Marriage was a sexual association in the highest sense of the term. It rested on the mutual attraction of the sexes, on the direct tie binding the man to the woman and the woman to the man. But it also contained an ethical element, transcending the physiological. No man can be one flesh with two women, no woman with two men. A husband who enters into a union with another woman in the lifetime of his wedded wife commits adultery, whether he has obtained a divorce under the laws of the day or not. As there is no divorce in the religious sense, so also there can be no second marriage so long as the first partner is alive. Only death can part man and wife. This is the new faith.

The Position of Women

The Christian dogma of marriage was not at first the law of any land. It was an appeal to the faithful. As St. Paul's Epistles show, the missionaries at first trod very delicately when introducing the new doctrine in countries in which quite different matrimonial customs, often including bigamy or polygamy, prevailed.[67] Nevertheless, the number of the Christian communities whose members followed strictly the new doctrine, steadily increased.

What were the results? The first and inevitable consequence—seeing that impotent husbands and barren wives could no longer be got rid of by divorce—was a rise in the number of childless marriages. The natural increase of Christians was thus reduced. This factor must not be underestimated, for in old days, when the treatment for many women's ailments was imperfect or non-existent, there were undoubtedly more childless marriages than today.

There was another consequence, affecting well-to-do families who wanted to have sons to whom to leave their wealth. The right of inheritance was the basis of all family law in antiquity. Now came a moral doctrine which ignored it altogether and, worse still, did not allow a young, healthy man who was unable to have children by his wife to take another partner in wedlock. The prohibition of divorce was not only a moral precept, it also had an economic aspect which the rich found dangerous. This was undoubtedly a main reason why Christianity so long remained a religion of the poor, at least among men.

The positive advantage to be weighed against these drawbacks was the increased solidarity of the family. The bond between man and wife was strengthened as never before, and with it, also, the bond between parents and children. Family relationships were simplified. Since widows and widowers were allowed to re-marry, step-children and step-brothers and sisters were still to be found, but they became rarer and the blood-relationship became the usual one (which had ceased to be the case in the Rome of Christ's day).

The most important consequence of the indissolubility of marriage was undoubtedly the security which it gave women. Since in most divorces it was the woman who suffered, many women presumably benefited by the prohibition of divorce. An indissoluble marriage was not necessarily always a happy one; but a woman had no longer to fear being thrown out of her home for no fault of her own. She could feel safe, even if her marriage proved childless. She was assured of a roof over her head to the end of her days, or at least for her husband's lifetime. This feeling of security contributed appreciably to the high rate of conversions to Christianity among women.

This, however, was the only gain which Christianity brought women. The general inequality of the sexes before the law remained as great as ever. The status accorded to women by the new religion was rather a step back compared with the position which they had already achieved in Rome. There was no equality even inside the Christian community. Whereas women could rise to high sacerdotal office in most Asiatic countries, in Egypt, in Greece, and above all in Rome—the Vestal Virgins were among Rome's chief dignitaries—the Christian cult excluded them from any such office. Still less were they man's equals in private life. In marriage wives were bidden to be subject to their husbands.[68] Not even Greece had proclaimed their subjection in so wide and comprehensive terms; the Greek woman was the undisputed mistress in the household's internal affairs and the Roman *domina* still more so.

The inequality which the new religion brought with it was probably not so large in practice: the custom of the country set the tone. Nor should it be forgotten that the family law of Greece and Rome, as of the Eastern countries, was cut to the measure of the propertied classes. Legislators troubled their heads little with the poor, where there was nothing to inherit, distribute or administer. The first Christian communities, on the other hand, were mainly recruited from among poor people. None the less, the personal subjection of the woman to the man remained the governing principle of Christian family law even after Christianity had penetrated into well-to-do circles. If a domestic conflict or a difference of opinion arose between man and wife, the will of the husband prevailed. The husband was bound to love and cherish his wife but the wife had to obey her husband.

Women seem to have regarded this division of rights and duties as perfectly natural; otherwise they would not have adopted Christianity so readily. Yet in the first century A.D. women had quite ceased to be prisoners unable to leave the house without their fathers' or their husbands' permission. Even in the East they were admitted to public life. They knew what was going on in the town and the State; they were intellectually awake; they took a lively interest in the new religious movements of the age (the Christian doctrine was only one among many new creeds). Except where the new sects were specifically masculine communities of monastic character, as in the case of the Essenes, their adherents always included women. The great religions of the age, the cults of Osiris in Egypt, of Attis in Phrygia, and of Adonis in Syria, are typical women's religions. Death and resurrection, suffering and redemption, are the constantly recurrent religious *leit motifs*. Except for the Mithras cult, which, originating in Persia, quickly became the favourite cult among the Roman legionaries, they are all gentle religions. There are no more battles between gods and giants, demi-gods and monsters. If blood is shed it is a sign that wrong has been done. All these religions contain, moreover, a strong mystic element. Their symbolism is addressed rather to the heart than to the head. The rituals are designed to transport the faithful into another world, or to prepare them for it. They are religions of escape.

Mary Magdalene

If Christianity from the first had a particular attraction for women—and all contemporary reports agree that it had—this cannot have been due solely to the mystical and metaphysical elements in it, for these were equally present in other religions. But Christ's doctrine gives mankind more than this; it offers a new order of values. Driven by its wish to make itself universally comprehensible, to the extreme and the paradoxical, it champions even the 'fallen woman'. A woman who prostitutes herself is a sinner: that is stated quite unequivocally. Nevertheless, *il y a fagots et fagots*. Even if the prostitute lives as luxuriously as the rich men, she is one of the poor, the exploited, and therefore still a degree better than the really great sinners.

In the course of a dispute with the Pharisees, Jesus told his opponents flatly: 'Harlots go into the kingdom of God before you.'[69] This phrase is reminiscent of his other saying that it is easier for a camel to pass through a needle's eye than for a rich man to enter into the kingdom of Heaven. Even harlots can hardly hope to achieve eternal bliss so long as they persist in their sinful ways; but their case is still less hopeless than that of the Pharisees and the rich men, for fallen women can be taught and converted; they are capable of repentance and improvement.

The great example of a converted sinner in the New Testament is that of a notorious harlot, one Mary Magdalene, who practised her trade in a certain city of Galilee, probably Capernaum. Later legend invented a lengthy earlier history for her. She had been wife of a rich landowner in Magdala (hence the name), but being left prematurely a widow, and having squandered her wealth on frivolous pleasures, she had gradually sunk into harlotry. This version, however, appears for the first time in the Court literature of the ninth century, in a biography dedicated to the great sinner by Alcuin's pupil, Hrabanus Maurus. It is unknown to the early Christian writers.

In the Gospels, Mary Magdalene appears in quite another light. She is one of the women who accompany Jesus and the disciples on their missionary journey through Galilee, caring for them out of faith and gratitude because Jesus has freed them from their ailments, physical and spiritual. Mary Magdalene was severely psychopathic: she believed herself possessed by evil spirits. But the 'seven devils' had left her, and in their place had come a good spirit, so that her eyes were opened. She saw that the rabbi of Nazareth, who had healed her, was more than man, and felt herself spiritually bound to him.

All that the Gospels tell us of the profane life of this strange woman is that she was 'a woman in the city, which was a sinner'.[70] We do not even know whether she was a small prostitute or a great hetaira. The later world, which has been tireless in glorifying her in ink, in paint, and on the stage, has come down in favour of the more colourful hypothesis. A modern cleric, for example, who has devoted an interesting book to her, tells us that she owned a luxurious villa and appeared at the supper in the house of Simon the Pharisee splendidly attired in a gown of purple embroidered with filigree and pearls.[71] None of these details, again, appears in the Gospels. The only possession credited to her by Luke the Evangelist is an alabaster perfume jar which she humbly brings to anoint the Master's feet. Add the fact that some philologians derive the Greek word *Magdalene* not from the place Magdala but from a word meaning 'hair-dresser', and we have gathered all that contemporary sources have to say on the profane life of history's most famous courtesan.

It is not much, but it is enough to produce a remarkable effect in contrasts. Everything in this woman's life seems exaggerated into extremes. It would be nothing very extraordinary for a public sinner to turn into a repentant and virtuous woman. But Magdalene, the sinner of Capernaum, is not the same woman as 'the repentant Magdalene', Lazarus's sister. She is much more than a quiet penitent: she becomes an active force in the movement of the Faith. It is she who first discovers that Christ's grave is empty, and carries the news to the disciples; she who first sees Christ in the body after his physical death, and hears his voice. Thus she is the first witness of the Resurrection. In no other religion does a female sexual-sinner figure in so important a role. The figure of Mary Magdalene typifies tolerance carried to the highest degree.

Gula *and* Libido

The age of tolerance, however, was short-lived. Towards the end of the first century A.D. a progressive reaction set in, obviously the outcome of the pressure under which the adherents of the new faith were themselves suffering. Under the Emperor Domitian (A.D. 81-96) Christianity was forbidden throughout the Roman Empire. Baptism was made illegal and the cult had to take refuge in the catacombs. As physical resistance was out of the question, only moral resistance was left. For this, the faithful had to put on armour. Forgiveness of sins may be the indispensable preliminary to conversion, but for people already born in the faith the problem is a different one: they must not fall into sin at all.

Gula and *libido*, intemperance and wantonness, are mankind's two arch-enemies. They must be overcome by asceticism. At first it was small self-contained groups, notably the so-called Jewish Christians, who practised asceticism. The expression 'flesh' used by Jesus, and more often still by St. Paul, led them into confusion. They rejected the flesh both in the literal and the metaphorical sense: ate no meat and abstained from sexual intercourse. From the middle of the second century, serious scholars also occupied themselves with the problem and came to remarkable conclusions.

The first question, naturally, was: 'What does Holy Writ say?' This was not so easy to answer, for whereas the Gospels contain no single word which could be interpreted as a general command to practise sexual abstinence, many utterances by St. Paul point in this direction. Paul himself was, indeed, far from demanding that everyone should practise abstinence, but he did not conceal his view that a life of complete chastity was preferable, if only because it made it easier for a man to carry out his duties as a believing Christian and missionary of the Faith. 'It is good for a man not to touch a woman,' he once said.[72] The supporters of asceticism pinned their doctrine on this word. It is true that this was only one of the Apostle's sayings among many others which were far more liberal; and even granted that it expressed his innermost conviction, it was yet only a personal view, not confirmed by the opinion and conduct of other apostles. One of the twelve disciples who had received the Word directly from Jesus, Peter, was married. It was therefore not possible to argue by pure appeal to the founders of the Christian Church.

There was also the question of pre-marital sexual intercourse. Here the field was free for a grand attack against *libido*, for the writings of the New Testament contain practically nothing on the subject, for or against, to take hold of. At the most, the presumption might be legitimate that the founders and pioneers of the new doctrine tacitly accepted the ideas of the Old Testament. The Mosaic law demanded purity from girls, but not from youths. It was one of the biggest inequalities between the sexes. In this respect man was undoubtedly privileged. He was entitled to return his bride to her father if the bridal night showed that she had not come to his bed a virgin. It was not even necessary to divorce her; there had been a species of fraud, so the marriage was invalid.

The Christian prohibition of divorce complicated matters. If the indissolubility of marriage was founded on the corporal union between man and woman, was the husband still entitled to put away a woman who had lost her virginity, or must he accept his fate? It was a question for lawyers, but also one for moralists, for if virginity was indispensable, the further question arose: how is a man to live otherwise than chastely before marriage if unmarried women, and *a fortiori* married ones, may not have intercourse with him? The solution was prostitution. This was, in practice, the safety-valve in all countries which insisted strictly on the preservation of maidenhead and on marital fidelity, but permitted men pre-marital intercourse. Naturally, however, the advocates of asceticism rejected this solution indignantly as the most shameful form of libido—in theory, that is, for in practice it soon became obvious that things worked out differently, precisely among the proponents of sexual abstinence.

As neither common sense nor logic could provide a basis for asceticism, its advocates resorted to the most daring metaphysical combinations and the most far-fetched ingenuities. The first theory of this kind came from Syria. Its author, the philosopher Saturninus, or Satornil, believed the world to be full of angels and devils, fighting for the souls of men. At the head of the evil spirits stood Satan, who had bestowed on man that pleasure in the sinful flesh which drives him to generation and to marriage, which things are also only the devil's work. All that is good and pure comes from Christ, who is pure himself, not having been begotten of the lust of the flesh.

The idea that because men were begotten in concupiscence they were therefore sinful, dominated the debates of the Christian theologians and philosophers for centuries thereafter. The leading thinkers of the age shared it. The satanic and angelic frillings were gradually dropped and the theory made somewhat more mundane and more scientific. St. Augustine developed it into a sexual-moral theory of heredity, the doctrine of original sin. Sin is transmitted from generation to generation in a vicious sequence: concupiscence—generation—a sinful being comes into the world; concupiscence—generation—*da capo*. So it has ever been since Adam's fall. Pope Gregory the Great (A.D. 590-604) himself declared that the lust of our parents' flesh is the cause of our being, therefore it is sinful. The disobedience and undiscipline of the generative organs are the proof of original sin.[73]

As these pronouncements from the highest princes of the Church show, the problem of sin was becoming more and more a purely physiological one. When people spoke of the sins of the fathers, the reference was no longer, as in the Old Testament, a general one to ancestral errors which later generations had to expiate, but to something quite specific: the act of generation. Copulation was the Evil, whether committed in the brothel or the marriage bed. There is no material difference, wrote St. Augustine, between the *copula carnalis* between man and wife and the *copula fornicatoria*, or physical union with a whore. Both are sinful. And Pope Gregory, two hundred years later, endorsed St. Augustine's doctrine: even marital intercourse was never free from sin.

The Age of Asceticism

How can hereditary sin be escaped? The moderates inclined to compromise. They did not call for complete abstinence, but required men to eliminate libido as far as possible, even in wedlock. They should, as Augustine put it, not 'demand'. The radical party, however, advised men to withstand temptation and keep away from women altogether. For in the whole litera- ture of asceticism, which is a typical male literature, woman is the truly guilty party. She is the temptress, like her ancestress Eve; it is from her that the sinful thoughts proceed; she is more sensual and aggressive than man, albeit she knows better how to hide her thoughts. Clement of Alexandria, a born Athenian, a most learned and, in other respects, most liberal theologian, goes so far as to say: 'Every woman should blush at the thought that she is a woman.'

All the Church Fathers, meanwhile, agreed on one point: half- abstention was only half-emancipation from the evil. The truly pious man must abstain from all sexual intercourse; only so could he achieve inward spiritual peace. This lofty goal could not be reached without sacrifice; thus Origen, one of the greatest and most original thinkers of the Alexandrine School, chose to give mankind an example by emasculating himself. This, however, was more than could reasonably be expected of the most pious— and moreover, was it a solution of the problem? It was well known that eunuchs often entertained more sinful thoughts than ordinary men. He who would free himself from sin must first purify the spirit, then the body would follow. The best means was to take a vow of chastity.

The movement in favour of celibacy started in the East, where monasticism was a time-honoured institution. The mystic, Methodius, Bishop of Olympus in Lycia, was its foremost advocate. He polemicized vigorously against Origen, who had described women as daughters of Satan. Even if they are that, said Methodius, we must try to take them out of sin's clutches and lead them on to the right path. Methodius, like Origen, was steeped in Greek culture and looked up to Plato as his literary exemplar. This gave him the odd idea of writing a *Symposium of the Ten Virgins*. As in Plato the friends of love between men debate about Eros, so Methodius's virgins discuss all the advantages of virginity, which they concluded to be more desirable than the highest wedded happiness. The conversation takes place in the garden of Arete, the daughter of Philosophy, which lies on a steep hill—how fortunate that the Freudians were not yet there to read unchaste allusions into this picture! The dialogue is thoroughly monotonous, for Methodius is no Plato. Yet he produced one phrase which was destined to make history: the soul of a pure virgin may become the bride of Christ.

The idea was not new. It comes from the Song of Songs, in which the soul is made one with God. The God of the Jews, however, was himself only a thought, and it was unlawful to make a picture of him. Christ, on the other hand, had been a man, a handsome man, whose features were already enthroned above many an altar. The phrase 'bride of Christ' had a magical effect. It spread over all lands in which Christians dwelt. The theologians preaching asceticism added more touches, inserting further images and associations drawn from sex-life. Makarios represents the soul as a poor girl whose body is her sole possession. The Celestial Bridegroom, however, cares not for earthly riches. He loves her and seeks her in marriage. The betrothal thus becomes a marriage, and in many writers the soul of the pure virgin is already the bride of Christ. The libido is no longer extinguished; it is transcendentalized.

The West carried this even farther than the East. 'The complete transference to Christ', writes Harnack, 'of the sexual-feelings forbidden to them, is a peculiarity of the Western nuns and monks.'[74] Augustine's tutor, Ambrose, was the apostle of virginity in Italy. This Roman aristocrat, the 'Emperor of the Western Bishops', devoted five lengthy works to the subject. His book in praise of St. Thekla, the virgin of Antioch, who was abducted and placed in an oriental house of ill-fame but escaped and subsequently suffered a martyr's death, aroused such interest that young maidens came from Africa to Milan to take the veil under Bishop Ambrose's patronage.

The intoxication of asceticism reached its climax in the fourth and fifth centuries, just the period when the Roman Empire was falling swiftly into decay. Very likely many men found in the decline of Rome a reason for renouncing offspring. Long before this Tertullian had written in his *Ad Uxorem,* a book addressed to his own wife, that it would be better for her to remain a widow after his death, because in the Christian sense only one marriage could be complete and the wish for offspring could not outweigh all other considerations: in these unhappy times children were only a burden. This was in the time of the persecution of the Christians. After Tertullian's day Christianity had conquered Rome and become the official religion of the State. The times, however, had grown more unhappy still. The Christian writers who recommend asceticism hardly ever mention the fact that abstinence entails renunciation of issue. It was a sort of tacit agreement between the shepherd and the flock to leave propagation out of the equation.

Nevertheless, precisely this consequence was of the utmost historical importance. Almost all historians regard the diminution of its population as one of the causes of the decline of the Western Empire; many see in it the decisive factor. It is, however, still customary to ascribe the decline of the population to the corruption of morals.[75] Yet *gula* and *libido*—to use the Christian Fathers' expressions—are not so fatal to individuals—still less to whole peoples. In any case, the conquest of these vices by asceticism is a much surer means of decimating a population. It is, indeed, not possible to show statistically how far this was the case in Rome; but unless one assumes that the innumerable treatises in favour of asceticism were mere literary efforts and that no one except a few thousand monks and nuns ordered their lives after them, one is forced to conclude that sexual abstinence did more than excess to bring about the downfall of Rome.

6

POLYGAMY

THE sexual history of the Mohammedan countries is often depicted in terms of sultry nights of love, voluptuous women of the harem, and ludicrous eunuchs. But its beginnings were highly unromantic. A caravan agent in Mecca, Mohammed, son of Abdullah, son of Abdul Muttalib, married his employer, a rich widow named Khadija. She had been married twice before and was fifteen years older than her new husband. It is hard to suppose that the union between the twenty-five-year-old Mohammed and the forty-year-old Khadija was a love-match on his side. It was not the first time, nor would it be the last, that a man who felt himself called to a higher destiny smoothed his upward path by marrying money.

Mohammed's calculations proved correct. Now he was able to follow his meditative bent, unhampered by material cares. His marriage with Khadija was happy: it lasted for twenty-six untroubled years, until ended by her death. It was the pattern of a monogamous life-union. Even across the Red Sea, in the Empire of the Negus, where Christianity had by that time established itself firmly, there can have been no more perfect marriage. Notwithstanding her advanced years, Khadija presented her husband with six children, and Mohammed was completely loving and loyal towards her. His fidelity so impressed the worthies of Mecca that they nicknamed him *Al-Amein*—'the reliable'.

Not all men, of course, were as he. It is not in the nature of every man to content himself with one woman and not everyone finds a Khadija. Mohammed was aware of these truths, and allowed for them, for in the revelations which he received from

Allah there is no suggestion that a man should renounce the delights of love, or, if he fails to find them with one woman, not seek them with another. If they are denied him in this world, he can still hope for them in the next, where the good man who has confessed Allah and obeyed his commandments finds all his wishes fulfilled. When addressing prospective converts, Mohammed never forgot to picture to them the amorous delights which awaited them in the Seventh Heaven. Beds would be waiting for them there, and as many women as their hearts desired. And what women! 'Pure, immaculate virgins, maidens with great black eyes like pearls which are still hidden in their shells.'

But that was only for other people. Mohammed's own thoughts were all for Khadija; even in paradise he would certainly look for no other woman. When death bereaved him of Khadija he was inconsolable. Friends advised him to take another wife, a widow of unblemished reputation, but he rejected the thought; it would be treason to Khadija. It was, however, unseemly to remain unmarried, so he decided to marry a six-year-old little girl, Ayesha, daughter of his friend Abu Bekr. Child-marriages were nothing out of the ordinary in Arabia. There were even cases where a child in the womb was promised to a man, if it should turn out to be a girl. Marriages between elderly men and very young girls were, again, no rarity. Nevertheless, this marriage between Mohammed and Ayesha was something out of the ordinary. For him it was at first tantamount to prolonging his widowed condition, because early though women in Arabia mature, he would certainly have to wait for years before consummating the union. When Ayesha entered Mohammed's house she brought her toys with her, and her husband, who was old enough to have been not merely her father but her grandfather, took pleasure in watching the child at play.

Ayesha's Camel

When Mohammed was in his middle fifties, however, a second —it might be true to say a first—youth awoke in him. Sex acquired over him a mastery which it retained to the end of his days. His own countrymen had refused to listen to his prophesying: he emigrated to Medina, founded a State of the Faithful there, and became a successful military leader. Every victory over the Unbeliever was crowned by a new marriage. Mohammed's harem grew even faster than his empire. Some of the women on whom he bestowed his favours were the widows of fallen warriors, some were the daughters of enemies whom he sought thus to reconcile to him. There was also a Coptic girl called Marya whom the ruler of Eygpt sent Mohammed as a gift— causing much jealousy in the harem.

Mohammed's later love-life was by no means untroubled. The young women made fun of the old gentleman and intrigued endlessly against each other. More than once Mohammed was on the point of divorcing the lot, except only Ayesha, who remained his favourite wife and in whose arms he hoped to die. But even Ayesha caused him headaches enough.

Ayesha was the only one of Mohammed's wives who used to go with him on his campaigns—carried in a heavily curtained litter, so that no other man should set eyes on the Pearl of Allah. One day, however, she vanished; the camel and litter arrived at the halting place without her. Abduction was suspected; but who would dare carry off Mohammed's wife out of the midst of his armies? A few days later Ayesha came back, escorted by a young soldier. She had a moving story to tell. She had gone to wash herself at a halt and left her necklace behind. She had gone back to fetch it, and meanwhile the train had moved off, her camel with it. She had seated herself in resignation on the ground, like a poor little Bedouin girl, and waited for Allah to rescue her. Finally the deliverer had appeared, in the person of this gallant soldier.

The sages of Mohammed's entourage shook their heads. What would the Prophet do? Would he put Ayesha away from him? Would he have her put to death as an adulteress, as he had himself not long before ordered the Faithful to do in such cases?[76] But Mohammed was sager than the sages. Unlike Julius Caesar, who required that his wife must be above suspicion, he proved himself a gallant and understanding husband. He took Ayesha's side and thundered against her accusers: 'Why have they not brought four witnesses? Unless they bring witnesses, verily they are liars in the eyes of Allah.'[77]

Mohammed did even more than this to protect female honour —and his own. The incident touched him so nearly that he issued a new law on adultery. In future the punishment for the adulteress and the adulterer (i.e. the woman's lover, for the husband could ignore the marriage bond as often as he liked) was not to be death, but only flogging. Each was to receive a hundred strokes. If, however, they abstained from committing the sin absolutely in the public market-place they had very little to fear, for if anyone accused an honourable woman of adultery, and could not bring four witnesses to prove his charge, he was to receive eighty strokes—almost as many as the punishment for adultery—on the spot.[78]

Today, even these penalties may perhaps seem very servere, but compared with the codes of Eastern antiquity the *Lex Ayesha* was unexampled in its mildness. For himself, Mohammed drew another conclusion from the incident (this is not recorded in the Koran, but vouched for by his disciples): thereafter he left Ayesha at home and took another and more experienced wife with him on his campaigns.

If we are to understand Mohammed's sex-legislation, we have to take some account of his own experiences with women, whether important or trivial. His laws are not only the product of history and geography, the laws of the desert and the caravan, of religious fanaticism and ruthless conquest; they also reflect the excitements and disappointments of a sexually abnormal individual life. It will perhaps be objected that the life of most founders of religions was sexually abnormal. This is true and is why most religious sex-laws are so wrong-headed. The Mohammedan law bears the characteristic traits of a man who grew young—so to speak—late, who in his mature years suddenly turned from monogamy to polygamy and now found women too much for him. He could only shut them up, and even that did not always help. Out of this mixture of pride and servitude emerges a world in which the men command and the women rule, a world of harem intrigue, of over-heated and unsatisfied sensuality.

The Taming of the Shrew

The Faithful credit Mohammed with having been, for his time, an emancipator of women, who before then had counted for no more in Arabia than so many head of cattle. The example of Khadija alone suffices to refute this claim, but there may be a grain of truth in it if the conception of freedom is taken to apply only to social relationships. Islam, like Christianity, began as a religion of the small man. Mohammed met with the same resistance from the rich merchants of Mecca as Jesus from the Sadducees. The Prophet's most devoted adherents were slaves and women. Mohammed did not emancipate either class, but he tried to improve their social status. He formulated a fixed law of divorce and appealed to husbands' consciences, if they put away their wives, to do it kindly, not to keep back any part of their dowries and to make some provision for them. If after the divorce the wife was found to be pregnant, there should if possible be a reconciliation, but otherwise a husband should not make it difficult for the woman to marry again. We know little about the marriage law of Arabia before Mohammed, but the marriage-tie appears to have been very loose, and all the advantage lay with the husband. Mohammed would assuredly not have issued such very detailed provisions regarding marriage if there had not been much to reform in this field.

The emancipation did not, however, go very far. Even under the new law a wife was subordinated to her husband in every respect. She was the inferior creature; Allah had willed it so when he created them, and there was no changing this. The woman must obey the man. If she was disobedient and showed even a sign of rebelliousness, her husband should warn her, separate his bed from hers, and chastise her.[79] Mohammed expressly grants husbands the right to beat recalcitrant wives. This was probably not uncommon in the East even before his day, but none of the old codes lays it down so frankly as the Koran.

If after these procedures the woman submits, all is to be forgiven and forgotten. If the punishments have proved ineffectual and the marriage seems likely to break up, the first stage is the convocation of a family council composed of relatives of both parties. This is one of the very few provisions which seem to treat husband and wife equally. Strictly speaking, however, it is simply the two families which have concluded the marriage contract. Furthermore, this court is not empowered to pronounce any final verdict. The ultimate decision lies with the husband. He can divorce his wife, while she has no right to divorce him, however badly he may have behaved. He should not do so: the Koran enjoins him repeatedly to live soberly and to respect his wife. But these are only warnings, and no punishment attaches to disregard of them. The woman, on the other hand, is punished, the full severity of the law is visited on her.

If the marriage is dissolved, the husband gets the children, for children are wealth. This maxim governs the whole Mohammedan law. It was new for the Arabs, for before Mohammed's day poor people who felt unable to bring up their children used to dispose of them in the most cruel way conceivable, by burying them alive. Now a man arose among them and called to them: 'Slay not your children because ye are poor—we shall care for them and for you. . . . Allah has made life holy.'[80] Mohammed promised the poor more than he was able to give them. The *sura* of the Koran which contains these words dates from the time when he was only a prophet. Later, when he became head of the new State, he was careful not to promise his subjects that he would provide for them however many children they had. He tried, however, to protect the lives of children and mothers, within the limits of practicability. His enactments for the protection of expectant and nursing mothers and infants are far in advance of anything on the subject in Roman law, or in either the Old or the New Testament. They are genuine social legislation.

It was only after Mohammed's death, when his disciples set out to conquer the world in Allah's name, that this evolved into the population-policy typical of all States which need more soldiers. Now, too, all sorts of pronouncements were attributed to the Prophet to prove that marriage has only one end: the production of children. Mohammed himself never went so far as this. Men marry for four reasons, he said once to one of his confidants: for the woman's money, for her social position, for her beauty, or for religion's sake.[81] These words reflect Mohammed's own marriage history. He never asked a husband to put away his wife because she had not borne him children. His marriage with Ayesha was childless, yet Ayesha was always his favourite wife. A man's wish to have children should not kill his love for a woman who is unable to bear them to him, for sex has its own rights. The sexual instinct and the reproductive instinct can be reconciled. Polygamy provides the solution.

The Limits of Polygamy

Polygamy is the stock-breeders' form of marriage. They borrow their practice from that of their animals. One bull can serve many cows, one stallion many mares, one he-goat many she-goats. The Arabs had observed that carefully: they were even the first people to practise artificial insemination. The birth-rate depends primarily on the female animal, on the length of the period of gestation and of lactation, during which a fresh pregnancy rarely occurs. So it is also with human beings. A woman's capacity to conceive is limited, but during the intervals a healthy man can bestow his semen on other women, beget children and at the same time satisfy his sexual appetite. One man is enough for many women. This is nature's will, or would be if reproduction was the only point at issue.

But reproduction is only one aspect of human sex-life. There are others which a law-giver has to take into account. A modern commentator on the Koran has defined the difference between the Christian and the Mohammedan doctrines of marriage in the following terms: 'For Christianity, celibacy is the strictest religious ideal; even monogamy is a concession to human nature. For

Mussulmans the ideal is monogamy, the concession to human nature is polygamy.'[82] This may be a trifle forced, but it describes the Mohammedan doctrine accurately enough. The Koran is by no means a paean to polygamy. Mohammed's dicta on polygamous married life, his own or other people's, are nearly always laments for the woeful state of the man with many wives. One wife may be shrewish, but many wives are much worse: they quarrel with one another, they are rash and indiscreet (Mohammed's permanent nightmare)—in a word, they are an affliction. It is no wonder that there are more women than men in hell. Polygamy, however, assures a man uninterrupted enjoyment of the pleasures of love and affords him better prospects of progeny than monogamy.

An old tradition lays down that a Mussulman shall not have more than four wives at once. This limitation, however, was interpreted into the Koran, retrospectively, by the Kadis. The texts which go back to Mohammed himself contain only one reference to the point, and that a very vague one. After the Battle of Uhud, in which the followers of the Prophet suffered heavy losses, he exhorted the survivors to care for their comrades' orphans and widows and to marry 'two or three or four of them', or—if that was too much, then only one.[83] This was obviously just a careless figure of speech, not meant for a law. Mohammed himself did not keep to it: he married fourteen times and when he died, he left nine widows. Nor did other Islamic rulers observe the limitations; the Sultans of Turkey allowed themselves seven wives, besides the concubines and slave-girls on whom they bestowed occasional favours.

It was, however, no accident that the interpreters of the Koran fixed the number of principal wives for ordinary mortals at four. Four was the Prophet's favourite number: the principle of order, applied by him on various occasions, just as Plato, and Hegel after him, favoured tripartite categories. The Prophet did not like the number three: it was associated with the Trinity and Christianity.[84] One or four seemed to him natural and reflecting God's will. Whatever was founded on four stood firm, like a beast of burden. Four witnesses proved a statement, four reasons affirmed a thesis. It was thus conformable to the Prophet's spirit to interpret his dictum on the warriors' widows as meaning that the Faithful might have four wives. The limitation was not founded on economic considerations, for Mohammedan law allowed any man to keep as many concubines as he liked, beside his wives, and to legitimize their offspring.

Although permissible to all the Faithful, polygamy can never have been widespread among them. This was not only because the vast majority of men were too poor to keep more than one wife; even demographically, polygamy is not practicable as a general rule for married life. A simple mathematical calculation proves this. Exact investigation has shown that rather more boys are born than girls, but that the mortality is higher among boys, so that the numbers of children of the two sexes a few years after birth is approximately equal. From that point up to puberty— and the Arabs married very early—the composition of the population by sexes does not alter appreciably.

If we suppose, then, that there are a hundred girls of marriageable age for every hundred young men, but that only one man in ten wishes to take full advantage of the Islamic rule and live 'tetragamously'—i.e. to marry four wives—the result of even this relatively small number of polygamous marriages would be to leave only sixty women for the ninety men wishful of contracting monogamous marriages, so that one out of every three male candidates for marriage would have to remain single. If fourteen of the hundred men live tetragamously, forty-four, or more than half, of the remaining eighty-six must remain unmarried. If there were twenty marriages with four wives each, only one man in four of the other eighty could find a wife, and twenty-five tetragamous marriages would force all the other men to remain unmarried. It is quite certain that no State, however authoritarian, could get its male subjects to accept forced celibacy on this scale. If even one out of every three 'monogamous' males had to remain unmarried against his will because the 'polygamists' had snapped up all the women, there would be a revolt against polygamy. The history of the Mohammedan countries, however, records no revolt of the kind.

Hired Wives and Bigamy

Polygamy on any extensive scale is possible only when, for some special reason, there is a surplus of women in a certain country. This condition probably existed in Mohammed's day and in the subsequent period of the great Arab wars of conquest, in which many men perished. This is, indeed, the background of Mohammed's exhortation to marry the widows of soldiers. There were also—as, again, the Koran shows—many marriages with women encountered on the march and with the daughters of conquered lands. Women were booty of war, precisely because there was always a demand for them in a polygamous society. The big demand for women is also the explanation of the Mohammedan legislation on mixed marriages with members of other faiths. Marriages with heathens were prohibited unconditionally. Mohammedan men were allowed to marry Jewesses or Christian women, whereas Mohammedan women were forbidden to marry Jews or Christians.

The shortage of women could not fail to become more perceptible still as soon as times grew more tranquil and losses in war lower. The extremely high rate of death in childbirth threatened to reverse the proportions between the sexes, so that polygamy had even less chance to become prevalent. True polygamy, what the ethnologists call 'polygyny', i.e. the contracting of permanent marriages with several wives simultaneously, can therefore never have been at all widespread except in periods of prolonged and expensive war.

Polygamy, however, allows for many degrees, which are most nicely distinguished in Mohammedan marriage law. Strictly speaking, no marriages are binding for life under Islam, since a man can put away a woman at any time, even without the pretext of adultery. But this procedure, if repeated often, would after all reflect disagreeably on any man's character. Mohammedan law allows him to contract a so-called *mut'a*, or marriage for a limited period. The *mut'a* is no unlegalized concubinage; it is based on a marriage contract, which a woman is entitled to conclude even without her family's consent. The husband is bound to support the wife for the duration of the contract, often to pay a fixed sum of money, but the woman has no claim to a financial settlement on the expiration of the period. It is thus a lease-marriage, which is more convenient for the man, and sometimes also for the woman, than a marriage of unlimited duration.

Women who repeatedly contract *mut'a*s naturally do not enjoy the best of reputations. In the Sunnite countries, particularly in North Africa, *mut'a*s have always been regarded as mere 'unions of pleasure' and the women contracting them as disguised prostitutes. Yet precisely in the more strictly orthodox Shiite States— Iran and, in part, Iraq—*mut'a* is regarded as a regular form of marriage; the legitimacy of the children born of these unions is not questioned, and they are fully entitled to inherit.

Polygamy in Mohammedan countries very often comes down to bigamy: an elder wife and a younger whom the husband has married after the other has ceased to attract him sexually, or because she has failed to bear him children. At least as frequent as this legal *ménage à trois* is the situation in which a man lives with one lawful wife and a concubine, usually a servant, under the same roof. The number of wives depends primarily on the financial circumstances of the husband—although this is not the only factor determining whether a Mussulman has few or many wives, or makes do with only one. The number of children, the profession, and the social milieu are other factors. In many North African tribes a sheik who had only one wife would be as generally looked down on as a high civil servant who lives in bigamy in a Christian country.

In other parts of the Islamic world sex-life has become so Westernized that it is no longer considered seemly for members of high society to have more than one wife at a time. The Aga Khan, who is the spiritual head of the Ishmaelite sect, the Ali Khan, and ex-King Farouk of Egypt may be taken as prominent representatives of the Western school. We shall have later

PLATE 1

The "Venus of Willendorf". Front and side view. 11 cm. high, limestone. Found 1908 near Krems in lower Austria.

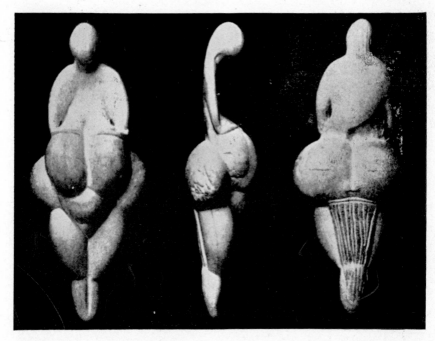

The "Venus of Lespugue". Front, side and back view. Carving in mammoth ivory. 14.7 cm. high. Found 1922 in the Grotte des Rideaux near Lespugue (Haute-Garonne).

PLATE 2

Naked woman with bison horn.
Relief from Laussel in South
of France. 46 cm. high.
Originally painted red.
Discovered 1912.

The three " Venus " figures
from the cave in the Roc aux
Sourciers near Angles-sur-l'Anglin.
Discovered 1950. Life size.

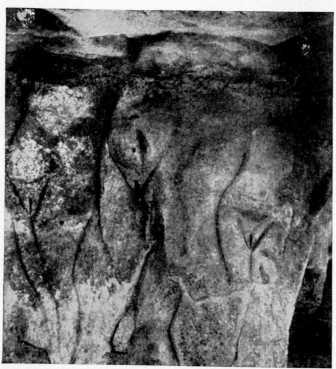

PLATE 3

Egyptian female musicians. Mural from the Nakht tomb in
Thebes. 18th dynasty. (16th century B.C.)

PLATE 4

The pursued Amazon throws herself down from the rocks.
Marble relief. 5th century B.C. Athens. Piraeus Museum.

Dancing scene with satyrs.
Picture on Attic vase,
figures in black.
4th century B.C.

PLATE 5

Female lute player.
Old Egyptian tomb
painting from Thebes.

The " Parisienne ".
Fresco from the royal palace
at Knossos in Crete.
2nd century B.C.

PLATE 6

Pair of lovers. Picture on Attic bowl. 5th century B.C.

Hetaerae. Vase picture from Euphronios.
5th century B.C. Leningrad Museum.

PLATE 7

Hetaera blowing flute at banquet.
Attic bowl of 5th century.
Paris, Louvre.

Female bird-rider. Phallic scene on Attic bowl.
4th century B.C.

PLATE 8

Erotic scene.   Base of bowl.   Greek.

to speak in more detail of the legal abolition of polygamy in Turkey, which is one of the most important events of modern sex-history.

The Office of the Eunuch

Polygamy in all its forms and nuances is under Islam a privilege reserved for men. Not in any circumstances may a woman have more than one husband. She is bound to remain absolutely faithful to him, even though he bestow his favours on countless other women under her very eyes. The men themselves have always regarded this extreme inequality as an inner contradiction and difficult to maintain in practice; it could not be introduced and maintained without compulsion. Women had to be shut up at home as far as possible, and when they left the house, must be thickly veiled from the eyes of other men.

Both institutions, the seclusion and the veil, are very old. It would be possible to trace a connection between them and the taboo codes of primitive peoples; but there is no need to look for any mystical background. Male jealousy, which exists in every human society, is motive enough to explain these mutually complementary devices for making woman, as it were, invisible. In Islam they are no special concomitants of polygamy; they apply equally to monogamous unions. It is obvious, however, that conditions of polygamy make it harder to keep an eye on women and therefore seem to men to call for stricter measures. Although the Koran made confinement within the house and veiling outside it religious obligations, they are not truly religious in character. They have no connection with the basic dogma of Islam, nor with its ritual. They are sexual measures, devised nominally to protect the woman against unchaste eyes; but really to safeguard marital fidelity, i.e. the husband's sexual property.

It is probable that both institutions were in existence before Mohammed in Arabia, as everywhere in the East, but in the more progressive countries they had already been abolished or greatly relaxed. Islam revived them, and also carried them into countries where they had previously been unknown. Up to this point, Mohammedanism must bear the responsibility for this cruel and degrading limitation of women's freedom. Woman is *de facto* isolated from the world, hidden and masked like a leper. Not only may she not show her face, her neck or her arms; she has to behave like a deaf mute. Even in the house she may only speak to her nearest relatives and her slaves.

Such a régime cannot without very strict supervision be enforced on women who are often half children. One might suppose that the most suitable person for this duty would be an elderly, experienced woman. Islam, however, answered the problem differently. Women did not possess sufficient authority over other women, and if they did possess it they could not be trusted. Women were all chips of the same block: they cheated, they intrigued, they conspired together. Men were needed to watch over women, but they must of course be men incapable of being dangerous to the women, i.e. eunuchs.

We have become used to regarding these guardians of female virtue in a comic light, as Mozart, for example, depicts them in *Il Seraglio*—bearish, malicious, but fundamentally harmless pot-bellied fellows who are always made fools of in the last act. But this is not what they were like in fact. Most of them were coarse, unpleasant creatures who embodied the despicable qualities of a spy and a Bumble. Even when they were humanly less repulsive, the institution remains one of the most loathsome ever devised. The warders of the marriage-prisons were not men who had vowed themselves to celibacy, like the eunuch priests of Eastern antiquity. They had been mutilated to prevent them from doing what they would have liked to do. They were qualified for their profession because they had been disqualified for adultery. They were unsexed physically, but psychically they belonged to the sexual sphere in which they lived. They were not ascetics, but emasculated men, sexual cripples.

It must be said for Mohammed that he neither invented nor promoted this institution. The Koran contains not a word about it, nor do the other early Islamic writings. It appears first at the

Courts of the Khalifs in Damascus and Baghdad, and thereafter
maintained itself for a full one thousand years in the entire
Mohammedan world. Remnants of it still exist today in some
Eastern countries.

Hierarchy in the Harem

The place in which the castrated guardians of marital morality
exercised their office was known to the Arabs as the harem, to the
Turks as the *haremlik*, to the Persians as *enderun* and to the
Indians as *zendnah*. Excavations in Tello suggest that there were
harems in Mesopotamia as early as 3,000 B.C., and ruins of harems
from pre-Mohammedan times have also been found in Persia.
It is unquestionable that in the Orient of antiquity, and even in
Greece, every princely palace and every large private citizen's
house contained special quarters for women. The only question
is how far the seclusion went. It seems never to have been carried
so far before as under the influence of Islam. The names are
significant in themselves. The Arabic word *haram* or harem means
something which is forbidden, unapproachable, sanctified, not to
be violated. Inside the mosque there is a place known as *al-haram*.
The word is applied not only to the place but also to the women
who inhabit it; they are *harim*.

But the harem is a special kind of sanctuary. It is not enough to
post a few sentries in front of the door; the inhabitants of the
harem are prisoners *de luxe*, who must be kept in suitable condition in order that the husband, when he visits them, may have
his proper pleasure. This calls for an outfit, with servants, mistresses of the wardrobe, craftsmen, jewellers, doctors. The harems
of great lords grew into regular courts, which it was impossible
to seal off hermetically against the outside world. Only poor
people can live hermits' lives; luxury needs human ministrations.
Even if the persons in question are nominally slaves, the daily
intercourse with them breeds a certain familiarity which may,
unless care is taken, lead to intrigue, indiscretion and possibly
even more directly intimate relations.

The Turks produced a monster organization for the solution

of these problems, the product of sexual ambition and sexual fear. A whole corps of men and women were employed at the Sultan's Court in Istanbul. They were organized in a strict hierarchy. The head of it was the Kyzlae Agha, the Chief of the Black Eunuchs, who were recruited in Africa. There were also 'brown eunuchs' from India, and 'white eunuchs', who were employed on other duties at Court. The white eunuchs formed the Sultan's personal bodyguard. It had been discovered that eunuchs can be trained like sporting dogs, and were very efficient in tracking down male-factors, even outside the harem. The head of the negro eunuchs was, however, something more than a mere officer of police. He was one of the high dignitaries of the Ottoman Empire and of equal rank with the Grand Vizier and the Sheik-ul-Islam, the highest religious official. He was Superintendent-in-Chief of all women's apartments, keeper of the keys of the harem, and had access at any time to the Sultan if he suspected anything amiss. This need not necessarily be only a love-affair; it might be a political intrigue—half the palace revolutions began in the harem.

The black guardians of the women of the harem were also their escorts if they were ever allowed to walk out. The word 'walk' is not appropriate, for it was not seemly for a lady of the Sultan's harem to walk. Either she rode on horseback, when not only she but also the horse was veiled, its head alone showing, or she was borne by four eunuchs in a litter closed as tightly as a coffin. Equally strict was the ceremonial inside the harem, especially for the merchants of silks and jewels who were occasionally permitted to enter it. They never set eyes on their customers: they were allowed only into an ante-chamber, whence they communicated with the Sultan's favourites through relays of harem employees. Not even the Court fools or the dumb door-keepers, who in other respects were the freest creatures in the seraglio, might approach the inner chambers of the harem.

The women of the seraglio were divided into five categories. In the first came the *kadyne*, the Sultan's official wives; in the second, the *quedikli*, or 'graduates', who served the Sultan at table when he chose to dine in the harem. The *quedikli* were, however, often required to perform more intimate duties, especially the favourite among them, the *ikbul* or odalisque—a word which only means, literally, chambermaid. The third category, the *ustas* or *khalfas*, were there to minister to the Sultanas and their children. After them came the *chagirds*, or novices, who could hope for promotion into a higher class; and finally, the army of *djaris*, or simple slave-girls.

Besides the women of serviceable age there was a host of superannuated women; for it was rare for a woman who had once entered the Sultan's harem to leave it again. It was a prison, but it also meant provision for life. The elder women therefore formed the majority, and the world experienced considerable surprise when Abdul Hamid's entire harem was carried away publicly, in omnibuses, after his overthrow by the Young Turks in 1909. Eye-witnesses testified that it looked like the evacuation of an almshouse for old women.

Sex-starvation

In the great princely harems, in which dozens, perhaps hundreds, of women were shut up, the most difficult problem was one of mixed physical and mental character. It is a problem common to all prisons—that of sex-starvation. The masters of the harem were not always fiery young lovers. Often they were elderly men to whom the harem was simply a drawing-room, and even when they succumbed to the women's charms the spur of conquest was lacking. He who owns a harem has no need to be a Don Juan. Rather, the plenitude of choice turns the heart to monogamy. The prince has his favourite. If, then, he occasionally bestows his favours also on some other woman, that is a proof of great kindness and justice. What happens to the others? They are more or less condemned to celibacy.

The sage princes of the East considered this problem very carefully, and sought to solve it by trying to divert their harems' minds from thinking only of sex. Harun al-Rashid, the great khalif who ruled in Baghdad at the beginning of the ninth century, is said to have had four hundred concubines in his harem, and required each of them to master some art. They might play a musical instrument, write, paint, do fretwork or anything else they liked, but they must have some occupation: not simply sit in idleness, waiting for him to tear himself loose from business of State and from his favourite, Zobeida, to sate their sexual appetites.

This recipe does not seem to have been very effective, for there were intrigues enough, even in Harun al-Rashid's harem. The problem proved insoluble. Lack of sexual satisfaction warps the character even of naturally good-hearted women: some grow dull and apathetic, others develop extreme irritability, a morbid jealousy of other women who appear to be favoured above them, or a nymphomania which not infrequently finds an outlet in sadistic excesses. This last type is particularly popular with the oriental writers, especially the Arabs, who have depicted harem life under the Khalifate. The woman is constantly preoccupied with deceiving her husband: she is sly, lascivious, and cruel.

Any means is good enough for her to achieve her end. Fear of punishment makes her keep her infidelities secret, but her greatest triumph is when she can prove to her husband that there are other men, besides him, who minister to her wishes. She is for ever chafing against the moral law which allows a man to have as many women as he likes, while a woman may have only one man, and him she must share with rivals. She cannot master her impulses; sex-starved as she is, she throws herself into the arms of the most hideous of her slaves.

Strangely enough, the legislators failed to enact that all harem slaves must be castrated, like the door-keepers. They obviously never supposed that free-born women could look so far beneath them. Yet the sex-instinct broke through even this social barrier. Moors and, in the stories of the later Egyptian period, Mamelukes are employed at the princes' courts, where the women are carefully shut away from the outer world and no worthier lover can gain access to them to satisfy their sexual hunger. The slaves seldom venture to approach them of their own initiative: it might cost them their heads on the spot. But the women command them to consort with them, and then the servants perform their duty zealously, usually to the satisfaction of their mistresses. But woe if her rightful lord and master grudges a neglected wife even this substitute for marital love! Of this situation are born the great tragedies of harem life.

Outwitting the Husband

This is the situation which forms the starting-point and the framework for the narrative of the Thousand and One Nights. One night King Shahseman surprised one of his wives in the arms of a negro slave. A far worse trick still was played on his brother, the Sultan Shahriyar. Shahseman was eye-witness of a most painful scene, which was something more than adultery—a veritable harem rebellion, a slaves' bacchanalia in which his brother's wife was a participant. Suddenly he saw the palace door open, and twenty slaves, male and female, issue from it, his brother's wife walking among them in all her beauty. They went to a spring, where they halted, disrobed, and stood waiting in a group. Suddenly his brother's wife called out 'Masud!' A black slave came up and embraced her. The others did the same, in couples, and ceased not until the sun went down. Yet a third time the sorely-tried brothers were shown how little faith can be placed in woman's virtue. On a journey they perceived that in spite of the closest watch, the Djinnai's wife sought to betray her honest husband with every comer.

It was then that the Sultan Shahriyar took the fearful decision to leave no woman alive with whom he had spent a night of love. He should not be betrayed again. If the eunuchs' vigilance was so ineffective, only death could ensure fidelity. He intended to deal thus also with Sheherezade, the beautiful and brilliant daughter of the Grand Vizier; she was to die on the morning after the bridal night. Sheherezade knew what fate was in store for her, but she succeeded in outwitting her jealous husband. Instead of tasting to the full the brief joys of love allowed to her, she began talking about literature and told her husband a story. And lo! the Sultan enjoyed her tale so much that he forgot that this was his wedding night and that the beautiful young girl at his side was doomed to die next day. He allowed her a period of grace to finish her story, and so it went on for a thousand nights. Sheherezade always broke off her story at the most exciting moment, and thus succeeded each time in getting the execution postponed.

Macabrely beautiful as it is, the story, if one strips off its oriental trappings, is only a literary *jeu d'esprit* with a deeper meaning: erotic literature can mean more to a man than the act of love itself. Modern Orientalists have discovered that the idea is not native to Arabia, but, like much in the Thousand and One Nights, comes from India.[85] In any case, it appears in two older Indian poems, the Story of the Seven Viziers and the *Sukasaptati*, in which, when a woman wants to go by night to her lover, her husband being absent, a clever parrot tells her a long story, always breaking off at the most interesting point with the words: 'I will go on tomorrow, if you will stay at home tonight.'

The Arabian author's adaptation of this ingenious idea is, however, characteristic: in the Indian version the moralizing bird restrains the woman from committing adultery, while in the far more dramatic Arabian version it is the woman who wins: she has prevented a suspicious, brutal husband from visiting the adulteries of her predecessors on her. It is the victory of female guile over the stupid male, who falls into her trap even while he thinks himself woman's absolute master. It is an episode out of the eternal sex-war, in which the victory always lies at last with the woman. But it is not only the arms of the spirit to which she owes her victory; in the last resort she is the stronger because the man is physically subject to her far more than she is to him. The strongest man cannot resist a beautiful young woman. That is the secret of her power.

This is most vividly illustrated in the story of the Sons of King Nooman. Sharkan, the mighty wrestler, whom no man has ever vanquished, sets himself to conquer the young queen Abrise. The issue is to be decided by a match between the champion and the queen. He seems certain to win, for Abrise is no Brunhilde, she is nothing but a beautiful young woman. But precisely this fact is fatal to Sharkan. The Thousand and One Nights tells 'How they seized one another, entwined their limbs and wrestled, until his arm was round her slender waist and his finger-tips touched her soft body. Then his limbs grew slack and he sighed and trembled like a reed of Persia when the storm-wind blows.'

The teachers of the Koran did not altogether appreciate this apotheosis of female guile and superiority. In the East the stories of the *Alf Laila wa Lalla* never enjoyed the esteem which they achieved in the West, after the archaeologist Antoine Galland made this masterpiece available to Western readers in his French translation at the beginning of the eighteenth century.[86] In Arabian countries the stories were regarded as literature for the people, to be told in the coffee-houses. Yet millions and millions of hearers have caught fire from these 'lying stories' by some unknown hand and have felt their youth renewed when they listened to them. No work in literature has given more pleasure to the Eastern and the Western worlds, or shown them deeper glimpses into woman's sex-life.

7

THE ART OF DISSIMULATION

NEITHER of the two great new religions had allowed the sex-instinct even as much freedom as the Law of Moses had granted it. Islam had delivered woman up to the mercy of polygamous husbands; Christianity practised justice by castigating both sexes. The difference, however, was fundamental. Under Mohammed's law a pious Mussulman could write: 'Praised be Allah who created women in their beauty, who formed their bodies with all the charms that awaken desire, who made their hair so beautiful, who fashioned their throats and the precious curves of their breasts.'[87] But at the Christian altars every evening the words were intoned which still form part of the official evening prayer of the Catholic Church: *Ecce enim, in iniquitatibus conceptus sum et in peccatis concepit me mater mea*— 'Behold, I was conceived in iniquity and in sin hath my mother conceived me.' And after man and wife had heard these words in repentance and had so prayed, were they to go back to the marriage bed and sin again, knowingly?

True believers were submitted to fearful pressure. Yet the sex-instinct was not to be repressed. It rebelled, even in men who had devoted themselves to the Church, body and soul. The struggle over the celibacy of the clergy lasted a full thousand years. For the theologians the question was one of dogma, but to the individual priest it meant a complete reversal of his life. The architects of the Church reckoned with this and went to work very cautiously. Even St. Paul, who favoured celibacy in principle and regarded it as especially desirable for missionaries, chose married men and fathers of families to be bishops.[88] The only limitation which he imposed on them was that they must not remarry if their wives died. Celibacy was not compulsory for the lower grades of the clergy during the first three centuries of the Christian era; it was only considered unseemly for men who had been consecrated priests when single, to marry afterwards.

The Struggle over Celibacy

It was only in the fourth century, when the preachers of asceticism were intensifying their campaign against the sins of the flesh, that the Councils occupied themselves with the question. At the Church conclaves, advocates of celibacy united to demand that married priests should put away their wives, or at least, abstain from all intercourse with them. One prince of the Church who was himself a bachelor, Bishop Paphnutius, came to the help of the married men and prevented sexual abstinence from being made compulsory on them. A few generations later, however, the pressure grew stronger. It came from the extreme West. A strong movement in favour of celibacy began in Spain and spread to southern France and Italy. Rome tried to mediate between the divergent views: in future, married men might still be consecrated priests, but once anointed they must renounce sexual intercourse. Pope Innocent I laid down that anyone refusing to accept this sacrifice rendered himself liable to punishment.

It was, however, still a long step from this threat to compulsory vows of chastity. Innumerable Councils debated the question and all its consequences. As late as the closing years of the seventh century the Council of Trullo confirmed the custom which allowed married priests to live under one roof with their wives. Only if a priest was consecrated bishop must his wife take the veil, and priests marrying after ordination were to be unfrocked. It was only very gradually, in the course of the next centuries, that complete celibacy was made the rule, even for the lower clergy. The resistance was particularly stiff in the East. The question of celibacy was one of the main reasons why the Orthodox Church, which tolerated married priests, split with Rome. Even in the West, however, there were many priests married or living in open concubinage—citadels of the sinful flesh. In vain did the Archbishop of Canterbury command all married priests in England to put away their wives. More vigorous still was the resistance in Milan, where the entire priesthood was married, and appealed to the precedent set by St. Ambrose.

Milan was too near Rome for the Church to dare tolerate such disobedience. It was the obstinacy of the Lombard priests that ushered in the last phase of the great struggle. Celibacy found support in the great monastic orders, whose importance was steadily growing. The monks had more adherents among the people than the priests, and their influence gave the struggle against priests' marriages the character of a popular movement. Married priests were pilloried as lustful voluptuaries, men who had succumbed to the woman-demon. No mercy for them! Rome still hoped, however, to bring the priests to see reason without expelling them from the Church. In 1018 Pope Benedict VII enacted that the children of clergy should be perpetual serfs of the Church. After the children, it was the women's turn to be blacklisted: wives of priests were placed on an equal footing with concubines.

Pope Leo IX (1048-54), the man who consolidated the Church after years of great disorder, went a step farther. Chastity was now formally enjoined on priests: to disregard this command was not only an offence against discipline but a heresy. This was serious, for the consequences of a charge of heresy could be extremely disagreeable. The Church did not need to see to the execution of the punishment itself. Mobs, incited by the monks, broke in on priests who refused to be parted from their wives. Even Milan had to capitulate. A Council held in Rome in 1059 took one more step to blacken married priests in the eyes of the faithful: the laity were forbidden to hear Mass from a priest who had a woman in his house.

The driving force in this struggle was the Tuscan monk Hildebrand who mounted the papal throne in 1073 as Gregory VII. The very next year a Council in Rome branded all commerce between priests and women as whoredom (*fornicatio*). All priests who were still living with wives were commanded to put them away instantly. As the Church did not recognize divorce, it could only order separation from bed and board, but this was to be enforced most rigidly. Yet even the unyielding monk-Pope who had forced the Emperor to his knees had a hard struggle to assert his will on the question of celibacy. He had to send out special legates to break the resistance of the priests outside Italy.

Stormy scenes took place at the Councils of Mainz, Erfurt and Paris, where the question was debated over again. Even high dignitaries of the Church were still found to speak for the married priests. The monks were called in once more to help the people vent its indignation. Nevertheless, decades more passed before celibacy was generally practised—at least nominally—in the West. No more priestly marriages were concluded, except in the Eastern Churches in union with Rome, where they are still allowed today. Concubinage went on, however, almost openly. Monastic morality, too, became laxer; there were innumerable scandals in the monasteries and convents. The question of celibacy continued to smoulder throughout the Middle Ages, like fire under ashes, till Martin Luther blew it into a leaping flame which split the Church for the second time.

The Castration of Abelard

Just when Rome looked to have succeeded in driving the woman-devil out of the priests' houses, there occurred one of the most frightful sex-tragedies of the Middle Ages. The love story of Abelard and Héloïse is a Faust and Margaret drama, but it is no fable. It happened in the student quarter of Paris about A.D. 1119, long before the birth of the Faust legend. Pierre Abelard, a most learned scholar of distinguished family, was born near Nantes in 1079, at the time when the monk-Pope Hildebrand was still ruling in Rome. He studied theology, but did not take Orders, finding a life without any woman in it too barren. He founded a school of philosophy and theology (which were one and the same thing, since at that time there could be no truth other than that of the Church) on the Mont Sainte Geneviève in

Paris, later the site of the Panthéon and the Sorbonne, and then already Paris's *quartier latin*. He was an extraordinarily successful teacher: hundreds of students flocked to his school. Although his lectures were often more liberal than was thought fitting for a man of learning, he was highly esteemed in clerical circles. The Bishop of Paris was his friend, and he lodged with the Canon Fulbert.

The austere Canon had submitted to the rule of celibacy, but he had taken into his house a young niece named Héloïse. She came of one of the noblest families of France, and had been brought up in a nunnery. Her uncle guarded her closely, wishful that when a suitor worthy of her sought her hand she should enter on married life a virgin. Yet even in this pious household the devil wrought his mischief. Héloïse was seventeen, Abelard nearly forty, but he was not only a great scholar but also a fascinating speaker, a wonderful singer and a gifted composer. She lost her heart to him. On the wings of spirit and song was born a love affair which did not remain without consequences. When Héloïse's pregnancy could no longer be concealed, Abelard sent her secretly to his sister in Brittany, where she gave birth to a boy. Abelard offered to marry her, but she refused, saying that men of genius must not encumber themselves with families; the theologians who wrote on celibacy said so. Héloïse knew the texts which she had studied with Abelard and quoted them, for she, too, was highly educated and corresponded in Latin like any scholar.

Meanwhile, however, the household in Sainte Geneviève had got wind of the matter, and the Canon took a dreadful revenge on the man who had seduced his niece and defiled his house. One night he forced his way into Abelard's bedroom, accompanied by several accomplices, who overpowered Abelard and castrated him on the spot. His students were infuriated at the outrage to their professor, but the scandal was so great that Abelard had to abandon his teaching and leave Paris. The Church hushed up the incident, Héloïse took the veil, and Abelard, too, retired into a monastery.

Yet the nun Heloissa (as Héloïse was called now) could find no
rest, even in the cloister. She wrote passionate letters to Abelard:

> Yet another still stranger experience has been mine. My love itself
> turned to madness, so that of its own volition it renounced the only
> thing it desired, without hope of ever recovering it. That happened
> when I obeyed thy will and undertook to change my heart with my
> gown, to show thee that thou alone art lord of my body and my soul.
> Nought have I ever sought in thee—God knoweth it—except thyself.
> Thee only did I desire, not what was thine. I sought no marriage, no
> wedding gift, I sought not to satisfy my desire and my will, but only
> thine—well thou knowest it. The name 'wife' might sound to thee
> nobler and more honourable, but to me it was ever more delightful to
> be thy 'beloved' or even—take it not amiss of me—thy 'mistress',
> thy 'strumpet'.[89]

Abelard sought to quieten her and to turn her mind to things
of the spirit, but Héloïse was not to be reconciled with her lot.
' 'Tis thou whom I would please', she wrote, 'not God. 'Twas thy
word, not the love of God, made me into a nun. Ah, look on my
unhappiness, do I not lead the most pitiful of lives when all that
I suffer is in vain and no thanks await me in the future?'[90] Abelard
could offer her no consolation but to trust in God's wisdom: 'In
his merciful counsel he has decided to save us both through one
of us, while the devil strives to destroy us together.'[91]

Gradually the devil relaxed his grip on them. Héloïse learnt
with pleasure that Abelard had been allowed to recommence
instructing the young. He had founded a new school on an
estate in Champagne, and over three thousand students streamed
out into the country (which says much for the open-mindedness
which then ruled in France) to be initiated by the mutilated
master into the doctrine of the *Universalia*, the relationship
between ideas and things. He founded a nunnery, in which
Héloïse also took up her quarters. Again, however, they were
soon parted. This time the monks were against him. Now that
sex no longer distracted it, his spirit became more rebellious than
ever; he became involved in a conflict with the Church, and it

was only the Pope's special dispensation that enabled him to end his troubled days in a monastery, as a simple monk. Héloïse outlived him twenty years. She, too, died in the cloister, but high in honour, for the sins of her youth had been forgiven her.

Intercourse with the Devil

Had Abelard and Héloïse lived a few centuries later they might have fared worse still, for meanwhile a new plague had appeared on the earth. The man or woman possessed by the devil of sex had now to reckon not only with his neighbour, but also with authority, and this usually meant death at the stake after frightful torture.

The devil seduced persons of either sex, but his victims were usually women. The women who were possessed of the devil, meaning that they committed uncleanness with him, were of many kinds. There were wrinkled old crones with dishevelled grey hair whom no man would look at any more, so they flew on broomsticks by night to the Witches' Sabbath, for the devil to sweep them. Although their personal sex-life could no longer do much harm, they were nevertheless dangerous, for they brewed love-philtres for maidens and adulterers, compounded salves which make men impotent, coupled unmarried women to lustful men and then destroyed in the womb the fruit of these sinful unions. In brief, they carried on many activities noxious to mankind.

More dangerous still, however, were the young witches, for they had dealings not only with the devil but also with men of this world, with a preference for married men and respectable citizens. As it was not always easy to distinguish between a witch and an ordinary whore, special tests were necessary. The surest proof was, of course, when a woman, or a man, was caught consorting with the devil or his assistants—for since the devil could not transact his own business singlehanded he kept assistant devils to carry out his will. These creatures were of various sorts, notably the male incubus, which descended on women at night and had sexual intercourse with them, and the female counterpart, the succubus, which had intercourse with men. Sometimes the devil would turn himself into a black cat as large as a medium-sized dog, or a he-goat.

Witnesses often testified to having surprised the accused in

Satan and a witch. Woodcut, *circa* 1500.

intercourse with the devil. The judges of the Inquisition were, however, conscientious after their fashion. They attached weight to confessions, and torture or the mere threat of it usually extracted the most absurd self-accusations from the terrified women. So, at one witch-trial in Toulouse, in 1275, the accused, one Angèle de Labarthe, 'confessed' that she had had sexual intercourse with the devil in person and had given birth to a monster with a wolf's head and a serpent's tail. Since this monster, her own child, had fed on the flesh of children, she had been forced to kill other children.

The Court's stock leading questions usually elicited identical answers, and thus a complete anatomy and physiology of the devil was built up. The women always said that coitus with the devil was very painful, since he possessed an excessively large and hard penis; it was shod with iron, or else covered with fish-scales —opinions on this point varied—and his semen was ice-cold. Although it would be assumed from this that the devil must have injured the woman's body severely, the contrary was the case. For since young, completely intact girls were denounced as witches, the explanation was found that women could have intercourse with the devil without being deflowered. Respected theologians agreed that this was entirely possible.[92]

The devil's particular sexual sphere, however, was his hindquarters, in which lustful women took especial delight. Numerous illustrations from the Middle Ages show women keeling down to peer beneath the devil's tail. If they succeeded in kissing the

Satan's train. Woodcut from the *Compendium Maleficarum*.

orifice, mysterious powers were believed to be conferred upon them. If anyone wanted more of the devil, it was necessary to conclude a pact with him. This was not always so formal as in Goethe's *Faust*. Often it was enough if would-be witches gave the devil four hairs as pledges for their souls. Blood-pacts with the devil were not always necessary, although it was, of course, more convincing to have something put down in red and white. Documents of this kind were at times produced in evidence at witch trials.

Often, however, the inquisitors had to content themselves with less certain proofs. Fortunately for the investigators, intercourse with the devil always left traces on the bodies of the persons bewitched. One of the most infallible was a sort of local anaesthesia. If needles were applied to the suspect and she did not twitch at every prick, this was a sign that the place had been touched by the devil's fingers, or it would not have been insensible. Freckles, warts or other trivial blemishes of the skin were often adduced as proof. Even sties which disappeared after a few days were regarded as devil's work, and might lead to fatal consequences for the persons concerned.

The Witches' Hammer

The Church has often been blamed for these absurdities. That is not justified. The Church of the Middle Ages was by no means a gloomy, sadistic, mystical-minded institution; on the contrary, it had emancipated itself from the mystic mists of Alexandria, the spiritual world of neo-Platonism, and had in the best sense of the word become latinized. It strove to spread clarity and light and to prove logically, in Roman fashion, what it believed and what it held to be right. It had taken over the conception of the devil (who has had a place in human creeds since time immemorial) from the East, particularly from the religion of Persia, and when it advanced northward it rediscovered this under another form. The spirit of evil was the necessary counterpart to the all-good God; without this dualism the existence of God would be too hard to maintain. It also served the cause of morality to dangle the corporeal devil and all his accoutrements before the eyes of the masses, who were not susceptible to theological argument. But the Church held the belief in witches to be a heathenish superstition which ought to be eradicated. Its first measures were directed not against alleged witches but against those who believed in them. The Synod of Paderborn itself pronounced that 'If any man, blinded by the devil, believes in heathenish fashion that someone is a witch, and burns her, let him die the death!'

Gradually, however, the line between belief and superstition became blurred. The devil blinded even the most clear-sighted

Burning witches. Broadsheet describing a witch-trial, 1555.

clerics. Albertus Magnus and Thomas Aquinas, the two leading theologians of the thirteenth century, were both firm believers in the existence of witches. Theologians who disagreed were themselves haled before the Inquisition and could count themselves lucky if, like Professor Guillaume Edeline of Paris, they got away with life imprisonment.[93] After the first wave of witch-trials, which began in southern France, had spent its force, a new epidemic of witch-hunting broke out at the turn of the fourteenth and fifteenth centuries, this time in the Alps. It spread like wildfire across Germany, France, and Italy, and within a generation half Europe had succumbed to the infection. It was often impossible even to credit the inquisitors with good faith. Accusations of witchcraft were simply used as a pretext to get rid of inconvenient people. The sexual motive was not always the dominant one, as the burning of the 'witch' Joan of Arc shows, although witch-madness was always coupled ideologically with sexual associations.

The Inquisition did its best to exterminate witches, but new ones constantly appeared. All previous methods having failed to put down the devil's handicraft, Pope Innocent VIII, son of a doctor and no ascetic in his own way of living, prepared a grand blow. In 1484 he issued the Bull *Summis desirantes affectibus*, in which he expressed his anxiety about intercourse with the devil: 'Not without immense grief have I recently learned that in certain parts of Germany, particularly in the regions of Mainz, Trier, Salzburg and Bremen, very many persons of both sexes, forgetful of their own weal and straying from the path of the Catholic Church, have sinfully consorted with devils in male and female form.' At the same time, the Pope appealed to two most expert witch-hunters, Jakob Sprenger and Heinrich Institoris, inquisitors for north and south Germany respectively, ordering them to collect all available information on the best way of recognizing and convicting witches.

The two experts set to work with the greatest zeal, and two years later presented the Pope with that masterpiece of juristic acumen and sexual idiocy, the *Malleus Maleficarum* or 'Witches' Hammer'. It was first printed in 1487, and thereafter constantly revised and brought up to date, reaching the twenty-eighth edition by 1669. But even the first edition justified its name: it was a true hammer. Now the witch-hunters could lay about them. The first two parts of the 'Witches' Hammer' give a sketch of witches' misdeeds and of the arts practised by them to conceal their wickedness; the third part shows how they can nevertheless be convicted if an exact judicial procedure is applied.

The magistrate had to put thirty-five questions to the suspect. The first question alone was enough to send the witch to the stake, irrespective of the others. It ran: 'Believest thou in witches?' If the accused answered 'yes' she was versed in witchcraft; if she answered 'no' she was guilty of heresy. If she tried to deny her guilt under further questioning, she was to be put to the torture, and other witches, especially those hostile to her, called in evidence against her. If there was still any doubt of her guilt, a judgment of God, similar to the old Babylonian ordeal by water against adulteresses, was to be invoked. She was bound hand and foot, and cast into the water. If she sank, she was a witch; if she floated, this was proof that the water rejected her baptism, so she

The witch's ordeal. After a sixteenth-century woodcut.

was still a witch. A woman was thus drowned for a witch on the Hela Peninsula, near Danzig, as late as 1836.

The 'Witches' Hammer' achieved instantaneous and general popularity in all civilized countries and quickly attained the rank of an international *corpus juris*. The great Popes of the Renaissance, Alexander VI, Julius II and Leo X, endorsed it. The inquisitors were now able to work freely, to the advantage not only of their consciences, but also of their purses, since the property of convicted witches was confiscated and part of it was the judges' perquisite. The witch-madness and witch-trials were not confined to the Catholic world; the Reformation provided them with fresh fuel from both sides. In England witch-hunts reached their climax under Queen Elizabeth; in the next century they spread to the North American colonies, but even in Europe witch-mania was still rampant in the century of Galileo and Descartes. It was not a case of individual instances, but of mass annihilation of human beings. A Saxon magistrate boasted that he had read the Bible through fifty-three times and had condemned twenty thousand witches.[94]

Knightly Morals: Virtuous Adultery

The history of the witch-trials itself shows that the Middle Ages were more tolerant in matters of sex-life than many earlier and later ages. No one except priests, monks and nuns—who constituted, indeed, a considerable fraction of the population—was required to repress his sexual impulses. They were not to be driven out, as the Fathers of the Church had wanted, only concealed. Subject to this condition, people could, in practice, do as they liked. If it is permissible to characterize a period so long and so changeful with a simple phrase, we may say: the essential was dissimulation. This applied to politics, and also to sex-life. On the surface, everything centered round loyalty. The entire feudal system depended on the fidelity of the vassal to his liege lord, and family life on a marital fidelity which left no place for other relationships. But the elaboration of the conception of fidelity brought with it as its corollary the elevation of infidelity into a fine art.

An act of infidelity was no disgrace, always provided that one preserved the forms of polite society and was prepared to draw the sword and if necessary (this was not often the case) to die for one's heart's passion. The art of adultery used the same terminology as the official code of morals: honour, purity, virtue, loyalty were part of the regular vocabulary of the heroes who seduced other men's wives. Any knight who contented himself with wedding a maiden before having himself grown practised in adultery and carried off several trophies of the chase was unworthy of his spurs. Adultery was a social diversion among the upper classes. A knight had to have a 'lady' whom he worshipped, to whom he devoted himself, and the lady had to be married, if possible to a husband of slightly higher rank than the lover, for in knightly love the eye was always turned upward. Everything was pure, delicate and noble—*honi soit qui mal y pense.*

To suggest any connection between these sex-relationships and the devil—to say nothing of witchcraft—would have been to inflict a mortal insult on the knight's pride and the lady's honour. Fortunately the suggestion was never made. Church and State alike tolerated the adulterous relationship between the young knight and the baronial lady. A cavalier might even bring religion into his affairs of the heart. It was the thing to choose a celestial patroness, and the usual practice, incredible though it sounds, was to invoke the Virgin Mary to patronize the liaison and soften the lady's heart towards her suppliant.

The Virgin Mary had been definitely recognized as *Theotokos,* the Mother of God, by the Council of Ephesus in 431. Since then, the cult of the Virgin had passed through many phases. She was more than a mortal woman; divine honours were paid her. In the period of transition from heathendom to Christianity she was identified in the East with Rhea-Cybele, the Great Goddess of the Greco-Roman pantheon. In Italy she borrowed the features of Ceres, the harvest goddess;[95] in northern Europe she took the place of the goddess Freya. Presently, however, the faithful installed her on a still higher throne as *Regina Coeli,* Queen of Heaven. It was only in the later Middle Ages that she became more humanized and was made the symbol of motherhood. Never before, however, had mankind committed such blasphemy as to make the Virgin the patroness of organized adultery—for the knightly *minne* service, divested of its romantic trappings, was just that.

The Sex-rebellion of the Minnesingers

Later ages would probably have passed severer judgment on the sex-life of the knights and their ladies had it not been sung by so many bards. The poetry of the *minnesingers* has sublimated these doings so completely that teachers give most of them to school-children to read, at the same time preserving a truly medieval discretion on what they are really about. It is true that not all the *minne* poetry is treated as meat for babes.

The first troubadour (the Provençal word *trobador*, like the Old French *trouvère*, simply means an inventor of songs) was the exceedingly merry Duke William IX of Aquitaine, a contemporary of the luckless Abelard. William had a spacious heart and made no bones about it. He was a cynic who anticipated the philosophy of Don Juan as only a very high independent lord could dare do in the Middle Ages. His belief was that a real man should endeavour to possess all women, and he acted accordingly. When, after long shilly-shallying, he consented to go on a crusade, he surrounded himself with a swarm of courtesans on his journey to the Holy Land, and the chronicler Geoffroy de Vigeois ascribes the failure of the expedition, in part, to the sensual pleasures in which he indulged.[96] Only fragments of his poems have survived; some are philosophic contemplations, others were crude obscenities.

This first ancestor of *minne* song was soon followed by worthier successors. Jaufré Rudel was a noble melancholic, always broken-hearted because women were reluctant to listen to him, and Bernard de Vantadour, a tempestuous lover, insistent on his rights. But in France at the same date a moralist named Marcabru, who was himself of no high lineage, but a foundling—probably a peasant's child from the Danube—lifted up his voice. He complained bitterly that the Court poets were corrupting morality and that 'the Tree of Perversity' overshadowed all things. It is not necessary to conclude from this that morals on the Danube were much better than in France. It was only a century before the *minne* poetry reached its climax there. Historians of literature distinguish between 'high' and 'low' *minne*, according to the degree of nobility of purpose and feeling inspiring the knights and poets. The 'high *minne*' had an educative purpose: it served to perfect a man and to make a true hero of him. The 'low *minne*' was more concerned with sensual pleasure, and was also looser in form, although poets of genius, such as Walther von der Vogelweide, practised this form or drew on the sources of the low *minne*.

This nice distinction is somewhat unilluminating for the history of sexuality, for even in the high *minne* the knights in armour and champions by no means rested content with platonic love, but set out to achieve complete conquest over the lady of their hearts. Their efforts always received their crown in bed. This was the reward for which they strove, and if the lady was obdurate, or too hesitant, the lover, jettisoning his oath of loyalty, turned to another fair one to try his fortune. We seldom hear of disappointed lovers retiring to a monastery or turning to asceticism, although special spiritual orders of knighthood existed for the purpose. *Per aspera ad astra*—'through toil to the stars'—or more exactly, *per aspera ad adultera*—through toil to adultery—that was the unwritten motto of this lofty society.

It sometimes happened, indeed, that a woman overshot the mark and, by demanding too much of her knight, ended by being disappointed herself. Thus it is recorded of the doughty knight Moritz von Craun that when, after excessive exertions, he reached his divinity's bed, he fell asleep from exhaustion; the lady naturally thought this unchivalrous and consequently broke with him. Then there was the young Styrian knight, Ulrich von Lichtenstein, a precursor of Don Quixote. He always carried with him a bottle of the water in which his mistress had washed, from which he was wont to refresh himself. He cut off one of his fingers and sent it to his lady as a token that he was prepared for any sacrifice; but she, who obviously had more sense than her adorer, now decided definitely to have none of him.

These are the tragi-comic accompaniments of a woman-cult developed to the pitch of masochism—a phenomenon unparalleled down to our own day. But there was also a more serious side to it. What happened, sociologically? As the history of *minne* service is known to us almost exclusively through love-poems and chivalric romances, it is not easy to answer this question or to say how much in them is pure invention and how much is more or less true to fact. The vassaldom relationship of the knight to the noble lady has been explained as a mere variant of the existing feudal law: young gentlemen of rank and status tried to win the favour of great ladies, who, especially in southern France, were sometimes very rich and powerful in their own right. But economic motives of this kind can only rarely have been an important factor; most frequently, perhaps, among the wandering minstrels of the small nobility, desirous of finding shelter for the winter in a rich man's castle.

If this theory had been correct, the whole *minne* service would be merely a form of literary patronage with erotic embroiderings. Probably, however, it was something more. Even if most of it was only literature, paraded in the ale-houses, or often in monastic refectories on the high-roads or in great men's banqueting halls, yet there was behind it a revolt against the existing lay and ecclesiastical legal order. What the bards and minstrels said to their audiences, indirectly, but plainly enough, was: 'Lo! everything you are told in Church about the sanctity of marriage applies only to the small man. The great do not need to trouble about it; neither do they. *Minne* law is above marriage law.'

This principle applied to women, as well as men. Wolfram von Eschenbach, the author of *Parsifal*, makes Parsifal's father, Gahmuret, forsake his wives Belahane and Herzeloyde to take service under his 'lady', the fair Amphlise. It is the same story with Tristan, who is also a married man. But the real novelty was the liberty which the *minnesingers* conceded to the married women. Love for their knights at once absolved them from loyalty to their husbands. The decisive factor was the sexual attraction—not the marriage bond, not the family, nor the children, who are hardly mentioned in the whole of *minne* poetry. As, however, marriages could not be formally dissolved, a secret liaison with the lover was the only way out. A few heretics, such as Gottfried of Strasbourg, went farther still, and openly bewailed the conflicts produced by the indissolubility of marriage. They did not, however, venture to demand divorce.

The *minnesingers* were great heroes on the battlefield of love, but they were no sexual revolutionaries. They clenched their fists in their pockets, but they were not prepared to challenge the existing order in open combat. On the surface, accordingly, nothing changed; it was only inside society that a transformation took place. Marriage became looser and woman more powerful than ever before.

Courts of Love and Chastity Girdles

In the later Middle Ages, when the old feudal system was in dissolution, and the princes and rich burghers growing stronger, the impoverished nobles attempted to turn the cult of woman into a sort of class shibboleth and, at the same time, a remunerative profession. The itinerant knights who broke a lance at a tournament for their lady of the day, were no longer interested in conquering her person; they were satisfied to get from her a tangible reward in the shape of a valuable prize of victory. Knights could even display their courage and skill in the service of imaginary ladies. Jacques de Lalaing, the champion of the itinerant knights, whose proficiency in the joust won him the hearts of two noble ladies at once, the Duchess of Calabria and Princess Maria of Cleves, made himself the impresario of the abstract woman-cult. He erected a pavilion on an island in the Saône near Châlons, in which he placed a statue of a mysterious weeping woman. No one knew who she was, but she could be fought for. Tournaments were held for a whole year in front of the *Fontaine des Pleurs*.

Although chivalry was obviously on the decline, new Orders of Chivalry were still founded; thus in 1399 Marshal Boucicaut founded the 'Order of the Green Shield with the White Lady', whose statutes pledged its members to defend ladies in their just causes against all comers and against all things.[98] These Orders were, however, in reality only aristocratic clubs in which one chattered about books, swapped amorous experiences, discussed preparations for festivals and occasionally made politics. They were, incidentally, purely masculine associations; women were not admitted.

Not very different from them was the famous *Cour d'Amour*, or Court of Love, which was founded in Paris in 1400 by Philip the Bold, Duke of Burgundy, and counted among its members the intellectual *élite* of the European Courts, Louis of Orleans, brother of the King of France, Ludwig of Bavaria, Jean de Bourbon, and also important humanists and even leading ecclesiastics.

The Little Garden of Love. Engraving by the Master of the Gardens of Love, *circa* 1440-1450.

In spirit and form the *Cour d'Amour* already resembled the Renaissance Academies of Italy, except that the subject of discussion in Paris was not Plato but love. Here, too, the most important item on the agenda was the service of women. In practice, indeed, the Court confined itself to organizing competitions for ballads in praise of women, readings and banquets. The literary productions were modest, the gains for women, nil. It had a great success, however, and it soon had a membership of six hundred and was widely imitated.

An important new element in this enterprise, which it owed not to the knights but to the direct influence of the Court, was a certain democratization. Ordinary citizens were admitted to membership, and they were naturally greatly flattered at being allowed to discuss the problems of love with noble lords. The wall which had made the cult of women a privilege of belted knights, was thus officially breached. The bourgeois took honest pains to show themselves deserving of this unexpected honour.

They outdid one another in the finesses of love poetry, and were scandalized at the assertion of the *Roman de la Rose*, the great French love-epic of the thirteenth century, that 'an honest woman is as rare as a black swan'. They instituted their own poetry competitions, and even admitted such dubious fellows as lyric poets into their homes. In the end, matters came to the paradoxical pitch described by Wagner in the *Meistersinger*, where a knight who is courting a goldsmith's daughter has to compete with a town clerk, and needs the patronage of a cobbler at that.

Generally speaking, however, the middle classes proved the bulwark of morals, even in this age of social upheaval. They defended not only their purses and property but also their women better than the barons. Swords were not necessary: the burghers had thought out another device for guarding their lawful spouses against adultery. When a merchant went away on business, he guarded his wife with a chastity girdle, a metal framework a handsbreadth wide, which left only a small opening which allowed a woman to perform her necessary non-sexual functions. The girdle was closed over the hips by a lock to which only the husband possessed the key.

This disgusting product of masculine jealousy derives directly from Homer. The *Odyssey* describes how Aphrodite (Venus) betrays her husband, Hephaistos, with his brother Ares. In revenge, Hephaistos forges a girdle to prevent her from further infidelities. It never occurred to the Greeks, however, to take this farcical fable seriously and to shut up their wives' persons in this fashion. It was only two thousand years later that this perverse idea occurred—first, apparently, to the Florentines, whose wives were not specially renowned for their fidelity. The horrible instrument was then copied elsewhere, and was popularized throughout Europe in the fifteenth and sixteenth centuries under the name of the 'girdle of Venus' or 'Florentine girdle'. It was technically perfected; rich men had their wives' girdles ornamented with gold. Ingenious women found ways to rid themselves of it; jokes about spare keys to the chastity girdle form part of the regular repertory of satirists. All the same, husbands

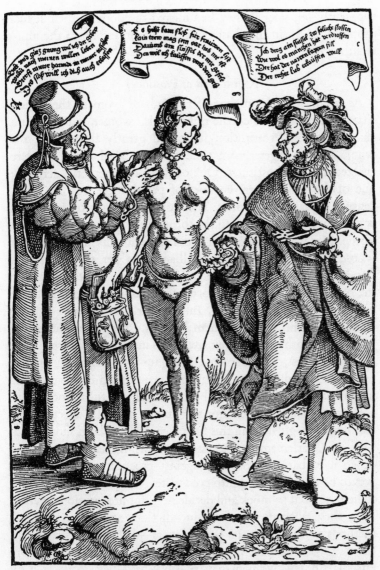

Woman wearing a chastity girdle, between two men. She is taking money out of the purse of the old man (presumably her husband) and giving it to her lover, who also has in his hand the key of the girdle. Woodcut, *circa* 1540.

apparently felt safer if they had locked the door to their sexual property. In Spain the chastity girdle was in use up to the nineteenth century.

Registration of Prostitutes

As in all ages, so in that of the cult of woman, the honest citizen naturally claimed the right to visit women who wore no chastity girdle. Prostitution flourished greatly throughout the whole Middle Ages. From time to time penal measures were enacted against prostitutes. One of the most energetic, certainly one of the most expert enemies of prostitution was the sixth-century Byzantine Empress Theodora, the Emperor Justinian's consort, whose own road to the throne had not been one of rigid virtue. Nevertheless, she dealt unkindly with the poor creatures whose careers had been less brilliant than her own. She sent five hundred prostitutes from the brothels of Constantinople to the other shore of the Bosphorus, there to spend their days and nights in cloistered seclusion. But the girls refused to enter the place of asylum. Many of them leapt into the water during the crossing and others took their own lives in their loneliness.

In the West, Charlemagne took up the campaign against prostitution. Adultery, whoring and prostitution figure together in his laws as the three sexual vices which are to be rooted out —how, the chronicles do not say. In any case, the effects of the Carolingian legislation in this field seem to have been short-lived. One of Charlemagne's successors on the Imperial throne laid down a barbarous procedure against prostitution: the woman was to be thrown naked into cold water, and passers-by were not to help her, but to mock and deride her. But prostitution survived even these aberrations of sex-jurisdiction, and the commoner methods of disgracing its practitioners—the pillory, shaving of the head, the stocks, flogging and whipping, were no more effectual. A few women may possibly have been converted by them to virtuous ways, but the institution went on—inevitably, for it is not there for women's satisfaction but for men's pleasure, and men always went unpunished, even if caught *in flagranti*.

The Crusades brought with them an extraordinary increase in prostitution. The pious warriors could face parting from their wives, painful as this was, but complete abstinence, perhaps for several years, seemed to them altogether too hard. The organizers of the Crusades fully understood the impossibility of getting and keeping an army together without women. The ports of embarkation themselves swarmed with women offering themselves to the Crusaders, and many went on board the ships. A calculation by the Templars (the Order which kept the accounts of the Crusades) noted that in one year thirteen thousand prostitutes had to be provided for.

When the Crusades ended, the problem of keeping the prostitutes under control became more urgent still. Many new towns had been founded. Women who formerly tramped the highways now followed the trend of the age and were practising their trade inside the town walls, or outside the gates. The citizens, even if they patronized the women, were scandalized. The nuisance must be abated. The Church appreciated the position. It would be vain to attempt to eliminate prostitution altogether; this would do more harm than good. St. Augustine himself had said: 'If you put down prostitution, licence and pleasure will corrupt society.' After long consideration, the authorities reverted to the methods of antiquity: putting the prostitutes into public houses, under police supervision, seemed the lesser evil. In many places the Church itself took control of the problem. In the Papal city of Avignon a public house of ill-fame was established under the name of 'Abbaye', Abbey, and the official patronage of Queen Joanna of Naples. The women employed there were required to keep the hours of prayer punctually and not to miss any service, for, depraved as their trade was, they were to remain good Christians. The customers, too, were subject to a rule of religion: only Christians might enter the house; heathens and Jews were specifically excluded. The enterprise seems to have prospered so well that Pope Julius II afterwards founded a similar house in Rome.[99] In other towns the Church refrained from active participation in the business, but brothels were not infrequently established in houses which were owned by priests or Mothers Superior of convents. One Archbishop of Mainz, a highly educated man, was said to have as many prostitutes in his houses as books in his library. An English cardinal bought a house in which a brothel was situated, with no intention of shutting it down.[100]

It was, of course, a great advantage for a brothel-keeper if he could carry on his business on such premises, for he was then safeguarded against any slanderous accusation of commerce with the devil. Even lacking such extraneous protection, however, the profession was not very dangerous. The Inquisition paid small attention to brothels, unless for some special reason. It persecuted prostitutes who worked on their own account and at their own risk, for they might be witches; but women working as the employees of a brothel-keeper were obviously not consorting with the devil, but with honest citizens, and they could not be stopped from doing that. Brothel-keepers were forbidden only to employ renegade nuns, married women or girls suffering from dangerous contagious diseases—all prohibitions which were often difficult to enforce.

A brothel. Engraving by the Master of the Bandrolles.

Virtuous citizens, however, did not rest content with placing
the brothels under police supervision. They genuinely desired the
welfare of these women, who were called 'free' but in reality were
half prisoners. When a sinner tired of her profession and wished
to return to the paths of righteousness, the doors of civic society
were not to be shut against her. The Church encouraged these
endeavours; in 1198 Pope Innocent III recommended well-
intentioned citizens to reclaim prostitutes by marrying them.
They could not, of course, be taken at once into a respectable
burgher's house, as maids or even something higher; first they
had to go through a sort of purgatory, to reaccustom them to
discipline and order. Nevertheless, the world wanted to make
their path to repentance and reform as smooth as possible. To
this end some places, while not closing down their brothels,
established special 'Magdalene Homes' for repentant sinners.

The Penitents' House at St. Jerome's in Vienna, known to the
populace as the 'Soul House', was a model of this kind of institution. It was founded at the beginning of the fourteenth
century, on the private initiative of a few rich citizens, and was
given a charter in 1384 by Duke Albrecht III as a recognized
institution for 'penitent women'. From outside it looked like a
convent, but no excessive asceticism was required of its inmates,
who were not asked to vow themselves either to chastity, or to
poverty. It received so many endowments that it soon became
the richest institution in Vienna. The best of the vineyards outside the city walls were its property. The penitents were able to
build themselves a magnificent church, and when they married
they were given handsome portions. Not a few respected citizens
chose their wives from among the former 'pretty ladies' of the
Soul House.

The educative method having yielded such good results, the
Emperor Frederick III, in 1480, incautiously granted the penitent
women a retail licence for the sale of produce of their vineyards.
The foundation of St. Jerome now became witness of animated
scenes. Many of the women reverted to their former way of life,
led by one of their Superiors, Maria Kleeberger, who contracted

a marriage with the institution's priest, Laubinger (this was during
the confused period of the Reformation, when Vienna was
preponderantly Protestant), while practising her former trade on
the side. The scandal which ensued proved to be the end of the
Soul House. The bedrooms of the incorrigible penitent women
were now occupied by austere Franciscan monks, who recon-
verted Vienna to Catholicism and re-established the old order.
Thereafter the gay city contained many brothels, but no more
Magdalene Homes.

Woman-houses and Baths

By the later Middle Ages every town had its *lupanar*, as in the
old Roman Empire. Where German was spoken, the establishments were called *Frauenhäuser* ('woman-houses') and this
neutral, uncompromising name became usual in other countries
also. The house was usually situated in a side street near the
church. It bore no sign, but everyone knew where it was. The
business was less often combined with the sale of liquor than in
antiquity, but a new attraction had been invented. The public
baths were not great mansions as in ancient Rome, but modest
utilitarian establishments, often simply disguised brothels. The
hub of such a place was not a drawing-room, but a basin with
room for five or six people, not to swim, but to enjoy physical
contact. The women presented themselves to the guests undressed,
and welcomed them hospitably. Larger tubs were provided for
more intimate enjoyment, unless the customers preferred to
withdraw into a dry chamber to carry out the real purpose of their
visit. Paris, whose population of two hundred thousand made it
far the largest city of Europe, had thirty such establishments at
the beginning of the fifteenth century.

Every large town also contained many street-walkers, who
gave the police endless trouble. It was the dress of these women
that particularly occupied the authorities: the problem was not
so much to check the prostitutes from displaying too much of
their charms, as to prevent confusion between them and honest
women. Here, again, people reverted to the example of ancient

The pleasures of the bath. Pen and ink drawing by the Master of the House Book, *circa* 1480.

Rome, in which street-walkers were allowed to wear only a short *tunica*, in distinction to the virtuous matron's long gown. The problem had become more complicated, however, since fashions changed faster and the dress regulations had therefore to be frequently revised. Around 1425, for example, the *filles communes* of Paris were forbidden to wear golden girdles, spreading skirts or fur-trimmed collars. The ban on edgings of grey fur was particularly strict, these being the fashion in high society.

Man and woman in a bath-tub. From the
German Calendar, Augsburg, *circa* 1480.

Every age has its own problems. But with or without fur trimmings, the girls of the street, the woman-houses and the bathhouses found their customers—usually married men with wives at home. What could a neglected wife do? Despite all the Orders of Chivalry, with their fine promises, they had no device but to appeal to their own woman's wit. A 'knight', who in reality was probably a comfortable bourgeois of Paris, tells in a book on sex-education[101] how a clever wife brought her husband to give up his nocturnal excursions. She left out a burning candle, water, and a towel, and when he came home uttered no word of reproach but only asked him to wash his hands. The husband felt so ashamed that he ended by staying at home.

8

THE REVELATION OF THE BODY

THE Renaissance era brought mankind one revelation in the true sense of the word: the revelation of the human body. For the first time in a thousand years, men saw themselves as nature had created them. They made this discovery not in the mirror but through old broken marble statues dug out of the earth. The first finds made by the handful of architects and sculptors who practised this hobby among the ruins of Rome were of fairly crude images of gods or colossal athletes; these could not greatly affect taste. But then, either in a villa of Grotta Ferrata, in the Alban Hills, or, according to another version, farther south, in Anzio, someone dug up a marble statue of a young man which silenced all criticism. It obviously represented a Greek god, the Archer Apollo, but it had nothing warlike about it, and for all its majesty it was human. Its masculine beauty, its gracious youthfulness, seemed, to quote Winkelmann, like the personification of eternal spring.

This was what men looked like, before the religion of suffering commanded them to veil all that was lovely in them, to turn men into haggard martyrs and to swathe women in grey cloths like mummies, hardly leaving their hands and their faces free! Cardinal Giuliano della Rovere, the later Pope Julius II, on whose estate the statue had been found, was liberal and artistically minded enough to take the young god into his house, and afterwards to give him a place of honour in the Pavillon de Belvedere in the Vatican, after which the statue has since been called.

Meanwhile the Apollo Belvedere had produced a veritable revolution among the young artists. Now they had found that ideal representation of the nude human form of which some of them had assuredly dreamed, but none dared depict undisguised. Hitherto the nude had still been treated as in the Middle Ages: if represented at all, it had to be distorted and caricatured, lest it awaken sexual lust in the beholder. The second stipulation was that it must be coupled in some way with sin. It was permissible to surround the devil in a fresco with naked malformed sinners, male and female, and Adam and Eve at the Fall were allowed to appear naked, although it was preferable that all sexual characteristics should be decently covered by hair, hands or leaves. Now painters and sculptors felt free to forget this chaste obligation. He who had seen the Apollo Belvedere without fainting from shame could also bear a Dionysus or a Narcissus of modern minting. Even saints were undressed and 'antiquized', i.e. humanized. Leonardo's John the Baptist and his Bacchus (both of which are in the Louvre) are as alike as twin brothers.

The Naked Woman

After some hesitation, the veil was now gradually lifted also from women. First, the bandages which had constricted their throats disappeared. The line of the throat and neck was freed; then artists moved down a little and gave their subjects a square-cut décolleté, which presently showed the first swelling of the breasts. Here, too, little difference was made between the fashionable ladies of Florence and Ferrara, and biblical figures. The pictures of the Madonna soon went a step farther still. The Mother of God not only carried her Babe at her breast, but suckled him, and this meant parting the dress over the maternal bosom. Boltraffio, Solario, Andrea del Sarto and many others depict this intimate scene with increasing emphasis on the maternal and womanly elements in it, at the expense of the religious.

A few bold spirits then ventured to disrobe the entire female body, under the pretext of representing scenes out of mythology. The Florentine painters, however, were still obviously daunted by their own daring. Their antique goddesses of Love look like medieval nuns forcibly undressed. Botticelli's Venus Anadyomene climbs out of her shell with so dismal a face and covers her intimate parts so chastely that one might think her an angel of innocence captured by pirates on the high seas and now only looking for some clothes to enable her to retire into a convent. The Umbrian painter Signorelli's *School of Pan*, in the Berlin Gallery, is one of the first pictures to show a totally naked woman among naked men.

But the sensual art of the nude was born in Venice. Whatever the reason—the proximity of the East, the climate of the lagoons, or the wealth of the merchant princes—Venice made no bones about admitting that Olympus was only interesting in so far as it excited the senses. Frosty marble nudity found no advocates here; rather sumptuous garments and colourful finery on which the eye could feed!

A young painter of Castelfranco, Giorgio Barbarelli—named by his first biographer (Vasari) Giorgionc, or George the Great, and so known to the later world—found out how to reconcile the formal conventions of antiquity with Venice's joy in the senses. He was uniquely fitted for this task. The illegitimate son of a patrician of Venice, he had passed his childhood outside the city, but had gained an entrée to the luxurious Court of Catarina Cornaro, the dethroned Queen of Cyprus. He entered Giovanni Bellini's studio in Venice, and now his genius developed rapidly; at the same time, he passed for a model of elegance and chivalry. Women besieged the handsome youth, but he was invulnerable, ever faithful to a mysterious love. A love-legend attached to his very end: it was said that his adored one had succumbed in an epidemic of the plague; he kissed her on her deathbed, and thus contracted the infection which slew him in early manhood.

So much is certain, that he died of the plague when only thirty-two years of age, but that short life was long enough to make him one of the greatest and most influential painters of the Renaissance. Of the few authentic pictures by his hand which have survived, the most famous is the *Sleeping Venus*, now in Dresden: a completely nude woman at rest in a landscape setting.

The proportions of her limbs are as perfect, the contours as delicate and harmonious, as in the best statues of antiquity, but the red-gold hair and the golden tint of the skin give her a direct, living humanity unachievable in marble. In his *Rustic Concert*, now in the Louvre, Giorgione enhances the charm of the nude female form by placing behind it two fully clad male figures—a contrast subsequently repeated by many painters, down to Manet, in his *Olympia* and *Déjeuner sur l'herbe*, but then new and surprising. The woman shows herself naked, while the men are clothed. In the Middle Ages it was just the reverse: a woman's body had to be veiled.

Giorgione's fellow-countryman and contemporary, who, however, outlived him two full generations, Tiziano Vecellio, carried on the painting of the nude and made it internationally renowned. Emperors and kings competed for the 'Venuses in repose' which Titian turned out in endless variations to satisfy the wishes of the great. His women are more erotic, more of the courtesan, than Giorgione's classic forms. We see them in a different light today: the flesh-tints have darkened and the golden-brown tone translates the nakedness into the super-sensual. For Titian's contemporaries, however, they were sexual pictures, excitingly true to life. They were all the more interesting to men because many of them were known to be portraits of grand ladies: the Duchess of Urbino sat to the painter as model for his *Urbino Venus*, now in the Uffizi.

The Italian fashion was widely copied. Even north of the Alps, ladies of high rank had themselves painted in the nude. The master of this new art in Germany was Lucas Cranach the Elder. His over-slender, mincing women have not entirely emancipated themselves from the limitations of the Gothic, but Cranach tries conscientiously to make them as sensual as possible. His naked little ladies have eyes as lustful as any inmate of a woman-house. The more to emphasize their nakedness, Cranach sometimes crowns them with waving feather hats. France, normally Europe's leader in the field of eroticism, lagged behind in this epoch. It was only comparatively late that French art adopted the cult of the

nude, as in the twin portrait of the d'Estreés sisters, by an unknown hand, in the Louvre. In this, two young women sit side
by side in a bath, one touching the other's nipple, a symbolic
gesture indicating that Gabrielle, the sister whose breast is touched,
was expecting a child by her royal lover, Henri IV.

The sexual attraction of representational art was enhanced when
painters began to make the naked woman the central figure in an
anecdote, and to impart movement to the figures. Biblical,
mythological, and historical motifs were enlisted, the most popular
being Susannah in the Bath. Here, too, it is a Venetian who bears
away the palm; the masterpiece in this guise is still Tintoretto's
Susannah in the Kunsthistorisches Museum in Vienna, a voluptuous beauty with carefully parted legs which leave nothing un-
revealed; one can credit this Susannah with anything, except
chastity. But even that was not enough. People had become
accustomed to the sight of nudity, and a woman who displayed
everything no longer caused a sensation. Only the sexual act
itself was not depicted, although even here there was an advance:
the amours of Zeus gave painters their chance to show the
woman's reaction, the expression on her face and her bearing at
the moment of supreme sexual ecstasy. Leda and the swan,
Danäe and the shower of gold, Io and the cloud, furnished
material for Titian, Correggio, even Michelangelo, to display
their virtuosity, their observation, and their sexual imagination.

The Sonnets of the Divine Aretino

Was it possible to go farther still, and to depict man and
woman embracing, as a natural happening, without mythological
and romantic trappings? Three highly-placed and respected
artists ventured it—not in free Venice, not even in Florence,
where perhaps not everything but most things were allowed, but
in the papal city of Rome itself. The painter who seems to have
concocted the plan was Giulio Romano, at that time a young
man of only twenty-five, but widely regarded as Raphael's real
successor. He had been Raphael's favourite pupil, had helped him
decorate the loggias and halls of the Vatican, and after Raphael's

death in 1520 had been loaded with orders from high dignitaries of the Church. His decorations to the Villa Lante had ventured into the field of erotics, but they were still nothing compared with his next enterprise. He proposed to portray the different postures of coitus in sixteen pictures. Other young painters before him had probably made similar drawings for their own amusement, but had kept their sketches to themselves. In any case, the charm of the theme for Romano seems to have lain in its novelty. Pompeii had not yet been re-discovered, and the Indian and Persian representations of the theme had not penetrated to the West.

Giulio Romano completed the sketches in 1524, and was so well satisfied with them that he commissioned Marc Antonio Raimondi, the best engraver in Rome, to make copper-prints of them. They were, of course, destined only for private circulation, but some of them got on to the market.[102] Nothing remained a secret in Renaissance Rome. Within a few days the news reached the Vatican, and was brought to the notice of the Pope by a zealous prelate. Clement VII, a Medici by origin, was a friend of the arts, but he was shocked that a thing like this could occur in Rome, and among artists who worked for the Vatican to boot. Almost more shameful than the pictures themselves he found the caption: *In quanti diversi modi, attitudini e posituri giaccino i disonesti uomini con le donne* ('in how many different ways, attitudes and positions loose men lie with women').

The Pope wanted to have the artists arrested on the spot and brought to trial, but one of his advisers, the poet and diplomatic agent Pietro Aretino, intervened for them. Aretino was a man of good reputation; he had just composed a panegyric on the Pope and been granted a pension in reward. A few weeks later, however, it transpired that Aretino had not only been privy to Giulio Romano's project, but had composed a highly illustrative sonnet for each of the pictures. This was too much. The Pope ordered his men to destroy the plates and all copies on which they could lay hands, and to put all persons concerned under arrest. Giulio Romano had, however, got away meanwhile to Mantua, with the help of Count Baldassare Castiglione, the Mantuan envoy to the papal Court; Aretino, too, escaped, taking refuge in Milan with a relative of the Pope, the Condottiere Giovanni de Medici. Only the least guilty of the three, the engraver Raimondi, was caught and thrown into prison, whence, however, influential well-wishers soon procured his release.

The Pope's action nevertheless brought about the complete disappearance of Romano's drawings, while of the engravings only one copy survives, allegedly safely shut up in the Biblioteca Corsiniana in Rome.[103] The drawings 'after Giulio Romano' which still occasionally turn up (a set was recently privately printed in France[104]) are in fact reconstructions on the basis of tradition, with the help of Aretino's text. Aretino, on the other hand, less timid and more resourceful than Romano, salvaged his own contribution to the *Modi* and saw that it was preserved for posterity. His *Sonnetti lussuriosi* are among the most famous and sought-after products of pornographic literature, but also some of the dullest. It is extraordinary that the pictures of so great an artist as Romano should have inspired a man so intelligent and educated as Aretino to such ineffably crude obscenities. The sonnets contain not a trace either of the wit of the Pompeian *Positiones* or of the poetry of the *Kâmasûtra* or the late Indian *Anangaranga*. Aretino gives, so to speak, a dynamic explanation of each drawing. He describes the whole course of the *Modo* in question, but apart from a few mythological allusions each poem is merely a coarse enumeration and interminable repetition of the most vulgar expressions for the genitals and the sexual act.

In Venice, where Aretino established his literary workshop in 1527 (he employed a large number of assistants) he could give freer rein to his sexual imaginings, for here there was no censor to stop him. Anything not directly dangerous to the security of the Venetian state could be freely written, printed, and circulated. This of itself sufficed to make Venice the main centre of pornographic literature in the sixteenth century. Aretino took ample advantage of this licence. His main work, the *Ragionamenti*, in which he describes the unfaithfulness of married women, the sensuality of nuns, and the education of a young girl to be a complete courtesan, contains chapters hardly less outspoken than the *Sonnetti lussuriosi*. Obscener still is his *Dialogue between Magdalene and Julia*, an imitation of Lucian's *Hetairic Dialogues*, but much coarser than the original. These works, too, are today safely stowed away on the 'reserved' shelves of the few libraries which possess them, but Aretino's contemporaries found nothing objectionable in them. They bestowed on their author, in his lifetime, the soubriquet *il divino* 'the divine'.

It is true that this side of his work was not the only one to which Aretino owed his fame. He was a versatile man and fulfilled any order placed with him, provided the customer paid well. He also wrote books of overflowing piety, for example, his *Humanita di Cristo*, in three volumes. Pope Julius III forgave him his sins and kissed him on the forehead, and the poet of the *Sonnetti* only just missed becoming a Cardinal. King Francis I of France and the Emperor Charles V availed themselves of his talent as a political agent and go-between; painters such as Titian and Michelangelo (whom he stabbed in the back afterwards) were among his friends. Wherever questions of aesthetics and morality were raised, the voice of Aretino was heard. Nevertheless, he was known chiefly as the poet of sex, and since the Renaissance liked ascribing to famous men a cause of death appropriate to their lives, a typical story was invented for Aretino: it was said that certain kind friends were telling him suggestive stories about his sisters, who were living gallant lives in Venice, and that these so tickled Aretino, who was then sixty-five years of age, that he fell out of his chair with laughter and died on the spot.

Nature and Convention

Aretino's smutty poetry and his adventurous career are typical of his age, but are, after all, an extreme example. Of more general and lasting interest is his philosophy of sex. Aretino put down the essentials of his creed in a letter in which he sought to justify the *Sonnetti lussuriosi*.

As both in ancient and modern times poets and sculptors have found diversion of the spirit in writing or fashioning lewd works—witness, for example, that marble satyr attempting a boy, displayed in the Palazzo Chigi—so did I compose to those *Modi* sonnets of voluptuous memory, as they are to be read under the engravings and as I dedicate them to you, defying all hypocrites. The devil take that miserable opinion and so-called propriety which forbids our eyes to see precisely that which gives them most pleasure! What is the harm if we see how a man mounts a woman? Shall animals enjoy more freedom than men? My opinion is that we ought to carry representations of that instrument which Mother Nature has given us for our self-preservation, hung round our necks and clasped on our caps.

Few would have dared to state these views so bluntly, but they were in fact very widely held at the time. *Humana non sunt turpia* —'What is human is not shameful': this old Roman maxim, long repressed, was again in honour. Especially—to the profit of mankind—did it pervade scientific thought. In spite of the great discoveries of the Arabs (or more exactly, the Persian and Jewish physicians who wrote in Arabic), medicine had made but little progress in the Middle Ages, because men shrank from examining the body closely and studying its anatomy. This could not be done without dissection, and the Church forbade the dissection of corpses. Even as late as 1515, under so liberal a Pope as Leo X, a son of Lorenzo de Medici, Leonardo da Vinci was forbidden to conduct autopsies in hospitals.

The University of Padua, however, which at that time was under Venetian sovereignty and thus automatically anti-Roman, was more enlightened, and Padua thus became the cradle of modern anatomy. Its true founder was Andreas Vesalius, a young scholar of Brussels, to whom the Paduans gave a chair when he was twenty-three years of age. Six years later Vesalius produced a work such as the world had not yet seen: a great anatomical atlas in which all parts of the human body were portrayed and described with an exactitude previously unknown.[105] The title-page of this epoch-making work shows Vesalius dissecting a woman's body. A generation earlier this would have been regarded as most heinous heresy, but now even opponents bowed to the new knowledge. Vesalius's anatomy laid the foundations for a complete revolution in surgery. Here, too, the Renaissance did pioneer work. People even began to improve and beautify malformed or diseased limbs and features, particularly noses, by plastic surgery.

Loving couple. Woodcut from the *Hypnerotomachia Poliphili*, 1499.

The body was all. The Renaissance was less interested in the soul, and its few considerable psychologists, such as Pomponazzi of Padua, contributed practically nothing to the psychology of sex. The interpretation of sex was left to the poets and writers, and they, too, have said little on the spiritual relationship between man and woman that was not already to be found in mediaeval literature. Sex-life occupies a dominant position in Renaissance literature, especially that of Italy and France, but fundamentally it is always the same problem: law and convention stand in the way of two lovers; complications ensue, comic and tragic, but in the end the sexual urge always proves the stronger force. Tragic turns to the conflicts are rarer than in the Middle Ages; happy endings are now preferred. There are, however, a few real tragedies, such as the story of Romeo and Juliet, which originated in the Middle Ages but was popularized in 1524, when Luigi da Porto, antedating Shakespeare by two generations, made it the theme of a touching story.

Two main themes recur constantly: the married woman who betrays her husband, and the young girl who holds secret tryst with her lover, in defiance of her parents' prohibition, often sacrificing her maidenhead to him before marriage. The parties do not regard the sacrifice as very serious, and so far one may find a difference from the views of the Middle Ages; yet the frequency with which this situation recurs in stories and on the stage is, probably, proof that bourgeois circles still held it important that a girl should preserve her virginity up to her wedding night.

A man might, of course, do anything, before and after marriage; only married men had sometimes to put up with a beating, or some other punishment, from their wives. This again was nothing new. The physical chastisement of the unfaithful husband by his wife is a standard scene in the popular literature of the later Middle Ages, especially the German carnival farces. At the Renaissance it was developed, with features borrowed from classic Roman comedy. The formidable old harridan-wife is, so to speak, man's judgment on earth. Such episodes, however, always remain on the plane of comedy. For a wife to break with her husband because he was unfaithful to her was outside the bounds of possibility. If she was young enough she could revenge herself by betraying him in return; if she was too old for that, she had no remedy but to greet him with a stick or a broomhandle when he came home from his amorous escapades.

Male Potency

On the whole, the Renaissance was a masculine age. The obligatory proof of manliness was no longer heroic deeds, as in the age of the knights and the *minnesingers*, but sexual virility.

Probably the most prominent feature of the erotic literature of the Renaissance is the stress laid by it on this quality. Women seem to be insatiable, and men who are incapable of satisfying them cut absurd figures. The very fact that virility is taken as the true measure of manliness gives young men the advantage over their elders. The young men are always in the right, because they are the stronger in bed—Renaissance writers, incidentally, do not fail to enumerate the embraces exactly and generously. A husband is allowed a maximum of three in a night, but the lover who cuckolds him, seven or more. The woman often consumes the one and then the other without the slightest trace of fatigue. However tempestuous the night has been, she is always dewy fresh next morning, and ready for new adventures.

In order to be able to do justice to such exacting women, men not infrequently resorted to drugs and other methods of increasing their virility. The most famous comedy of the Italian Renaissance, Machiavelli's *Mandragora*, is built round this question, and consultations of doctors or helpful neighbours about magical herbs, incantations and similar recipes figure largely also in innumerable other plays and stories. To enhance the comic effect, old men are usually made to have married women much younger than themselves and then to be at a loss how to satisfy their wishes. Needless to say, none of these artificial remedies ever works. The woman's only recourse is invariably a young lover.

As in other epochs, we must ask again of this: how far does its literature reflect the age in which it is born? How far is it working with the traditional properties of olden days and other lands, and how far did it itself influence ways of life and thus anticipate the manners of later ages? When, about the middle of the fourteenth century, Boccaccio initiated the new literature with its exclusive obsession with sex, it still bore many medieval and exotic traces. Boccaccio's passionate love for 'Fiammetta', who was the illegitimate daughter of King Robert of Naples, is very much the same at bottom as the knight's adoration of his lady. The new elements, apart from the form and the verbal felicity, are mostly importations from books.

Boccaccio is the Marco Polo of eroticism. Not that he had made any long journeyings before finding his happiness at the Neapolitan court; he was the illegitimate son of a Florentine merchant. But most of his art of love comes from the East, not the West. A considerable proportion of the string of witty anecdotes of which the *Decameron* is composed, Eastern fashion, come ultimately from Arabia or India. Some of the themes are found in earlier Provençal poetry and others are drawn direct from antiquity. Even where Boccaccio had had ample opportunity to make his own observations from nature, he preferred to rely on well-proved models: his description of the plague of 1348, which forms the setting of the *Decameron*, is closely modelled on Thucydides and Lucretius, and it is no different with his eroticism. Gradually, however, he emancipates himself. His own observations, made in the rich burghers' houses of Florence or at the Court of Naples, are worked into stories based on antique or classic plots, or are sometimes utilized for independent tales, such as the 'Caccia di Diana' and the 'Ninfale Fiesolano'.

As early as the eighteenth century philologists got to work on Boccaccio and painfully traced back each of his tales to the age and place of its origin.[106] The men of the Renaissance were not interested in such refinements. They were collectors, not analysts. They did not mind if Boccaccio gave Troy a bishop in the days of Priam. Boccaccio was for them a generic term. Love had, presumably, always been as he depicted it. Out of the wealth of figures and adventures which he portrayed for them they evolved a general picture, a philosophy: the decisive thing is not the great, individual love of some man for a specific woman, but the attraction of the one sex for the other. Monogamy is a self-deception which lasts only until another man or another woman comes along and attracts one more. This is nature's rule for men, and he who fights against nature is a fool. Boccaccio himself formulated this natural law two centuries before Aretino in the words: 'Nature has created nothing without a purpose, and she has given us these noble parts also to be used, not to be left lying idle.'

Illegitimate Children

The naturalism which dominates Renaissance sexual morality is perhaps in some measure due to the circumstance that the period was, especially in Italy, one of mass mortality. Terrible epidemics repeatedly ravaged the country, carrying off large parts of the population. On top of this came the losses occasioned by wars which were more devastating in their effects than the Second World War. The population of Rome, which had been about ninety thousand in the Papacy of Leo X, sank to thirty thousand after its sacking by Charles V's mercenaries in 1527. Fifty years later it had only recovered to forty-five thousand.

People troubled little whether a child was legitimate or not. There was hardly a married man of rank who was not the father of illegitimate children. Of the famous personalities mentioned in this chapter, the majority—Giorgione, Aretino, Leonardo da Vinci, Boccaccio—were the offspring of extra-marital unions, and we did not select them for that reason. Any other assortment of great painters and poets would show the same picture. It is possible that genius and great talent were particularly frequent among illegitimate children. Not being entitled to inherit, they more often took up free professions, and had to fight harder to make their way, but their fathers or other relatives usually looked after them, and in matters of education, too, it made little difference whether a child was legitimate or not. No one was excluded from society, nor even from the courts of princes, because his parents had not married legally before his birth, or legitimized him after it. To be an illegitimate child entailed no social stigma.

Illegitimate children were even commoner in princely houses than in those of the middle classes. There, too, little social prejudice attached to illegitimate birth. The contemptuous word 'bastard' had practically fallen out of use. The prince's 'natural' sons and daughters belonged to the Court and were treated as princes and princesses. It was only when the time came for them to marry that difficulties sometimes arose. Even illegitimate children were given big dowries and appanages, but they were excluded from the succession of the ruling houses. The result was that they often married one another. There was a special class of nobility composed of the illegitimate issue of princes, which took rank and title as punctiliously as their legitimate brothers. The illegitimate son of a duke married the illegitimate daughter of another duke, but if he took the illegitimate daughter of a person of lower rank to wife, that was a *mésalliance*. The weddings of illegitimate children were celebrated in the presence of the whole family, and with all splendour. The wedding of Pope Paul III's thirteen-year-old son to an illegitimate daughter of the Emperor Charles V was to have been one of the most gorgeous events of the Renaissance. It was called off at the last moment, because the bride refused her consent at the altar, but this was not because her youthful bridegroom was illegitimate, but because he was all too obviously a cretin.

One factor helping to efface the difference between legitimate and illegitimate birth was the ambiguous conduct of the Princes of the Church. The most vigorous and uninhibited lead was that from the Borgia Rodrigo Lanzol, afterwards Pope Alexander VI. When still Archbishop of Valencia he had contracted a liaison with a noble Roman lady called Rosa Vannozza dei Cattanei, who became the mother of five children. Whether all of them were Rodrigo's we do not know, but the future Pope was a *galantuomo*, recognized them all as his children, and set himself to make princes and princesses of them. His daughter Lucrezia was betrothed at twelve to a Spanish grandee. The engagement was broken off a year later to enable Lucrezia to marry a Sforza of the great Milanese dynasty. This marriage, too, was dissolved, on the grounds of the husband's impotence, yet, soon after, Lucrezia gave birth to a child. Events of this kind were nothing extraordinary, and most likely no one would have asked who the father was, had not Alexander VI himself insisted on producing a surprising explanation. He issued two successive Bulls, in the first of which he named himself as the father, and in the second, his son Cesare.

The too seductive Lucrezia was released from these over-close family ties when she took for her next husband the Duke of Besaglia, an illegitimate son of the King of Naples; but Cesare Borgia, being still enamoured of his beautiful sister, strangled his brother-in-law with his own hands. At twenty-two Lucrezia at last found lasting happiness by the side of the Duke of Ferrara, and thereafter only good is recorded of her—that she was a true and loving wife to her husband, a patron of the arts and devoted to good works. She died an early but peaceful death at the age of thirty-nine.

Her marital and extra-marital relationships—not least the public confirmation of twofold incest—have given Lucrezia Borgia a posthumous fame which she does not altogether deserve. She was obviously a rather passive woman, who submitted to the wills of her father and brother, and got into situations which were not at all congenial to her character. The reason why she has achieved so lasting a fame is, however, a different one. The Italian Renaissance in fact produced very few women who were eminent in any field: neither important rulers or heroines, nor interesting courtesans, much less famous artists or poets.

The last-named fact is remarkable, for at the Courts of Ferrara, Mantua, and Florence, women had unlimited opportunities to develop and display their talents. Men had, indeed, outgrown the childish and hypocritical aberrations of the medieval woman-cult, but they were anything but misogynists. Women were greatly desired, and women of the upper classes freer than ever before in history. The ladies of the nobility and *haute bourgeoisie* were admitted into the Academies, given the best tutors, and encouraged to take up philosophy, mathematics, or natural history, to paint, compose, write—whatever they would. But the harvest of this unaccustomed freedom was exceedingly meagre. In an age which has produced more genuises than any other, the list of famous thinkers and artists includes no single name of a woman. Woman remained in the modest role of the 'muse' worshipped by the poet. When, like Raphael's mistress, the Fornarina, they intervened more closely in the artist's life, they usually pulled the man down, rather than up. This was perhaps one of the chief reasons why the very great masters led abnormal sex-lives, Michelangelo seeking the friendship of young men, Leonardo da Vinci eschewing sex altogether. In the Renaissance woman was for the first time given the chance of competing with man on equal terms in the arts and sciences, and the result was a fiasco.

A New Plague: Syphilis

For sex-life the most momentous event of the Renaissance was the sudden appearance of syphilis. In December 1494, twenty-one months after the return of Columbus and his crew from their first voyage to America, a new sickness broke out in Naples. Its symptoms were the formation on the exterior of the genitals of a tumour, which was not painful, and after a time, disappeared; but soon after, the patient got eruptions, sores inside the mouth, and next, festering, malignant ulcers on the legs and other parts of the body. As the first cases of this illness to be exactly observed and described occurred among soldiers of the French army garrisoning Naples, the disease was called the *morbus gallicus*, or French sickness. The doctors, however, soon saw that the sickness could not have come from France, where it had not previously been known, but had probably been brought via Spain from the newly-discovered lands across the ocean. Naples was subject to Spain, its traffic with Spain was very lively, and it might well be that the disease had been imported direct from the West Indies by men who had sailed with Columbus on his first voyage.

The true facts could not be ascertained, for Columbus and his men were already away on their second voyage to the New World. It was only some years later that a Spanish physician, Rodrigo Diaz de l'Isla, gave clearer details. The sickness had been first observed in a certain First Mate Pinzon, on the return voyage from Hispaniola, as the newly-discovered island of Haiti was then known. Another Spaniard, the writer Oviedo, who rose to be Governor of the West Indies, confirmed this version, adding that he had his facts direct from Columbus, whom he had met at Barcelona in 1493.[107] These were important testimonies, but there were also other indications suggesting that the sickness had existed in Europe before that and had been carried to America by Columbus's crew. The origin of syphilis is one of the unsolved riddles of sex-history. At the beginning of the twentieth century leading specialists made another attempt to reach the truth, but came to no certain conclusion; one school held by an American origin for the sickness,[108] while others insisted that it was a legacy from the Old World.[109]

Only so much is certain, that whether or not syphilis had existed previously in Europe, it appeared in the Mediterranean countries towards the end of the fifteenth century with the virulence characteristic of new plagues. Shortly after, it crossed the Alps. It made no distinction between friend and foe. The prostitutes and wenches in the seaport taverns on whom the French soldiers had bestowed it yesterday passed it on to the German mercenaries. At first a typical soldiers' disease, it soon infected the civilian population, and assumed such alarming forms that the authorities were impelled to issue warnings. As early as 7 August 1495 the Emperor Maximilian issued a proclamation on the subject of the *pöse plattern*—the bad pox—a new sickness previously quite unknown and unrecorded.

The pious Emperor expressed the view that the disease, unlike those by which his lands had previously been visited, was no consequence of famine or earthquake, but sent over the earth as punishment for its ungodliness. In fact, if one avoided the haunts of the sex-devil, one could most probably escape the disease, but even that was not quite certain, for the primitive condition of hygiene and medical knowledge made it possible for quite innocent girls and even children to contract the disease. Sometimes whole families got the 'bad pox'. The Emperor's warning failed to affect moral standards appreciably, but had the good result of making physicians study the scourge more closely. A voluminous literature on it sprang up on both sides of the Alps; we still possess ten treatises from the years 1495-1498 alone.[110] The most thorough study is one by a Spanish doctor named Caspare Torrella, who was employed in the Vatican as physician-in-ordinary to Pope Alexander VI and there had the opportunity of observing seventeen cases in the months of September and October 1497 alone.[111] If the papal Master of Ceremonies, Paride de Grassi, is to be believed, the later Pope Julius II himself contracted the disease.

The name *morbus gallicus* thus became more and more inappropriate; it could now equally well have been called the Roman sickness. The physicians of the age, however, knew and loved the antique. They sought through the writings of antiquity and found certain indications that the disease might have been known to Hippocrates. One of the most brilliant scholars of the Renaissance, the Veronese physician Girolamo Fracastoro, conceived the idea of combining the 'American' and the 'antique' theses in poetic form by locating the origin of the disease in America, but bringing Greek gods and figures from classical mythology into the story. His didactic medical poem, the

Broadsheet with astrological explanation of syphilis. Attributed to Dürer, 1496.

Syphilides, sive morbi gallici libri tres, published in Verona in 1530, tells how a fearful drought afflicted the island of Haiti, in consequence whereof the shepherd Syphilus rebelled against the Sungod. That god punished his impiety by visiting the earth with a new scourge, the syphilis, and the shepherd was its first victim. The poet obviously took his name from Niobe's son, Sipylus, who in the Greco-Roman legend had been punished by Apollo for a sin of his mother's.[112] In one edition of Ovid his name was written with an 'h' as Siphylus, and from this Fracastoro took the name, which was soon generally adopted by the medical profession.

Only France was reluctant to allow the son of Niobe this dubious honour. The French had never accepted the name *morbus gallicus*, which laid them under the unjust imputation of having brought the pestilence on the world. They called it the *mal de Naples*, the Neapolitan sickness, after the place from which they themselves had first taken it, or simply *vérole*—pox. Voltaire himself wrote an epigram to that effect:

> Quand les Français à tête folle
> S'en allèrent dans l'Italie,
> Ils gagnèrent à l'étourdie
> Et Gêne et Naples et la vérole.
> Puis ils furent chassés partout,
> Et Gêne et Naple on leur ôta,
> Mais ils ne perdirent pas tout,
> Car le vérole leur resta.

('When the French went hot-headed to Italy, they easily won Genoa and Naples and the pox. Then they were driven out everywhere, and Genoa and Naples were taken from them, but they did not lose everything, for the pox remained with them.')

One French doctor, however, Jacques de Béthencourt, thought that diseases ought to be named after their causes, and that the appropriate name for the new scourge was *morbus venereus*, 'the sickness of Venus, goddess of Love'. This name, too, was widely adopted. The term 'venereal diseases' came to mean all diseases derived from sexual intercourse, but it was long before the plural form came into usage with the recognition that there were several such diseases. The physicians of the Renaissance did undeniable good work in diagnosing syphilis and also in devising remedies against it; it was only a few decades after the first appearance of the scourge that an Italian doctor, Giovanni de Vigo, introduced mercury treatment, which four centuries later was still the most effective cure known. The doctors committed, however, a fatal error in assuming that there was only one venereal disease, to wit, syphilis, and that gonorrhoea, which had been known since classic times, was only a symptom or first stage of syphilis.

This confusion, the author of which was a doctor named Antonius Musa Brasavolus, was presumably due to the fact that many persons suffered simultaneously from both diseases, or contracted syphilis after previously suffering from gonorrhoea. It was, however, one of the most unpardonable and fateful blunders ever committed by medicine. The treatments for gonorrhoea, many of them very effective, which the Arabic physicians, in particular, had evolved, were increasingly neglected. As soon as anyone was suspected of having clap he was subjected to mercury treatment, on the assumption that this was a symptom of syphilis. The mistaken treatment afflicted innumerable persons with ruinous induced diseases, while their real malady remained uncured. The immensely increased incidence of gonorrhoea in Europe was largely due to this error, from which medical science only finally freed itself in the second half of the nineteenth century, when the microscope revealed the cause of gonorrhoea, the gonococcus.

9

MORAL REFORM

THE Renaissance was one of those great revolutions which take place without changes in the law. Rome tried hard to avoid anything which looked like a breach with tradition, but the transformation was too striking. Between the law and the reality there existed a gulf which had somehow to be bridged over. Either the law had to be changed, or public morals, or, preferably, both. The movement which had this for its purpose was the Reformation. Getting no hearing in Rome, the reformers made new laws for themselves and cut loose from the Pope. This stiffened the resistance of the Curia, because any legal reform now looked like a concession to the rebels. Its only resort was therefore to strengthen the old canonical law and enforce it. This reaction is called the Counter-Reformation.

Problems of sex play a leading part in both movements; in particular, two old disputed points which have shot up, again and again, like fission-fungi, since the first days of the Church: the celibacy of priests and the indissolubility of marriage. There were, however, others as well: not the least of them the question, might the Church derive profit from immorality? In this respect, the practice of Rome had been extremely broad-minded. The Curia had partly financed the building of St. Peter's by a tax on prostitution, on the classic model: this brought the papal exchequer 22,000 ducats, a vast sum for that age—four times as much as Leo X expected from the sale of indulgences in Germany. Had it been possible to squeeze a little more out of the prostitutes, the whole transaction in indulgences might have been unnecessary.

Even this trade was for many only a way of buying off the penalties attaching to their sins of sex. If one dropped one's penny into the offertory box, one could go into the nearest woman-house without qualms. No purgatorial fire threatened the adulterer who had proved his repentance by contributing to the good works of Rome.

The sinners' money which the Curia pocketed, this way or that, naturally inflamed beyond bearing those men who had taken the oath to live in poverty and chastity. One of those who took their oaths seriously was the Augustinian monk, Martin Luther. On a visit to Rome he had seen with his own eyes the debauched life led by the prelates. The rule of celibacy was obviously regarded as applying only to the lower clergy and monks in Orders: the high dignitaries of the Church need not trouble about it. Not that all of them kept mistresses or visited prostitutes, but those who did were not punished or even rebuked. It was a régime which applied two standards, for the benefit of a small upper class. Luther did not want to become one of that class and do as they did. Although already an established university professor, he was still a monk at heart: He would have been ready to go on living a life of extreme asceticism and sexual abstinence if the rule had been genuinely enforced on all who had devoted themselves to the Faith. This, however, was not the case. Rome measured with two scales, and that revolted his sense of justice.

If sexual intercourse was irreconcilable with priestly office, then logic demanded that the higher priesthood should be the first to submit to the rule. This was the practice in the Eastern Church. It made a distinction between the lower clergy, who were allowed to marry, and the bishops, to whom marriage was forbidden. In Rome it was the exact opposite: the higher a priest's rank, the less he troubled with the rule of celibacy; only the formal prohibition of marriage was respected. At one moment it looked as though the higher clergy would be freed from even this limitation; this was when Pope Alexander VI, father of many children, was thinking of turning the Church State into a hereditary monarchy. That the plan fell through was due, not to any moral qualms, but to the opposition of the great Roman families, the Orsinis, the Colonnas, and the Savellis, who feared that it might exclude their own members from the papal throne. The prohibition of marriage for priests had thus become something quite different from its founders' intentions: not a protection against sinful lusts, but a means of assuring the elective character of the papal monarchy.

Even this safeguard did not keep the Holy See from being the preserve of a few families of great nobility. Leo X, who was Pope when Luther started his movement, was not even in Orders when he was elected. But he was a Medici; that was enough. He was only thirty-eight years old, but it was apparently not difficult for him personally to vow celibacy. His interests were centred on intellectual and artistic enjoyments. He did not, incidentally, insist on the men of his entourage living as he did. His Court was as worldly as that of any other prince, and a Court implies women.

Protestant Marriage Law

The pioneers of the Reformation were unanimous in believing that celibacy, as then practised, was endangering the Church. They wanted sexual equality between priests, but this ideal could not be achieved through celibacy, only through allowing priests to marry. Only this could put an end to the higher clergy's mistresses and the lower clergy's resentment against Rome. The first man to re-raise the question of marriage for priests was Philipp Melanchthon.[113] He did not go very far; he wanted celibacy to be provisionally suspended, and the final decision left to a Council of the Church. Melanchthon was twenty-four years of age and not himself a priest. For all his precocious learning, he did not possess the authority to pass judgment on such a question. A little later, however, a weightier voice was raised. Ulrich Zwingli, the secular priest in the Great Minster at Zürich, started a campaign for the unconditional abolition of the celibacy rule. Zwingli was also the first of the reformers themselves in Orders to practise what he preached; in April 1524, then forty years of age, he married one Anne Meyer, née Reinhard, the widow of a judge. No priest of the Roman Church had ventured as much for five hundred years.

Luther followed the next year. His heresy was even more conspicuous. The excommunicated monk married a nun named Katherine von Bora, who had fled from her convent with eight fellow-sisters after reading Luther's works. After great difficulties she had found a lodging in Luther's own town, Wittenberg. She was young, beautiful, and intelligent, deeply attracted to the new doctrine and its founder. When he made up his mind to marry, Luther was in his forty-second year, fifteen years older than his bride. The marriage was, however, extremely happy; six children were born of it. It was only after Luther's death in 1546 that hard times came again to Katherine, who was left destitute, for the man who reformed Germany died as penniless as a mendicant friar.

The third of the great reformers of the sixteenth century, Jean Calvin, the son of an official of the magistracy in north France, also married; he was then thirty. For him there was no question of conscience, since he had not been either priest or monk. Marriage was only a brief interlude in his life, however, for his wife and his only child died early. In practice his life was that of a weak, sickly bachelor with no interest in women, and this outlook is reflected in the austere legislation on sex which Calvin enacted when he ruled in Geneva. Young men and women were forbidden the most harmless diversions; dances were punishable with prison. Lucas Cranach, who bought an apothecary's shop in Wittenberg and then opened a bookshop there, was able to paint his seductive naked women under Luther's very eyes; in Calvin's Geneva they would have led him to the stake. Nevertheless, Calvin, having set the example himself, still maintained that priests of the new faith might lawfully marry.

The example of the religious leaders naturally brought about a sexual revolution among the young clergy who adhered to the Reformation. Within a generation celibacy vanished from the Protestant countries of the Continent; a parson's wife was an integral feature of a parsonage. There is no doubt that the abolition of the rule of sexual abstinence was an additional reason for many priests, monks and nuns on whom the oath of chastity had been imposed, often in their childhood years, to adhere to the new movement. Not all of them landed at once, without shipwreck, safely in the harbour of matrimony. There were sex-scandals in Protestant circles in no way behind those of papal Rome. The opponents of the Reformation thus found plenty of material with which to prove their contention that the reform movement owed its success to the sex-devil.

No less a figure than the great humanist, Erasmus of Rotterdam, associated himself with this reproach. Erasmus was the world oracle of his age. He succeeded in holding the balance so delicately between Romans and reformers as to win high esteem in both camps. It was all the more serious when he remarked that the great drama of the Reformation was ending, like a stage comedy, in a denouement of weddings, with monks throwing off their cowls and marrying nuns as the curtain fell. Although the point of this was obviously directed against Luther, Calvin could not refrain from parading his virtue again, and showing that he was not as Luther was. In his *De Scandalis* he complained bitterly that people were saying of the leaders of the Reformation that they had begun a set of second Trojan wars for women's sake, as the Greeks had waged the first for Helen; as for himself, it must be conceded of him that he was entirely immune from such temptations.

So he was. Neither did anyone dare make such reproaches against Zwingli, who by now had died for his faith in the field, as an army chaplain. But Martin Luther was regarded by his enemies while he lived, and still more after his death, as the sex-devil incarnate. When he died the story went round that his grave was found empty, and a fearful stench issued from it: even those who did not believe such fairy stories held him for an arch-sinner whose main purpose in starting his movement against Rome had been to get rid of celibacy.

If Luther was really governed so entirely by sex, it is remarkable that he should have been able to subdue it so long. He always insisted that he had come to the marriage-bed a virgin, and there is not a scrap of evidence that he did not preserve chastity for

PLATE 9

"To the Sisters". Sign-board of a brothel. Roman.

Female dancers. Mural from a caliph's
palace in Baghdad. 8th century.

PLATE 10

Pair of lovers.   Persian miniature.   17th century.

PLATE II

The minstrel, Jacob von Warte
in the bath. Manessic
Manuscript. 1st half of
14th century.

Count Kraft von Toggenburg
climbs up a ladder to the lady
of his heart. She hands him
the wreath, and with it her
love. Manessic Manuscript.

PLATE 12

Love-magic. A naked woman entices a man with magic arts.
1st half of 15th century. Formerly Leipzig, Museum der
bildenden Künste.

PLATE 13

Pair of lovers in the bath.
From a drawing by the
Master of the Housebook.

PLATE 14

The Belvedere Apollo.
Copperplate engraving by
Hendrik Goltzius (1559-161...

Pair of lovers. From the erotic " Posizioni " series.
Ascribed to Guilio Romano, Raphael's master pupil.

PLATE 15

The Courtesans. Painting by Vittorio Carpaccio (1455–1525).
Venice, Museo Correr.

PLATE 16

Recumbent Venus.
Painting by Giorgione (*cc.* 1478–1510).
Dresden, Gemäldegalerie.

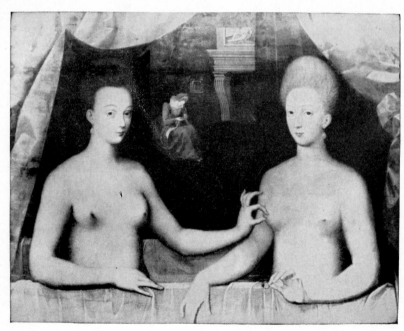

Gabrielle d'Estrées and her Sister in the Bath.
Painting of the Fontainebleau school.
2nd half of the 16th century.

forty years and more. Whether this was healthy for him, physically and still more psychologically, is another question. He was a strong, very masculine man. The frequent fits of anxiety from which he suffered in youth may have been due to self-imposition of a restraint against which his nature rebelled. When, at last, he felt entitled to throw off his restraint, it was at an age at which sex has normally ceased to be explosive. The change to a normal sex-life obviously did him good; in the first years of his marriage he was psychologically more balanced, a man who has found inner peace, weighs issues calmly, and avoids extreme solutions.

A true man of the Renaissance in this respect also, Luther in his later years never hesitated to speak very openly on sexual questions. He thought this neither immodest nor indiscreet, even when dealing with details which today are regarded as falling within the doctor's province. Hence his famous advice to married couples:

> A week two
> Is the woman's due.
> Harms neither me nor you,
> Makes in a year, twice fifty-two.

The verse is often quoted in abbreviated form, leaving out the second line, although that is not unimportant, for it makes the 'two' a sort of minimum which the wife has a right to expect. Even so, however, it may safely be regarded as no more than the well-meant advice of an elderly man married to a wife much younger than himself. Had Luther married at twenty-two, instead of forty-two, his rule for marriage might have run differently. In any case, he saw in marital intercourse both a right and a duty for both parties; the woman, too, was entitled to it. He allowed a woman the same equality of rights when a marriage proved childless. If impotence in the husband was to blame, the wife should seek herself another husband, just as the husband might remarry if the wife proved sterile. This reversion to the marriage law of the Old Testament implied recognizing divorce, even in cases where there had been no adultery.

That Luther was not narrow-minded about divorce, at any rate in exceptional cases, was shown when his fellow-Protestant, the Landgraf Philip of Hesse, wanted to put away his wife, Christine of Saxony, and marry another. Luther gave him permission. The affair stirred up a lot of dust. But although the legalization of divorce occasioned certain misunderstandings, it soon became clear that the Reformation had greatly strengthened marriage. The last mists of chivalric romanticism, with its semi-legal adultery, were blown away, the secret liaisons which crept in with the institution of separation from bed and board became rarer, and it was no longer assumed as obvious that a man had 'child and chick' (*Kind und Kegel*), i.e. both legitimate and illegitimate children. In a word, marriage had become cleaner.

Henry VIII's Divorce

Whereas on the Continent divorce became legalized without great friction as a consequence of the Reformation, in England it became the direct occasion of the Reformation. Obviously, other motives, spiritual and profane, played a part, factors of foreign and domestic policy, questions of power politics and economic interests, but the great conflict with Rome arose directly out of a question of sex-law: whether a prince can marry as often as he pleases, or whether he must submit to the decision of the Pope.

The general prohibition of divorce had developed during the Middle Ages into one of the most potent instruments of papal power. The Pope himself could not dissolve a marriage, but he, and only he, could do what amounted to the same thing, declare a marriage invalid and thereby enable the former spouses to contract new marriages. As all Catholic princes admitted this papal prerogative, the Curia held a strong trump card to be played on occasion against the temporal rulers. The most powerful prince, if he wanted to put away his wife and marry another, must apply to Rome as a supplicant, while the Pope could decide as he would. Since political reasons were most often behind the request—a remarriage being a way for a prince to acquire land or conclude an alliance—these cases were treated also in Rome as questions of high politics, and the Curia sometimes drew great advantage from them.

The exercise of the right of annulment varied, some Popes being more generous than others. Usually, however, Rome treated this valuable privilege carefully and took care not to devalue it by over-frequent consent. The way of the petitioner was made difficult. Sometimes the suits dragged on for years. A prince had to be very interested in his new marriage for it to be worth his while; and it was only for this purpose that he approached Rome. If he just wanted to be rid of his wife, he found simpler ways and means. A suit for annulment of marriage was thus, put in terms of modern civil law, not a divorce suit but an application for a new marriage licence, the entire world being aware in advance which woman the Prince in question had chosen for his future consort. This, again, was not irrelevant to the decision, presuming that it was a woman of a princely house.

A case of this kind was the application made at the end of the fifteenth century by Louis XII of France for the annulment of his marriage with the daughter of his predecessor's predecessor on the throne, so that he might marry the widow of his immediate predecessor. From the point of view of family law, the question was rather complicated, but politically it was clear and simple. The desirable widow was the Duchess of Brittany, and Louis wanted to save Brittany from being lost to France.[114] The Pope, Alexander VI, who had proved his broad-mindedness on questions of canonical law over the marriages of his own children, displayed complete understanding for political necessities in this case also. When a treaty advantageous to both parties had been safely negotiated, Cesare Borgia in person brought the king his marriage licence, and Brittany remained with France.

Encouraged by this precedent, King Henry VIII of England sent an emissary to Rome in 1528 to request the annulment of his marriage with Catherine of Aragon, to enable him to marry a lady of his court, Anne Boleyn. Every request coming from London was benevolently received in Rome, for Henry VIII was a pious son of the Roman Church, and a stout opponent of the

Reformation; he had even personally written a book against Luther. But on closer inspection the case was found to involve difficulties. Louis XII had petitioned for his annulment immediately after his marriage, allegedly before it had been consummated. Henry VIII, however, had been married to Catherine for nearly twenty years. Six children had been born of the marriage: that, of them all, only a single daughter had survived was nothing extraordinary in those days. Henry's union with the ugly Spanish princess, six years older than himself, had certainly been unhappy from the first; it had been a political *mariage de convenance*, forced on Henry while yet a child. He had, however, known how to console himself. Before succumbing to Anne Boleyn's charms he had had a liaison with another court lady, Elizabeth Blount, by whom he had an illegitimate son. Henry was very proud of this boy, for he saw in him proof that he would be capable of begetting a sturdy heir to the throne if only he had the right woman.

For the king this was a powerful argument, but the Pope had to take account of other factors beside it. Queen Catherine was a scion of the mightiest ruling house of the world. She was the daughter of Ferdinand of Aragon and Isabella of Castille, and, more important still, aunt to the Emperor Charles V, of whose help the Pope stood in urgent need in his struggle against the Reformation. And who was Anne Boleyn, for whose sake the king wanted to pluck the crown off Catherine's head? An unimportant young girl of the minor English nobility. Was the Pope to endanger the vital interests of the Church just to gratify the whim of a gay gentleman who later, perhaps, would bestow his favour on yet another woman? This seemed irresponsible. Clement VII, a serious man whose life had not been easy, rejected the request.

The refusal set Henry beside himself with rage, and Anne Boleyn fanned the flames by her continued refusal to become his mistress; she was not going to bestow her maidenhead on her royal adorer except in return for the Crown of England. The real need was to change the Pope's mind. Henry mobilized the lawyers of all Europe for the purpose. Ingenious jurists discovered new arguments for him: his marriage had never been legal, for when Henry married her, Catherine had been the widow of his elder brother. One passage in the Old Testament does, indeed, enjoin a man to take his elder brother's widow to wife, but another passage forbids anyone to marry his or her sister or brother-in-law; this was surely the relevant text. The universities of Oxford, Cambridge, Paris, Padua, and Bologna delivered opinions to this effect, and the French Ambassador in Rome intervened in Henry's favour. But the Pope had to be more careful of the Emperor than ever. He was a Medici, the Medicis had lost the throne of Florence, and it depended exclusively on the Emperor whether they were reinstated.

In September 1530 the Pope pronounced his second verdict: Henry VIII's marriage with Catherine of Aragon was valid and could not be annulled. In other circumstances, Henry's love for Anne Boleyn might perhaps have cooled, for although lively and attractive she was no extraordinary beauty, and the king was a tempestuous but unstable lover. But the question for him had now gone beyond that of conquering a woman. He felt the need to prove to himself, to his subjects, and to the world that he was King of England and that his will prevailed. As Rome refused to give way to him, there remained only one solution: to split with the Pope and announce the divorce himself. He had himself proclaimed Head of the Church of England, and a conclave of theologians pronounced his marriage with Catherine invalid. Now Anne Boleyn could have her wedding ring and her Crown.

For three years she was allowed to call herself Queen. During those years she gave birth to one daughter, the later Queen Elizabeth, and had one miscarriage and a still-born child; but she did not give the king a son. Doubts began to gather in Henry's brain. Perhaps what prevented Anne from presenting him with an heir was lack of virtue. Henry sought and found. Persons were there to testify that before marriage with the king, Anne had been secretly married to another man, that she had committed incest with her brother, and had betrayed her royal spouse with a series of lovers. A court of twenty-six peers, presided over by Anne's own uncle, pronounced her guilty. The executioner did the rest. The lovers had to be content with having their heads chopped off with an axe in the customary fashion. For Anne Boleyn, Henry, gallant as ever, fetched a specialist over from Calais to do the operation with a sword.

Of the four marriages which the inexhaustible king concluded in the next seven years, one ended in exactly the same way, one in divorce, one in death in childbirth. It was only when Henry was over fifty that his sixth wife, an experienced widow, managed to keep on the throne and to survive her husband. It rounds off the picture of this most uninhibited of all Renaissance princes if one adds that, even at the height of his orgies of blood and sex, Henry VIII insisted strictly on piety at Court, demanded the oath of chastity from the priests under his rule, and made the bishops nominated by him put away their wives. As, however, he was successful in war, he has gone down in history as a great king, and in the twentieth century the film industry has even discovered him to have been, really, a delightful Don Juan.

The Purge of the Council of Trent

After the waters of the Reformation had already flooded over half Europe, Rome, urged by the Emperor Charles V, at last steeled itself to set up a dam against them. A Council should remind men, and particularly the clergy, of the old dogmas and examine what measures were necessary for the purpose. The decisions of this great conclave, which sat—it is true, with long interruptions—for eighteen years (1545-1563) in Trent and Bologna, dealt, among other matters, with problems of sex. A decision taken by the Council of Florence a century earlier, which had indeed been little regarded, was reaffirmed and marriage again declared to be a sacrament and indissoluble. To strengthen the marriage-tie, it seemed necessary to make weddings public and solemn acts, and to place them under the control of the Church. Even though this made marrying more difficult, it was still better than allowing the thoughtless contracting of unions which as easily went to pieces afterwards, leading to bigamy and total separation of man and wife.

The Council of Trent tried to sanctify marriage through two devices: so-called secret marriages, i.e. marriages not contracted in the due form, were no longer to be recognized. The ceremony was to be preceded by notification through threefold calling of

Holy wedlock. A bridal pair in bed receiving a blessing from a bishop. Woodcut, *circa* 1480.

the banns in Church, and at the wedding itself three witnesses had to be present, one of them a Clerk in Orders, personally acquainted with either the bridegroom or the bride.

The second innovation, which cut into sex-life deeper still, was the rule that candidates for marriage must show their parents' consent. It proved exceedingly difficult to comply with this condition, which had repeatedly occupied earlier Councils, and most countries did not insist rigidly on it. The promotion of this precondition of marriage to a law of the Church was, however, not unimportant, for it gave parents more rights over their grown-up children than they had enjoyed for centuries past. Sons, in particular, were thus placed in a dependent relationship on their fathers which recalled the legal systems of antiquity. In some countries the temporal authorities hastened to pass enactments further confirming the Church law. In France, a whole series of royal decrees was issued to this effect between 1556 and 1639. Sons and daughters marrying without their fathers' consent were automatically disinherited, and when that remedy proved ineffectual, such marriages were pronounced equivalent to rape, the penalty for which was death.[115]

Another chapter of the decisions of the Council of Trent dealt with the problem of priests' marriages. Here, too, the conservative view won the day. Although Charles V, in view of the great difference of opinion prevailing on the subject in Germany, had recommended abolishing the celibacy rule, the clergy were again required to take the vow of chastity in its strictest form. No pardon was allowed, even for trivial offences. Scandalous literature was submitted to close scrutiny; Boccaccio's *Decameron*, which had long ranked as a classic in Italy, was placed on the index of prohibited books. The representation of the nude in visual art was outlawed no less strictly.[116]

It is true that precisely the secular patrons of the Council, and many of the ecclesiastics also, were not particularly qualified to pose as censors of morals in respect of this last point, since everyone knew that the walls of their palaces were covered with pictures of naked women. Charles V was an enthusiastic collector of Titian's Venuses, and his still more pious son, Philip II, in no way yielded to him in this respect. Philip's monastically simple study in the Escorial still testifies today to the pleasure which he took in seeing naked women about him. For a little while, however, the decisions of the Council were observed, at least in the case of apartments open to the public.

Michelangelo and the Breeches-maker

As usual with such purges, people did not begin by inquiring what was the essence of the sensual and where the line between art and pornography ought to be drawn. They decided that what is naked is immoral and must be erased or covered up. This new prudery made its début in art's noblest home, the Vatican, and its first victim was Michelangelo. A quarter of a century after Michelangelo had created the painted ceiling of the Sistine Chapel, Pope Clement VII commissioned him to decorate the wall behind the altar in the same chapel. He himself gave the master his subject: the fall of the rebellious angels and the Last Judgment. As always, Michelangelo found certain objections to the wishes of his noble patron, but when Clement's successor, Paul III, repeated the order, he gave way. The theme accorded well not only with the spirit of the age but also with his own genius.

While Michelangelo was engaged on the preliminaries of his work, he received from Pietro Aretino a letter, loaded with compliments, in which the dubious aesthete of Venice gave him sundry good counsels on how to interpret the Last Judgment. Michelangelo was well aware who this gentleman was, and that it was inadvisable to incur his enmity. He answered the letter with an equally courteous epistle beginning 'Magnifico Messer Pietro, my master and brother, whose merit is unmatched in this world', and took no further notice of the advice of this uninvited counsellor, for he had decided on his plan: he was going to depict the Last Judgment in an apocalyptic spirit, as a battle between Gods and Titans. Every figure in his picture—Christ, the angels, even the Virgin Mary herself—was to be nude. The plan sounded monstrous and audacious, but Michelangelo was not to be dissuaded from it. The Pope's Master of the Ceremonies, Biagio da Cesena, objected to it; Michelangelo punished him by perpetuating his features among the damned, deep down in hell.

When the gigantic work was completed, after seven years of labour, a shudder ran through the Vatican, but no one dared protest to the master. The only man bold enough was Pietro Aretino. The pornographic Aretino wrote an open letter to the master of the Sistine Chapel, accusing him of obscenity—'when heathen sculptors created, I will not say, a clothed Diana, but even a naked Venus, they made her cover with one hand the privy parts which are never revealed. A Christian for whom faith counts more than art regards neglect of martyrs' and virgins' dress, and the act of rape by seizure of the genitals, as a forbidden spectacle. Things are carried so far that the very denizens of a brothel would shut their eyes, your art would beseem a bawdy bath-house, not a lofty choir.'

Coming as it did from Aretino, it was not surprising that the letter should contain certain personal allusions which smelt of blackmail. When already approaching the sixties Michelangelo had found pleasure in handsome young men; Febo di Poggio, Gherardo Perini, and, most recently, the slender Tommaso di Cavalieri had bewitched him, and the elderly sculptor had written ardent sonnets to Tommaso. Aretino must have learnt of this, and he made transparent allusions to it in the letter.[117] Michelangelo had more important things to do than to bother about denunciations from a notorious slanderer and blackmailer. Aretino's letter did not, however, fall on deaf ears. Michelangelo's enemies in the Vatican muttered and pressed for his Last Judgment to be removed from the Sistine Chapel. So long as Paul III, the last of the Renaissance Popes, lived, they could effect nothing; but when in 1555, Cardinal Giampietro Carafa, the head of the Inquisition, mounted the papal throne under the name of Paul IV, one of his first tasks was to order Michelangelo's Last Judgment to be taken off the chapel wall. As it was a fresco, that simply meant destroying it.

A storm of protest arose from the artists of Rome, and even those prelates in whom the spirit of the Renaissance was still alive declared that such an act of vandalism ought not to be perpetrated in the Vatican. The aged Pope saw that his zeal had carried him too far. He refused, however, to renounce his purpose altogether. He ordered clothes to be put on the heavenly hosts in the Last Judgment; the Virgin and the angels were to be given robes, Christ and the saints at least a loin-cloth apiece. One of Michelangelo's pupils, Daniele de Volterra, was entrusted with this delicate task. While his master was painting away lustily next door in the newly-built St. Peter's, Daniele, who was himself an excellent painter and sculptor (the best busts of Michelangelo are by his hand) painted billowing clothes on to the offending figures. The other painters made mock of him: they nicknamed him *Il Braghettone*—The Breeches-maker. He was not, however, the only one to earn this name, for later observers thought that he had been too hesitant. Girolamo da Fano, Stefano Pozzi, and others of smaller talent still, carried on the tailor-work. For two hundred years various hands fiddled with Michelangelo's masterpiece until even the damned in hell got a shred of cloth.

In his old age Michelangelo had to endure another outbreak of barefaced prudery. He had painted a *Leda and the Swan* for the Duke of Ferrara. Until this, Ferrara had been the most liberal and art-loving court in Italy. Now, however, when a different wind was blowing in Rome, and the Inquisition had set up a Court there which claimed jurisdiction over all Italy, the Duke of Ferrara thought it wiser, after all, not to expose himself to any unpleasantness. He passed the picture on to France, assuming that it would certainly be safe from any harm in a castle of the gay Francis I; but he was wrong. One day, an attack of false modesty overcame even Francis's court. Michelangelo's picture was covered over and put aside until a virtuous Minister of Louis XIII's happened to set eyes on it one day, and was so scandalized that he had it burned.

The number of pictures which fell victim to the Counter-Reformation was less than the number of human beings. Giordano Bruno had not yet been burnt for a heretic in the flower-market in Rome, nor Galileo forced to retract that the earth revolved round the sun, before the cult of the nude was again flourishing gaily. Carracci and Caravaggio, Guido Reni, Francesco Albani and hundreds of their contemporaries paid their tributes to the beauty of the nude body with an energy and passion which stressed the sexual element even more than the painters of the Renaissance had done. The Grand Master of the nudes, however, was a painter from the north, Peter Paul Rubens. The

Courts of all Europe loaded him with orders and honours. Only Spanish painting, sensual though it was, remained clothed.

The Figure of Don Juan

In literature, too, the Counter-Reformation did little to banish sex. The pastoral plays which now came into fashion were less highly spiced than Machiavelli's and Aretino's comedies, but not much less sensuous. The kiss took the place of everything else on the stage, and there was an inordinate deal of kissing and of talk about kissing. The romances and lyrics, however, did not stop at that, but described the more intimate processes of love as explicitly as in the Renaissance. Boccaccio's *Decameron* was released again, after a commission of theologians had expunged a few passages, and was imitated everywhere, even in Spain, where Tirso de Molina's *Los Cigarrales de Toledo* and *Los tres Maridos Burlados* showed that marital morals had not changed greatly since the Council of Trent.

Tirso de Molina, otherwise Gabriel Telléz, is also the inventor of a literary figure which posterity turned into a general type: Don Juan, the insatiable woman-hunter, the sex-driven adventurer who finally perished of his sins. Molina, who wrote over four hundred pieces for the theatre, assuredly did not himself realize what a hit he had made when *El Burlador de Sevilla y el Convidado de Piedra* (the Mocker of Seville and the Guest of Stone) was first performed in 1630. It was one of the innumerable 'cloak and dagger' melodramas in which hot-blooded cavaliers duelled and murdered for a woman and met a well-deserved bad end in consequence.

Molina's Don Juan is set in the Middle Ages; his sorry hero, Don Juan Tenorio, commits his villanies not only in Seville but also in Naples. He has already seduced one society lady and two girls of the people, and is now searching for his fourth victim. His especial sinfulness, however, lies not so much in the number of his victims as in his cynicism. After murdering the father of the virtuous Doña Ana, he throws suspicion on to another cavalier and, worse still, makes mock of the stone effigy of the murdered man, the noble Don Gonzale de Ulloa. Then the ghost of Don Gonzale seizes the evil-doer by the hand and carries him off to hell.

It was thus more a villainous murder-story with nocturnal duels, churchyard ghosts and hell-fire, than the punishment of a sexual profligate. The audience of the drama, however, felt that they were seeing before them a figure which they all knew, but had never before beheld in such recognizable flesh and blood— the conscienceless sexual insatiate, who inevitably became a criminal. The *caballeros* in whom even a spark of the Don Juan lurked, the decent lads who had lost their girls to a more adroit wooer, the severe paterfamilias, the young women who had lost their virtue, even the innocent virgins who were waiting secretly for a Don Juan, by the end of Act II were all of one mind: may the devil fly away with this scoundrel! And so he did. At the end of Act III the balance of guilt was struck, justice was done, not indeed with the help of the police, which had failed again, but thanks to the higher Judge.

The drama had an enormous and instantaneous success. It appeared in book form immediately after its first stage perform-ance. The Italians got hold of the material, Molière took it over from them, Lorenzo da Ponte worked it up into a libretto for Mozart's opera, Byron made a satire out of it, Nikolaus Lenau twisted it into the melancholy mood, and many more tried their hands at it, investing it with ever more nuances. Thus Don Juan was inexhaustible and indestructible, like the natural force of sex.

After Don Juan had conquered the world, the philologists set themselves to searching out his real origin. Was an otherwise not exceptionally original writer like Tirso de Molina capable of inventing such a figure, or was some greater genius, such as Calderon, its father? An Italian literary historian showed that the Don Juan legend was no specifically Spanish product, but found throughout the world, especially in Italy.[118] This, again, wounded the pride of the Spaniards, who comprehensibly wished to preserve for Seville the fame of being the cradle of Don Juan. To prove that Molina's hero, Don Juan Tenorio, was a true son

of Seville, they unearthed from the old archives his 'original' a
rich citizen named Miguel de Manara, who, after a life rich in
love affairs, had made over his earthly wealth to the monastery
of the Caridad, and whose monument had long stood in Seville,
facing the Caridad church.

That Manara had been a great sinner, before he became a
humble penitent, is attested by his own testament: 'I, Miguel de
Manara', we read, 'have served Babylon and the Devil, its Prince,
with a thousand abominations, acts of arrogance, adulteries,
blasphemies, scandals and robberies. My sins and my offences
are innumerable, and only the great wisdom of God can tell
them all.' Further research has showed that Manara had, indeed,
been born in Seville, but of a Corsican family, and that his
real name was Vincentelo de Leca. As Corsica belonged at that
time to Italy, several nations might claim a share in the glory of
having produced the original of Don Juan. There has been
repeated talk—most recently in the spring of 1955—of canonizing
the repentant sinner.

Meanwhile it is certain that Miguel de Manara was born in
Seville on 3 March 1627, thus only three years before Molina's
play saw the light of day, and the first three years of life are too
short a span even for a born Don Juan to establish his fame as
seducer and woman-hunter. The Don Juan of literature must
therefore renounce this particular model. One may, however,
freely admit that he was not the product of a poet's unfettered
imagination. In the age in which this human type put on tangible
shape on the stage, there were in Spain, as in other lands, among
the great lords and also among lesser men, plenty of Don Juans,
who ended their sinful lives sometimes in the odour of hell-fire,
sometimes not.

Perversion in Court Society

What gives the true sex-life of this era its special character is
a tendency to the extreme and a pleasure in the perverse, which
does not always seem to derive from natural tendencies, but
rather to be fostered by the new code of morals. A lurid light

is cast on the life of high society in Rome by the trial of Beatrice Cenci, who was executed in 1599 on the Monte d'Angeli for the murder of her father, Francesco Cenci. The father had committed incest with his daughter and had shut her up, but Beatrice was not the innocent angel of Shelley's and Stendhal's romanticized versions of this family history. She had conducted herself more freely with her lovers than was seemly for a young woman of good family in Rome. As Rome now kept a sharper look-out for unlawful love-relationships between men and women, which consequently entailed certain risks, homosexual relationships, especially between women, became very frequent. The best-informed historian of the morals of the age, Brantôme (Pierre de Bourdeilles, Abbot and Lord of Brantôme), has left a detailed description of this side of sex-life in his posthumously published *Memoires*,[119] and particularly in his *Vies des dames galantes*.[120] The general use at the time of the expression *donna con donna* itself shows that Lesbian love was particularly prevalent in Italy, but it was also common enough just then in Spain and even in France, which normally was little addicted to this aberration. Brantôme expressly remarks that the practice was still new in France; a 'lady of quality' had introduced it from Italy.

This lady of quality, whose name the Count of Brantôme (ordinarily no very discreet writer) carefully refrains from mentioning, was assuredly none other than Catharine de Medici, the mother of three kings of France and for thirty years the *de facto* ruler of the country. The true authoress of the massacre of St. Bartholomew's Eve, Catharine has earned the reputation of being one of the craftiest sadists of modern history, and it would be vain to try to cleanse her memory from the deeds of blood for which she was responsible. In mitigation, it may perhaps be remarked that it was a thwarted sex-life that turned her into the paths of cruelty. She was brought up in Rome under the guardianship of her uncle, Pope Clement VII, and sent to France at the age of fourteen to be married to Francis I's second son. It was a political *mariage de convenance*, like many others. No one in

France bothered about the little, inconspicuous Florentine, who had not even brought with her a big dowry, as had been expected. She was overshadowed by other women, the powerful Duchess of Étampes and the beautiful Diane de Poitiers, Francis I's mistress.

Catharine's position became even more difficult when the death of his elder brother brought her husband to the throne. Henri II, as he now was, was very dependent on other women, but not on his wife. Diane de Poitiers changed over from the father to the son, who in his turn, although eighteen years her junior, became a slave to her charms. Henri's union with Catharine remained childless for ten years and there was some talk of divorcing her for sterility. Then, suddenly, her womb grew fruitful, and she bore her husband seven children in quick succession. She remained a shadow-queen, however, until her husband lost his life in a tournament in 1559. Now at last she was able to evict her elderly rival Diane. She herself was no longer interested in men—her interest had, obviously, never been very lively; all she desired was power.

On the other side of the Channel another frigid woman was now ruling and sacrificing sex to power—Elizabeth of England, the daughter of Henry VIII and Anne Boleyn. Catharine de Medici became Elizabeth's great rival. Her ambition was to exterminate Protestantism and become the matriarch of a Catholic Europe. She married one son to Mary Stuart, Queen of Scots; another received the crown of Poland, and one of her daughters became wife to Philip II of Spain. Her children, however, were degenerates, some of them sexual perverts. Her favourite son, Henri III, was a chaser of petticoats who neglected the business of government for his mistresses, until the age of twenty-three, when he underwent a curious sexual change. Thereafter he was only interested in young men. His *mignons*, the friends of his bosom, made him a laughingstock in the eyes of the world. One of Catharine's daughters, Margot, who married the King of Navarre, afterwards Henri IV of France, was a nymphomaniac. Her consumption of men grew so inordinate that her husband, although very liberal even in this respect, parted from her and divorced her.

At the Court of the most pious of all lands, Spain, the sexual irregularities were even greater. Don Carlos, Philip II's son, has little beyond the name in common with the hero of Schiller's drama. His undoubted tenderness for his step-mother, one of Catharine de Medici's daughters, was only an insignificant episode in his sex-life. He was a physical cripple from childhood and mentally a sadist who loved tormenting women and animals. When he was only ten years old his outrageous behaviour caused so much scandal that his grandfather, Charles V, advised keeping him away from women. He had little girls whipped, and mutilated horses after shutting himself up at night with them in a stable. His dagger was always in his hand. Even when he had passed his childhood no woman was safe from his importunities. Withal, he was impotent and none of the innumerable remedies which he tried availed. The Courts of Europe knew it, and no prince would bestow his daughter's hand on this cretin. When he took to political intrigue, Philip had him shut up. His early death saved Spain from being ruled by a monster.

His step-brother, Philip III, on whom the Crown of Spain now devolved, watched most severely over the morals of his subjects, but life at his Court was more exuberant and profligate than ever. He was democratic in his affairs of the heart, bestowing his favours on ladies of the Court, but also on courtesans. He is credited with thirty-two illegitimate children, a figure hitherto matched only by Arabian sheikhs.

When his son, Philip IV, mounted the throne in 1621, Spain put on a winding-sheet. The new king began as a zealot. He issued strict ordinances against the luxurious lives of the grandees and the bishops. The brothels were shut throughout Spain, gluttony forbidden, the menus of banquets strictly regulated. The king directed especial attention to the etiquette of dress. Already under Philip II it had been made black and severe. Now women were forbidden more strictly still to reveal their charms; nor might men expose themselves. The king, too, submitted himself to a strict rule, which extended to his sleeping-chamber. When he visited the queen at night, he was, indeed, allowed to wear slippers, but a black cloak had to be laid about his shoulders; on his right arm he bore a shield, bringer of good fortune, and in his hand he carried his cavalier's dagger, while the Mistress of the Bedchamber preceded him to the bed with a candle and a chamber-pot. His wife, Maria Anna of Austria, who found it hard to accustom herself to the Spanish Court ceremonial, wrote in a letter: 'I would rather be the last nun in Graz than Queen of Spain.'

But mirth soon returned to Madrid, and Philip IV's Court became almost as luxurious as that of any of his predecessors. One feast followed another, and the dress regulations again allowed *décolletés*. Don Juan had conquered the 'Guest of Stone'.

IO

THE AGE OF DISCOVERIES

THE discoveries of which we shall speak here relate neither to America nor to the sea-passage to India, but to the new light thrown on the knowledge of sex. Up to the middle of the seventeenth century what was known of the origin of man —generation, fertilization and the development of the first stages of the embryo—was little more than what Aristotle had taught two thousand years earlier. Any new doctrine was mainly compounded of errors and vague hypotheses. What happens when copulation takes place? What is the physiological effect of the generative act? Of what is the semen compounded? Is its quantity or its composition decisive for fertilization? How far does it penetrate into the woman's body? Where and how does conception take place? Must the woman be disposed to it in any particular way? Does emotional excitement play any part, or is the physical disposition the only factor to count, and what governs this? Does the woman play any active part in fertilization, by herself emitting a kind of semen, or is the male semen the sole active force? And how, after that, does the fruit grow?

So many questions, so many insoluble riddles. Nature seemed determined to keep all her secrets in this field. Even the observations of botanists and animal-breeders added very little to knowledge, leading rather to the conclusion that the human process was quite different. Laymen were chiefly interested in practical questions. They wanted to know what was the moment most propitious to ensure fertilization and what they must do to produce a boy. But the scholars could not answer this question, or else they gave married couples such ridiculous recipes that presently people stopped asking.

The *Compendium Medicinae* of Gilbertus Anglicus, one of the most famous English physicians of the Middle Ages, who had excellent work to his credit in other fields of medicine, recommends childless husbands to drink a herbal tea and, while drinking it, to write a magic formula on parchment and wear the same words, written on a card, round their necks. Then they would have a boy, while if their wives went through the same procedure it would be a girl. By comparison with such recipes, which remained in use long beyond the Renaissance, it seemed more profitable to consult an astrologer, when one could at least make sure that the child was born under a propitious star.

The theologians concerned themselves mainly with the question 'When did the embryo get a soul?' Thomas Aquinas, the most influential doctor of the medieval Church, decided that this did not happen immediately on conception, but on the fortieth day of pregnancy in the case of boys and the eightieth in that of girls. This dictum, for which there was not the slightest trace of justification in biology, was of great importance, especially in cases of induced miscarriage, for although the Church condemned on principle all devices for preventing or interrupting pregnancy, there was yet a difference between doing away with a still lifeless embryo and with a foetus possessing a soul sent of God. Above all, the difference of dates gave authoritative recognition to the superiority of the male even long before birth. This was the more important because, when the child came into the world, it was not perceptible to the parents that boys had more mature souls than girls. On the contrary, little girls often developed earlier than little boys. This, however, was clearly an illusion. In everything connected with the life of the soul, boys had priority and superiority. Boys were accordingly, as a rule, sent to school earlier than girls.

The Doctrine of the Egg

Aquinas's basic theory, although differently worded, agreed in essentials with Aristotle's teachings. The two sexes were not entirely unlike, and each had its function in life to perform, but man was better equipped from the outset than woman. In the reproductive process also, he was the active and more important partner. According to the prevailing view, fertilization was bisexual. The woman did not only receive the man's semen, but also contributed towards the formation of the fertilizing element. As late as the eighteenth century natural historians still wrote of a female semen which was emitted in coitus in the same way as the male. How the two semina then mingled, and what happened after that, was unclear. Even the acutest thinkers resorted to vague metaphors when discussing this question. The most popular idea was that the semen dispersed itself like an aura, a mist or steam, but there were other variants. Descartes, in a posthumously published treatise[121] expressed the view that the process of generation resembled chemically that of beer-brewing, in which the froth of beer could be used as yeast for other beers: 'The semina of the two sexes mingle and act as yeast, each on the other.'

The 'bi-seminal theory' formulated by Descartes, was appropriate to an age in which women wielded so much influence on the destinies of humanity. Descartes himself was in the service of a queen, Christina of Sweden. Yet science had discredited his theory even before it appeared in print. It was sharply attacked from two angles. One school maintained that the ovum, the female egg, was the decisive factor, and that the role of the male in reproduction was only to stimulate. Others said that all important elements in reproduction derived from the male, that there was no female semen, and that the woman was only the recipient and nurse of the specifically masculine product through which reproduction was effected.

The first blow against the bi-seminal theory was delivered by an Englishman, William Harvey, the discoverer of the circulation of the blood. Harvey was then over seventy. He had suffered misfortunes. Having been Physician-in-Ordinary to the Stuarts, he had been driven into exile when his royal patient, Charles I, ended his life on the scaffold. Nevertheless, every biologist in Europe listened very carefully to every word that came from the grand old man. In 1651, one year after Descartes' death, Harvey published a treatise on reproduction in animals (*Exercitationes de generatione Animalium*) which caused a sensation in the world of learning. It attacked Aristotle's doctrine, hitherto regarded as impregnable, in two respects. Harvey maintained that there was one reproductive principle common to all living creatures, the ovum; the semen was irrelevant. The female element was thus the decisive one in reproduction.

Aristotle had taught that the lower forms of life were derived from inorganic matter, mud, the decomposition of the earth by water and heat. Harvey denied this. His observations had, indeed, been made on the higher mammals, chiefly on does shot by the courtiers for sport, but he generalized. Modern historians of biology have found that Harvey's views were, basically, not so very radical, and quite easily reconciled with those of Aristotle.[122] But his contemporaries, and the following generations, thought him a revolutionary. Linnaeus reduced the quintessence of Harvey's theory to the epigrammatic formula: *Vivum omne ex ovo*—everything living comes from the egg.

Harvey was the author of *ovism*, the doctrine which makes the female the more important partner in reproduction. It was a hypothesis, nothing more. It is almost the rule in natural science, however, for the great intuitive ideas, the hypotheses, to come first, and to be followed by the proofs, the exact observations of individual cases. So it was now. Once Harvey had broken the ban that had lain on everything not strictly Aristotelian, evidence in favour of the ovum very soon appeared in plenty. The most illuminating material came from the researches of an Italian scientist, Marcello Malpighi, into hens' eggs.[123] Shortly after, a young Dutch anatomist named Reynier de Graaf made even more remarkable discoveries.[124] He demonstrated the changes which take place in rabbits' ovaries in the first days after fertilization, and concluded that similar processes must take place in human beings.

The Discovery of the Spermatozoon

The ovists' victory seemed complete, but it was short-lived. In 1677 a student named Ham brought the famous optician Leeuwenhoek of Delft a glass bottle containing the semen of a man who suffered from nocturnal emissions, saying that he had put the semen under a microscope and observed in it small living creatures, *animalcula*. Leeuwenhoek listened to the young doctor's report with attention, but without great surprise, for in his researches he had seen so many extraordinary things under the microscope that nothing could surprise him now. Just ten years before he had found in a drop of apparently pure, clear rainwater minute living creatures which he had named *infusoria*. His visitor's animalcula might simply be the same creatures. But he kept an open mind, smeared a drop of the semen on a slide and put it under his keenest lens.

Ham had been right. The grey fluid was in fact full of innumerable tiny, moving living creatures quite distinct from the infusoria and other animalcula which he had discovered in water. They had round bodies and tails five or six times as long as their bodies. They made swimming movements with their tails, like an eel. When Leeuwenhoek looked at them again a few hours later, they were no longer moving: they had, apparently, died in the interval. But their form was still clearly recognizable and their existence was indisputable.

As these animalcula came from the semen of a sick man, it seemed probable that they were a specific product of his illness, perhaps the result of disintegration, for, although the ovists denied it, many scientists thought it possible that life derived from some inner process of decay. Leeuwenhoek therefore examined the semen of healthy males, and found the same result: a vast number of living creatures, a thousand or more in the space of a grain of sand, moving about. They seemed to possess more power of resistance than those which he had observed first, but the length of their lives depended on the temperature. In the cold they died after twenty-four hours. If the semen was kept in a warm place, they were still moving after two or three days, but on the fourth day they were all dead.

Antonius van Leeuwenhoek was no specialist scholar. He came of a family of spectacle-makers and glass-grinders, a profession which was at that time a Dutch speciality; his contemporary and fellow-countryman Baruch Spinoza had also been a glass-cutter before taking up problems of cosmogony and morals. Leeuwenhoek's father had thought that there were enough polishers of lenses in Holland and apprenticed his son to a cloth-merchant, but Antonius found the family profession more interesting and soon returned to it. He showed an extraordinary skill in this field; his lenses were sharper than those of any of his competitors. In the course of a long life (he was born in Delft in 1632 and died there in 1723) he constructed over two hundred microscopes. He kept the best ones for himself, for he was not simply interested in making magnifying glasses but hoped, with the aid of his lenses, to penetrate to the inner structure of things. He examined everything that came to his hand, but was especially attracted by organic objects. Here, too, he displayed the same keen eye as in his making of instruments, and thus a world hitherto unsuspected revealed itself under his eyes.

Taken all in all, Leeuwenhoek's discovery must rank as one of the greatest of all times. His descriptions of primitive organisms entitle him to be regarded as the true founder of microbiology, but he was also the first to recognize cross-striature in muscles, the dental channels, the spiral ducts, and scalariformity (ladder-like formation) in plants. And at an advanced age he made another great discovery, that of parthenogenesis, or a-sexual reproduction. Although he had never attended a university and understood no language except Dutch—not even Latin—the specialists treated him with respect, knowing that this craftsman, unhampered by any load of book-learning, had a sharper eye than they. He pored over no theories, but had an uncannily keen gift of observation. If they sent him material for examination they could count on getting a clear, wholly reliable report.

All the same, his discovery that the human semen was full of life made Leeuwenhoek rather uneasy. He was convinced that these were living creatures and the essential components of semen, not some sort of parasite feeding on man. He called them *spermatozoa*. Nevertheless, the question was a little delicate. People might not like his having pried into human semen. In any case, he thought it best to submit his discovery to a learned society for the specialists to check it and publish if they thought fit.

In November 1677 he accordingly approached Lord Brouncker, President of the Royal Society of London. The Royal Society was the most advanced scientific association in the world, if not entirely the freest. Only a little while before, one of its most active members, Henry Oldenburg, had been thrown into the Tower and kept there for several months for having conducted correspondence with Leeuwenhoek, Spinoza, Malpighi and other foreign scholars which aroused the suspicions of the authorities. To be in touch with the Royal Society was, however, an honour in itself. Scholars from every country in the world sent the results of their researches to London to receive the blessing of the Society. The modest optician of Delft was at the utmost pains to show the great gentlemen in London his respect for them. In an almost servile tone he protested that it was far from his purpose to shock the esteemed members of the Royal Society. He was aware that they might find his observations disgusting or scandalous; he therefore left it to their free discretion to publish them or to suppress them.

To his surprise, however, Leeuwenhoek very soon got an encouraging answer back from London: he was to extend his investigations and look into animals, dogs, horses, and other quadrupeds. Leeuwenhoek could not at once procure a stallion's semen, but he soon made his observations on dogs and rabbits, and posted back a paper, complete with drawings, of living and dead spermatozoa. It was published in the proceedings of the Royal Society in 1678[125] and was a milestone in the history of the modern science of sex: taken together with the work of Malpighi and Graaf, its starting point.

The scientists of all Europe pricked up their ears. Here was something quite unparalleled, no mere experiment on an animal but an investigation conducted on a living man, on a question of universal concern. All the great universities counter-checked Leeuwenhoek's experiments, and everywhere they were confirmed. The glass-cutter of Delft had been right again. Even the Pope's physician, Lancisi, expressed his admiration for Leeuwenhoek. As with many great experiments and discoveries in all ages, a dispute over the priority had arisen even before the opposition had given tongue. Another Dutchman, a certain Hartsoeker, announced that he had observed the spermatozoa three years before Leeuwenhoek and had shown them to the famous physician, Huyghens, but had refrained from publishing his discovery out of 'excessive modesty'. Now ambition awoke also in Leeuwenhoek and he declared that he, too, had seen spermatozoa under the miscroscope years before. However this may be, the credit for this great scientific achievement undoubtedly belongs to the medical student Ham and the lens-polisher Leeuwenhoek.

The Secret of Fertilization

The discovery of the spermatozoon was a hard blow for the ovists and a triumph for the adherents of the Aristotelian doctrine. Clearly Aristotle had been right after all: the male principle, the semen, was the original source of life, the active reproductive force, not a mere external stimulant to the development of the ovum, but the germ out of which the future generation proceeded. De facto, nothing was known about the ova of mammals, still less of human beings. No one had ever seen such an egg. One female organ was called an ovary, on the analogy of the male scrotum, but whether the ovary really contained eggs out of which the embryo developed, was by no means certain. A hundred and fifty years were yet to pass before Karl Ernst von Baer found the egg-cell in a mammal; but the contents of the semen could be seen by anyone possessed of a microscope.

There was no more need of the hypothesis of the *aura seminalis*, of the semen spreading out like a cloud of vapour. The spermatozoa could move themselves. But could they ascend into the

womb, where the fruit developed? It was behind this question
that the ovists dug themselves in. Their original leader, Harvey,
had never observed semen in the uterus, and neither had his pupils.
Once again the Royal Society of London was called in as supreme
referee. This time it was the Society's secretary who addressed
Leeuwenhoek, sending him a list of seventy distinguished
physicians and biologists who shared Harvey's view.

Leeuwenhoek felt confident. He had already found the spermatozoa of animals in the uterus shortly after copulation, but to
give incontrovertible proof, he made an experiment. He had a
bitch covered several times, then killed her and examined her
sexual organs. The uterus and the vagina leading to it were full
of spermatozoa.

The ovists were now silenced for a while. The animalculists,
champions of the male principle, had won the first round. The
role of the female in the reproductive process seemed even less
important than Aristotle had thought it. The strict animalculists
regarded the female as simply furnishing the nutriment for the
fruit, the sole origin of which was the male semen. They denied
that human beings and viviparous animals had any ova at all;
this was an erroneous hypothesis, excluded by the new knowledge. Man was man enough to get children, woman's part was
to carry them. That was her only function, until birth. Such was
nature's decree.

When the ovists had the upper hand, they used to show a
drawing of a woman's ovum, deduced from the analogy of
Malpighi's description of the evolution of a hen's egg, and already
containing the child in embryonic form. Now the animalculists
turned the tables on them and produced drawings showing the
child already present within the spermatozoon. The first person
thus to exercise his imagination on the inside of a spermatozoon
was Hartsoeker, the Dutchman who had claimed to have been done
out of his proper credit by Leeuwenhoek. His semen-mannikins
are reminiscent of the Basle physician Paracelsus's *homunculus*, that
laboratory creature brought into the world in a glass bottle by
mysterious forces, out of a mixture of human semen, horse's

dung and some chemical ingredients, without calling on a woman.

Some mocked, others believed, for from new scientific discoveries to the crassest superstition is often only a step. The biologists went on wrangling throughout the eighteenth century and into the nineteenth, on the respective roles of the male and female principles in reproduction. It was long indeed before they agreed to recognize both sexes as equal partners in the foundation of the coming generation, for sceptics who regarded one or the other as more important could always say: 'First show me a male cell penetrating a female cell, then I will believe.'

In 1877, exactly two hundred years after the discovery of the spermatozoon, a Swiss biologist named H. Fiol succeeded in observing the entry of sperma into the ovum of a starfish,[126] and it was longer still before microscopic evidence was produced of the fertilization process in higher animals. The confirmed sceptics could still argue that the process in human beings might possibly be different, for, often as it has been illustrated on paper, the fusion of the male and female human cells has never yet been observed.

Telegony

The epoch-making discoveries in the biology of sex which marked the latter half of the seventeenth century were at first followed by scientists with keen attention. Afterwards, however, interest flagged somewhat, not only because the pundits could not agree but also because the new knowledge was of so little practical use. The world now knew more than before about semen and ovaries, but as many men as before remained impotent, as many women sterile, and no one had found a convincing explanation, let alone a remedy. The interest of the public therefore concentrated on side-issues, to the solution of which science seemed able to contribute more.

First and foremost, there was the strange doctrine of telegony, which held that a woman's first pregnancy—not her first coitus —decisively affected all her later pregnancies. The first pregnancy brought about such great changes in the woman's body as to leave behind permanent after-effects. The result was that the children of the same mother but different fathers all took after the father of the first child. This doctrine was derived from observations allegedly made in stock-breeding, and many breeders still believe today that a single crossing with a male not of pure pedigree affects detrimentally all the subsequent progeny of the female animal. Inconsistent as it was with the rest of his views, William Harvey had adopted this theory in the middle of the seventeenth century and had furnished it, so to speak, with a scientific foundation. The first conception, the *primus conceptus*, and none other, produced in the female ovary chemical changes which passed into the blood and penetrated the entire body. It acted as an infection of which the woman's organism could never again rid itself. The later pregnancies, by contrast, were more superficial, affecting only the uterus.

Since a man so important as Harvey had made this assertion, other doctors were soon found ready to swear by telegony. The doctrine of the *primus conceptus* became a magic formula which was used to explain many awkward surprises in married life. For women who had been unfaithful to their husbands it was a useful excuse. However close the child's resemblance to her secret lover, the woman could always put this down to chance, and jealous husbands could console themselves with the thought that the children would always take after them, even if their wives had lovers. A man who had married a virgin could never get a cuckoo's egg laid in his nest, however often his wife was false to him, whereas a man who married a widow cuckolded himself in advance, since his children were really the children of his wife's first husband. But the question had a more serious side, especially for widows, who now found it harder to get husbands. Even if they had had no children, one pregnancy, one miscarriage, sufficed to set on them for the rest of their lives the stamp of their first husband. Physiologically speaking there was no second marriage. Views on blood-relationships became confused, and in thousands of hitherto untroubled marriages doubts arose as to whether the fathers were related to the children.

Harvey's theory also gave rise to another confusion, this time less serious. Since his discovery of the circulation of the blood, blood was all the fashion in medicine. Sir Christopher Wren, the architect of St. Paul's, who was interested in biological problems, was the first to recommend injecting medicines into the veins. Sheep's blood was transferred into human veins; it was believed that old men could be rejuvenated by blood-transfusions from young men, and soon expectations ran higher still. If, as was believed, all a man's qualities were contained in his blood, it must be possible to harmonize temperaments through blood-transfusion. The hot-blooded and the cold-blooded, passionate husbands and phlegmatic wives or, vice-versa, sluggish husbands and over-exacting wives, could equalize their respective temperaments and achieve harmonious lives by mutual blood-transfusion. After the Royal Society had led off in 1666 with a basic work on blood-transfusion by Richard Lower, a Berlin doctor named Sigmund Elsholz proposed that 'all unhappy marriages should be reconciled by mutual blood-transfusion between the incompatible spouses'.[127] Unfortunately the annals of medicine do not record how far the ingenious German's advice was taken, or with what results.

Political Arithmetic

It must be regarded as a real indication of progress and spiritual liberty that the State and the Church put no great obstacles in the way of biological research, and even of the propagation of the new theories on sex. In other respects the seventeenth century was by no means a tolerant era, even when the religious wars had died down; but the new microcosm, the world made visible under the microscope, and the theories derived from it, did not seem to the temporal and spiritual authorities to be particularly dangerous. Not a few members of the clergy, especially in Italy, participated in the laboratory experiments and made unprejudiced contributions to the knowledge of natural processes.

The State, however, had other cares. It was not particularly interested in whether the male or the female principle played the larger part in reproduction: what governments wanted was that their subjects should multiply quickly and vigorously. Germany had been depopulated by the Thirty Years War, Vienna and London had suffered severe visitations of the plague, and the population of other countries, especially Spain, was being drawn off to America. It was primarily on military grounds that a dense population had hitherto been thought desirable, but now economic considerations also began to enter into the calculation. Everywhere in Europe the authorities were growing afraid that there would soon be not enough hands to till the soil and fill the workshops.

These fears were most acute in the most highly industrialized countries, England and France. In those countries were born the demographic theories which thereafter held the field, uncontradicted, up to the end of the eighteenth century. Put shortly, they amounted to the proposition that density of population was decisive for a country's wealth. The more people, the better. A dense population was not the result of economic well-being, but the precondition for it. One need not therefore fear to bring children into the world, or to admit foreigners; immigration was better than emigration. Above all, one should not let oneself be misled by the fact that large families often lived more scantily than small ones. The important factor was not the circumstances of the individual family, but the national wealth, and this was increased by a higher birth-rate. The larger the families, the larger the labour-force, the more one could export, the more money would come in. *Ergo*, producing children meant making the country richer.

Who profited by the wealth, the whole population or only a small upper class, was an aspect of the question with which the theoreticians of population did not concern themselves, or only in passing, for it was a dangerous one. The age concerned itself little with social problems. It is true that Poor Laws had been enacted in England as early as the reign of Queen Elizabeth, but sentimentality of this kind consorted ill with the objectives of the new economic policy, the development of trade and industry. If large families fell into any great difficulties, the parents could better their condition by sending their children to work in factories at an early age, and if the children were not strong enough for that, they could still earn a few pennies by crawling up chimneys as sweeps. Child labour was cheap and consequently in demand—one reason more for wise parents to bring as many children as possible into the world.

Statesmen—Cromwell in England, Colbert in France—had been practising this policy (later known as mercantilism) for some time with apparent success, but the theoretical foundation for it was lacking. The man who provided this was a doctor named Sir William Petty, the son of a tailor from a London suburb. He had travelled in France and Holland and was a man of many parts. He lectured on natural history, and also on music, became Surgeon-in-Chief to the army in Ireland when not yet thirty, proved a successful manager of estates, and himself acquired wealth through practical speculation. He was also one of the founders of the Royal Society and connected with the circle of men who acted as supreme referees in the field of sex-science.

The lesson which he drew from these manifold activities and observations was that the life or death of the individual mattered less than the general phenomena affecting the entire people, and that these were calculable. Petty called this process, which to-day we call population policy, 'political arithmetic'. If statistics of births and deaths could be exactly calculated, as another music teacher, John Graunt, had tried to do before him, it would be possible to predict with great accuracy by how much the population would have risen in twenty-five or fifty years, and this was very important for the economic development of the country. On this basis it would be possible to make plans, form industries, and regulate immigration and emigration, without groping in the dark.

The idea was then new. For all the advance of medicine, death still seemed to be entirely in God's hand and no one dared prophesy about it. Births seemed to be more uncertain still.

Who, when he married, knew how many children he would have? If one looked at the families of one's acquaintance, the number of births was so unequal that it seemed impossible to draw general conclusions on the subject. Whether the decisive factor was the sex-instinct, the man's virility, or the woman's fertility, everything seemed quite fortuitous; some had many children, some few, some none at all. Petty, however, showed that the fluctuations in the number of births and deaths, taken over a large city like London, or if possible over the whole country, were not so great but that the same phenomena recurred regularly, and certain tendencies were apparent.

Petty's doctrine was received with acclamation. Doubtful as some of his assertions might be, they yet provided a foundation on which to build. For the first time sex-life had been linked with politics and economics, independent of all laws of morality and all individual accidents. It had been fetched out of its isolation and made part of a scientific system which embraced natural and social processes. It is true that the *modus operandi* were still very imperfect. The available source-material consisted chiefly of the parish registers of baptisms and funerals; for which reason alone, the clergy's part in the investigations was an especially prominent one.

Petty's most important pupil in the first half of the eighteenth century was a Berlin pastor named Johann Peter Süssmilch. He gave his *magnum opus*, which appeared in 1741, a theological title: *The Divine Order in the Relationships of the Human Kind, from Birth, Death and Reproduction*; it was, however, a sober investigation of population policy, in many respects a big advance on its English forerunners. Süssmilch's conclusions were similar to those of the Englishman: the numbers of the human race, unless decimated by wars and especially violent epidemics, increase, and that is well, for increase of population means greater well-being. It was only half a century later that another clergyman, Malthus, dared to attack this principle and dangle before the eyes of mankind the spectre of the famine which awaited them if they multiplied too fast.

II

THE AGE OF GALLANTRY

THE one hundred and fifty years from the Thirty Years War to the French Revolution are the Golden Age of royal mistresses. Throughout history it has of course been common enough for princes to keep mistresses who outshone the legitimate consorts at Court and even in political life; no age has been quite without them. But now the practice became an institution. A ruler who did not keep a mistress in addition to his legitimate spouse was certainly either an eccentric or a barbarian.

The King of Denmark greeted Peter I of Russia, by then already a very powerful prince, with the condescending remark: 'My compliments, brother; I hear that you, too, have mistresses.' To which Peter replied, not very gallantly: 'My whores cost me less than your Majesty's concubine.'[128] This crude answer only showed that Peter was still half an Asiatic. To be accepted as a true prince, it was not enough to build palaces which could vie in splendour with Versailles: one must also be lavish in one's affairs of the heart. Peter's love affairs were, it is true, copious and various, but they were a farm-labourer's amours; furthermore, he was full of medieval cruelty towards his wives. He had relegated his first wife, the daughter of a small country nobleman, to a nunnery. During his Swedish campaign he had picked up in a camp a Lithuanian peasant girl called Martha Skavronskaya who had been servant in the house of a Baltic Protestant pastor and afterwards served the general purposes of the Russian army. She was one of the market-women types described by Grimmelshausen in his *Landstörtzerin Courasche* in 1670: rough but good-hearted, a hard drinker, always obliging, accustomed to sleeping on straw, or even on the bare ground. After she had lived with Peter for ten years she prevailed on him to marry her.

The other European Courts looked down their noses at this misalliance. Peter continued to take his Catherine, as she was called after she had been baptized into the Orthodox Church, with him on his campaigns, leaving her behind only on his official journeys to western Europe.

She looked round her for consolation and betrayed him with William Mons, brother of one of Peter's earlier mistresses. When Peter discovered this, he had Mons executed. Catherine was forced to witness the scene and as she continued laughingly to protest her innocence, Peter had her lover's head pickled in spirits and put in her bedroom. When even this failed to break Catherine's iron nerve, the Czar of All the Russias himself capitulated; he was reunited with her, and when he died a few months later—probably of a venereal infection—the Lithuanian serving-maid ascended the throne, where for two years she proved herself completely incompetent to rule, but satiated her sexual hunger with numerous lovers.

The rise of Catherine I is untypical, either for her age or for royal mistresses at any time. There is probably no other case in history where the whim and personal taste of a prince has sufficed to make a woman of the lowest social classes ruler of a great country. Catherine is described by contemporaries as neither particularly beautiful nor particularly intelligent—unlike the Byzantine Empress Theodora, and Theodora, although she dominated her husband Justinian, never became ruling sovereign. Princes' mistresses in western Europe in the seventeenth and eighteenth centuries were even less likely than their predecessors to attain the title of queen or empress. Even the extremely intelligent and ambitious Madame de Pompadour, Louis XV's mistress, could not achieve this. She was known as Madame XV, but she never became *Reine de France*. Similarly Madame de Maintenon, whom Louis XIV married secretly, was not given the rank of queen. For precisely in this age, when sex figured so prominently and with so few inhibitions at royal Courts, it came up against dynastic considerations and the barriers of tradition.

Noblesse de Lit

No limits were set, physiologically speaking, to the polygamy and polyandry of princes and princesses. It was only in backward countries that marital fidelity was asked or expected. But socially and politically, sex-life was ordered by a strict hierarchy to which even the most powerful rulers submitted. The women with whom a prince had sexual relations, and also the men whom ruling princesses admitted to their bedchambers, fell into three categories: consorts, lovers, and partners in pleasure.

The consort, male or female, had to come of a ruling House, or a House which had once enjoyed that status. Only children of such a union were entitled to the succession. Consorts who failed to bear children to a prince were not as a rule put away; far fewer princely marriages were annulled or declared invalid in that century than in the sixteenth. In this respect, while sex-life was laxer, the marriage-tie was better respected.

The second place in the sex-hierarchy was occupied by the *maîtresse-en-titre* or favourite—the official lover, male or female as the case might be, of the ruling sovereign. The *maîtresse-en-titre* corresponded up to a point to the junior wife in Eastern countries of antiquity, but there were important differences. Now only one woman held this rank. There were not several junior wives at the same time, as in ancient Babylon. The standing of the *maîtresse-en-titre* in social life was a very high one; in political life it was often unrivalled. Courtiers, ministers and foreign diplomats sought her favour in the hope of obtaining in the bedchamber, through her help, what the sovereign had refused in audience. The Austrian minister Kaunitz used the Pompadour to draw France into war against Prussia. He sent her a valuable writing desk inset with jewels and a portrait of Maria Theresa—this to make her believe that the straightlaced Empress regarded her as her equal.[129] Sex being more powerful than all arguments, even mistresses who were totally uninterested in affairs of State often came to play important parts in national and international politics. A typical example is the influence exercised by Du Barry,

Louis XV's last mistress, whom foreign ambassadors used to seek out when they wanted to get something out of the old, vacillating king.

At the same time, even the most powerful mistresses were entirely dependent on the favour of the ruler. They enjoyed no legal security, and might fall out of favour from one day to the next and be cast out of the Court circle. The usual solution was for them to retire to a convent, but there are also cases in which the ex-mistress of a prince continued to live a gay and active love-life or made a brilliant marriage.

Although few mistresses succeeded in retaining the favour of their royal patrons to the end of their lives, the relationship usually lasted several years and took on the forms of normal married life. The unions were often very fruitful; Louis XIV had four children by La Vallière and eight by Mme. de Montespan. The children, like their mothers, were given high titles of nobility. Most mistresses further showed themselves possessed of a strong family feeling, and saw to it that their brothers and even their remoter kinsfolk were given fat jobs and imposing titles. The European Courts were soon swarming with marquesses, counts, princes and dukes who owed their high-sounding names and their estates to the sexual needs of the monarch. The old landed and military nobility and the newer *noblesse de bourse* were now reinforced by a *noblesse de lit*, descended from princes' mistresses. Ancestresses of this category figure in the family trees of the most famous families of the high aristocracy.

There was little difference in this respect between West and East, unless that the founder of the East European families of this type was usually a male. For after the death of Peter the Great, Russia was ruled for seventy years almost exclusively by women, and all the four who presided over the sumptuous Court of St. Petersburg in the eighteenth century—Catherine I, Anna Ivanovna, Elizabeth Petrovna, and Catherine II—were big consumers of men.

The lovers who performed their tasks with especial distinction were soon raised to the rank of counts or princes, regardless of whether they had been officers of the guard or simple peasants. Catherine II, if we are to believe the Prince de Ligne, bestowed her favours on eighty-two men, not one of whom went unrewarded.

The West, and particularly Versailles, was not quite so 'democratic'. Not that monarchs, in choosing their mistresses, asked many questions about ancestry, but the choice itself was more difficult. The reigning monarch had few opportunities of meeting women of the people. Under the old régime it was not the thing for the ruler to promote a woman who took his fancy straight from the street to his palace, as Napoleon did. The Court was the prince's world, and to become a prince's mistress a woman had first to gain entrée to the Court through the recognized channels. La Pompadour, who was the illegitimate daughter of a rich land-agent and had married a small country nobleman, had absolutely to stalk Louis XV and to employ all sorts of ruses before she reached the king. Du Barry, who began her career of gallantry as a milliner, had first to charm her way into the position of legitimate wife of a count before she could cast her spell over the elderly monarch.

Most princes' mistresses had been ladies of the Court. Often it was one of the queen's maids of honour who caught the monarch's eye; sometimes, a lady in attendance on some other member of the royal family. In Louis XIV's day the Court of 'Madame', the King's sister-in-law, produced several of the most famous mistresses. This circle supplied not only La Vallière and Mme. de Montespan, but also Louise-Renée de Kéroualle, *maîtresse-en-titre* of England's Merry Monarch, Charles II, who became Duchess of Portsmouth and played an important part in the negotiations for the Anglo-French alliance of her day.

Very far behind these great mistresses, who were 'ruling' in the true sense of the word, came the third category of women, the recipients of a prince's occasional favours: enjoyed for a night, or at the most for a few weeks, they too were popularly known as 'mistresses' and are sometimes so called in the history books, but their function was simply that of any courtesan. They were admitted by discreet back doors into the prince's bedchamber, or into some special pavilion where the prince amused himself unbeknown to his wife or—what was more important still—to his *maîtresse-en-titre*. Such were the heroines of the crude orgies in which the Regent Philip of Orleans was wont to seek relaxation after the day's labours in the Palais Royal. Of such were the *biches* or hinds of the nocturnal parties which Louis XV used to organize in his deer-park. Although women bearing famous names sometimes figured among them, they yet constituted the *demi-monde* (to use a later expression) of Court society.

Transvestites *and* Castrati

As time went on, this last category came to be drawn increasingly from ladies of the stage—dancers, singers, actresses. When employed at a Court theatre such ladies belonged, of course, to the Court world, if only to its servants' hall. But their colleagues from private theatres were often welcomed to the nocturnal amusements of Court society. They clearly exercised a magic attraction on the gentlemen of the Court—if not on the princes themselves, at least on the higher courtiers; not, most often, because they were distinguished by any special physical charms or remarkable intelligence, but because they represented something out of the ordinary.

The profession of stage artiste was new. For two thousand years acting was a man's profession. Women never appeared on the stage in antiquity, except in the vulgar mimes, a sort of sketch in which the performers gradually unveiled themselves to the accompaniment of erotic music of cymbals, flutes and tambourines—something like the American strip-tease, except that Greece and Rome carried the unveiling process much farther than is customary today. Women who took part in these mimes were of dubious reputation, as were the female dancers, acrobats, and flute-players who used to appear at private entertainments.[130] It was little more than a disguised form of prostitution, which, incidentally, explains how some 'stars' made very big fortunes. Even in the Roman Republic, in Sulla's day, a dancer named

Dionysia made an annual income of 200,000 sesterces, at least 20,000 dollars in modern values. All female parts in tragedy and literary comedy were played by males, often adolescent youths.

Thus from the first the theatre was, sexually speaking, always a travesty. When the Renaissance revived the classic theatre, further evolving new art-forms of its own invention, it at first maintained the Greco-Roman tradition. In Shakespeare's plays all female parts were still played by youths. In the operas, too, which became popular at princely Courts from the beginning of the seventeenth century (the fashion spreading from Italy) men took the female parts, singing falsetto to imitate women's voices. Connoisseurs of music found this device unsatisfactory, so another solution was adopted: Italy supplied all Europe with *castrati*. Even before this, the soprano parts in church choirs had been sung by *castrati*, one of whom, Hieronymus Rossinus, joined the papal choir in the Vatican in 1562.

Some *castrati* had highly successful careers. The Abbé Malani, once a *castrato* at the Court of Louis XIV, became the ambassador of the Duke of Tuscany. The Neapolitan Farinelli, whose original name was Carlo Broschi, did better still. He came of a good family, notwithstanding which he was castrated as a child to save his beautiful voice from breaking. He made his debut in Rome in 1722 at the age of seventeen. The Emperor Charles VI invited him to Vienna, and he made a triumphal appearance in London. The most brilliant part of his career, however, was in Spain, where his *bel canto* consoled Philip V's melancholy. He remained in high favour under Philip's successor, Ferdinand VI, and became an influential figure in politics—a development which, indeed, led to his being expelled from Spain after the accession of Charles III. His enemies bestowed on him the derisive soubriquet of 'the Capon', but he built a sumptuous palace in Bologna and there lived the life of a grand seigneur until his days ended at the age of seventy-seven.[131]

Joseph Haydn, the composer of *The Creation* and *The Seasons*, narrowly escaped castration in his young days. He was a chorister in St. Stephen's Cathedral in Vienna, and the choirmaster, anxious not to lose the boy's lovely voice, and probably also desirous of helping Haydn to a brilliant career, planned to have him castrated, or, as it was then called, 'sopranized'. He was scrupulous enough, however, to ask Haydn's father first. The old man hurried up to Vienna, and fearing that the operation had already been performed, asked his son: 'Sepperl, are you in pain? Can you walk?' Sepperl was still intact and, thanks to his father's vigorous objections, lived to have his voice break and to lead a normal sex-life—though not, indeed, at all a happy one.[132]

Castrati continued in favour at the Courts and among connoisseurs of music up to the first decades of the nineteenth century. Napoleon had an Italian *castrato* named Arien to sing to him after the burning of Moscow. Rossini was an admirer of the *castrato* Velluti, who appeared in London with great success as late as 1825. By that date, indeed, the *castrato* voice was regarded as a separate type, not as a substitute for a woman's. Meanwhile women had not only won their own rightful place on the stage, especially that of opera, but had begun to oust men from theirs. 'Boy's clothes parts', or 'breeches parts', in which girls play young-men roles, and travesty proper, in which women are disguised as men, have remained the stock in trade of opera to our own day. German opera in particular is full of such figures. Cherubino in Mozart's *Figaro*, Leonora in Beethoven's *Fidelio*, and, among Richard Strauss's works, Octavian in *Der Rosenkavalier*, the Composer in the Prologue to *Ariadne auf Naxos* and the heroine's sisters in *Arabella*, are only a few examples of this disguise of sex. Authors, including those of the most delicate taste and the longest experience, still clearly believe that the theatre-going public takes a special pleasure in seeing women dressed in costumes which flatten their breasts and emphasize their posteriors.

Woman conquers the Stage

Girls dressed as boys are a survival from the age of gallantry, which took inordinate pleasure in all forms of sex-disguise. It was, indeed, a long time before women were able to show themselves on the stage in such costumes. Woman's conquest of the stage was an arduous one. The assault came from two sides: from the lowest and the highest social classes. The wife and the daughters of the director of the company of strolling players who performed farces in the market-place had to perform, otherwise the troupe could not pay its way. The first entry of the 'revolution from above', the appearance of women on Court stages, was a very diffident one. The break-through came from the ballroom. Ladies were always allowed to dance at Court. That being so, it could not be improper for them to display their proficiency on a dais or a stage fitted with technical devices by taking part in a ballet. Allegorical ballets, featuring the gods and heroes of antiquity, and seasoned with contemporary allusions, became the rage in Court circles.

Princes themselves took part in these performances with relish. They enjoyed acting: it was, so to speak, part of their profession, as practised daily *vis-à-vis* their subjects. Louis XIV owed his nickname of *Le Roi Soleil* to a role played by him as a boy of fifteen in a *Ballet of Night*. He was not the first royal ballet dancer, for his father, the austere Louis XIII, had appeared on the stage before him and had danced in ballets, preferably in comic roles. And Louis XIII's father, Henri IV, had been a passionate devotee of the ballet, although he preferred not to dance himself, but rather to stand in the wings, where he could get a close-up view of the ballerinas.

It is of Henri IV that the first love-stories connected with ballet are told.[133] He appeared unexpectedly at a rehearsal, and one of the Amazons, Mlle. de Montmorency, pointed her spear precisely at the spot where he was standing. The situation was delicate. It was recalled that one of the king's ancestors, Henri II, had met his death from a lance-thrust in a tournament. This time, however, all went smoothly. The spear of the fair de Montmorency was not of iron, and neither was her heart. She became the king's mistress until replaced by another society ballerina, Mlle. Paulet, daughter of the Court banker. Mlle. Paulet was the gallant king's last mistress. He was on his way to visit her when the dagger of the fanatic Ravaillac struck him down.

French Court ceremonial insisted on a proper distance being kept, even in intimate circles. When the queen and the princesses danced in a ballet, no male dancer might be in the dance, and when the king danced, no woman was allowed on the stage. It was only quite exceptionally that *ballets mixtes* were allowed, in which gentlemen—but only those of the highest aristocracy—performed in the same dance as a princess. It was this point of etiquette that made 'travesty' usual in court ballet. There were either only men or only women, some in each case dressed as members of the opposite sex.

But the disguise of sex only enhanced the sexual stimulus of the stage. However modest the treatment, however reticent the movements, nevertheless the theatre, and above all the ballet, did give out an erotic atmosphere by which neither old nor young could remain unaffected. There was no need even to be performing. Henri IV showed wealthy cavaliers the way to approach the ladies of the stage. Before long, life behind the scenes of the private theatres, and also of the Court theatres when professional actresses were allowed in them, was thoroughly uninhibited. Gallants made their way into the dancers', singers', and actresses' dressing rooms, or invited them during the intervals into their own boxes, which were so arranged that one could chat or do anything else there unobserved. Writers enough have dwelt on the social function performed by the theatre boxes. Their erotic function was even greater. In Paris theatres in the eighteenth century there were boxes the backs of which were curtained off, and contained comfortable couches.

The *filles de l'opéra*, the chorus-girls and members of the *corps de ballet*, were expected not only to dance and sing competently, but also to put their charms freely at the disposal of the *habitués* of the theatre, the renters of the boxes. The stars of the ballets naturally aimed higher. Of the three leading ballerinas of Louis XIV's reign, two owed their fame largely to their gallant adventures. Only the most accomplished actress of the three, Marie Sallé, was uninterested in men: she was a Lesbian. Her rival,

Camargo, who had been born in Brussels of an old family of Spanish nobility (her uncle was Grand Inquisitor), had been seduced while very young by a certain Comte de Melun. The impressive list of her later lovers included the Duc de Richelieu and the Comte de Clermont.

The love-career of the third, Barberina, was more adventurous still. Her real name was Barbara Campanini. She left her Italian home at a very early age and made a hit in Paris with grotesque dances, through which, however, connoisseurs discerned her real beauty. French aristocrats and English lords fought duels for her. Frederick the Great engaged her for his opera in Berlin, and when she lingered in Venice, enjoying a love-affair, after she was due in Berlin, he sent to the Senate of Venice an official demand for her extradition. Incredible though it may sound, La Barberina was brought by force to Berlin.

But this caprice was soon forgotten. The place which she came to occupy in the society of Berlin and Potsdam was one which no other artist, before or after, ever achieved. The king, usually no great admirer of women, was a regular guest in her house, and was almost inconsolable when she married the son of the Grand Chancellor, Cocceji, and went to Silesia with her husband. The marriage soon broke up, but Barberina's amorous career was over. Like Camargo, she spent the evening of her days in pious works. She founded and presided over a particularly strict convent for ladies of the nobility, who had to go about in grey penitents' gowns. Frederick William II rewarded her services by creating her Countess of Barschau, and conferring on her armorial bearings with the motto *Virtuti Asylum*.

Meanwhile the Paris opera had witnessed the rise of a new star who surpassed all her predecessors, if not in artistic talent yet certainly in the scandalous variety of her love-affairs. This was Marie-Madeleine Guimard. She lived in unprecedented luxury, but employed part of the large sums which her talents and her charms brought her in patronizing the arts lavishly. The Revolution put an end to her glory and she died in complete destitution. Edmond de Goncourt wrote a moving account of her life. Many of her contemporaries cherished less agreeable, and lasting, memories of her, for she infected some of her lovers, who included princes and dukes, with syphilis. This was, indeed, no rarity among the grandees of the world of love. Princess Liselotte of the Palatinate writes of the Court of Louis XIV that Prince Frederick Karl of Würtemburg contracted the same disease from the dancer Dechats, and died of it.

A Marshal recommends Temporary Marriages

Dancers were the first to penetrate into high society, and reached it the most easily, but singers and, still more, actresses, were not far behind them. Among the ladies admitted to the bed of the Regent, the Duc d'Orleans, was an actress named Florence (her surname is unknown). The son born of this union received a bishop's mitre and the title of Duke, but that was not enough for him: he wanted to become a *pair de France*. That was denied him for, as the Duc de Saint-Simon remarked maliciously,[134] one must know who a peer of France is, and the Regent had not recognized him as his legitimate son. To console him, however, he had him made Archbishop of Cambrai. The actress Quinault, another of the Regent's intimate circle, prevailed on the Duc de Nevers to marry her secretly. The actress Duclos, who numbered Voltaire among her earlier admirers, was the mistress of the Comte d'Urès. The tragic actress, Clairon, who starred in Voltaire's plays, led a thoroughly gay private life: her lovers included the Prince de Soubise, the Duc de Luxembourg, and the Marquis de Bissy. The famous singer Sophie Arnould, who sang leading parts in Rameau's and Gluck's operas, had a passionate love-affair with the Comte de Brancas. In brief, the stage and the high aristocracy got on excellently together.

Nevertheless, stage folk remained a pariah caste. The Church denied them the sacraments and a resting place in consecrated ground: they were buried in the sinners' cemetery outside the town. No exception was made, even for Adrienne Lecouvreur, mistress of Count Maurice of Saxony, who was accounted the most faithful and virtuous of them all.

It is a fact that in no age did sexual relationships help so little to bridge social gulfs as in the age of gallantry. The women who made their way into the highest circles of society via the bedroom still remained outsiders. The highest success which they were ever able to achieve, and that rarely, was the morganatic marriage. This ensured to them and their children a certain status in law, but not the recognition of society. Occasionally some highlight of society would find his conscience smite him. Maurice of Saxony, himself the illegitimate offspring of a union between the Elector Augustus the Strong and Countess Aurora of Königsmark, sought to find a solution of the marriage problem. He wrote a book on marriage in which he recommended temporary marriages.

Marriages, he thought, should be contracted for a few years only; if the partners agreed, the contract could be prolonged, but marriage for life was a betrayal of the self, an unnatural compulsion. The view was a daring one for the age and gave rise to numerous *bon mots*, but was not taken seriously at the Courts, although the author, the 'Maréchal de Saxe', who had taken service with Louis XV, was one of Europe's most famous generals. It probably went to show that even though his father had recognized him as his legitimate offspring, he still felt himself not quite inside the pale.

The Order of Sodomites

The sex-reform carried through in the age of gallantry, and within the gallant world, was in another direction. It was precisely something which its opponents afterwards claimed as their own: a 'back to nature' movement. Long before Jean-Jacques Rousseau gave this phrase a social-revolutionary content, high society had usurped it and was living in accordance with it. The sex-instinct, it was argued, was a natural one, and therefore nothing to be ashamed of. Women were made for love, but they were by no means created simply for the pleasure of men. They had themselves an active right to love: they were entitled to choose their lovers and to change them if another pleased them better. There was no subordination of the weaker sex in love-life, as there had been in the ancient world and in the Renaissance.

If there was any difference of rank between man and woman—assuming that both belonged to the same social class—it could only be that the woman stood the higher. She was at the centre of private and public life. Everything revolved around her, and every well-brought-up man must be at pains to make women's life as agreeable as possible. But this new cult of the woman differed fundamentally from the woman-cult of the Middle Ages. The cavalier of the rococo age had nothing in common with the knight of the *minnesingers*, who felt that he had to cloak his adultery in romantic and, if possible, transcendental garb. Now people behaved much more naturally. They spent less time on preliminaries, and did not seek to turn their love-affairs into dramas of passion.

In that age, as in every other, there were, of course, affairs of honour which ended tragically, but people no longer thought it heroic to kill other men or to hazard their own lives for the sake of a woman. Duels over women were much rarer than in the nineteenth century; this kind of chivalry only came back into fashion with the romantic movement and when the growth of modern capitalism re-awakened the sense of property, including property in women. Love and possession are not mutually compatible. Even if a woman gave herself to a man out of material interest, she did not become his chattel. She herself had something to give, which she exchanged against another pleasure, but she had not sold herself: she had not become the man's property, to do with as he pleased.

Love between men was altogether forbidden. In the reign of Louis XIV there was one last great homosexual scandal at the Court of Versailles. Some members of the highest nobility, including the Duc de Gramont, the Prince Conti, and the Marquis de Béran, had founded a society whose members had to pledge themselves to have no relations with women. They wore under their coats a golden cross showing a man trampling a woman underfoot. The Director of the Court theatre and Court opera, the famous composer Jean-Baptiste Lully, a Florentine by birth, was involved in the affair. He was styled 'the King of Sodom', and the members of the Order were known as Sodomites. Louis XIV intervened energetically and put an end, for a long time to come, to this and all other paederast associations.

This obviously did not banish homosexuality from the world. There must have been as many constitutional homosexuals in this woman-ruled age as in any other. But men of these tendencies had to indulge them discreetly, with their friends. Even kings whose tastes ran in this direction (as Frederick the Great's were said to) had to keep them dark. Homosexuality was regarded as unnatural, meaning 'ungallant'. The age had no understanding of such aberrations, even when their origin was physiological. Only in Britain, where manners differed in many respects from those of the Continent, did homosexuality rank as 'fashionable' in the eighteenth century.[135]

The dominant position of woman in social life, the innumerable deifications of woman on paper and on canvas, suggest that men had become rather soft and effeminate. That, however, was not the case. The rococo cavalier was neither henpecked nor a physical weakling. Virility was no longer a measure of a man's worth, as it had been in Renaissance days; to please women a man needed to be no stallion. Obviously, however, a man did what he could to satisfy his partner in this respect also. There are on record some performances which prove that the men of the age of gallantry were by no means inferior in this respect to those of earlier days.

After Louis XV's wedding night with Maria Leszczynska, his Premier, the Duc de Bourbon, reported, as tradition demanded, to the young queen's father, Stanislaus Leszczynski, King of Poland. Everything had gone off well. 'The king', the report runs, 'went to bed with the queen and during the night bestowed on her seven proofs of his affection. The king himself sent one of his gentlemen to me to tell me this, and repeated it to me personally.' Maria Leszczynska presented her husband with ten children, and the number of Louis' illegitimate children is also imposing. It has, indeed, been suggested that Louis ruined himself, physically and mentally, by his too intensive love-life. Nevertheless, he lived to be sixty-four, enjoying life to the end.

Wigs and Crinolines

Sex-life in the age of Louis XV was in many respects more natural than in the age of his great predecessors. The proof of this does not lie in the pseudo-naturalism of the pastoral poems and pictures which now became fashionable, reaching their most perfect expression in Boucher's drawings. The pastoral affectation was no invention of the rococo age. It goes back to sixteenth-century Italy, where it was regarded as highly moral. The Jesuits cultivated it, and the severe censors of the Spanish Inquisition found nothing objectionable in shepherds and shepherdesses saying pretty things to one another in polished verse. The French rococo only gave it pictorial expression, and struck louder the erotic note in the pastoral scenes. And they were not meant to be solely symbolic. Rendezvous out of doors, pastoral episodes in a meadow or under a tree, were now part of the mode; even gentlemen and ladies of rank indulged their affections without need of boudoirs or hunting boxes.

But love out of doors, at least in a bosky park, even if not under completely pastoral conditions, could not be practised in the pompous costumes of Louis XIV's age. The beginning of the great dress reform antedated even Louis XV's accession. The decisive turning point in fashion took place during the Regency, which showed so many liberalizing tendencies in various directions. It can be dated with some accuracy: it was about 1718 that ladies began to revolt against the stiff dresses and demeanour[137] which the Spaniards had introduced and *le Roi Soleil* had maintained.

Under the influence of the severe Mme. de Maintenon, Louis XIV had become a disciplinarian in his old age. His disappearance was hailed with relief. In internals and externals alike, there was a general relaxation. The heavy, ceremonious women's robes gave way to dresses made of lighter materials. Women wore dresses of cotton and soft muslin which moulded their forms. *Décolletées* were deep, sometimes allowing the breasts to show. In the home, comfortable *négligés* were worn. Skirts were full, lacing less tight. Men's fashions, too, adapted themselves to the new trend. Watteau's *Indifférent*, painted in 1716, is still mincing round in a Spanish ruff and a silk dress, cut quite tight. A few years later it was permissible for the most courtly gentleman to show himself in an easy coat almost devoid of ribbon and lace. Necks gradually became quite free and were protected only by a scarf.

More striking still was the change in the manner of wearing the hair. The long full-bottomed wig vanished; gentlemen now wore only a flat wig ending in a short, dainty plait; some venturesome spirits did without wigs altogether, and simply powdered their hair. Women, too, wore their hair short, in little curls—a feat of daring unknown since the days of the Roman Empire. Much of this was, indeed, only a whim of fashion, and fashions are not eternal. When, in the middle of the eighteenth century, the bourgeoisie began to ape the comfortable dresses of the Court, the ladies of Versailles turned to building up their hair on frames; in Marie Antoinette's day the coiffures were veritable towers. The wide, fluttering skirts, too, were reinforced underneath with whalebone and reed frameworks. The French crinoline, the *vertugadin* or *vertugade*, which now became the polite wear throughout all Europe, was an old Spanish fashion from the days of the Counter-Reformation. The name suggests that it was originally designed as a protection, or at least a symbol, of virtue, a sort of enormously enlarged girdle of Venus. Now, however, it was by no means an impregnable fortress. It could easily be lifted with a few deft twists, which men quickly learned. The crinoline with a man hiding under it was one of the caricaturists' most popular themes.

Love is a game, a game of hide-and-seek with nature; but the search must not be dragged out too long, or the partner will grow impatient and turn to less difficult playmates. As in all ages, so now, the true *ars amandi* consisted in holding the balance between hiding and seeking, between refusal and surrender; and the erotic literature of the eighteenth century was tireless in its descriptions of all the excitements and delights of the art of love. Although the tendency of the age was towards didacticism, writers tried to invest the subject of love with an aura of poetry. Dry treatises on sex failed to interest: the customary form was the love-romance, in which the tenderest spiritual emotions and physical processes could be displayed with equal realism. Some authors, such as Claude Crébillon or Restif de la Bretonne, whose works owe their survival precisely to this quality, are exceedingly outspoken, and rococo literature has consequently acquired a reputation for extreme salacity. Its lasting value, however, lies in the subtlety of its psychological analysis. To this day no more closely observed description of a woman's amorous impulses has ever been written than Choderlos de Laclos's *Liaisons Dangéreuses*, which appeared shortly before the Revolution.

The Enigma of Casanova

Dalliance, hide-and-seek, which has a very definite objective but enhances the player's pleasure by putting barriers in his way, was only one aspect of the love-life of the age of gallantry. The other was the surprise attack. Often, indeed, the surprises had been carefully pre-arranged by both parties, for nature has endowed mankind with a brain which must not be left entirely out of account in love. The sex-life of the age of gallantry almost always contained an intellectual element, even when it appeared to derive exclusively from the emotions. To be enjoyable, an adventure must be carefully prepared. Men of violence can violate women, but violation usually takes place only in a man's imagination. In the *Liaisons Dangéreuses* a woman writes to her adorer, who has been posing too much as the irresistible Don Juan: 'Do you then believe, you pining lover, that every woman you possessed was taken against her will?'—and many society women shared this point of view. The pleasure in adventures sometimes assumed extravagant forms. A sister of Rousseau's patroness,

Madame d'Épinay, gave a singer whom she admired a first rendezvous: they were to meet in bed.

The love-life of the eighteenth century was indubitably less inhibited than that of other ages. Why should one conceal from others that one enjoys love, that one has a lover, or several lovers? In the crowded Courts—and ten thousand men and women were cooped up together in Versailles—everyone knew everything about everyone else, in any case, and invented more. Why then play at being an angel of virtue? Nor were the men noticeably discreet. Stories about gallant adventures served to while away the time. It should be noted, however, that most of what we know today of the love-life of the age of gallantry comes from memoirs or letters posthumously published, or secret police or diplomatic reports. The two most famous of the memoirs—Saint-Simon's twenty-one volumes, which cover the last decades of Louis XIV and the Regency, and Casanova's almost equally voluminous autobiography, which ranges over Europe in the ages of Louis XV and Louis XVI—did not appear until the nineteenth century, and then almost simultaneously, between 1820 and 1830. Both are the work of old men wishful of living through their youthful years again by recalling them. Saint-Simon's reflect the arrogance of a reactionary for whom even the age of Louis XIV was 'the rule of the common bourgeoisie', while Casanova's are tinged with the heart's melancholy of a man who never achieved satisfaction in all his life, and is left at the end with nothing except the memory of a few precious moments enjoyed with beautiful women.

Why Casanova became the symbol of a type practically identical with that of Don Juan, only still more gallant and charming, is a mystery. His merits are purely literary: he was a brilliant writer, but his fellow-men have refused to believe it. Not one of his numerous writings, except his description of his escape from the Venice *piombi*—at that time the most dreaded prison in the world—attracted any attention in his lifetime. He was a keen observer and endowed with a phenomenal memory. Almost everything which he noted down in his old age about the important figures of his day has been confirmed from other sources. But he had, after all, only a walking-on part on the world stage, and his personal adventures, his quack-doctoring and bucket-shop keeping, his fraudulent lotteries, his petty thefts and his conflicts with the authorities who chased him from one country to another, are no more than can be read in any newspaper today; in his day they were even commoner.

Equally unimportant are his love-affairs. Most of them are connected with the stage. Occasionally he takes a maidenhead, and is as proud of it as an Indian taking a scalp. When he is short of money he makes up to elderly Court ladies, but he is second-rate in everything, even as a gigolo. He is a self-possessed, good-looking man, successful with women, but not often with ladies, whose conquest requires special skill. Possibly his boldest conquest is that of the somewhat overblown wife of the burgomaster of Cologne, whom he entices away from a lieutenant-general. That is about as high as he gets. Weary of his love-odyssey, he found a refuge as librarian in a Bohemian nobleman's castle. Like all the little adventurers of his day, male and female, he repented in his old age and invested himself with an aura of sanctity. His last words (which he had probably thought up before) were: 'I have lived a philosopher and die a Christian.'[138]

12

BACK TO NATURE

THE gallant world, from which the age of gallantry took its name, was the world of the lords and ladies; but it was, after all, only a small upper class that was able to live that life, and took pleasure in it. The great majority could not afford so intensive and extensive a love-life. Polygamy is expensive, and people were not prepared to descend to general promiscuity. The sexual looseness of the propertied classes thus inevitably awoke if not the envy then the indignation of those poorer than themselves.

The fomenters of this indignation were by no means prudes. The philosophers and writers who gave birth to the Enlightenment, the struggle against the existing legal and social order, were no saints living according to the tenets of their faith. They were far too intimately connected with the ruling class, and materially too dependent on it, for that. They lived from the crumbs which fell from the rich men's tables, from the bounty of the princes and nobles. Most of them had to make do with meagre pensions, but some received princely appanages which enabled them to live on the same scale as the great lords, and to keep expensive mistresses. Elderly noble ladies were especially lavish patrons, not always on a purely platonic basis.

Conditions of this kind are not calculated to turn intellectuals into subversives; nor were the leading spirits of the Enlightenment revolutionaries by temperament. They believed that education, persuasion, literary propaganda—in a word, *Enlightenment*—would be strong enough to effect the peaceful abolition of public scandals and remould the structure of society. Up to a point, too, they were successful. Even before the great

storm broke, much had changed in Europe; France itself had
become more 'bourgeois'. The adherents of the Enlightenment
included many young nobles who took an active part at the
outset of the revolution in putting through the social and sexual
reforms advocated by the masters.

Nevertheless, the Enlightenment failed to achieve its great
aim of establishing, without force, a uniform morality for all.
The morals—or absence of them—of the gallant world were
specifically class morals. The ruling classes never tried to impose
their own morality on other classes—that would have meant
renouncing their own privileges; on the contrary, they were at
pains to keep the morals of the lower classes uncontaminated.
The eighteenth century was as rich as any earlier age in decrees
and laws against vice, licence, laxity in marriage, sexual excesses,
rape, seduction of young persons, and perversion, but the upper
classes were not required to obey them.

Fallen Women

There were, of course, no absolute class distinctions in sex-life,
for sex overleaps all barriers. It was the frontier incidents that
fired the zeal and the imagination of the bourgeois moralists.
They did not object if great lords occasionally took their
mistresses from the lower classes; that would have been too
dangerous and, in any case, women of that sort were too depraved to deserve the compassion of bourgeois society. But
there were plenty of other border-line cases, which merit closer
examination.

The *romans de mœurs* which deal with these cases are all constructed on approximately the same pattern: the gallant comes
from a better social class than his mistress; he is the seducer, she
the victim whom her lightness ruins. Alternatively, she resists
the temptation and the story then ends happily. She is, indeed,
not always an angel of innocence, but the man is the culprit in
chief. He is the mephistophelian element, into whom the sex-
devil has entered. This allocation of the responsibility is new.
Previously all the blame, when at all possible, had been piled on

the woman. For centuries, Eve had been the temptress; now Adam was the tempter.

It is odd that bourgeois literature should have made a sacrificial lamb of woman in an age in which women played a dominant role in the social life of the ruling classes. Yet she is always represented as the weaker party, the sufferer, the one to be pitied, paying for her sin with social outlawry, banishment and even death, while the men clear out and usually escape due punishment.

The theme of the fallen woman is one of the stock *motifs* of world literature; it is found wherever value is attached to maidenly purity before marriage. Now, however, it was treated from a specifically social angle. It was no longer the same, even from the man's point of view. The Spanish Don Juan had seduced women of every class, and for him they were all alike—the objects of a night of love. The Don Juans of the eighteenth century, at least in literature, made a special set at innocent girls of the lower classes, hence the tragedy. If the girls seduced by them had belonged to the same class as themselves, the end of the story, too, would have been different: the frail beauty would have taken the veil or withdrawn into a convent for noble ladies, instead of ending miserably in a brothel or being deported to perish in the jungle.

The man who created this new sociological type of novel about women was a Catholic priest, the Abbé Prévost d'Exiles. When, in 1731, he published his *Histoire du Chevalier des Grieux et de Manon Lescaut*, he already had behind him an adventurous life spent as friar and soldier. He had fled from his home and settled in England, where class distinctions were even more strongly marked than in France.

The later world put *Manon Lescaut* in the first rank of erotic literature; contemporaries, however, preferred another novel of morals, Samuel Richardson's *Pamela, or Virtue Rewarded* (1740). This was the story of a servant—a remarkably educated one and uncommonly fluent with her pen, for the whole book is in the form of letters written by the virtuous heroine, who, unlike many of her kind, resists all temptations. As the title of the

book itself shows, virtue finds its reward; Pamela becomes the
lawfully wedded wife of a young count, who had failed to win
her on other terms. *Pamela* was the most successful novel of the
century. The Abbé Prévost translated it into French, and it was
as well received on the Continent as in England. Voltaire drama-
tized it, Goldoni based two plays at once on it, and thirteen other
authors brought Pamela on to the stage.

Richardson first hurriedly wrote a sequel, *Pamela in her Exalted
Position*; then another novel, *The History of Clarissa Harlowe*,
depicting the ghastly fate of a girl who allows herself to be
seduced and is consequently cast out by her family. Rousseau,
Gellert, Lessing, and even Goethe drew on *Clarissa* for inspiration.

Simple repetitions and variations on the literary theme of the
fallen woman could not achieve the goal. Romances and dramas
of this kind, however high their literary quality, have never
exercised much moral effect on the public. People read them or
see them in order thus to pass a few hours in the hell of vice,
unscathed. He who would influence the sexual morals of his age
must come to the point; he must say clearly what positive
reforms he has in mind.

At this point opinions became divided. The English puritans
had nothing to set against the licence of the Royal Court but
the fustiest philistine morality: wives must be subject to their
husbands and occupy themselves with housework and children;
girls must sit at home crocheting, and wait modestly and obedi-
ently until their father married them off. Even an appreciation of
good cooking was regarded as unseemly. These were the counsels
given by the moralists to English fathers of families, and middle-
class women were usually trained accordingly. 'By 1750', writes
an English sociologist, 'women were at the lowest point of
degradation which had been reached for centuries; they were
useless, they were uneducated, they were unnatural, their morality
was false, their modesty was false.'[139]

On the Continent, in Frederick's Berlin, Maria Theresa's
Vienna, even in Paris, things were not very different. Close under
the walls of the castles and parks in which Court society diverted

itself and beautiful women exposed their charms, lived well-situated bourgeois families where strict patriarchal rule prevailed, where almost everything was allowed to a man and nothing to a woman, where a daughter who had made a 'slip' was thrown into the street without mercy. On the one side was the family, on the other, prostitution, which was frowned on but winked at and recruited its clientele mainly from among reputable fathers of families. No intermediate stage was tolerated.

Rousseau's Sex-morality

It was a bold enterprise upon which Jean-Jacques Rousseau set out—to replace the cruel, out-of-date family law of bourgeois society by a new and more liberal sex-law. His basic ideas were simple—too simple, his critics would say. It is nature's dispensation that love should bring human beings together, and that two human beings who love one another should live together and found a family. But the social order, which is founded on property, does not allow this pure, innocent human cohabitation. Property interests are opposed to the natural bond of love, and marriage is commercialized and corrupted. Nature, however, rebels. The consequences are adultery and disintegration of the family. The family cannot be strengthened by compulsion from without, but only by putting marriage back on its natural basis, the free and unimpeded union of human beings who love one another.

Rousseau's 'back to nature', however, does not at all mean free love in the sense of a short-term association, dissoluble by either partner at will. He believed monogamy to be the form best suited to human nature. A native of Geneva, grown up in a world of Calvinism, he applied Calvin's doctrine of predestination also to love-life. Men and women who are destined for one another will end by finding each other, and once they have found each other they will not part again. This is God's will and nature's, and the will of the Moral Law which is nothing else but the uncorrupted law of nature; it is also the will of Reason, which can have no other objective but human happiness.

After the fashion of the times, Rousseau set out his ideas on love and marriage in a novel in letter form; Julie, the 'new Héloïse' had been married against her will. She loved another man. Her husband, a rather simple but goodhearted man, was so incautious as to invite the former lover into his house, with the inevitable result. The two lovers endure frightful spiritual torments, but nature is stronger than convention. When the woman's heart is already ripe for adultery, a misfortune—fortunate for the prevailing morality—occurs which saves her from this shame; her child falls into the water during a family outing; Julie saves it from drowning but in doing so loses her own life.

This simple story, far less dramatic than that of the original Héloïse, Abelard's lover, is told with a sentimentality almost intolerable to modern taste. Everyone concerned oozes nobility— and yet the catastrophe occurs. Why? Because social institutions are faulty. In this work, however, Rousseau still refrains from saying anything which might offend the ruling classes. He neither pleads for the abolition of private property, although he regards it as the root of all evil, nor for divorce, still less for the right to adultery, which he condemns as severely as the Church. 'If there is anything to reform in public morals', he writes in the preface to *La Nouvelle Héloïse*, 'one must begin with domestic morals, and they depend entirely on the fathers and mothers.'

In other words, to reform institutions one must first change human beings, and this must be done through education. Yet when his great educational romance, *Émile*, appeared a year later, in 1762, Rousseau was forced to admit that it was impossible to change human beings while keeping existing institutions intact. As his educational reform involved secularization, he was listed as a heretic. For safety's sake he had published his book in Amsterdam, where there was no censorship. It was condemned by the Sorbonne, and the Supreme Court of the French judiciary, the *Parlement*, ordered it to be burned. Rousseau himself only escaped arrest by hurried flight. Even in his Swiss home and in liberal Holland he was a controversial figure.

Good society might have been less enthusiastic over *La Nouvelle Héloïse* if it had known more about the author. Rousseau was not in fact the ideal man to give the world a new sex-code. Not only had he for many years led an unsettled, vagrant existence, in many respects not unlike that of his contemporary, Casanova, but, much more important, his own sex-life was thoroughly warped. Towards the end of his life he set this down on paper with unprecedented exactitude. His *Confessions* and his *Rêveries du Promeneur Solitaire* are thus among the most interesting works of sex-literature.

Rousseau laboured under a severe mother-son complex—an Oedipus complex, in Freudian terminology. 'Many a man in his dreams has seen himself in his mother's arms', says Sophocles in his *Oedipus Tyrannus*.[140] Rousseau never knew his mother; she died in childbed, a few days after giving birth to him. He missed her; all his life he was searching for a 'mother', a substitute for the maternal care, the tender embraces which were lacking in his childhood. He grew up in a world of men. His father, a watchmaker of Geneva, troubled little about him and left him to an uncle, who boarded him out with a pastor. An old maid named Mademoiselle Lambercier kept house for the clergyman and Jean-Jacques was put in her charge. A woman, a mother at last! The little boy climbed into her bed and there conducted himself as freely as though she had really been his mother. He took pleasure whenever she touched him, even when it was to box his ears. His behaviour towards the highly-respected lady provoked scandal. The pastor sent him away, as unmannerly and apparently incorrigible.

Now Jean-Jacques began a picaresque existence. He had grown into a good-looking youth and could certainly have had many a girl lover; but they did not attract him. He satisfied his sexual desires by onanism, always imagining the innocent Mlle. Lambercier before him. He remained an onanist all his life; intercourse with women, who were generally elderly, was for him really only an interruption of the visions of his erotic soul-life. When he was twenty-one, a woman of thirty-five, Mme. de Warens, initiated him into the secrets of heterosexual love. In his *Confessions* he describes this, his first normal embrace, as one of his most revolting experiences: 'I felt as though I had committed incest.' Mme. de Warens became his mistress, or, rather, she made him her minion, and kept him; but for him she was never more than his *maman*. A second partner, Mme. de Larnage, was of the same type, again a woman much older than himself, who fell on him and pulled him into her bed. This time, however, he took more pleasure in the embraces.

When for a short time he was employed as secretary to the French Ambassador in Venice, he made some excursions into the baser purlieus of gallantry, mainly out of curiosity and because it was the thing to do; any visitor to the city of the Doges had to pay his tribute to the world-famous courtesans of Venice. But Rousseau was obviously not made for such adventures. The first courtesan to whom his friends guided his reluctant feet, the proud Padoana, left him completely cold. He would soonest have run away without enjoying her favours, if only for fear of infection. Only when she refused to accept a ducat from him without giving anything in return did he offer up his manhood to her, but at once went to a doctor to be examined and ran about quite distraught for three weeks, until it became clear that he had come to no harm.

His second adventure with the beauties of Venice ended more lamentably still. This lady, the hot-blooded Zulietta, made more appeal to him, but when she disrobed herself he saw to his horror that one of her breasts had no nipple. While he was poring over this phenomenon, Zulietta flew into a rage and dismissed him with the appropriate words: *Lascia le donne e studia la matematica* —'Leave women and study mathematics.' Greatly to his own discomfiture, Rousseau did not take this advice. He let two friends, Baron Grimm and the Duke of Coburg-Gotha's chaplain, lead him into the dirtiest haunts of Paris prostitution, a visit which ended in a fearful hangover. He tried his luck in the highest society. The gallant mistress of the Château of Montmorency, Madame d'Épinay, who gave him hospitality, was too thin for him. His friendship with her sister-in-law, the Comtesse d'Houdetot, also remained a platonic flirtation. He knew this brilliant lady was no stickler for marital fidelity; she was the mistress of a marquis-poet. But her face was disfigured with smallpox scars, and her figure too slender for his taste. Jean-Jacques liked full-breasted, robust women—that was part of his 'back to nature' programme.

Foundling Homes and Infanticide

The only woman who kept his interest for many decades, although he never really loved her, was a little Parisian laundress, Thérèse Le Vasseur, a nice but quite unimportant little thing, who did not even profit from the association. She kept house for him and gradually brought all her relatives into the house (Jean-Jacques Rousseau is not the only great spirit to have suffered thus). As soon as he got to know her he told her that he would never leave her, but never marry her either, and he kept his word on both points. She never became his legal wife, although late in his life he had a domestic marriage ceremony performed with her, with friends to witness.[141]

His aversion from registrars and church marriages may perhaps be explained by his philosophic views, that love is a private affair with which no authority is concerned. But Rousseau also applied this principle in another way which the world has taken very ill. Thérèse Le Vasseur bore him five children, and all five were, on his orders and against their mother's will, put in a foundling home without their father's ever setting eyes on them.

Rousseau writes in his *Confessions* that he had no scruples whatever in doing this, because it was the best thing for the children: 'I believed myself to be acting like a citizen and a father, and I regarded myself as a member of Plato's Republic.' It is easy enough to convict him of a breach of his own teaching, because his moral and sexual doctrines were entirely different from those of Plato's collective State of the future. In fact, however, Rousseau's behaviour was nothing very exceptional at the time for a man of his standing and in his precarious economic circumstances, and it is assuredly no chance that neither his friends nor his numerous enemies had anything to say against it.

The practice of leaving new-born children, legitimate as well as illegitimate, outside foundling homes had become very prevalent in France in the eighteenth century. We have exact data on it. According to Buffon, the number of children left in a year at Paris foundling homes rose from 3,233 in 1745 to 5,604 in 1766. In 1772, 18,713 children were born in Paris and 7,676 left at foundling homes. Even if (as a police report shows) some 2,000 of the children came from country districts where there were no foundling homes, yet it remains truly astonishing that roughly one third of all the children born in Paris were exposed by their parents and abandoned to public charity.[142]

The procedure was made extraordinarily easy for the parents. The infant was placed in a *tour*, a turning box at the door of the foundling home, and was at once taken in; this is what the midwife did with Jean-Jacques Rousseau's children. But it was also possible to hand the child over openly, and no one asked the parents' names. Parents who were quite callous, or over-nervous, still followed the barbaric custom of the Middle Ages and exposed their children, often in bitter cold, in front of church doors and hospitals, where they sometimes perished before anyone took notice of them. The encyclopaedist d'Alembert was a foundling, who was fortunately picked up alive from in front of the portal of Notre Dame.

The foundling homes were no specifically French institution. They existed in antiquity, and in the Middle Ages were found all over Europe. In the Nordic countries, however, they soon took on the characteristics of orphanages, and more attention was paid to formalities. In Latin countries, on the other hand, the foundling home retained its original character up to modern times, that of a place in which parents unable or unwilling to bring up their newborn children might leave them without any names passing, and without becoming liable to any legal penalty. Besides pure motives of charity, there were now considerations of population policy which made the State extremely liberal in this respect.

In the eighteenth century, as in the seventeenth, States were at great pains to increase their population and were unwilling to let future soldiers slip through their fingers.

It is needless to say that the methods by which poor or conscienceless parents rid themselves of their children in Rousseau's day offend the moral canons of today, and that even the reception arrangements of the time would no longer be regarded as a solution of the problem, either social or demographic. For their age, however, they were indubitably a boon and averted many worse consequences of the morality of the time.

In the frivolous France of Louis XV, and even in the last decades before the French Revolution, we hardly ever hear of infanticide or of suicide by unmarried mothers choosing this way of escape from their 'disgrace'. The German literature of the same age, on the other hand, is full of these topics. Goethe's boyhood friend, the Baltic German poet Lenz, treats the problem in two of his plays, *Der Hofmeister* (1774) and *Die Soldaten* (1776). Goethe himself held it to be so important that he made *Faust* revolve around it. Gretchen's fate was no poet's imagining. It was an acute and burning problem over which pedagogues and doctors puzzled without finding a practical solution. Attempts to introduce the French system were made in Electoral Hesse and Denmark, but met with opposition. Their opponents said that they put a premium on moral laxity. So there remained only the old maxim: 'seduce not poor girls and punish the seducer'—and that did not help.

In France, just before the curtain fell, a great satirist arose, who for the last time showed the lords of the old régime their true faces. Pierre-Auguste Caron, better known in literature under the name of Beaumarchais, was even less fitted than Rousseau by his own example to prescribe codes of morals to the world. He was an adventurer on the grand scale, and before he wrote *Le Mariage de Figaro* he had behind him a life of varied experiences which included a number of delicate affairs with women. Yet he put so much wit and grace into his criticism of society that even its victims listened and laughed. His chief reproach against the great

PLATE 17

Secret marriage in England. It took place without publication of banns. After the marriage ceremony by the priest the wedding guests brought the bridal couple to the marriage bed. Engraving by Bernard Picard.

Chevalier Charles d'Eon de Beaumont (1728-1810), a French adventurer, often showed himself in women's clothes, so that doubts about his sex arose. On 9th April, 1787, he fought a duel in London with Monsieur de Saint-George. Etching by James Gillray (1757-1815).

PLATE 18

Nocturnal meeting of the Adamites, a religious order with an erotic tendency. Engraving by Bernard Picard (1673–1733).

Giant wigs. Caricature of the exaggeratedly high hairstyle of the Rococo. Drawing by Louis Marin Bonnet (1743-1793)

PLATE 19

Françoise d'Aubigné, Marquise
de Maintenon (1635–1719).
Mistress of Louis XIV.
Miniature by Jean Petitot.

Françoise, Marquise de Montespan
(1641–1707). Mistress of Louis XIV.
Painting by Mignard.

Marie Jeanne, Countess du Barry
1743–1793). Mistress of Louis XV.
Contemporary engraving.

Jeanne, Marquise de Pompadour
(1721–1764). Painting by Boucher.

PLATE 20

"The Gust of Wind". Contemporary caricature on the fashion of the Incroyables.

In Token of Divorce. Napoleon informs his wife, Josephine, in the park of the Malmaison Palace, that he intends to divorce her.

PLATE 21

Food for wild beasts.
Illustration to a novel by
the Marquis de Sade.   1798.

Erotic scene.   Illustration to Casanova's Memoirs (edition of *c.* 1845).

PLATE 22

Catherine II, Tsarina of Russia
(1729–1796).

The Venetian adventurer, Giovanni
Casanova (1725–1798).

Madame Theresia Tallien
(1773–1835).

PLATE 23

A women's duel. Painting of the end of the 19th century.

Cartoon on the masculinisation of women.
About 1848.

PLATE 24

George Sand
(Mme. Dudevant), the
novelist. (1804–1876).

Parisian women rowers.
Coloured cartoon on
female emancipation.
Coloured lithograph.

lords was their habit of seducing poor girls in their service. It was
not only that they claimed the *jus primae noctis*, the prerogative
of deflowering the bride—Lope de Vega had castigated this
abuse on the Spanish stage two centuries earlier, and it is probable
that few landlords in France still practised it—but, what was

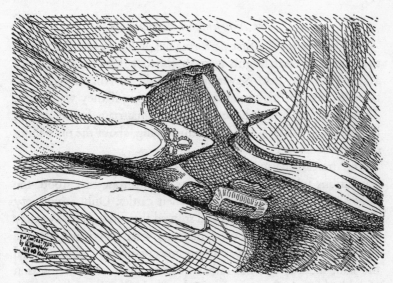

Love scene. Satirical broadsheet by James Gillray on morals at the
English Court

worse, if their eye fell on a pretty chambermaid they forbade her
to marry at all.

Beaumarchais illustrated this form of sexual tyranny through
the story of the blasé Count Almaviva, the wily maid Susanna,
and the resourceful valet Figaro. For caution's sake, he set the
action in an imaginary Seville, which, however, bore an uncanny
resemblance to the Paris of Marie Antoinette. Naturally, virtue
triumphed, and with it the *tiers état* of working men and women,
who want nothing better than to marry among themselves and
to be left in peace by the gentry. Of the many plays written in
the eighteenth century on the theme of Seduction and Innocence,

Le Mariage de Figaro is perhaps in essence the least truthful, especially when one thinks who its author was. Yet it hit the mark: never had the great lords in the stalls heard so many pointed truths addressed to them from the stage. Nevertheless, they still felt secure enough to take the whole thing as a joke, and to applaud.

The Anti-feminist Revolution

Five years after the first performance of *Figaro*, the jest turned to earnest. All feudal rights were abolished, at least on paper, with a stroke of the pen. Never more would an Almaviva be entitled to prevent his servants from marrying if they wanted to. They would no longer have to pay him a marriage fee on leaving his service. But that was, for the time being, about the only thing changed in sex-life.

The transformation did not take place so suddenly as in revolutions which follow lost wars. The throne still stood, the nobles still sat in their offices and their castles. Only a few very timid souls had gone abroad and stowed their money away safely outside the country; the great majority were convinced that the storming of the Bastille was only a mutiny, not a rebellion. Social life had, indeed, become rather quieter; the first winter season after the historic Fourteenth of July was less brilliant than usual. 'Paris is a night-cap', wrote the Comtesse de Seneffe in February 1790. 'No balls. Everyone stops at home. They have even decided not to give any more concerts.'[143] Other contemporary accounts show that the gay lady was exaggerating a little. There were still plenty of fêtes and entertainments. The salon, the opera, and the comedies went on as usual.

Gentlemen of taste still wore long waistcoats and knee-breeches and made merry over the handful of young men who ventured to appear in good society clothed in the English fashion of short waistcoats and long trousers. Yet this folly of fashion, the harbinger of a new age in male dress, had arrived before the Revolution. The pioneers were called *sans-culottes*, which does not mean 'without trousers', but 'without knee-breeches'. It soon became a derogatory term for the revolutionaries of the street.[144]

The men who were bent on extirpating the *ancien régime*, root and branch, had more urgent things to do than to trouble their heads about sex reform. Many of them did not even want it. The aims of the great French Revolution, like those of every revolution, were highly moral. Virtue was its highest good. Feudal society was vice incarnate. When that had been liquidated, virtue would return automatically, since mankind was virtuous by nature, as Jean-Jacques Rousseau had taught them.

Virtue is love of one's country, love of one's neighbour, respect of the young for the old, of children for their parents. As regards the relationship between man and woman, the position was not so clear. For many good revolutionaries, the conception of virtue differed little from that of the old *romans de mœurs*. Libertinage and adultery were symptoms of social corruption; they belonged to the old régime and in the new social order there should be no place for them. For the same reason, however, not too many concessions should be made to women. It was true that many excellent women had marched with the men from 14 July onward, and had proved themselves staunch adherents of the Revolution. One must not forget, however, that women had been deified under the old régime. That fact alone rendered them suspect.

The Revolution was thus anti-feminist *a priori*. In this it followed the principles of Rousseau, who was against allowing women any place in public life. The first manifestoes of the Revolution hardly mention women. The *Droits de l'homme et du citoyen*, proclaimed by the Constituent Assembly three weeks after the storming of the Bastille, is sometimes translated 'human and civic rights', but a more accurate rendering would be 'the rights of men and citizens', for women were excluded from most political rights. They were neither actively nor passively enfranchised, and they could not hold any high office. The women of the people who filled the galleries of the popular assemblies, parliament and the courts, and made themselves conspicuous by their violent interruptions, were regarded by the politicians only as unwelcome spectators. In the National Convention special posters were pasted up enjoining the women in the gallery to keep quiet.

Nevertheless, the turbulent and amorphous mass of the *tricoteuses* produced one of the first political women's associations. In order to win the men's ear more easily, it called itself the *Société Fraternelle des deux Sexes*. Its founder was a provincial actress, and it had something of the air of a melodrama. Its members ran about in men's long trousers; many of them, to show their fighting spirit, stuck pistols in their belts. Their behaviour in their political demonstrations was also extremely radical. The men of the Revolution, however, mistrusted these street-Amazons, especially when they saw that the women of the upper and middle classes who tried to take a hand in politics were becoming increasingly the mainspring and tools of the reaction. Madame Roland, a Republican of Roman stamp, linked up with the *Girondistes*, the party of the Right. Charlotte Corday, also at first an enthusiastic revolutionary, murdered Marat, the President of the Jacobin Club, to avenge his attacks on the Girondists. Both women ended their lives under the guillotine in 1793.

About the same time, that fate also overtook Olympe de Gouges, the authoress who had championed equal rights for women at the very outbreak of the Revolution. She had drawn up a Declaration of the Rights of Women, modelled on the Declaration of the Rights of Man, but this had found very little response in France. Her ideas did, however, influence the movement for women's rights in England. In 1792 Mary Wollstonecraft, the spiritual ancestress of the English suffragettes, published her subversive book, *A Vindication of the Rights of Women*. In the same year the burgomaster of Koenigsberg, Theodor Gottlieb von Hippel, a friend of Kant's, wrote a treatise *On the Position of Women in Bourgeois Society*. He did not go so far as the champions of women's rights in west Europe, but it was a beginning. It is true that these beginnings never led to any tangible result, after political feminism had been nipped in the bud in 1793 by the prohibition of the Paris Women's Club.[145]

Civil Marriage and Divorce Law

Nevertheless, the French Revolution accomplished enduring work also in the field of sex-legislation. Civil marriage before a registrar was first made voluntary, then on 20 September 1792 it became the only legally valid form of marriage. At the same time, divorce was legalized. The demand for divorce was no slogan of the Revolution. It came from the fastnesses of the *ancien régime*, where, in any case, marriage was not taken too seriously. The first person to raise the question—as early as 1789— and strongly to advocate divorce, was the Duc d'Orleans. The bourgeois members of the Revolutionary parliament showed only a very lukewarm interest in the question, and long debates were required before a majority in favour of the principle of divorce could be whipped up.

Then, however, France at once went far beyond the Protestant countries, in which the right to divorce had existed since the Reformation but in practice had been made very difficult to exercise. In England, in particular, divorce had become absolutely a privilege of the rich, for each case had to be sanctioned by Parliament, by a long and expensive procedure, and only adultery and impotence were admitted as grounds for divorce. The new French legislation made things easier for couples who did not wish to go on living together. They only had to hand in a joint declaration that they wished their marriage to be dissolved; they had not even to tell the authorities their reasons.

Pessimists prophesied a regular epidemic of divorce; but nothing of the kind occurred. In the first fifteen months of the new dispensation, a bare 6,000 divorces were registered in Paris. As Paris then numbered 700,000 inhabitants and well over 100,000 married couples, it is clear that only a small fraction of the population took advantage of the right to divorce. It was obviously not only tradition that held them back. The convinced revolutionaries did not want to acquire the reputation of being libertines. Even if marriage was, to quote the words of Chaumette, Solicitor-General of Paris, 'no longer a yoke or a chain', yet the government laid even more weight than its predecessors on the maintenance of the marriage relationship among its citizens. One of the new national holidays was the Feast of the Married Couples. The family was to be the basis of the new State, and anyone finding it necessary to divorce should re-marry as soon as possible, for the leaders of Revolutionary France were even more anxious than the statesmen of the old régime to see the population grow quickly.

To beget and to bear children was regarded as patriotic duty, especially when it was seen that the Republic would have to defend itself against foreign enemies. Women paraded the streets of Paris with banners bearing the inscription: *Citoyennes, Donnez des Enfants à la Patrie. Leur Bonheur est Assuré* ('Citizenesses, give children to your country; their happiness is assured'). The children's future was not, indeed, so assured and carefree as the banners promised, yet it must be conceded that in this respect also the revolutionary governments did more than their predecessors. The foundling system was reformed and placed on a better social basis. Parents who were not in a position to bring up their children themselves could entrust them to the *Service des enfants assistés*, where they were brought up and educated at State expense without being finally separated from their parents. After this reform, the number of anonymous exposures of children fell substantially. In Paris the figure during the Revolution was only 4,000 a year, half as many as twenty years previously under the old régime, when the city was considerably smaller.

There were, indeed, plenty of abuses and dubious innovations to set against these reforms. Ingenious business men made capital out of the State marriage policy. In Paris, Liardot founded the first marriage agency, under the name of *bureau de confiance*, combining it with a boarding house for daughters of marriageable age. The undertaking prospered so well that Liardot soon added a bi-weekly gazette, entitled the *Indicateur des Mariages*. The agency itself gradually developed into a pleasure resort in which clients danced and gambled, and could make female acquaintances without any serious thought of marriage. M. Liardot's idea, however, caught on and out of it there developed a flourishing business branch of sex-life.

A Prostitutes' Price-list

As in all revolutionary periods, the market for venal love flourished greatly. As propaganda and the press were now free from restriction in France, the world—and posterity—learnt much that was hitherto unknown about the institutions in question. On the first anniversary of the 14th of July a price-list was published in Paris, in several instalments, of brothels, *maisons de rendezvous* and women working on their own account; it was entitled *Tarif des filles du Palais-Royal, lieux circonvoisins et autres quartiers de Paris, avec leurs noms et demeures* (Tariff of the girls of the Palais-Royal, the neighbouring districts and other parts of Paris, with their names and addresses). The author claimed in his preface to be doing a patriotic service by thus supplying information to the innumerable visitors who came to Paris for the national holiday, and apart from that were 'attracted here every day by the love of freedom'.

Whatever the editor meant by 'freedom', the list was long and alluring. A visit to Madame Dupéron and her four young ladies cost, we learn, twenty-five livres (at that time as many gold francs) whereas at the *Victorine* or the *Paysanne* love could be purchased for six livres and a bowl of punch. An especially famous lady, *La Bacchante*, had a graduated tariff: six livres for young gentlemen, twelve for their elders. There were, of course, also gallant ladies with special social qualifications and luxury apartments of their own, and others who were prepared to look after and amuse a tourist during his whole stay in Paris. One of Kotzebue's comedies is built round one of these.[146]

The police allowed gallantry a certain freedom of movement, but the new men now sitting in parliament were more austere. As early as July 1791 the Constituent Assembly laid down that prostitutes whose bearing endangered public order or offended modesty might be arrested. Two years later the Jacobins in the Paris city parliament set their hands to a great cleansing. One afternoon in July 1793 the Palais Royal, the centre of the *demi-monde*, was suddenly cordoned off. The women and their guests feared the worst, but the police only scrutinized the political records of the priestesses of Venus. A few months later, however, the matter was taken in hand seriously. The virtuous and energetic Chaumette himself took charge of the purge, and the pavements of Paris were swept clean of all sinners precisely at the moment when the Terror was at its height, under Robespierre. But the women outlasted Robespierre. He was hardly gone before they returned to their usual haunts, and there began one of the most extravagant periods that Paris had ever seen.

13

THE PLEASURE OF POWER

THE great French Revolution was conquered by a woman—and a Spanish woman at that. It was an act of feminine revenge for the wrongs inflicted on herself and her sisters. The process had a certain logic: the Revolution was an uprising of men against a régime and a form of society in which everything pivoted on women, and during which women ruled not only over men but also over the greatest lands of Europe. Where, as in Austria and Russia, they sat on the thrones themselves, as rightfully constituted rulers, they were perhaps well enough; but in France, where women were excluded from the throne and exercised their sway from the bedroom, their influence on the country was fatal, whether, like La Pompadour and Du Barry, they exercised it as mistresses, or as lawfully wedded queens, like Marie Antoinette. Such a régime could go on no longer. In 1789 this was felt by many who were neither natural misogynists nor desirous of seeing the form of State altered, much less a social revolution.

The Revolution had fulfilled these expectations. Women had been banished from their places of power. In five years they had lost all they had gained in two centuries. The one equal right allowed them was the right to perish on the scaffold. Most women overtaken by this fate accepted their lot; many faced their judges more courageously and manfully than the men. One, however, thought this was the wrong way; the point was not to die nobly, but to get rid of the executioner. She therefore mated herself with one of the most evil, bloodthirsty, and unprincipled terrorists practising in France, the ex-apprentice Tallien.

Notre Dame de Thermidor

The woman who ventured on this desperate remedy when the knife was already at her throat was a twenty-year-old marquise. Her maiden name was Juana Maria Ignacia Theresia Cabarrus; her father was a rich banker of Madrid, who came originally from the northern side of the Pyrenees, but acquired Spanish citizenship and was created Count by Carlos III for services in manipulating the currency. Theresia had come to Paris with her mother to learn the manners of polite society in the last years of the *ancien régime*. She was married at fifteen to a French marquis named Devin de Fontenay, as rich as her father and of equally recent title. The young marquis was neither an Adonis nor a model husband. He was unfaithful to his wife, and she to him, but neither bore the other a grudge, and the marriage would have remained perfectly successful but for the storming of the Bastille.

The Marquis de Fontenay fraternized with the people, after his fashion, by taking a shop-girl into his house as mistress. Theresia coquetted with the Revolution and was so fired by the happenings in Paris that she opened her heart to every revolutionary. Many profited by the beautiful Spaniard's generosity. She was passed from hand to hand. She was, indeed, not entirely undiscriminating. She preferred men who were just in the public eye and, in general, she was against radicals. When things began to get out of hand in Paris, she found it wiser to move to Bordeaux, near the Spanish frontier, whence she could take refuge in her own home, if necessary. She had divorced the Marquis de Fontenay, who wanted to go to Martinique and begin a new life there. That did not appeal to her. She was not yet ready to give up; she meant to rise higher. She proposed to conquer Paris—if it could not be achieved with the revolution, then against it.

For a few months more she tried playing the drawing-room revolutionary in Bordeaux; but the time for that was past, even in the south. One day she found the door of her apartment sealed, and a warrant for her arrest pinned to it. She tried to hide, but in vain, and a few days later she was under lock and key.

Fortune, however, favoured her. The commandant of Bordeaux, who bore the proud title of Proconsul, was one of the pseudo-revolutionaries to whom she had made up at an earlier stage: Jean-Lambert Tallien. She succeeded in getting taken before him, and by the next day she was his mistress. That settled her case. 'Citoyenne Cabarrus', as the young marquise was now called, was not only at liberty, but the uncrowned queen of Bordeaux, courted by all, while her protector carried on with his butcher's work. She succeeded in saving one or two of her friends from the guillotine, but Tallien was nervous of becoming suspect in Paris if he showed too much mercy. Once he had the entire audience in the Grand Theatre arrested, brought two hundred of them before a revolutionary tribunal and reported triumphantly to Paris: 'I have destroyed a nest of aristocrats.'[147]

Yet his murderous zeal did not avail him. In Paris they knew that he was unreliable and connected with a woman who was coquetting with counter-revolutionaries. He was summoned to Paris to justify himself. Now Bordeaux became too hot for Theresia, too. Taking a young lover with her, she made her way secretly to Paris, where it was easiest to go underground. She was soon discovered, however, and a warrant for her arrest, signed by Robespierre himself, put an end to her escapades. A warrant from Robespierre usually spelled certain death. In her despair, Theresia indited a defiant letter from her cell to Tallien, who was himself fighting for his life and had publicly repudiated his mistress: 'The police officer has just left me; he had come to tell me that to-morrow I must appear before the court, which means I must mount the scaffold. This is very different from the dream I dreamed last night: Robespierre was no more, and the prisons were open. But thanks to your characteristic cowardice, there will soon be no one left in France capable of turning this dream into reality.'

Theresia's words shook Tallien into action. This was his last chance. He was still a member of the Convention. Whether he would be so on the morrow was uncertain. Only a surprise attack on Robespierre could save him.

The improbable happened. The accusations of a demagogue so smeared with blood and filth as Tallien sufficed to overthrow the 'Incorruptible'. Everyone knew, however, that the real author of the victory was not Tallien, but Theresia Cabarrus. Parisian wit soon found a nickname of honour for her. Robespierre had fallen in the month known in the new calendar as Thermidor; Theresia was dubbed *Notre Dame de Thermidor*. She was, in fact, adored as a saint. Her train of votaries was composed of the *jeunesse dorée*, young aristocrats and bourgeois sons who had gone in fear of their lives the day before and were now on top again.

'Sexa': an Illness

After the first intoxication of victory was over, Theresia married her inconstant protector and now became Madame Tallien. This did not, however, bring any change in her love-life. She betrayed her new husband as often as she had betrayed his predecessor, and would presumably betray his successors. Her sexual appetite was strong; no man succeeded in satisfying it completely. Although undoubtedly an intelligent and purposeful woman, she was not conspicuous either for wit or for charm. Her real attraction was obviously physical, for all contemporary reports rave over her extraordinary beauty. Many portraits of her still exist, but it is not easy to say just what she was like. She looks different in each. In the early pictures she still has the stereotyped smile of a rococo damsel; later she becomes an ample, dignified matron—'every inch a queen'.

In any case, she was undoubtedly herself largely responsible for this change of fashion. Madame Tallien is the accepted authoress of the *Directoire* style, in which women are transformed into goddesses of antiquity and men into figures out of a Venetian carnival. Women's clothes were no longer sewn, but draped round them, leaving as much as possible undraped. When an actress walked along the streets of Paris with her bosom completely exposed, a sensation ensued but no scandal; society ladies were acting not very differently. With the pseudo-classical robes went coloured wigs which might have left Nero envious;

Madame Lange had twenty, and Madame Tallien thirty, although when sitting for her portrait she preferred to display her own luxuriant black hair. On top of the wig was balanced an enormously magnified jockey's cap with a peak standing up like a carving-dish.

The ladies affecting this fashion were known as *les merveilleuses*, and the *merveilleuse des merveilleuses* was Madame Tallien herself, who let no week pass without finding some new touch to embellish herself and her sisters. Men's costume was no less eccentric, but in the opposite way. Fashion demanded of its male devotees to wrap themselves up to the limit. Summer and winter they wore a cravat wound six times round the throat and just allowing the nose to appear; also *lorgnons*, whether they needed them or not. Above all, however, they had to master a special genteel language, as a sign that the plebeian revolution was over. They were so blasé as to be unable to pronounce the letter 'r', and they ended every sentence with the words *c'est incoyable, ma paole d'honneu*! Hence they were called the *Incroyables*.

When these novelties were coming in, the Paris papers wrote of a new sickness, the *sexa*. This, fortunately, was not a new form of venereal disease, but only a disease of fashion. The word *sexa* was a witty abbreviation of the question *Qu' est-ce que c'est que ça?* The pun on 'sex' was, however, justified. The *Directoire*, the period of transition between the Revolution and Napoleon's dictatorship, was laden with sexuality. It was definitely a period of women's rule.

The undisputed queen was the over-sexed Madame Tallien, the woman who had freed France from the terrors of revolution. She held her court in a house which from the outside was still disguised as a chalet in the Rousseauesque 'natural' style, and was accordingly called *La Chaumière*. Inside, however, the whole cold, classic pomp of the Empire was displayed. The bosom friend of Theresia was a Creole from Martinique, Joséphine Tascher de la Pagerie by name. Before leaving Martinique this lady had married a Vicomte de Beauharnais, who died under the guillotine in 1794. The widow had, however, soon consoled herself. The list of her lovers is as long as Theresia's own, and includes names of note. She had just made an especially good catch: she had become the mistress of the Vicomte de Barras, an unscrupulous aristocrat who had been an ultra-radical during the Revolution but had changed sides in time, shouldered Tallien aside, and was now the richest and most powerful man in the government.

Theresia did not long leave her friend in possession of this exotic prize. In other ages a rivalry of this sort would have given rise to the most envenomed scenes of jealousy, but under the Directoire things were settled amicably. No passion; that led to no good! 'Change, change, little tree!' Madame Tallien became *maîtresse-en-titre* of Barras, Member of the Directorate and Generalissimo, without even troubling to divorce her husband.

The kind-hearted but shrewd Joséphine de Beauharnais allowed herself to be compensated with the hand of a rising young general of artillery who had distinguished himself under Barras's command. His name was Buonaparte (the 'u' still figures in the Corsican version of the family name) and he was destined for great things. At the time, however, it cost Joséphine, who came of the highest Parisian society, some effort to marry this penniless little officer, who not long before had had to beg the material for a new uniform from Madame Tallien. Barras and Theresia sweetened the pill for Joséphine by standing witnesses at her wedding.

The free sexual morality which prevailed in the *Chaumière* circles penetrated to other classes of society. The bourgeoisie had lost its inner stability under the privations of the Revolution, followed by monetary inflation of unprecedented dimensions. Love was a commodity like any other. The first to feel the effects of this unfair competition from the wives and daughters of the bourgeoisie were the prostitutes, whose business suffered heavily, even though at this period the police never troubled them at all. The divorce rate had gone up fantastically, and divorced men and women no longer remarried at once, as during the revolution. Only the rise in illegitimate births saved France from depopulation.

Spanish Flies

Directoire society was loose enough to find room for a figure that the world had either shunned before or had kept under lock and key—the Marquis de Sade, after whom sadism, the most repulsive of all sexual perversions, is still called today. Although an ex-revolutionary and an aristocrat—two attributes highly prized in that circle—the ill-famed marquis appears never to have been admitted to the *Chaumière*; but he is found in another circle which had evolved a remarkable way of passing its time. In 1795 the famous gourmet Grimode de la Reynière had founded a dining-club in the Palais Royal, under the enticing name of *Diner des Mystificateurs*, whose members amused themselves not only with the delights of the table but also with the art of turning other people's brains by more or less harmless methods, including, in particular, love potions.

No better expert in black arts of the kind could have been found than the crazy marquis. He had taken his degree in sadism a quarter of a century earlier. On a visit to a brothel in Marseilles he had treated the prostitutes to wine and liqueurs, and had then handed round bonbons containing a strong dose of cantharides, an exceedingly dangerous aphrodisiac. Cantharides, which is extracted from the Spanish fly, has been used since early times as a sex-stimulant, especially for men, and, often before, its use had certainly resulted in accidents and dangerous after-effects. This time its effect was catastrophic. The women rolled about in agony and screamed until people came running from the neighbouring streets. One threw herself out of the window and suffered severe injuries, while two others succumbed to internal burns.

Such at least was the evidence given by the first witnesses before the court at Aix, and since the Marquis de Sade and the valet who had accompanied him to the brothel and helped him hand round the sweets had fled, instead of defending themselves, the Court condemned them both to death *in absentia* for murder by poisoning. The sentence would seem, by modern ideas, over-harsh, for the marquis had certainly not meant his jest to have such consequences. Even if the witnesses' evidence was correct —and this was afterwards contested—the offence was manslaughter, not murder.

Moreover, the marquis already had one sexual crime to his score. Four years earlier, when a young officer in Paris, he had enticed into his summer-house a young girl who had begged from him on the street. He pinioned her, threatened her with a knife, and inflicted slight wounds on her. That too, he maintained, had been meant only as a jest, a mystification, the thrill of which lay in watching another's terror of a death which would not be inflicted. In fact his victim had managed to free herself and to escape by jumping through the window. The scandal was great, and intervention from high quarters had to be invoked in order to get de Sade off with a short period of detention in a fortress.

On this second occasion, too, the marquis's family pulled all possible strings to save his life and liberty. The Comtes de Sade (the eldest son always bore the title of Marquis) were of the leading nobility of Provence. The marquis's father had been French Ambassador in Russia, his son had already inherited from him the dignity of Governor-General of the provinces of Bresse, Bugey, Valmorey and Gex, and the king had appointed him a colonel of cavalry, in spite of his earlier sentence. Were the de Sades now to admit that one of them was a poisoner?

After long intrigue the death-sentence of the Aix court was quashed and the marquis represented almost as a martyr. All charges against him were dropped, except 'excessive debauchery' and failure to appear before the court, for which he was ordered to pay fifty livres into the poor-box. If the first sentence had been over-harsh, the second, which was tantamount to an acquittal, was an obvious perversion of justice for the benefit of a great lord. Justice under the *ancien régime*, however, had its own methods. If a man was once caught in the meshes of the law, and if he had influential enemies—and de Sade had enemies enough— he did not get out of them so easily. He should have been released in May 1779 at the latest. In fact it was not until 1790, when the National Assembly ordered the release of all persons imprisoned without due process of law, that he regained his freedom.[148]

The Novels of the Marquis de Sade

Seventeen years of prison had shaken his nerve, but had not broken his resistance. With liberty, his health came back. He seemed even to have been cured of his old sadistic tendencies. He lived peacefully with a former mistress, herself the daughter of a great family, and tried to adapt himself to the new world in which he found himself. He did not even resent the fact that the revolutionaries had looted his castle; he had suffered worse things from the *ancien régime*. But now, at fifty, he had for the first time to earn his own living.

In the Bastille he had begun work on a novel which purported to describe all imaginable forms of perversion. Now he turned professional author. He wrote a number of mediocre plays, one of which was performed at the Théâtre-Français. But the bees were back in his bonnet. He sought adventures, if no longer in life, then on paper. His imagination was constantly haunted by sex and violence, and these two impulses became confused in him into one. In 1791 he published, anonymously, the first and most famous of his novels, *Justine, ou les Malheurs de la Vertu*. It is hard to understand today how this piece of scribbling became so famous, for, at bottom, it is simply one of the *romans de mœurs* on fallen women of which eighteenth-century literature had been full since the Abbé Prévost set the fashion sixty years earlier with his *Manon Lescaut*. De Sade, however, exactly reverses Prévost's system of rewards and punishments. Vice is rewarded, virtue humiliated and ground down—that is the way of the world.

The Marquis de Sade describes the careers of two girls left to make their own way through life after the death of their father, a Paris banker. Juliette, the elder, who is the stronger and the less scrupulous character, enters a high-class brothel, marries one of her customers—who is, of course, a count, for de Sade's romances are all set in the highest society of the old régime—gets him to make a will in her favour and then poisons him, ruins a number of other men of rank and standing, and ends up as the mistress of one of the highest dignitaries of France.

On the other hand, her younger sister, the shy and tender Justine, who tried to defend her virtue, is violated, unjustly accused and thrown into prison, out of which she is only rescued by a terrible act of arson committed by a fellow convict. Even this, however, does not help her. Soon after she is again assailed by counts and their lackeys, bound hand and foot, and spanned between four trees, while blood-hounds are set on her, and so on. She takes refuge with a surgeon; he tries to vivisect her. Even in the cloister she finds no rest; monks assault her. Finally she falls into the hands of a sex-murderer of exquisite cruelty who specializes in cutting off women's heads with a sabre. She escapes this fate, but just because she has survived it, is suspected of being the mass-murderer's accomplice and is unjustly condemned to death.

In *Juliette, ou les Prospérités du Vice*, his second novel in this style (he also wrote others in a less sensational strain), de Sade described some further episodes in the life of the elder sister. She sets fire to a peasant's cottage in order to gloat over the death of its inmates; participates in an enterprise, founded by an English-woman, to depopulate France; flees to Italy and tries to convert the Pope to the cult of the French Revolution; and robs King Ferdinand IV of Naples, with the complicity of his wife, the dreaded Queen Marie Caroline. King Ferdinand and his wife were the implacable enemies of France. They had just concluded an alliance with England, partly through the instrumentality of Lady Hamilton, dancer in the nude, wife of the English minister and afterwards mistress of Lord Nelson. The romance thus turns into a political satire. It appeared in 1796, under the Directoire, when people were no longer exclusively interested in horrors, as during the Revolution, but wanted also to be amused.

But contemporary interest has its dangers. When de Sade com-posed a thinly-disguised romance about Madame Tallien and Joséphine de Beauharnais, entitled *Zoloé et ses deux acolytes*, and even had the audacity to send a copy to the Consul Bonaparte, retribution quickly descended on him. One day he was arrested at his publisher's, nominally not on account of *Zoloé* but of *Juliette*. Now he learnt to his cost that a man could be caught in the toils again, as under the monarchy. He was not even put on trial, but dragged from prison to prison, under a police warrant. He sent in countless petitions for release, but all he achieved was to get put in a lunatic asylum, where he was allowed occasionally to stage plays. He died there in 1814, at seventy-four.

Posterity has made a monster of the Marquis de Sade. If one reviews his life, however, one finds no reason to rank him among the notorious sex-criminals. The two evil deeds of his youth in Paris and Marseilles appear to have been his only acts of sadism. It is possible that what prevented him was the extreme severity of the law, but even during his few years of liberty he committed no further crime than one of which greater writers, before and after him, have been guilty: of depicting sadistic situations. He was simply a pervert of the pen.

Napoleon's Love Strategy

Had the Marquis de Sade refrained from mixing, so to speak, in affairs of State and dropping unfriendly remarks about Joséphine, Napoleon would perhaps have treated the old man, who could no longer be a danger to anyone, less harshly; for the new master of France had no desire to turn it into a land of monks and nuns. He troubled his head little about the sex-lives of his subjects, and less still about their sex-reading. France under Napoleon was certainly a police State, but its severity was mitigated by corruption. The Prefect of Police of Paris, Dubois, introduced the laudable innovation of making prostitutes submit to regular medical inspection, but for that they had to pay a fee, a proportion of which went to the Prefect's own privy purse. It was the same in all spheres; with money and influence a man could evade or turn to his own advantage any decree of the Dictatorship. For a woman it was still easier: she could pay in kind.

Napoleon I's Empire was first and foremost a military State, and the Emperor himself saw to it that civilians looked the other way where soldiers were concerned, however freely officers and soldiers behaved towards the wives and daughters of the bourgeoisie. The military were to constitute a privileged class in this respect as in others. Napoleon thought that the best way of keeping young men with the colours was to allow them sexual freedom; soldiers could therefore commit with impunity many sexual offences and crimes, not only in the field—that was understood—but also in the garrisons and against their own compatriots.

Even during the period of his great military successes, most Frenchmen were by no means over-eager to risk their lives in the service of the Corsican's lust of conquest. In 1810, 160,000 persons in France had already been sentenced for desertion or for harbouring deserters, and as it had proved impossible to apprehend the persons of most of them, fines totalling seventy million gold francs had been imposed on their families. To raise the soldiers' spirits, Napoleon gave them unlimited wine and bread, while the civilian population went short. Even this, however, was not attraction enough; the soldier also needed something for his heart.

The result was that in Napoleon's army a sort of 'red-coat' morality developed which recalled the days of the Thirty Years War. The *Chronique Scandaleuse* is full of sexual crimes, offences against public morality, and acts of sadistic violence perpetrated by Napoleon's soldiers in the heart of Paris, and in broad daylight.[149] Once six soldiers violated a woman, a complete stranger to them, and then threw her into the Seine. When things got too bad, the government would issue a new decree, or the military authorities themselves intervene, but it was an unwritten law that such rules and prohibitions were only for the subordinates, not for those who enacted them. Sexual morality in the corps of officers was no better than among the rank and file. A true warrior had to be 'gallant'. That meant that he had to pester any girl who caught his eye, and if the attraction of the uniform proved insufficient, storm her *manu militari*.

Napoleon himself set his officers a bad example. At the beginning of his career he was shy and rather clumsy as a lover, and had not much success with women. At one moment he thought of smoothing his path to promotion by marrying a sixty-year-old woman for her money. When, however, he achieved power he made up for lost time. Power need deny itself nothing. Napoleon disposed of women as though they were his property. He ordered them to him; if they objected, he had them brought by force. He kept them for a night, a week, or occasionally a few months, and sent them away when he pleased. If a man was in his way—even if it was the husband of the woman of his choice—he sent him abroad on some mission, as Nero had done.

Some husbands profited by the transaction, but usually Napoleon was not very generous to his rivals. When he was held up in Cairo on his expedition to Egypt and felt bored, he ordered his adjutant to bring him a lady whom he had glimpsed when out riding, the wife of a French lieutenant. As the young woman loved her husband, and refused to give herself to the Generalissimo on the spot, the unfortunate lieutenant was sent on a dangerous naval expedition, being given a small ship and ordered to run the British blockade and proceed to Malta. He was promptly taken prisoner by the British, and now Napoleon was able to console his subordinate's wife at leisure.

After he had become absolute dictator, he hardly needed to use such forceful methods. Women threw themselves on his neck. The highest ambition of any actress, singer or lady of the new Society, was to spend a night in the great man's bed. Even at this time, however, Napoleon took a strange pleasure in picking up young women off the street. This was how a Berlin girl (usually he preferred southern women) came to occupy a place in his love-gallery.

After his entry into Berlin, Napoleon held a parade. The security precautions were strict, but a young girl accompanied by her mother succeeded in making her way into the Emperor's presence to present a petition to him. She was uncommonly pretty. Napoleon cast one look at her, and it was enough. That evening he sent his First Chamberlain, Constant, to order her to his quarters in the Charlottenburg Palace. The mother was made to wait in the antechamber; only the daughter was admitted to the Emperor's presence. The visit lasted till morning, and ended with Napoleon's rewarding the girl with two hundred gold pieces. He said openly to his Chamberlain that he found the girl very attractive, but rather dull since she spoke no word of French.

A few months later Constant encountered the girl in Paris in a street near the Palais-Royal where prostitutes carried on their profession. She told him a remarkable story of her adventures. A French colonel had married her, obviously in the hope of getting promotion through her, but as she had been unable to do anything for him he had left her, and she had had to find another way of earning her living. Napoleon thought of sending for her again, but changed his mind after all, sent her another four thousand gold francs and advised her to go back to Berlin as quickly as possible.

The list of the women on whom Napoleon bestowed his favours is a long one. We know of several dozen—partly, of course, because his love-life has been studied particularly closely, but also because he was himself very indiscreet on this point. He used to talk to his intimates with the utmost lack of reserve about his various love-affairs, often giving them regular bulletins about the preceding nights—always, of course, accounts of victories. No woman on whom his eye fell could resist him, but not because he was particularly attractive physically. Women submitted to him either out of ambition or out of fear, or because they promised themselves some advantage from the connection with the most powerful man in Europe.

Napoleon was a tempestuous lover. When he had a new woman in front of him, he would fall on her like one possessed. But he could be charming, too, and knew how to beguile women by lover-like attentions. He would write them glowing love-letters, care for them when they were indisposed, and display sympathy with their personal interests. Only if they troubled him too much with such matters would he become rough and even brutal. He treated his women as he did the soldiers under his command. It was, in fact, much the same thing for him; his pleasure was always to conquer and command other human beings.

He was, however, no sadist. The sufferings of others gave him no pleasure. He wanted his partners to carry away as happy a memory of their night of love as his own. He was imperious, but not cruel. At times he indulged in youthful tricks in the course of his gallant escapades. When already a mature man, he climbed one night through a window to reach a lady of his choice. He aspired to be a Don Juan, but he was only Napoleon, and women succumbed not to his manliness and his seductive arts but to his worldly position. That was the inner tragedy of his love-life.

Precisely because the gods had not created him a woman's darling, he was anxious to prove his manhood in women's estimation and in his own. Throughout years he spent each night with some woman; never more than one at a time, *tête à tête*. He hated the orgies which were fashionable under the *ancien régime* and the *Directoire*; but that one woman with whom he was alone had to be shown that he was all of a man. It is amazing that he should have been able to combine this extraordinarily intensive sex-life with his extreme activity as general, statesman and administrator of a great empire, without overstraining his capacity for work and concentration. His strength clearly lay in his ability to switch his attention instantaneously, at any moment, to other men, other objects, other interests. Even this quality, however, does not explain everything. Even a genius needs sleep.

Was Napoleon exceptional in this respect also? Apparently not. Mademoiselle George, of the Comédie-Française, who remained his mistress longer than most others, has described in great detail her nights of love with Napoleon. When she had assuaged his sexual hunger, he used to sleep as peacefully as a child, his head pillowed on her breast, and awoke in the morning rested and refreshed.

Conquest of an Empress

Although Napoleon not infrequently returned for a few nights to earlier mistresses, change was for him an absolute necessity. This did not prevent his being genuinely devoted for years to three women: Joséphine de Beauharnais, the Polish countess Marie Walewska, and the Habsburg archduchess Marie Louise. Joséphine was six years his senior, and this difference in age, if nothing else, drove him to younger women. He saw in Hortense, Joséphine's daughter by her first marriage, the image of her mother, and it is probable that he was on more than platonic terms with his step-daughter, as he was with his beautiful and much-desired sister Pauline, his junior by eleven years. The thought of incest did not trouble him; such considerations were all right for the code which bore his name, but not for its author.

Marie Walewska, the Polish patriot, was his *femme fatale*, the only woman whom he allowed to influence him even in politics. It was she who dragged him into the fatal East European policy which began with the slogan of 'liberating Poland from the Russian yoke' and ended in the catastrophe of Moscow. It was, indeed, not the physical charms alone of the lovely Pole that enslaved him. She had given him the proof of his potency by conceiving a child by him. Shortly before, another of his mistresses had borne a child which might possibly have been his, but the mother was a very light-minded lady and, to boot, the wife of a scoundrel who had just served a two-year sentence for fraud. Napoleon created this dubious offspring a Count and put him down in his will for a princely legacy, but he could not acknowledge the paternity openly.

He needed to have no such doubts with Marie Walewska. Her son could only be his. This raised the dynastic question in an acute form. His marriage with Joséphine had remained childless for twelve years. As Joséphine had had children by her earlier marriage, the fault seemed to be his. This reproach, which had always lain heavily on him, was now refuted. From that moment his resolution was fixed—to divorce Joséphine, marry a princess of one of the great Courts, and beget a blue-blooded heir to his throne. The diplomatic marriage-brokers first thought of a Russian princess, the sixteen-year-old sister of the Czar Alexander; but while Petersburg was still hesitating, Metternich, alarmed at the possibility of a Franco-Russian alliance, stepped in and offered Napoleon the seventeen-year-old daughter of the Emperor Francis of Austria instead.

Marie-Louise was not precisely Napoleon's favourite type of woman. She was rather stiff, and out-topped her forty-year-old suitor by a head. But she was 'available immediately'. The marriage contract was, in fact, as business-like as an order for a ton of herrings. The marriage took place by proxy in Vienna, the bridegroom not being present; Marie-Louise was then packed into a State coach and sent off to Paris. Much though Napoleon had coveted this marriage, he was not quite easy in his mind. It was the first time in his life that he had to take to himself a woman known to him only from pictures and report—and a real princess at that.

That, too, was something new for him. Before that, he had never risen very high in his love-affairs. The many women with whom he had shared his nights had been lights-of-love, actresses, opera singers, dancers (including one tight-rope dancer), little girls from the middle classes, wives of his subordinates, ladies of the Court, only occasionally women of the old aristocracy. He had never tried his luck with the princesses of the little Courts whose existence or non-existence depended exclusively on his will. In other words, he had always kept sex and politics strictly apart. Marie Walewska was, after all, a woman of no official position, who committed him to nothing. But now he was to subordinate his sex-life to the *raison d'état*, and to adapt himself to the Spanish-Austrian Court ceremonial, if possible even in the bedroom.

This was too much for a man who never put off the conqueror, even in his relations with women. It was not enough for him to have his new consort sent to his home. He would fetch her, and make her his wife before the marriage bells pealed. Unannounced, he rode to meet Marie-Louise, jumped into her coach on the road, and spent his bridal night with her in the Château of Compiègne, anticipating the civil and Church ceremonies. He was very pleased with this exploit. The next morning he reported to his entourage. 'Marry a German, my dear fellow,' he said to one of his intimates. 'They are the best wives in the world: good, simple and as fresh as roses.'

Marie-Louise's simplicity did not last long. When Napoleon was banished to Elba, she soon threw herself into the arms of an Austrian general of cavalry, whom her family had sent to be her escort, Adam Adalbert von Neipperg. While remaining officially Napoleon's wife, she presented her lover with an illegitimate child. She was a trifle nervous about the consequences of this lapse, but the Court of Vienna showed no annoyance over the way Neipperg had carried out his mission; he was loaded with titles and honours. It made it all the easier to liquidate the episode of Napoleon.

Napoleon, too, sought consolation. In spite of all fortune's blows, his heart was still young and romantic. In Elba he had three mistresses, and even on St. Helena, a sick man, he contracted liaisons, first with the fifteen-year-old daughter of the caretaker, then with several other women. Yet his erotic swan-song had a touch of greatness. In his last will—he no longer had much to leave—he bequeathed to Marie-Louise his lace and his heart. This was to be preserved in spirits of wine and sent to the Empress, as proof, he wrote, 'that I have loved her tenderly, and have not ceased to love her'.[150]

14

POLICE STATE AND ROMANCE

THE fall of Napoleon ranks as one of the great turning-points of history. What follows it, obviously belongs to another epoch. Is that true also of sex-history? Did laws, morals, and views on the relationship between the sexes so alter after 1815 as to enable one to say: 'From now on, a new era of sex-life begins'?

Obviously, questions like this cannot be answered with a stop-watch in the hand. Even the greatest military and political events do not usually exercise a direct effect on sex-life, which is the most private part of human existence. Even the battle of the Milvian Bridge, which decided the victory of Christianity in the Roman Empire, did not itself produce an immediate revolution in sex-life. What was one to expect of Waterloo? The Napoleonic wars were no wars of religion, the Napoleonic Empire no totalitarian régime as we understand the term today. Napoleon had inter-fered as little as possible in the private lives of his subjects.

This kind of freedom now seemed to be over. The victors wanted to 'restore', i.e. to eliminate, everything that had survived from the revolutionary years into the Napoleonic era. This could not be achieved completely. A quarter of a century of radical change could not be simply washed out. Some things, however, could be erased with a stroke of the pen.

In France itself, the most important restoration in the field of sex-life was the abolition of divorce. This was one of the first measures taken by the new Bourbon government. The law per-mitting divorced persons to remarry was annulled as early as 1816. All that married couples could now get was separation (*séparation de corps*) in certain cases: e.g. where severe excess and injury could be proved and, in particular, when the wife had committed adultery. Adultery on the part of the husband did not give the wife ground for divorce unless the husband had taken his mistress into the home. The wife was not required to sleep under one roof with the concubine; that was the sole concession made to women.

The practice of the courts did gradually somewhat restrict the husband's privileged position by interpreting as 'injury' especially flagrant cases which took place outside the home. On paper, however, these monstrous laws remained in force not only throughout the Restoration but even under Louis Philippe, under the Second Empire, and even under the Third Republic, until divorce was reintroduced in 1884. After that, in cases of adultery, the spouses could themselves choose between divorce and *séparation de corps*. For religious reasons, the latter form was usually chosen, until modern times, unless the parties preferred to close one eye and remain together.

The other Continental countries, too, began by returning undisguisedly to the ways of the old régimes. The Holy Alliance, the league of the victors, prided itself greatly on having restored the Christian morality shattered by the French Revolution. What it really restored was, however, the morals of the Pompadour, with the sole difference that this code of morals had now spread to the wealthier bourgeois circles. Governments were tolerant in this respect. A citizen's sole duty was simply to be an obedient subject and not to meddle in public affairs, which were the preserve of a small upper class. But in questions relating to sex he was allowed considerable licence. The State only wanted to know exactly what he was doing; but so long as this did not endanger authority, he could give free play to his amorous instincts, under the watchful eye of the secret police. This was, above all, the guiding principle of the man who had, in a certain sense, entered into the heritage of Napoleon.

Espionage in the Boudoir

The man who restored Europe was a cavalier of the old style: a Rhinelander in Austrian service, Clemens von Metternich.

He was four years younger than Napoleon and thus only forty-one when he presided over the Congress of Vienna. As propriety demanded, he was married to a lady of a great house and was father of seven children, but he lived apart from his wife. His diplomatic duties and his personal inclinations required him to pay court to other women. He was not only a powerful man, but also a handsome one, and enjoyed making himself out even more diabolical than he really was. It was not difficult for him to make conquests, but he was less indiscriminating in his choice of loves than Napoleon. They had to have at least a coronet with five points and be of use to him politically, for even in the boudoir he was always concerned with receiving information about his opponents and his allies. His sex-life was only the continuation of politics by other means.

When Austrian Ambassador in Paris, he had been the lover of one of Napoleon's sisters, Caroline Murat. The Duchesse d'Abrantès, General Junot's wife, who for a while sweetened Napoleon's nights, was another who yielded to him. She was the most indiscreet woman at the French Imperial Court. Around the time of the Congress of Vienna, Metternich's favourite was the Duchess of Sagan; before that she had had a liaison with an English secret agent, and her sister was Talleyrand's intimate. At the Congress of Aix-la-Chapelle in 1818 Metternich succumbed to Princess Lieven, the wife of the Russian Ambassador, who now remained his Egeria for ten years. The correspondence between the Russian princess and the Austrian Chancellor was published only in 1936; it shows that she passed on to him a vast quantity of gossip from the English Court, but also a good deal of valuable political information.

But Metternich, too, was astonishingly loquacious to the ladies who had won his heart. Even during the Congress of Vienna, his closest collaborator, Friedrich von Gentz, noted in his diary: 'At seven I went to dine with Metternich. The whole tribe of Courland whores was there, so anyone else was superfluous. In the last week Metternich has initiated these women into all the political secrets; it is incredible what they know.' A secret report by the

Vienna police—for even the Chancellor was spied on—has more to say on the subject: 'Metternich is out of his mind with love and injured vanity; he wastes every morning, for he never gets up till ten, and then, hardly dressed, goes to sigh at Sagan's feet for five or six hours. Princess Bagration [one of his women friends from the Baltic], to avenge herself on Metternich for his neglect of her, tells everything she knows or has ever heard that tells against Austria.'[151]

Metternich would never admit to himself how much he was dependent on women, but he was convinced that other men were so dependent. Women had therefore to be brought into politics and used as go-betweens, to collect information or to disarm some adversary. He employed these methods in domestic politics also. Women occupied an important place in his police State. They could not, indeed, be entrusted with official duties; that would have been contrary to tradition, a revolutionary action, and thus against the principles of the Holy Alliance. But women were good enough for spying on men and carrying to the police everything that their lovers confided to them in weak moments.

Not every woman, it is true, lends herself to this dirty business; the best agents would therefore be those who had most reason to fear the police, viz. the prostitutes. Metternich's Vienna developed this into a system which in its technical perfection was far ahead of the methods evolved in Paris by Napoleon's Minister of Police, Fouché. Metternich's Fouché was Count Josef Sedlnitzky, Chief of Police in Vienna for thirty years, from 1817 to 1848.

Europe's biggest Love-market

After the brilliant overture of the Congress of Vienna, Metternich probably dreamed of making Vienna not only the political but also the social capital of Europe. If this was his plan, it failed. London remained the pattern for all questions of male elegance. Dandyhood became a British export, almost as important as British steam engines. In everything which makes up female charm, Paris retained the supremacy.

It was only in one field that Vienna succeeded in out-distancing Paris: in the Metternich era it became the world's biggest love-market. In the 1820s, when the total population of Vienna was still under 400,000, the number of prostitutes in the city was estimated at 20,000.[152] This seems an enormous figure; it gives one prostitute for every seven or eight adult males of the population. But the loose women who gathered in Vienna worked, first and foremost, for the tourist trade, which was very active. They were also exported, for, as in old Rome, visitors to Vienna could hire and take away 'free girls' for long periods. An army of pimps and bawds facilitated the customers' choice. The penalty for procuring was very low, and was exacted only if the offence was committed too conspicuously in the public streets.

The police clearly encouraged this traffic, for the prostitutes were, in fact, their assistants. The queen of the Vienna prostitutes from the 1820s to the 1840s was the brown-haired Henriette Rothman, who enjoyed the special protection of Sedlnitzky himself. She 'worked' in her own house on the Elendbastei (Misery Bastion), a name quite inappropriate to the luxurious orgies which took place in her house. It was useless denouncing her; she was impregnable, because she was herself informer No. 1 for the police. There was another Henrietta following the same trade, whose high price earned her the nickname of Tausend-guldenkraut.* On her patrols she used to wear boots with spurs, and sometimes also male clothes, but never came into conflict with the police. One of her colleagues was known in specialist circles as 'the eternal virgin', because—supposedly out of fear of pregnancy —she used to offer men everything except normal intercourse.

Even these fine flowers of Viennese prostitution were not distinguished by any special graces. Taste on the Danube was somewhat oriental, and corpulence was prized higher there than on the Seine; one of the most famous love-ladies of Vienna was known as the elephant girl (*Elefantenweibl*), on account of her enormous dimensions. The streets of Vienna were no place for a delicate, phthisic *dame aux camélias*. There was consumption enough in the home; every third family suffered from it. Women offering their charms for sale had at least to look healthy. Syphilis

* Literally, 'the thousand-gulden weed', or centaury.

and gonorrhoea, which were still thought to be the same disease, were rampant. Between 6,000 and 7,000 women suffering from venereal disease were admitted annually to three public hospitals in Vienna; most of these were prostitutes.

In other respects, too, the statistics of Metternich's Austria show a demoralization which left the France of the Age of Gallantry far behind. In 1811 there was one illegitimate birth in Vienna to every four legitimate; in 1847 the proportion had risen to 1: 2. Between 1821 and 1840 nearly a million foundlings were registered in the Austrian monarchy.[153] In the course of two decades the number of children exposed by their parents had doubled. This may in part be accounted for by the fact that more foundling homes had been established, but it also shows that under Metternich's régime, family life steadily disintegrated.

Joy in Suffering

The French historian and diplomat, Paléologue, has called Metternich a romantic.[154] It is perhaps arguable whether this description is accurate, for whether he was engaged on the conquest of a province, or of a woman, the Austrian Chancellor was always concerned with very real objectives and tangible advantages. He was for extending frontiers, but never strove for the unlimited, which is an accepted characteristic of the romantic. Undoubtedly, however, he contributed more than any other statesman to make romantics of his contemporaries. For many, the romantic was an escape from the political servitude to which young people were subjected, from the forced inactivity imposed on them. In times of war this could be borne, but, in the long period of peace, some substitute was needed.

In so far as eroticism provided this substitute, it took on the protective colouring of suffering. Love was the most beautiful thing on earth, but it brought unhappiness—that was the usual strain. Love always brought suffering with it, and not only if one was unhappy in one's love because the lady of one's heart remained deaf to one's prayers, or because one's own parents, or hers, were against the match, or some other obstacle placed itself in the lover's path. These themes, the leading ones in eighteenth-century romance, now became secondary. Even love fulfilled brought unhappiness; indeed, even more than love unfulfilled.

The talk is always of the pains, the suffering, the torments of love. The founder of this poetry of *Weltschmerz* was Lord Byron; he found imitators from North America to the Caucasus. Long before a tubercular spine condemned Heine to his 'mattress grave', he had fashioned his little songs out of his great pains. Alfred de Musset absolutely revelled in the worship of pain—the memory of sorrow and unhappiness was far more precious than the recollection of past joy:

> The only good that remains to me on earth
> Is sometimes to have wept.

Comte Alfred de Vigny, the panegyrist of military discipline unto death, went so far as to cry: 'I love the majesty of human suffering.' The singers of suffering quoted here were no doleful poets in attics, but elegant young gentlemen who lived thoroughly comfortable lives and helped themselves generously to pleasures of all kind, especially pleasures of sex. But suffering was now part of the profession and of the enjoyment. A poet had to suffer inwardly, or he was no true poet. This masochistic feature attaches to the whole generation that was born round the turn of the century and was setting the tone about 1830. Only the older generation felt the perversity of it. Goethe, now eighty years old, branded the Romantics as 'weak, sickly, and sick', and forged the lapidary formula: 'I call the classic the healthy and the romantic the sick.'[155]

Were the many thousands of readers, male and female, who gulped down the outpoured sorrows of their favourite poets, masochists too? Did they feel the suffering as their own—was it the expression of what they themselves felt but were unable to put into words, or were they just aesthetically interested spectators, or even sadists, gloating over the souls' torments of the poets? The question is not easy to settle. There is no doubt that in the later Romantic Age, i.e. in the 1830s and 1840s, the sadistic leanings of the public were once more very pronounced, and the poets and writers pandered to them. The ballads, plays, and novels dripped with gore; he who did not do murder or let himself be killed for a woman's sake was no true cavalier.

This code of morals applied not only to the past, in which most of the literary moralities were set, but also to the present. Duels with pistols belonged to the *bon ton*. For the rising middle classes they were a proof of self-respect and class pride, and the burgher must not lag behind the aristocrat in the defence of a woman's honour. Many adulterers, and at least as many cuckolded husbands, met their end in duels. The list of victims of these romantic contests includes the two greatest Russian poets, Pushkin and Lermontov.

Sex-appeal of the Spirit

By comparison with the Revolution of 1789 and the era of the Napoleonic wars, the Romantic Age, as, despite its many counter-currents, the period between 1815 and 1848 may be called, was a feminine era. Men were yielding and sentimental, women very often masculine and domineering. Men worshipped women, but it was no longer the situation of the Age of Gallantry, less still of the medieval woman-cult. In those earlier epochs woman occupied her lofty position because man set her in it. He was sexually more desirous, less disciplined, and had to pay for it. What gave woman her social position was no *jus maternum*, but the Right of the Beloved. Man submitted himself voluntarily, because the submission enhanced his sexual enjoyment. Now woman began to make her own way, in her own right, with the help of her intelligence, her energy, her accomplishments in fields which hitherto had been almost exclusively masculine domains.

Undoubtedly she continued to take advantage of the privileges which her sex bestowed on her. When she did not do that—when she tried to make her way by completely a-sexual means, neglecting herself physically in the hope of thereby the better asserting her spirit, or making herself ugly to avoid the reproach of coquetry, she only moved men to laughter. That was what

happened to the female intellectuals in England, the blue-stock-
ings. The women of the Continent knew that education by itself
was not enough. No learning, no literary talent or mental agility
would open any doors to them if they looked like scarecrows.
They could only force the breach in the male citadel if they had
success with the young men, preferably the very young men, over
whom they could exercise a certain maternal authority. Yet they
wanted to be neither their mistresses nor their housekeepers
with the titular rank of wife. They wanted to be equal comrades,
in the bed and at the writing-table.

Among the first to strike out along this path were two German
middle-class wives, both daughters of distinguished scholars.
This, however, was still in the turbulent age of the early Romantic
period, which borrowed some licence from the French Revolution. Caroline Michaelis, daughter of a well-known Orientalist
of Göttingen, having been early widowed, began an intellectual-
erotic picaresque life. In Mainz she got caught up among the
'Clubists', who sympathized with the Revolution. She had an
illegitimate child by a Frenchman; she was arrested and imprisoned by the Prussians as politically and morally suspect, and
hunted from place to place; she was expelled even from her native
Göttingen. At last she landed in the arms of the poet August
Wilhelm Schlegel, married him, and divorced him to marry the
philosopher Schelling, who was twelve years her junior. Her
literary output was small, but historians of literature see in her the
genius which inspired the Jena circle of romantics.

In Jena, Caroline had a rival in Dorothea Veit, daughter of the
philosopher Moses Mendelssohn. Dorothea had run away from her
husband, a rich Frankfurt banker, by whom she had already had
two children, to set up house with the young philologist, Friedrich Schlegel, the brother of August Wilhelm. She was nine
years his senior. They lived together for six years, then married
in Paris. She wrote a mediocre novel and translated Madame de
Staël's *Corinne*; Madame de Staël, meanwhile, was touring round
Europe with August Wilhelm Schlegel. A French-Swiss by birth,
a Swede by marriage, she was a romantic *à la* Rousseau; a *grande*

dame whose pleasure it was to converse in parks with poets and scholars on things of the spirit, with an occasional pastoral interlude. For all the tribulation which she had undergone during the Revolution, and through Napoleon's malice, she had retained a heart both loving and motherly; at forty-five she married a man half her age.

For the outer world, Madame de Staël became the harbinger of the German romantic movement. Germany was for her the land of dreamers. In love, too, everything was lofty and sublime; purity and depth of the spirit justified an attitude more liberal than that prescribed by law and convention in the rest of Europe. Stendhal, who wrote his famous treatise on love twelve years later,[156] saw the national differences in sex-life somewhat more realistically, although he, too, judged them in an entirely Rousseauesque spirit. He contrasted the sexual morality of France, misshapen through convention and vanity, with the simple, natural love-life of Protestant Germany, where young people were allowed to dance and make friends freely, while their fathers chatted to each other, and their mothers passed the time in innocent games. He was even more pleased with the local custom of the Bernese Oberland, where young men and girls tried one another out before marriage, with their parents' knowledge, to see whether they suited each other.

Stendhal recommends pre-nuptial intercourse as the best method of choosing one's mate and preparing oneself for marriage. In a country like France, in which a married woman might do anything and a young girl nothing, that was a courageous piece of advice, and was, in fact, not well received. More friendly was the reaction of the public to a piece published a few years later by a young and at the time still unknown writer named Honoré de Balzac, under the provocative title of *Physiologie du Mariage*. The advice which the youthful Balzac gives his fellowmen, under a mask of worldly wisdom, is not very different from Stendhal's: a man should study female anatomy and physiology before he marries—not, of course, in medical textbooks, but on the living object.

Balzac's breviary on marriage is studded with witty aphorisms which have become almost proverbial, as that 'the woman who lets herself get caught deserves her fate', or 'the destiny of a marriage depends on the first night'. He ends with the consoling conclusion that marriage is a provision for old age, not of the wife but of the husband: 'If men didn't age, I would not wish them wives.' Apart, however, from such flashes of illumination Balzac contributed little, either in this book or in his later works, to the physiological or psychological knowledge of sex-life. His strength lay in other fields.

The Intermediate Sex: George Sand

The laws of love-life are more complex than those of mechanics. The Galileo who worked them out, discovered the most delicate relationships between the physical and the psychic, and described them with the ruthless accuracy of a natural historian, was a woman: Aurore Dudevant, *née* Dupin. This lady wrote some hundred novels under the pseudonym George Sand. Most of them are unreadable today, but a few, especially among her earlier works, contain passages which assure her a lasting place not only in literature but also in the science of sex. She was a romantic, who sought absolute happiness in love, and did not find it. She gave herself to a whole host of men, but none of them satisfied her. She suffered in pleasure and she found no joy in remembering the pains of love. She was no masochist; she really suffered, not on ideological grounds, not out of morality or snobbery, as so many of her male colleagues and lovers did, but from temperament: she stood midway between the sexes.

Physiologically, she was undoubtedly a woman, and a beautiful and charming one at that, with thick black hair and deep dark eyes, finely-chiselled features, and a delicate, well-proportioned body: a southern type, like one of the fisher-girls from Capri of the then fashionable pictures. Her family tree, however, indicated Nordic ancestry. She came of an illustrious stock, of which she was more than a little proud. Her great-great-grandfather was the Elector Augustus the Strong, her great-grandfather the

Marshal Moritz of Saxony, her grandfather an extremely rich French aristocrat, her father a gallant officer in Napoleon's army. The distaff side of the tree was, it is true, less feudal; most of the unions had been unlegalized. Yet it, too, started with a lady of quality, the Brandenburg-Swedish Countess Aurora von König-smark, but the partners gradually grew more and more common. George Sand's mother, if her daughter's not very affectionate description of her is true, was a suburban singer of the lowest class, 'of the degenerate vagabond race of the gypsies of this world'.

This ancestry may be one explanation of the freedom with which George Sand changed her lovers. But then what is known about inherited moral qualities? No gene of original sin has yet been discovered, nor any psychological laws why some children seem, sexually speaking, to be throw-backs to their ancestors, others not. In any case, George Sand did not grow up in any sort of bohemian atmosphere, but in the sheltered surroundings of the family château. She received the usual schooling in a nunnery, showed no symptoms of rebellion, and at eighteen married a wealthy young baron. Everything seemed in perfect order; they had a child, to which Aurore was and remained an affectionate mother.

Then came the first lover, a magistrate's clerk, so shy that he did no more than kiss her in the grotto of Lourdes. The next lover was more enterprising; he was most probably the father of Aurore's second child. The third lover, a writer named Jules Sandeau, persuaded her to break with her dull provincial life at the side of a boring and jealous husband. She packed her trunks and went to Paris. To make a living she began to write, and thereafter to the end of her life wrote twenty pages a day. She took her profession very seriously and despised men who did not do the same. One reason why she worked so hard was in order not to become materially dependent on her lovers. If she condescended to be their mistress, she wished to be it in the original sense of the word: exercising the mastery.

From the men with whom she lived, whether for a few days or a few years, she demanded complete subjection, this applying also to sex matters. This sometimes occasioned difficulties. It looks as though men did not like renouncing the role of leading partner in intimate contacts. So long as the goal is still to be reached, men are as abject as slaves; but once there, they become masterful, brutal, inattentive, interested only in their own pleasure and their own need of repose. They have learned nothing of the lessons Balzac tried to teach them. The anatomy and the physiology of the woman seem not to interest them.

In a novel called *Lélia* George Sand expresses her nightly love-torments more explicitly than any woman had ever done before her. Here is one of these passionate confessions:

> As I lay beside him, I felt a sort of strange and frenzied greed which no embrace could satiate. . . . When he had fallen asleep, satisfied and satiated, I remained motionless and still at his side. I must have passed hours like that, watching him while he slept. He seemed to me so beautiful, this man! . . . I felt a violent temptation to wake him, to take him in my arms and evoke his caresses, which I had not yet been able to taste to the full. I withstood my sufferings' deceptive wish, for I was well aware that he would be unable to soothe it. . . . Sometimes in dreams I felt myself borne away with him. Then I swam on the floods of an indescribable voluptuousness, and casting my limp arms about his neck, I fell on his breast and murmured vague words. But he awoke, and then my happiness was fled. I found man again, man, brutal and voracious as a wild beast, and I fled shuddering. But he followed me, he claimed the price for his broken sleep, and in the lap of a swooning, half-dead woman he drained his savage pleasure to the dregs.[157]

On whom, then, did Lélia, who was none other than George Sand herself, concentrate her sex-impulse? Did the man serve her only as stimulant for a narcissistic self-satisfaction? In her dreams and her wishes did she seek a man other than the one who lay beside her? Probably neither. What she sought but could never achieve was a woman. That she gave herself a male pseudonym, dressed as a man and smoked cigars, were probably at first only tricks to attract attention. Soon, however, she needed no such advertising. Everyone knew that she was a woman; her very first novels had made her famous. That she went on dressing and behaving like a man was a sign that this behaviour really satisfied a masculine element in her. Nor was it only in externals that her masculinity found expression. She had a female friend to whom she wrote the tenderest of love-letters; but this lady, a Parisian actress, wife of a journalist and at the same time mistress of Alfred de Vigny the poet, had clearly no use whatever for Lesbianism.

George Sand's other female friendships, too, seem never to have got beyond the platonic. To the outer world she thus remained a huntress and devourer of men, a wild nymphomaniac; whereas in reality no man brought her satisfaction. In the 1830s, to share the bed of this famous woman was regarded as the crown of intellectual glory. Not everyone achieved it. Heinrich Heine, who long courted her, was rebuffed, perhaps because his seven years' seniority made him too old for her. She needed young flesh to stir her senses. Nearly all her lovers were younger than she. But even youth, wit, and beauty were not enough to pass the test before this capricious Princess Turandot.

Alfred de Musset, at twenty-three, had to put up with being called impotent by her. They went to Venice together, and when he fell ill and was tossing in high fever, she betrayed him with the doctor who attended him. It was thought at one time that a thoroughly pornographic novel entitled *Gamiani, ou deux nuits d'excès*, published anonymously in Brussels soon after, constituted de Musset's revenge on her. That is a mistake; he never sank so low. His answer, a less tasteless one, is to be found in his melancholy poetic cycle *Nuits*. He did not long remain inconsolable; duchesses and beautiful actresses helped him to forget George Sand's 'treachery', but in his poetry he remained ever after the great man of sorrows.

More disastrous, even in the artistic sense, was the end of George Sand's liaison with Chopin. When the romance began she was already in the middle thirties; he was twenty-seven and engaged to a young Polish girl. He resisted for some time, then fell into the lioness's den. She mothered him, but life with this tyrannical woman was for him a prison, from which, at the end, only George Sand's daughter, the adventurous Solange, kept him from fleeing. When at last he freed himself, after ten years' imprisonment, he was a wreck.

Other men of genius were less ready to expose themselves to this woman's caprices. Prosper Mérimée, the author of *Carmen*, known throughout all Paris for a Don Juan, laid siege to George Sand. It was a failure. After he had spent two nights with her, and she had not thawed, he withdrew. He put the blame on her, she on him. 'If he had loved me,' she complained afterwards, 'he would have subjected me; and had I been able to subject myself to a man, I had been saved, for freedom gnaws at me and slays me.'[158] But her first reaction is contempt. She remarks disdainfully, with the frankness with which she always reported her most intimate experiences to friends: 'Last night I had Mérimée; there is not much to him.' Victor Hugo hastened to repeat these words everywhere. Mérimée was made to look foolish; even his lion-tamer's arts broke down on George Sand.

She could not achieve Franz Liszt; he remained faithful to his mistress, the Countess d'Agoult. Marie d'Agoult, granddaughter of the Frankfurt banker Bethmann and mother of Cosima Wagner, was, like so many women of the Romantic Age, considerably older than the man for whom she had left her husband. She too dabbled in writing under a male pseudonym, but she was all woman. George Sand made no concealment of Liszt's attraction for her. She spoke to her fortunate rival in an image which needs no Freud to interpret it; her keenest wish was to lie under a piano on which Franz Liszt was hammering with a force that no instrument could resist. Possibly the Countess's vigilance saved her from another disappointment.

Individual and collective Bride-inspections

Never before had poetry and music exercised so strong a sexual attraction as in the Romantic Age. Verses and chords worked like love potions. They made women languishing and men foolish. The gifted of God who were able to produce such wonders, the creators and, even more, the interpreters—often they were both at once—formed the goal of all desire. The virtuosos were the kings of the age. If a society lady lost her heart to a great pianist, her husband had as little right to sulk as in the old days when a crowned head took the wife of one of his subjects for his mistress.

The circle in which this free marriage of art and sex was tolerated and appreciated was, however, limited. It would be wrong to generalize. In *petit bourgeois* circles parents were still enraged if a daughter of theirs slid down into the *vie de bohème* because a poet had taken her for his muse, or a painter for his model. And between the small upper caste and the masses of little men there still stood, firm in principle and stout in self-confidence, the real bourgeoisie, which had grown stronger everywhere since the July Revolution of 1830 in France. Money had carried it to political power, or where, as in Austria and Prussia, the achievement still lay in the future, to the hope of it. This already gave money a brighter lustre. It was therefore no mere hucksters' morality when money and property were held holy. Since the old caste privileges had been undermined, money had become the chief standard.

The new scale of values also influenced family life. The family was now, even more than before, a property institution. This made it all the more necessary to look carefully who one's son married, who came courting one's daughter, what the prospective in-laws were like. The dowry became the decisive factor. It was no longer a contribution towards the setting-up of a new establishment, but a mark of social distinction. The man able to give his daughter a princely dowry, or the son-in-law receiving it, had a social status. Never had there been so much talk of marriages for money as in the Romantic Age.

The commercialization of marriage did not mean, however, that daughters were simply bartered, without their knowledge or consent; the time in which that had been possible was gone for good. Parents themselves liked the choice of the right son-in-law to take place in a social setting. A suitor had, of course, to approach the future father-in-law for his daughter's hand, but a sensible father contented himself with a right of veto. The young people were allowed, and expected, to make their own choice within the social limits set by the money element.

In small towns, or in the country, where the choice was limited, individual bride-inspection long remained usual. The would-be bridegroom was taken to the home of the girls' parents by relatives, common acquaintances, or not infrequently by a professional marriage broker, with the undisguised purpose of preparing the way for the betrothal and, if possible, concluding it on the spot. Only after he had been thoroughly inspected and cross-examined by the girl's parents and other experts from the family was he presented to his future bride. It would be as fitting to speak of a bridegroom-inspection, as a bride-inspection.

Increasingly, however, this form of individual inspection—which has been depicted, with all its comic sides and frequent tragic consequences, in innumerable nineteenth-century novels and plays—gave way to a sort of collective inspection. Daughters of marriageable age were taken by their parents or, at least, under their mothers' supervision, to wherever the most suitable candidates for marriage might be found. The best place for rich people was at a spa. The great fashionable spa in the Romantic Age was Baden-Baden. People journeyed thither even from Paris in search of a good match. The middle classes, however, could not afford the luxury of so expensive a journey without the certainty of success. The most important marriage-mart for the daughter of not very well-to-do parents was still the ball.

Balls of all kinds, private, arranged by clubs and associations, or, for a special occasion, even public, provided the antechamber to marriage in the larger towns. Ball-dresses with all coquetry's adjuncts, especially artistic fans, programmes in which dancers put down their names in advance for a particular number, dancing lessons—for many new dances came in in this period—played an enormous part in the social life of this age. In Berlin, public balls were held weekly in the Court opera-house and Court theatre.[159] To read contemporary reports is to get the impression that a real epidemic of dancing had broken out in Europe, like that which followed 1918. It was, however, not the same thing. The ball-fever of the 1820s, 1830s and 1840s was no spontaneous erotic release after manless years of war; it had a very rational background. It was at the ball that one made the acquaintance of one's future partner in wedlock. This end also justified the extraordinary expense in which even thrifty bourgeois indulged when they took their daughters to the ball.

A Scandalous Dance: the Waltz

The new dances now coming into fashion differed from the older ones chiefly in being far more erotic. Sexually the most exciting was the waltz. Dancing and sex always go together, but in varying proportions. Bacchantic dances had been banned in the West, in good society, since the victory of Christianity. The Court dances of the seventeenth and eighteenth centuries, precisely the time when sex was allowed so much free play in other directions, were particularly restrained. The cavalier only offered his lady his hand or his arm; any other contact was regarded as improper. Only peasants and their wenches grasped one another by the shoulder or the waist; even the plebs of the cities eschewed such coarse doings.

It was only at the end of the eighteenth century that quick dancing came in at public balls, in which the gentleman seized his partner by the waist and dashed round the room with her at frantic speed. The waltz itself—the so-called two-step waltz—was originally one of these quick dances, two steps followed by a hop or a turn—a *Drahrer* (spin)—as the Viennese used to say.[160] It was, however, a considerable time before the 'whirl' turned into an elegant rotation, for it was not so easy to turn smoothly in 3/4 time, especially since the right music had still to be written. It was only after Weber had found the rhythm in his *Invitation to the Waltz* (1819) and Josef Lanner and Johann Strauss, father of the 'Waltz King', had composed their waltzes, that dancing acquired its real sway.

It was something new, not only in musical and choreographical respects but, above all, in its erotic effect. The couples no longer raced and hopped, as in the gallop or the polka. The gentleman's arm enfolded his partner's waist, his hand rested on her shoulder, as in a tender *tête à tête*. In the quick dances, the physical contact had been a clutching, a sort of grapple to save oneself from losing one's balance and falling. Now it became an embrace. The partners could be closely enfolded for minutes at a time, look into each other's eyes and exchange endearments, without having to watch for the next figure, as in a quadrille, and give up one's partner to one's neighbour. In the waltz a couple was really one. The mothers sitting against the wall were radiant at seeing their daughters thus happily united with a young man who might be her betrothed the next morning.

Naturally, there were protests against this new, public form of eroticism. It was not only the puritans who objected to the dance of vice from the Danube which was over-running Europe. Lord Byron, himself scarcely a pattern of virtue, raised his voice in warning against this sort of promiscuity. In general, the English dandies were no friends of dancing, which they regarded as a plebeian kind of sport. But even in Paris the opposition was strong. Alfred de Musset, who, his tempestuous youth over, had grown into an aristocratic aesthete, warned the young girls of society not to lend themselves to such exhibitionist pleasures and allow themselves to be publicly caressed by men. Yet even the idol of the Romantic drawing-rooms was powerless against the might of sex, especially since, this time, a large proportion of the parents were in league with the young people. The waltz remained in fashion for a hundred years.

A Forerunner of Kinsey

The new system of making a man's acquaintance obviously had its dangers, however careful parents might be. What happens when young people, inflamed by the dance, go too far, make secret rendezvous, and perhaps even enter into sexual relationships, possibly with disastrous results for the girl? The bourgeoisie still made a great point of a girl's preserving her virginity till marriage. How far this was achieved it is hard to guess, since a husband who discovered on the bridal night that he was not the first, now had in practice no basis for contesting the marriage. The parents' great anxiety was also not that their daughters should not lose their virginity prematurely, but that they should not produce illegitimate children; for in that case their prospects of marriage, and the honour of their families, were gone. Hebbel's *Maria Magdalena* (1843) depicts this conflict in a *petit bourgeois* family; but the views of the well-to-do middle classes were no different.

The ban on pre-nuptial sexual intercourse for women did not, however, tend to ensure the purity of marriage; rather it proved detrimental to monogamy. For curiosity, which is not the least powerful cause of polygamy, was thus transferred to married life. Women who had had experiences with other men before marriage, and knew that there was no great difference between them, accepted strict monogamy after marriage more easily than those for whom a new man had the thrill of a fresh experience. This may be one of the reasons why adultery by wives was so frequent in France, precisely where, up to the beginning of the present century, girls of middle-class families were kept under very strict sexual discipline before marriage, and nearly always educated in nunneries or boarding-schools.

The fact that ever since the Middle Ages female infidelity has been a favourite theme of French literature has given rise to an exaggerated impression that adultery is a French speciality. Divorce statistics, police reports, and the observations of sociologists and investigators of sexual habits show just the opposite picture. In a German document of the Biedermeyer period, the author, who was a member of several learned societies, appears as a forerunner of Kinsey. In the 1840s he conducted a private investigation into a hundred marriages, and came to the conclusion that of the hundred, forty-eight were unhappy, thirty-six indifferent—that is, immoral, in spite of which the partners lived together peacefully—only fifteen happy and one completely virtuous. Another classification of the same hundred marriages counted fifty-one as 'loose and dissolute' and fourteen as 'purposefully immoral'. In thirty of the unhappy marriages the husband was at fault, in twelve the wife. In fifteen marriages professional vice and procuration occurred.[161]

We cannot guarantee the exactitude of these astonishing figures. The compilation of precise statistics on adultery is not easy, even today, and must have been far harder then. But even if the percentages of moral, immoral, and totally corrupt marriages are not quite correct, and even if the number of cases observed is too small for safe generalization, this inquiry nevertheless shows that adultery was no rarity even in Germany, among either wives or husbands. The chief difference, as compared with France, seems to have been that in Germany marriages which had become intolerable were dissolved, and the cloak of charity drawn over others. Divorce was easiest in Prussia, where the law recognized insuperable aversion as a ground for divorce, and permitted the dissolution of a marriage when both parties consented. The pious King Frederick William IV, whose own marriage was childless, tried to tighten up the law of divorce, but without success.

That austere monarch was even more desirous of weaning his subjects from the temptations of houses of ill-fame. He may have been influenced by personal experiences; in any case, he died of creeping paralysis, i.e. of the consequences of syphilis. His efforts to improve his subjects' morals led to the abolition of brothels in Berlin in 1844. There had been about a hundred such houses in Berlin in 1780, under Frederick the Great, each with seven or eight girls;[162] a considerable number for a city with a population of barely 150,000. Under Frederick William III, however, the police had repeatedly taken action, and the number had fallen sharply. When the complete ban was enacted, there were only twenty-six brothels left, but some of them large establishments; the number of registered brothel prostitutes was 240.

The abolition had the usual results—the same as were observed when the brothels were shut down in France in 1946: an increase of near-brothels and of street prostitution. In this last field, especially, Berlin led all European capitals for several decades.

15

PRUDERY AND DEMI-MONDE

THE revolution of 1848 made a clean sweep of the old sinners. In Vienna, Metternich and the Chief of Police, Sedlnitzky, had to take to hurried flight before the popular wrath. The pretty ladies who had formerly been their helpers were so intimidated that some of them could think of nothing better than to dress up in men's clothes and volunteer for service with the Civic Guard. In Munich, Ludwig I paid for his love for the 'Spanish' dancer, Lola Montez (really she was Scotch) with his throne. Lola Montez turned suffragette.

For some time a wind of puritanism blew across Europe. It came, however, not from the barricades, but from the country which had been spared the revolution—Britain. In 1837 an eighteen-year-old princess had mounted the British throne. Many good patriots were anxious. What was going to happen? Would Britain again have a Virgin Queen who played with men and gave the country no heir to the throne? Or one like Queen Anne, who erred in the opposite way? The example of the women who were at the time to be on the throne of other countries was not encouraging. Marie-Louise, Duchess of Parma, although a daughter of the Emperor of Austria and once Napoleon's wife, had twice contracted morganatic alliances with her Court chamberlains, besides having a liaison with a French man of letters, Jules Lecomte, who had had to leave France in a hurry because he had paid a courtesan with a worthless cheque. Marie Christine, the Queen Regent of Spain, had gone even farther: she had married a soldier of her bodyguard and created him Duke of Rianzares.

These fears, however, were soon allayed. Things like that

didn't happen in Britain. Young Queen Victoria proved a model of virtue, diligence, and statesmanship. At twenty she sent for her cousin Albert, a Coburg prince of the same age as herself, made him a declaration of love, and formally sought his hand, as a queen's prerogative requires. It was a model marriage. Victoria presented her husband with nine children in quick succession. When the Prince Consort died, hardly forty years old, she put on widow's weeds, never to doff them again.

This loyalty, stronger than death, worked wonders in itself. As recently as 1825 a king of England had divorced his wife by methods which were universally regarded as scandalous. Under Victoria, divorce could not be mentioned at Court. Divorced husbands or wives were not admitted to Buckingham Palace. Even foreign Powers had to submit to this rule: no diplomat who had been divorced was accredited to the Court of St. James's. This unwritten law has remained generally valid to this day.

England is no country of abrupt upheavals. The moral transformation of the Victorian Age itself took place slowly, imperceptibly, without the invocation of draconian laws. Sex was not forcibly stuck into a strait-jacket, but carefully put in plaster, like the victim of an accident who must not be hurt. Only occasionally was the machinery of the law set in motion to lead the people into the paths of virtue. The example of the Court, the practice of treating vice as 'unmentionable', the social boycott of outsiders, were stronger weapons. If everyone knew what was 'shocking', what offended the sense of propriety of his fellow-men, he would somehow continue to be virtuous himself. Moral conformity needs no orders from above; it rests on recognition.

No one, for that matter, even in Victorian England, asked people to mortify their flesh and to live like monks. They had opportunities enough to exercise their vitality. The arena of politics stood open to them, no one interfered with their business operations, they could spend their money as foolishly as they liked. Half the world was English, English travellers were highly esteemed everywhere, and, if one felt like a little diversion, Paris was across the way. All this was calculated to console a sensible man for having to put up with a few limitations at home. Even there, no one asked what went on within the four walls. Certain things were not to be talked about; that was really all that was asked.

The Blacksmith of Gretna Green

The sex-questions which were still allowed as subjects of public discussion, and which occasionally occupied the attention of Parliament, were mostly of a touching innocence: as, for example, the stories of Gretna Green,[163] on the Scottish border, where rich young Englishmen had contracted runaway marriages ever since the Union. The famous blacksmith of Gretna Green, round whom a whole legend has clustered, was not a blacksmith at all, but a tobacconist who was also a Justice of the Peace, and therefore entitled to solemnize marriages. At other times fishermen and weavers performed the same duty. Since Scottish justices were empowered to issue marriage certificates which were also recognized in England, a marriage-mill for hurried weddings grew up in Gretna Green, like the Mexican divorce-mills which later served American couples. The businesslike registrars also kept a 'wedding chamber', in which the newly-married couples could taste the first pleasures of love.

Basically, this was an unexceptionable institution, even from the point of view of official morals, since it kept young people who were able to afford the journey to Gretna Green from the sin of extra-marital intercourse. The Victorians, however, did not favour romance. Even though Church marriage was not obligatory, a marriage should take place in due form, in the presence of the parents, or at least with their consent. Moreover, cases of bigamy occasionally occurred at Gretna Green. Deceivers took advantage of the institution, as also did couples who never meant to marry at all and only used the wedding chamber as a rendezvous.

About the middle of the nineteenth century, storm clouds gathered around this rustic shrine of love. The annals do not record how many couples spent a bridal night there, but the number was in any case large enough to make the local clergy anxious. A noble lord in London made himself their mouthpiece, and called on the peers of England to make war on this hotbed of sin. He declared that the bigamy, seduction and begetting of bastards fostered in the place was beyond description. The House of Commons, on the other hand, was more interested in the financial aspect. One member divided the Gretna Green marriages into two categories: if the bride had money the man regarded the marriage as valid; if she proved to be poor, he tried to contest it. Even the most moderate moralists saw the point of this, and Parliament decided that in future at least one of the candidates for marriage must have resided in Scotland for twenty-one days before the marriage could take place.

This was a hard blow for the Gretna Green marriage-mill, but not a fatal one. Impatient couples continued to cross the Scottish border, in the hope of achieving their hearts' desire there sooner than in England. Many went away disappointed when they heard that there were no more valid marriage certificates to be had; others found that the historic wedding chamber nevertheless had its own romantic charms, even without the certificate.

Shakespeare Expurgated

More momentous than the attack on Gretna Green was the witch-hunt for obscene literature. As usual in such cases, the guardians of virtue began by turning on real filth without any literary value. The Lord Chancellor repudiated any desire to attack literary freedom. A book like Dumas *fils' La Dame aux Camélias*, descriptive of the life of a Paris cocotte, which was all the rage at the time, would, of course, not be touched. After receiving these assurances, Parliament gave its consent in 1857 to an apparently harmless law which was, however, later invoked to justify the arrest of a bookseller who had sold Zola's *La Terre*, while it was on the strength of the same law that Joyce's *Ulysses* was banned eighty years later.[164]

The chief concern of the authorities was to see that no obscene literature was smuggled into England. The hunt was even extended to manuscripts. A poet who had written a love-poem might see it pulled out of his luggage and confiscated. There was no appeal against the moral judgment of the customs officials.

Soon, of course, virtuous men turned to the examination of the whole corpus of classical literature to see whether it contained anything offensive to the modesty of modern readers, male or female. They reaped an abundant harvest. The Bible turned out to be a most dangerous book to fall into the hands of anybody of unchaste mind; and the great English poets, too, were really corrupters of morals. Shakespeare, considered to be worst of all, was expurgated in editions which omitted passages known by heart to every educated Englishman. *Robinson Crusoe* was subjected to the same treatment. As always happens when the police take literature under their wing too intently, pure pornography flourished secretly in Victorian England. Edward Sellon, himself a pornographic writer of the first order, issued, under the pseudonym of Pisanus Fraxi, a comprehensive catalogue of erotic literature [165] which remained a standard work in England until it was superseded, long after, by Reade's even fuller catalogue.[166]

A third matter in which moral legislation intervened with only moderate effect, was the fight against prostitution. In this regard, London possessed an old tradition, for in the seventeenth century it had housed the biggest love-market in Europe until Paris, and later Vienna, again took the lead. At the beginning of Queen Victoria's reign police statistics gave only 7,000 prostitutes in London, a moderate number for a city with a population of 2,000,000. Unofficial estimates, it is true, put the figure much higher and the Chief of Police himself admitted the existence of 933 brothels and 848 houses of questionable reputation, which suggests that his own figure for prostitutes was too low, for London always had a large number of street-walkers.

It was the street-prostitutes, above all, who were the victims of the official 'campaign'. Wanton doings behind closed doors were sinful, but at least did not offend the eyes of the virtuous. Thus brothels were encouraged, while no one troubled greatly what happened to the prostitutes in them or how they got there. Up to the 1880s no penalty attached to inducement to prostitution, while prostitution itself was punishable as a cause of public scandal.

Ladies have no Legs

Any enactments look trivial, however, beside the prudery which enforced itself with no outer compulsion, simply through social pressure. Unlike the other periods in which sex was taboo, Victorian England was not unerotic: it had acquired a sort of love romanticism of its day, which was, indeed, very different from that of the Romantic Age. Its love-romances had to be strictly monogamous, and centred exclusively on one point: the wedding. The decent betrothal kiss stood for all permissible sex-relationships. After that there came the dressmakers sewing the bridal dress and the dressed-up pages carrying the train.

The convention of ignoring or covering up everything connected with sex led to the strangest absurdities, even in dress. In the Romantic Age women in Britain, as everywhere else, wore long lace pantalettes fastened coquettishly over the ankles; a glimpse of them going upstairs, or in the course of a curtsy, created no embarrassment. In the Victorian Age ladies had no legs. Anything which might suggest that women possessed nether limbs, even for the purpose of walking, was regarded as objectionable. Even the thought of the anatomy of the lower half of a woman's body was 'shocking'. Below the waist there existed nothing but a skirt, or rather a whole array of skirts so starched that they could stand up against the strongest wind.

This did not, however, solve the most delicate problem of dress. Even if the legs were covered by a dozen petticoats, that still left unprotected that part of the body for which the whole system of fortification was constructed. So there was nothing for it but to allow drawers reaching down over the thighs. But men must not know that they wore such things. The illustrated advertisements always represented this underwear as though it had no opening and was cut out of one piece. The 'woman with no abdomen' was no jest of the circus tent; it represented the prudes' ideal.

Prudery, however, had also its serious side, and the women themselves were the sufferers from it. It was not decent for a respectable married woman, still less a young girl, to let a doctor inspect and auscultate her whole body, as a thorough examination often required. Doctors helped themselves by putting up dummies in their consulting rooms, on which the patients showed where they felt pain. The doctor was then allowed to touch the place through the underclothing, or through a cloth—even that, of course, only in the presence of the patient's husband or mother. It was as compromising for a woman to go unaccompanied to the doctor as for her to visit the rooms of a strange man.

Another consequence of prudery was the lack of sexual hygiene. In the Victorian age British industry supplied the whole civilized world with hygienic appliances. The first modern water-closets, baths and showers came from England and Scotland, but bidets— a French invention dating from the age of the Pompadour—were unknown in Great Britain. Regular washing of the genitals might induce impure thoughts in a girl and lead to masturbation, if to nothing worse. That alone was enough to ban it from any Victorian home.

In boys and youths, however, nature would have her way, however hard parents tried to distract their minds from the sphere of sex. Recent investigations have shown that 85 per cent. of all men have practised masturbation in childhood or youth. It was certainly not otherwise in earlier times. The phenomenon had been known of old, and from the end of the eighteenth century onward doctors and teachers occupied themselves with it very seriously. Most of them regarded it as a pathological habit, to be attacked by drastic methods. In Victorian England industry interested itself in the problem and produced its own answers. Cages were manufactured which were fitted over a boy's genitals at night and carefully locked; some, for better protection, had spikes sticking out of them.

Erotomania on the Imperial Throne

The excesses of prudery only awakened derision on the Continent, but the wind of exaggerated morality which blew from Britain left its traces on the other side of the Channel. Britain was the world's leading great Power, and power is always widely taken as a model. British views on morality and sex-habits might be thought exaggerated, but they were regarded as genteel: anyone who wanted to pass for a gentleman had therefore to adapt himself to them.

French society set the more store on doing as Britain did, since a man had ascended the French throne for whom it was a matter of urgent necessity to legitimize himself as a true gentleman. Napoleon III was at first regarded at the other Courts as a mere adventurer, and his early private life inspired as little confidence as his record of political conspiracy. That he had remained a bachelor till over forty was in any case no good sign in a man who aspired to the throne of France. He was reputed to be as indiscriminate and shameless a woman-hunter as his great-uncle had been. In his years of exile and even in the fortress of Ham he had had liaisons with women of the people and was father of a number of illegitimate children.

Everyone knew, moreover, that a pretty English actress, Miss Henriette Howard (whose real name was Elizabeth Anne Harryet) had been his mistress in London, had followed him to Paris, and had established herself in the palace of Saint-Cloud as a new Madame de Pompadour in the years when he still called himself President of the Republic. It was she who had supported Prince Louis Napoleon, out of her own purse, during the last years before his rise to power, and had financed Bonapartist propaganda. The sums expended by her on the Pretender to the French throne were immense: reports estimated it at £2,000,000 sterling. The money could not possibly have come from the salary drawn by Miss Howard in the course of her brief stage career at the Haymarket Theatre, London. According to one version, an earlier lover, a rich Englishman, had made her his sole heiress—

such things did happen in Victorian England. According to another, several previous patrons had contributed to her wealth. The latest investigations indicate that most of it came from a rich Guards officer named Francis Mountjoy Martin, by whom she had had a child.[167]

A lady with so chequered a past seemed even less suitable than Joséphine de Beauharnais to become Empress of France. Napoleon III saw that, and Miss Howard was honourably dismissed in a manner befitting the venerable royal tradition. She recovered her expenses, with compound interest, and got also a large estate, a castle, and what she probably valued even more, the title of Comtesse de Beauregard. Her apartments were searched in her absence and all letters and papers connected with her august lover vanished. Napoleon III did not, however, part from her without tears and he entrusted to his ex-mistress the charge of the children whom he had had by another lover, Eléonore Vergeot.[168] After some resistance, Miss Howard perforce accepted her destiny, and the Emperor was able to enter on an immaculate married life, such as the nation expected from its ruler, unsullied by traces of his past.

The new Emperor's confidants had already picked out a whole collection of agreeable princesses for him. They included, indeed, no daughters of ruling princes, but a niece of Queen Victoria, a Swedish princess and a Hohenzollern figured on the list which had been got together in Paris. But the Dictator, who was now forty-five years old, disappointed the hopes of the unsolicited marriage brokers. He had already made his choice: he meant to marry a Spanish girl, or, more precisely, a Parisian girl from Granada, with whom he had already been carrying on a flirtation for some years—Eugénie de Montijo. The Tuileries was aghast. What would the other Courts say if the French Emperor began his reign with such a *mésalliance*? It was true that Mademoiselle de Montijo came of a family of grandees of Spain and that her sister had married the Duke of Alba; nevertheless, she had no royal blood in her veins.

Little was known of the earlier life of the lady to whom

Napoleon had given his heart, but rumour was not very reassuring. She was already twenty-seven years of age and had acquired more experience of male society than was fitting for a young princess. For years her mother had been dragging her round the fashionable watering places of Europe in search of a good match. Madame de Montijo was the daughter of an Irish wine-merchant who had gone bankrupt in Malaga. She appears to have laid no excessive stress on marital fidelity, and had, like many great ladies of the day, sought ready consolation in the company of famous writers: Stendhal was one of her intimate friends, Mérimée had been her lover and remained her adviser. Was there not a danger, if Napoleon carried out his purpose, that Eugénie might take after her mother and the French Court become a hotbed of continuous scandal? Was France to be ruled again by a Spaniard of the type of Madame Tallien?

Napoleon's relatives and all his ministers and advisers were against the marriage. The Foreign Minister tendered his resignation in protest against it; the moralist Prévost-Paradol, afterwards to become Imperial Ambassador, declared that the marriage was 'the fantasy of an erotomaniac'. It is still the general opinion today that, having failed to persuade the beautiful Spaniard to become his mistress, Napoleon had been obliged to marry her as the only means of achieving his purpose. There is, however, no proof that Napoleon had really only wanted Eugénie de Montijo as his mistress, or that he could not have had her in that capacity. It is certain that, on her mother's instigation, Eugénie went all out for marriage. She behaved as coquettishly as a flapper and left her admirer sexually unsatisfied; but, as she herself later admitted,[169] she had not been at all averse from romantic adventures in her youth, and women less passionate and even more pious than she had bowed to the insistence of ruling princes. Even in the nineteenth century the position of *maîtresse-en-titre* of the ruler of a great country was regarded as a desirable one.

In this case, however, Napoleon was clearly not acting as an erotomaniac, but as a power monomaniac—a dictator who refuses in the field of sex, as in any other, to submit to the will of his entourage or to tradition. When Napoleon I divorced Joséphine to marry the daughter of the Emperor of Austria, he had still been submitting himself to the old dynastic rules. Napoleon III rejected such compulsion, not because he was to a certain extent already the heir of a dynasty, with no need to marry his way up, but because he refused to recognize the principle. He wanted to found a new form of personal dictatorship, which should embrace also the sphere of sex. An absolute monarch is entitled not only to sleep with whom he likes, but also to marry the wife of his choice. In a speech from the throne to the chief dignitaries of France on 22 January 1853, Napoleon expounded this new, subversive sex-doctrine with complete unambiguity:

The marriage which I am contracting is not in accordance with the old political tradition. That is precisely its advantage. If a man has been raised to the level of the old dynasties, in the face of the new Europe, by virtue of a new principle, he does not make himself acceptable by making his quarterings older and by trying at all costs to make his way into the family of kings. His right course is rather to be constantly mindful of his origin and openly, before all Europe, to accept the title of *parvenu*, a noble title when the suffrage of a great people has conferred it. . . . I shall therefore say to France: 'I have preferred a woman whom I love and honour to an unknown woman, to marry whom would have brought its advantages, but also have involved sacrifices.'

The effect of this speech in Paris was decisive; after it, no one dared oppose the Emperor's marriage. The other Courts smiled at these high-faluting phrases and at the democratic pretexts with which the tyrant of France strove to justify his step, but even the old dynasties bowed before the *fait accompli*; Eugénie was respectfully acknowledged as the rightful Empress, and she played her new part better than her opponents had expected. Even she herself was surprised. On the day after the coronation in Notre Dame she wrote to her sister: 'Since yesterday I have been addressed as "Your Majesty". I feel as if we were playing in a comedy.' Soon, however, she learnt how to be a true Empress. Her Court was brilliant, and the fêtes in the Tuileries and Saint-Cloud as sumptuous as those of Louis XIV's Versailles. At the frequent fancy-dress balls the Empress liked to appear dressed as the maiden Diana, but she no longer went hunting after men, nor did she allow herself to be hunted. She was a model wife and mother. Although she never really loved her elderly husband and knew all about his everlasting infidelities, she remained constantly loyal to him and also required the ladies of her Court to be modest and virtuous.

Sexual Diplomacy

If there were, nevertheless, abundant sexual affairs at the French Imperial Court, the fault was entirely her husband's. Napoleon III remained an incorrigible erotomaniac even after marriage, and to an advanced age. Foreign Courts knew this weakness of the Emperor's and took advantage of it. If a bait was dangled before him, he would snap at it and then agree to much that he would otherwise have refused to concede.

The most uninhibited practitioner of this art was Comte Cavour, Minister-President of Savoy. Cavour was working for the unification of Italy and rejected no means which might lead to this great goal. One stage on the way was the expulsion of the Austrians from Lombardy and Venetia, and this could not be done without France's help, which really meant Napoleon's favour. In order to win the Emperor for the cause of Italy, Cavour sent his own beautiful nineteen-year-old niece, the Countess Castiglione, to Paris, with precise instructions to ensnare Napoleon. How she did this was her affair; she was free to choose whatever means she thought most appropriate.

The young countess understood. There was only one means, and she adopted it promptly. The Emperor, then fifty years old, succumbed to the young Italian like any student. This was only the first act of the delicate mission, and the countess did not possess the diplomatic skill of her uncle. She went to work too directly, too indiscreetly. She appeared at the Tuileries in a cloak of white silk embroidered with innumerable red hearts, and behaved to Napoleon, in the Empress's presence, so imprudently that even the quiet and patient Eugénie lost her temper. The countess's beauty and the extravagance of her *toilette* caused a general sensation, and her behaviour evoked a scandal. She angled for presents, she even took money from Napoleon as the price of her body, but when she came to speak of the real object of her mission he hardly listened to her.

Nevertheless, sex-diplomacy paid Italy. The rendezvous between the Emperor and the beauty queen in the discreet Passy villa at least helped to neutralize the influence of the Empress, which was thrown into the other scale. The unification of Italy would inevitably reduce the influence of Rome, and the pious Spaniard was strongly against this. Wavering between rival nations and rival women's hearts, Napoleon decided in favour of the Italian solution, which brought him not only some delicious hours of love, but also two provinces.

A Storm on the Boulevards

When she intervened in high politics, Eugénie seldom had a lucky hand, and this made her less popular. Her moral influence, however, was considerable, stronger in many circles than that of the Emperor. The atmosphere created by her example was not very different from that of the Court in London. Prudery had its triumphs even in Paris. When Napoleon bought Ingres' late work *The Turkish Bath*, Eugénie insisted that this 'vicious' painting should be sent back to the artist. Of the younger generation, only a few outsiders still dared to represent the female form nude and undisguised. Courbet, the revolutionary, for example, depicted the embrace of two Lesbians; but Courbet, who was destined later, after Sedan, to overthrow the column of Napoleon on the Place Vendôme, was considered a good-for-nothing and shunned in official circles. None of his pictures was allowed into the Paris World Exhibition of 1855.

Edouard Manet was put in the same rogues' gallery. He had been bold enough to send in for the Salon a picture then entitled *Le Bain* (changed afterwards to *Le Déjeuner sur l'herbe*) which showed a naked woman sitting with two fully-dressed men, not disguised as mythology but completely realistic. This 'disgusting piece of pornography' had, of course, been rejected. But then something unexpected happened: the Emperor, who took an interest in anything that was modern, intervened in Manet's favour and ordered the picture to be exhibited outside the Salon, with other paintings of the new school. Eugénie's party grumbled. Their taste in painting was Franz Winterhalter's chocolate-box portraits of the ladies of the Court.

Even chillier was the wind of sanctimony that blew on sculpture. Fig-leaves no longer sufficed; gods and heroes had to be dressed. Muses in flowing robes and goddesses of wisdom and agriculture took precedence of Venus and Adonis, irrespective of aesthetic values. The favourite models for the decoration of house-façades were the chastely-clad Caryatides from the Erechtheion at Athens. Sculptors reluctant to submit to the new dress-regulations preferred to model animals, in which every anatomical detail could be shown. There was an enormous demand for these figures. Public squares and parks over which laughing Tritons and naked Naiades had formerly lorded it were now filled with wild boars, tigers and lions in bronze.

When Jean-Baptiste Carpeaux, the leading sculptor of the Second Empire, produced for the front of the new Paris Opéra a group symbolizing the dance and consisting of naked female dancers in dionysiac ecstasy, an organized storm of indignation broke out. Naked women on the boulevard! It would be scandalous, even if they were of marble. As Carpeaux and Garnier, the architect of the Opéra, who had commissioned him, did not at once give way, they were taught their lesson by an act of vandalism. One morning the group was found spattered with ink from top to bottom. To save it from further attacks, its defenders proposed to set it up inside the opera house, in the foyer of the ballet; but this suggestion, too, evoked howls of protest. The ballerinas were no vestal virgins, but such a defamation of the art of the dance offended their professional and personal honour. Dancers were required to wear the *tutu* (a voluminous gauze skirt), tights, and a corset which left little of their own form visible.

The dignified and substantial holders of season-tickets who commonly saw rather more of the *corps de ballet* in the foyer than did the ordinary public, took the side of these sensitive young ladies who were shocked by the suggestion of naked dancers— even stone ones—in their theatre. The Directors of the Imperial Opéra were in a quandary. Carpeaux's *La Danse* was allowed to remain provisionally at the front of the building. The temporary solution, however, proved permanent. The war of 1870 intervened, work on the opera-house was suspended and, meanwhile, views on the nude in art changed. So the much-abused monument to the dance still stands today in the Place de l'Opéra, and no evidence is forthcoming that it has corrupted Parisian morals.

When prudery was so widespread in the heart of Paris, it will be understood that the provinces were more sensitive still. For centuries French literature had written freely on the subject of adultery. When, however, Flaubert in his *Madame Bovary* drew the portrait of a provincial woman who tried to free herself from the strait-jacket of a tedious married life, and ruined herself in the process, the public prosecutor stepped in and had Flaubert prosecuted for indecency. Flaubert, who was personally the most respectable of bourgeois, could count himself lucky to escape with a severe censure. Baudelaire, the most important lyric poet of the age, was fined for his *Fleurs du Mal*, and for nearly a century, until the courts took a new decision in 1949, the poems could only be published in an expurgated edition. Less well-known authors, like Xavier de Montépin and the youthful Catulle Mendès, expiated their literary sins with prison sentences.

Two Kinds of Demi-monde

People were slightly more tolerant towards the theatre, but even then only provided that no unchaste word was uttered and that female sinners met their due doom. The master of the modern morality play was Alexandre Dumas, son of the less straightlaced author of *The Three Musketeers* and *The Count of Monte*

Cristo. Outside France, even the younger Dumas was not taken very seriously, but in his homeland he was regarded as an apostle of morals of puritanical severity,[170] who wrote not in order to tickle his public with lubricious themes and epigrammatic *bonmots* but to strengthen family life and emancipate the institution of marriage from the bonds of money and the errors of the Romantic Movement. His first and most lasting success, *La Dame aux Camélias*, published as a novel in 1848, adapted for the stage in 1852, and turned into opera by Verdi in 1853 as *La Traviata*, is a sentimental rehash of the life of the Paris courtesan, Marie Duplessis, who had died shortly before, not of nobility and a broken heart but, like many of her colleagues, of tuberculosis. In his later works Dumas forsook romantic melodrama and presented, though not without considerable distortion, a picture of Parisian society with its prudery, its hypocrisy, its double life, and all the gradations and intermediate phases between wedlock and venal love.

Not all women are either faithful wives or professional prostitutes. Between these two poles there lies a congested area for which, in 1855, Dumas invented the word *demi-monde*. *Demi-monde*—originally the title of one of his plays—thus meant to him something different from the world's later usage of the term. Its citizens were not the 'swarm of courtesans', but only that category of women who are morally superior to prostitutes and yet not honest wives. People do not fall at once out of the heaven of wedded virtue into the hell of sexual damnation. Many step down gradually, many rise again when they have found the right man, and many remain all their lives in this ambiguous realm.

The *demi-mondaine* in the sense in which Dumas used the word is the sex-haunted woman who degrades herself; the young girl of good family who goes wrong after a first slip and becomes estranged from her family; and, above all, the dissatisfied wife who runs away from her husband to her lover. Even if she acts out of true passion, without thought of material gain, she has blotted her record. Society is stronger than the individual, and the woman who offends against the moral laws of society ends by damaging herself. The Romantic writers failed to realize this, and Dumas, the anti-Romantic, tried to bring this simple truth home again to his contemporaries.

His moral was, at bottom, good Victorianism. A discreet lapse from marital loyalty may be overlooked, but defiance of the institution of marriage, never! The *demi-monde*, Dumas explains in the foreword to the bitter comedy which bears this title, begins where the legal wife stops: it ends where the legal wife begins. It is separated from honest women by public scandals; from courtesans by money.[171]

Dumas' warning really came twenty years too late. His acute definition of the *demi-monde* would have been more appropriate to the age in which Balzac wrote his *Femme de Trente Ans*. Baroness Dudevant (George Sand) ran off with a young man of letters, and Countess d'Agoult left her husband to live with Franz Liszt. Cases like this still occurred under the Second Empire, but they had grown less common. The influence of the Church had grown stronger again and, furthermore, women thought long indeed, on financial grounds, before leaving their husbands; romance in an attic was no longer popular. A lover's first duty was to maintain his mistress at least in the circumstances to which she was accustomed, and if he ruined himself for her that was proof that he was a *chevalier sans reproche*. But cavaliers also made their conditions. They demanded their own comfort and independence: they no longer staked their honour on fighting duels for the ladies of their hearts; and, above all, they reserved to themselves the right to wind up an affair when they liked.

Ladies of good society, however adventurous, naturally could not and did not meet these conditions, which called for a woman who was prepared to devote her entire life to the profession. Not, of course, common prostitutes, but *articles de luxe* of exquisite beauty, social expertize and a certain education, who lived by love, indeed, but never lapsed from the role of hostesses. It was to this class, which had little in common with the other class, to which Dumas himself was really referring and to which the word *demi-mondaine* came to cling. There was something contemptuous

PLATE 25

Sleep. Painting by Gustave Courbet (1819–1877). Paris, Petit Palais.

PLATE 26

" Alone at last ".
Marital romanticism
of the plush period.
Painting by Tofano.

Tannhäuser and Venus
(section). Erotic pathos
of the plush period.
Painting by Otto Krille.
Formerly Berlin,
Nationalgalerie.

PLATE 27

When the dance meant slow paces. Copperplate engraving by
M. Zasinger. About 1500.

Fast dance, 1845. The "Grand Gallop" to the music of
Johann Strauss. Engraving by Andreas Geiger after a drawing
by Schöller.

PLATE 28

Ball at Windsor Castle, 1855.

Waltz, 1909.

Rock and Roll, c. 1955.

PLATE 29

Can-Can Dancer, *c.* 1900.

"Folies", London, *c.* 1958.

PLATE 30

Bathing at Southend,
early 1900s.

Ramsgate poster, *c.* 1956.

PLATE 31

Fashionable corsets, 1890.

Cami-knickers, 1925.

PLATE 32

Bisexual people, from the *Livre des Merveilles* of 1395, Paris, National Library.

Sex change : Robert Marshall Cowell (top) 35 years old racing driver and fighter pilot, father of two children, became Roberta Elizabeth Cowell (bottom) as a result of an operation.

Leopold von Sacher-Masoch (1835–1895). The term " masochism " derives from his name.

in the name: all the same, one could not help admiring a *demi-mondaine* of this type. They formed an *élite*; they were the champions of their profession.

The most successful of them were known in Paris as *les lionnes* —the lionesses. Their standard of living was that of the upper classes. They kept their own carriages and riding horses and owned their own villas. Many of them presided over literary salons which were frequented by the best-known literary luminaries of the day. The most respected gentlemen of the Court used to visit them, not secretly but in the full light of day. To sit at their tables was not compromising and did not necessarily mean the existence of a sexual relationship. They had one rich lover who kept them, and sometimes bestowed their favours on one or two others, but the number of their intimate friends was not much larger than that of many ladies of true 'society'.

There had, of course, been real *hetairae* before this in Paris, as in every capital. But in the Second Empire they played a larger role than ever before. Their fame was not always entirely spontaneous. They had their press-agents, like the film-stars of today. The fashionable papers reported the toilets in which they appeared at the Opéra or the races; even if they missed some big event, the columns in *Figaro* used to report their names. Their patrons were proud to possess such mistresses, and they themselves needed this kind of advertisement, for they never knew when they would be requiring a new lover.

La Païva's Onyx Staircase

Gallantry, like music, is an international art. Not a few of the 'lionesses' were foreigners, and their distinguished clientele, too, was composed largely of rich foreigners. A famous example was Cora Pearl (*née* Emma Church), who, before finding her true profession, had made an unsuccessful début in Offenbach's *Orpheus in the Underworld*. Another recruit from the stage was Marguerite Bellanger, who at one time numbered Napoleon III himself among her clients; later, she married in England and ended her days as the respectable mistress of a château in Touraine.

More brilliant still was the rise of La Païva, who came into the world as daughter of a small merchant in Moscow, and was laid to her last rest in the mausoleum of Schloss Neudeck, in Silesia, as Countess Henckel of Donnersmarck.

The name of Païva has lived on as a sort of symbol of the luxury and licence of the Second Empire.[172] Thérèse Villoing, *née* Lachmann, did not earn her laurels easily. When quite young she married a French tailor in her native city. The marriage was apparently not happy. Soon after the birth of a child she packed her bags and fled—whither and with whom is unknown. She turned up in Constantinople, in Vienna, in Berlin. She was seen here and there in the casinos of the big watering places, but as one of the many; not, apparently, especially favoured either by fortune or by love.

By 1841 she was in Paris, the Mecca of all women desirous of making a romantic career. Even there the first stages were difficult for her. One day, in despair, she was sitting on a bench in the Champs Élysées when two fashionable gentlemen came up to her. The one (who has recorded the anecdote) was a well-known writer, Arsène Houssaye; the other, a famous Austrian pianist, Henri Herz, who had once made her acquaintance in Bad Ems. Houssaye took her for a night; her second meeting with Herz had a more lasting result. Although never legally married, they lived together for several years as Monsieur and Madame Herz. She presided over a musical salon which vied with those of George Sand and Chopin, of Countess d'Agoult and Franz Liszt. Herz, however, went on a long American tour, and in his absence Thérèse was too generous with his money and her heart. There was a break and she had to start afresh.

The social contacts which she had made in the previous years made this new beginning easier. Jules Lecomte—the Don Juan who had consoled Napoleon I's widow, Marie-Louise, in Parma —got publicity for her in the press, and the poet and critic Théophile Gautier, one of the great figures of the Romantic Age, rendered still more valuable services. The only thing lacking was the money to pay the dressmakers' bills, but a visit to London,

during which she conquered the heart of Lord Stanley, solved
this problem also. The death of her first husband enabled her to
acquire a well-sounding name by marrying the Marquis Araujo
de Païva, who thereupon returned gracefully to Portugal. Now
Madame Païva had everything that a woman needed to become
a 'lioness'.

A young Prussian Count, Guido Henckel von Donnersmarck,
who sought her favour was at first treated most ungraciously, but,
when it transpired that he had just inherited a large fortune from
his father, the situation was viewed in a new light. She followed
her youthful admirer to Berlin, and bestowed on him a love
which was almost maternal, for she was eleven years older than
he, though in her papers the difference afterwards narrowed
down to four. But when they returned to Paris she was still on
hire. She lived, it is true, in a luxury flat, but had to receive such
men as the prince of painters, Eugène Delacroix, the pope of
literature, Saint-Beuve, and the fashionable philosopher, Hip-
polyte Taine, in a salon which was not her own. Count Henckel
von Donnersmarck set to work to remedy this grievance. With
his help, La Païva bought a large building-plot on the Champs
Élysées, directly facing the bench on which Henri Herz had once
met her in her hour of need. Now the dream of her youth could
be fulfilled; precisely on this scene of her sorrows she would
erect a palace for which Paris in all its splendour could find no
match.

It was ten years in building. Fabulous tales went round of its
fittings, which swallowed up several millions of gold francs. La
Païva's state bed alone was alleged to have cost 100,000 gold
francs, and when she allowed her tried friend Théophile Gautier
a peep into her bathroom he exclaimed: 'Fit for a sultana out of
the Thousand and One Nights!' Next day all Paris knew about it.
Even more sensational was the onyx staircase, for which the comic
playwriter Émile Augier proposed the inscription (a free adaptation from an epigram by Racine): 'Vice, like virtue, has its
degrees.' When the 'Hôtel Païva', as everyone called it,[173] was
ready at last, Paris was the richer by a work of questionable art,

which, however, was later found worth preserving as a period piece. Meanwhile, Henckel von Donnersmarck had also bought his beloved a superb historical château, Pontchartrain. After the 1870 war he made her the most valuable gift of all: a wedding ring. By this time La Païva was already fifty-two, while he was only just over forty.

It seems paradoxical, and honest level-headed citizens will always wonder at it, that so cool and calculating a man as Guido Henckel von Donnersmarck, who was one of the leading financiers and most successful *entrepreneurs* of his day, should squander a fortune on such a woman. Surprise and even indignation were well founded. The palace in the Champs Élysées alone cost as much as a thousand workmen got in wages, in those days, in three years. Count Henckel von Donnersmarck's Silesian miners needed to work ten million hours underground to make as much as their noble master spent to indulge the wishes of a Parisian light-o'-love.

As always, it was Eve, not Adam, who was blamed. Hardly any woman in the second half of the nineteenth century was so bitterly attacked as La Païva. She had her defenders, however, even outside the narrow circle of her intimate admirers. In her later years she was especially praised for her business head, and many thought that if she cost her husband millions she brought him in still more millions. It is at least certain that La Païva was one of the very few gallant ladies to become a great business woman.

16

BIRTH LIMITATION

Each age has its own nightmare. A thousand years ago people believed that the clocks of the world were running down, and that the Last Judgment was just round the corner. Five hundred years ago men went in dread of witches and horned devils. Today we shudder to think that a handful of madmen might disintegrate our planet by exploding hydrogen bombs.

The great bogy of the nineteenth century was the dread of over-population. The man who infected mankind with this terror was an English clergyman named Thomas Robert Malthus, apparently the most kindly of men. He was not, however, as benevolent as he seemed, for his theory of over-population came down in the end to the proposition that he who had no money had no right to exist and, above all, no right to reproduce his kind. Moreover, since sexual intercourse, unless for the purpose of reproduction, was sinful, the poor had no right to indulge their sexual desires. In brief, coitus was a privilege of the well-to-do.

Malthus did not put it so bluntly as that: he left the conclusion to others. He himself raised the problem from the moral angle, and, put in that way, his theory sounded both more scientific and more gentlemanly. Human beings, he argued, were possessed by a fatal sexual urge which led them to multiply faster than the corn in the fields and the flocks in the meadows. This was the cause of all the misery, wars, and vice, which were the means by which population was brought back into a rough relationship to the means of subsistence. These consequences were most regrettable, but they were inevitable and unalterable so long as the poor refrained from bridling their sexual instincts and from bringing into the world children for whom they could not provide.

Malthus, the Hare and the Tortoise

Significantly, it was the debate on a new Poor Law that gave Malthus this idea. He had never himself suffered from poverty. His father was a prosperous and highly-educated gentleman who had given his son an excellent schooling and smoothed his path for him in every way. In his youth the elder Malthus had corresponded with Rousseau, Condorcet, and other luminaries of the Enlightenment, and their views on equality and progress had taken deep root in his mind. He thought that a pittance of poor relief was still better than none at all. His son, however, belonged to the younger generation of Englishmen whose minds had been steeled and their hearts hardened by the French Revolution, and who regarded even the most modest social-political measures taken by the British government as exaggerated concessions to the plebs. The younger Malthus's chief argument against poor relief was that it was a waste of money. What would happen next? The poor would produce still more children, and thus they would soon be as badly off as before, or even worse off.

Father and son argued for days and nights without either convincing the other. The father, however, was not a little proud to find his son able to produce such acute arguments against him, and to evolve a whole theoretical system out of them. He said to him: 'Put that down on paper. We will see what other people think of it.' Yet it was a risky venture for a young parson who had just received a small country living to touch on such questions, and even more risky to champion publicly so controversial a theory. The two Malthuses accordingly agreed to publish the son's essay on the problem of population anonymously, and under a completely non-political title.[174]

This caution proved to have been well advised. Other political economists before Malthus had maintained similar views, but the outspoken way in which he put his case attracted extraordinary attention and caused some scandal. The young Malthus was prepared to admit authorship, but that would not close the matter. He had advanced an hypothesis without bringing a shadow of proof, for the simple reason that he had not the material out of which to construct such proof. He made up his mind, hung up his parson's coat, and on ample means provided by his father spent a number of years travelling round Europe, collecting material to prove that human beings multiplied very much faster than the means of subsistence.

No strict proof could be adduced at the time, for there were no reliable statistics of agricultural production anywhere in existence. Malthus, however, brought back from his travels enough figures to give the impression that his theory was based on a solid foundation of facts. He allowed himself considerable licence in the interpretation of his figures and observations. From a few population statistics he deduced the conclusion that if no special factors to the contrary intervened, the population would double every twenty-five years, so that by A.D. 2000 Europe alone would have a population of over fifty thousand million, while there would not be food enough for as many as two thousand million. That was, of course, impossible. One must therefore expect mankind to be decimated in the future by famine, destitution, and a merciless struggle for the sources of subsistence still existing.

Malthus did not rest content with drawing this picture of horror. In the second edition of his work, which had now grown into a bulky treatise and was published five years after the first, under his own name, he gave advice to the poor on how to escape destitution: 'If we can persuade the hare to go to sleep, the tortoise may have some chance of overtaking him.'[175]

Malthus's hare is, in its own way, a highly moral creature. It would never give free play to its sexual instincts while trying to avert the consequences. For it, there were only the two alternatives—of practising continence, or of producing young hares. As men were better endowed with reason, but also morally less reliable than hares, Malthus gave them a further piece of advice: if they were unable to restrain their sex-instincts in marriage, they should marry as late as possible. They must, indeed, remain chaste until marriage. Malthus was aware that many would find this difficult, but believed that men of strong will and sound understanding would find it not beyond their powers. He himself set his fellow-citizens a shining example by not marrying till he was close on forty; and so far as is known, he had preserved strict celibacy up to that time.

In no case, said Malthus, should men try to avoid or to prevent the consequences of intercourse. Moral restraint and abstinence were the only lawful means of solving the population problem and, with it, the social problem. This decisive rejection of any prophylactic methods whatever restored Malthus's credit even in those circles which had at first regarded him as an enemy of morality. The East India Company gave him a Chair of Modern History and Political Economy at a college maintained by them. The Académie Française des Sciences Morales et Politiques and the Prussian Akadamie der Wissenschaften bestowed on him the distinction of corresponding membership. The great majority of university teachers of political economy throughout Europe declared themselves in agreement with his general thesis, even where they did not accept every detail and every conclusion of his doctrine.

In certain countries, particularly Austria and southern Germany, governments tried to draw practical advantage from Malthus's doctrine, or at least used it as an excuse for intervening in the private lives of their subjects. Up to the end of the eighteenth century marriage had, on the whole, been encouraged, since large families were thought to be beneficial, militarily and economically, to the State. In the Metternich era the authorities began to make marrying more difficult. Any person wishing to marry had to produce an official permit, which was not granted unless the applicant had a regular profession or other means of subsistence. Permits were, in principle, not issued to persons living on poor relief, but they were also frequently refused on political grounds. Relics of this system survived in the Austrian crownlands and in Bavaria up to shortly before the First World War.[176] Officers and civil servants were generally required to obtain permission before marrying. In the Prussian army, for example, officers were not allowed to marry before reaching the rank of captain, unless either they or their future wives possessed ample private means.

These restrictions produced no considerable effect on the population in the Malthusian sense. Once again, the figures showed that when marriage was made difficult, more illegitimate children were born; where the system of marriage permits was relaxed or abolished, the legitimate births increased and the illegitimate fell off. Thus the total number of births was little affected, except in so far as the figure for infant mortality was lower among legitimate children than among illegitimate.

Neo-Malthusianism and Eugenics

The strongest echo evoked by the Malthusian doctrine was among the English manufacturers. Not that they were themselves ascetics, or required their workers to live monastically. But Malthus had provided them with a first-class argument in the wrangle over wages, which was growing steadily more acute. It was not the employers who were to blame for the wretched state of their workers. The workpeople had too many children, and the remedy for their economic condition was in their own hands. If the hare could get used to going to sleep without thinking of his mate, everything would be all right. But the hare refused to be persuaded. This was the hitch in the Malthusian theory.

As soon became apparent, the theory had other flaws. That even a country whose industrial development was proceeding as rapidly as Great Britain's was able to procure as much foodstuffs as it would, was another matter. The essential point was that Malthus's recipe had failed because no one was willing to use it. Neither undernourishment nor over-work seemed to change this. When a working man or woman returned home after twelve hours in the factory and fell exhausted into bed, the hare still awoke. If people wanted seriously to attack the problem of population and to improve the condition of the workers, they

would have to try other methods. Exhortations to sexual abstinence would not suffice.

In Malthus's own lifetime some of his disciples accordingly
abandoned orthodox Malthusianism and evolved a variant of it
later known as Neo-Malthusianism. They admitted Malthus's
theory of over-population and continued to maintain the necessity, on social grounds, of restricting the number of births, but
agreed that it was neither practicable nor desirable to achieve
this by trying to suppress the sex-instinct. The sex-instinct was a
natural thing and to suppress it was unnatural. Sexual abstinence
for the sole purpose of preventing births was an unnatural
demand, and therefore an immoral one.

The problem, in their view, could be solved only by providing
parents who were not in a position to maintain large families
with the means of keeping the number of their children down,
without having to renounce sexual intercourse. The sexual
instinct and the reproductive instinct were not identical. They
must be separated in the measure necessitated by social considerations and wished by the parties. To help the poor, it was
therefore necessary to disseminate among them the knowledge
of preventive methods of avoiding pregnancy.

One of the first persons to maintain this thesis clearly and
openly was the social reformer Francis Place, who in 1822
published in London a book entitled *Illustrations and Proofs of the
Principle of Population*. Place was also probably the person responsible for the distribution of certain leaflets containing instructions
on contraceptive methods.[177] A few years later a handbook for
women was published in London under the innocent title *What
is Love?* It contained more detailed information on how to avoid
pregnancy.

From Britain, the propaganda quickly spread to America. The
first champion in that country of birth-limitation by technical
means was an English-born social philosopher named Robert
Dale Owen, the son of the famous philanthropist. The name
alone sufficed to ensure respectful attention for his book *Moral
Physiology*, published in 1830. An American physician, however,

one Dr. Knowlton, who gave a detailed description of the contraceptive methods then known, was prosecuted and sentenced, first to a fine, then to a term in prison. The fact that the author had been punished in the State of Massachusetts did not, however, prevent his book[178] from circulating freely in the rest of America, and even in Britain it was sold across the counter for more than forty years before the watchdogs of morality discovered it to be objectionable.

Generally speaking, Britain did not particularly quarrel with Neo-Malthusianism, although the age was precisely that in which prudery was celebrating its greatest triumphs in other fields. The Malthusian doctrine was now familiar in all educated circles, its correctness generally accepted, and every man was left free to apply it as he himself thought best. The only demand made by the authorities was that the subject should be treated with decency. The Neo-Malthusian propaganda had therefore to submit to many restrictions of form, and to juggle somewhat with words. Its most important work, the author of which was a physician of great attainments named George Drysdale, was entitled *The Elements of Social Science*. The interested public, however, pierced this disguise. The book, published in London in 1854, ran through thirty-five editions in Britain alone, and was translated into ten foreign languages.[179] The public of the day gave it much more attention than it did Darwin's *Origin of Species*.

The public interest in Darwinism was itself due in no small part to the large sex-element in the doctrine. The natural result of the suppression of everything even remotely connected with sex in general conversation and social life was that sexual curiosity concentrated on purely scientific works and problems. Darwin, incidentally, expressly acknowledged his debt to Malthus, from whom he had taken the basic idea of the 'struggle for existence'. Darwinism and Neo-Malthusianism were not only in their origins two branches from the same tree of knowledge, but also seemed logically closely related. Preventive measures to control over-population and raise individual standards of living were in close accordance with Darwin's doctrine. The 'fittest' in this field had the best prospects of surviving in the struggle for existence, while the indolent spirits who accepted an unlimited number of children as heaven's will doomed themselves to destitution and ruin.

Limitation of families was not, indeed, to be carried too far. In the early days of Neo-Malthusianism no one suggested going to extremes. The movement only aimed at showing fathers and mothers that it was harmful for themselves, the nation, and humanity as a whole, to bring into the world an indefinite number of children for whom there were no means of subsistence. The thing to aim at was not quantity but quality; to produce and bring up healthy offspring, fitted for the battle of life. A special branch of natural history and social hygiene, the science of eugenics, devoted itself to this great problem. The foundations of this, again, were laid in England around the middle of the nineteenth century. The true founder of eugenics was a cousin of Darwin's, the anthropologist Francis Galton, who also made some contributions to the knowledge of heredity, then extraordinarily meagre.[180]

Annie Besant

All this went on without the least concealment—itself a proof of the error of regarding Victorian Britain as wholly given over to hypocritical false modesty. People were prudish and narrow-minded on small points, but there was great interest in and complete understanding of the important biological questions and their social implications. They were discussed more freely in Britain than anywhere else in the world. Since 1860 the Neo-Malthusians in Britain had issued their own periodical, which bore a somewhat colourless title, *The National Reformer*. Its contents, however, were quite unambiguous. The paper appeared for seventeen years with little official interference, and the authorities would probably not have troubled with it even then, had not an incident, trivial in itself, started the avalanche.

In one of the periodical dredgings for obscene literature, someone discovered in a Bristol bookseller's a copy of Dr. Knowlton's *Fruits of Philosophy*, a book which had passed through repeated new editions for nearly half a century, with no one objecting. An over-zealous inspector of police now had the bookseller prosecuted for disseminating obscene literature, and the court found him guilty. This was apparently only a lapse, not an organized attack on the freedom of literature and of sex-life. The editorial board of *The National Reformer* had, however, reason enough to feel nervous, since the propaganda conducted in their paper went far beyond anything in Knowlton's old book. The editor and proprietor of the journal, Charles Bradlaugh, grasped the nettle and challenged the opposition. In order to settle, once for all, whether the propagation of methods of contraception was lawful in Britain or not, he immediately arranged a re-issue of Knowlton's book.

This was more than a scandal over a book; a great question of principle was now involved. The Public Prosecutor took action again. Bradlaugh was prosecuted in his turn and sentenced to six months' imprisonment and a fine of £200. The sentence evoked widespread indignation in England. Even many persons who themselves did not share Bradlaugh's views admired the courage with which he had stood up for his convictions. A group of American physicians of Harvard University in Cambridge, Massachusetts, the State which had sent Knowlton to prison forty-four years earlier, had the book reprinted. The sentence against Bradlaugh was not long-lived. The Court of Appeal in London reversed it in the same year, 1877—only, indeed, on technical grounds. This was nevertheless a great victory for the Neo-Malthusians. It was long before any authority in England dared proceed against them again.

The moving spirit in this struggle was a woman, as active as she was eccentric, named Annie Besant. Her name is even better remembered by later generations in other connections. This pioneer, who died in 1933 at a great age, was in her later years one of the leaders of the theosophical movement, the discoverer of the 'New Messiah' Krishnamurti, and, later still, a champion of independence for India. Her first battle, however, was fought in the field of sex-policy. She had been born in 1847, in London, but her father was Irish and had transmitted the Irish quality of pugnacity to his daughter. She was brought up as a pious member of the Anglican Church, and married, at twenty, a country parson named Frank Besant, from whom she parted after only a few years of marriage. The separation had been preceded by a parting of their faiths. Annie Besant had become a Freethinker and had joined a circle of progressive intellectuals in London. of which Bradlaugh was a member. She became his collaborator and soon his Egeria. Her temperament always drove her to extremes, whatever the subject of her immediate interest or faith. On the question of Neo-Malthusianism, too, she brooked no compromise: one must confess and fight for one's beliefs, not hide before the enemy or seek excuses in the eyes of authority. She wrote most outspoken articles, and also insisted on taking responsibility for the propaganda of others. She was accordingly prosecuted with Bradlaugh, sentenced with him and, like him, acquitted in the Court of Appeal.

Now she was the heroine of the day, and she knew how to take advantage of the situation. While the trial was still pending she organized the foundation in London of the Malthusian League, a militant body which set out to achieve complete freedom of discussion for the question of limitation of births, and to propagate among the people 'by all practical methods, knowledge of the law of population, its consequences and its influence on manners and morals'. A well-known doctor, George Drysdale's brother, undertook the presidency of the League, while Annie Besant was its secretary and real driving force. In the course of the following decades similar leagues were founded everywhere in the world, beginning with Holland and Germany.

Her work for the League left Annie Besant enough time to make literary propaganda for birth-control. Her *Law of Population* sold 175,000 copies. A Neo-Malthusian handbook for women sold more than half a million copies, and readers were still studying it closely long after Annie Besant had turned her attention to other problems. The driving-force of this unusual woman had turned the hobby-horse of a little clique into a mass movement.

A Cure for Poverty

The most lively agitation would certainly not have produced such a response, had the conditions of the day not been favourable to Neo-Malthusianism. All Europe was again suffering a severe economic crisis, and governments were doing little to alleviate the distress. Many hundreds of thousands were emigrating annually to America. An addition to the family meant for millions of men and women an almost intolerable aggravation of their burden. Wealth of children had become a curse instead of a blessing. A man so moderate as Gaston Schmoller, the German political economist, warned farmers against having too large families: 'It is a dogma characteristic of a semi-civilized stage of culture.'[181]

Even the socialists, who from the first had strongly opposed Malthus's teaching (the youthful Engels had called it 'a shameful, degrading doctrine') began to waver, or held their tongues. It was a poor consolation for the workers, and most of all for the unemployed, to be promised that there would be no population problem in the socialist State of the future. For the moment they were living under another economic system and had to contend with that fact in their sex lives as in other respects. But how were they to do it? Their leaders did not tell them.[182] In the most popular socialist book of the day, August Bebel's *Woman and Socialism*, they could read that 'the more wretched the condition of the proletarian classes, the greater, as a rule, is their wealth in children', but this dictum hardly helped them.

The Neo-Malthusians, on the other hand, promised them help. They turned the sentence round, and said: 'the more numerous the children, the more wretched is the condition of the proletariat'. The whole weight of Neo-Malthusian propaganda was at first directed against the problem of poverty. *The Malthusian*, the official organ of the League in Britain, took for its motto the words: 'A Crusade Against Poverty', and the president of the

League went so far as to say: 'Prophylactic intercourse alone and unaided is fully sufficient to eliminate poverty.'

In other countries, also, propaganda was conducted under this slogan. The first book in German on the English movement (published in 1880) was entitled *Neo-Malthusianism, the Cure for Pauperism*. Everyone at that time understood what the word 'pauperism' meant: it meant mass destitution. This was the great problem of the day. But unlike other remedies recommended against this mass phenomenon, the Neo-Malthusians had the advantage that anyone could apply it for himself. There was no need of plebiscites, alterations to the economic system, revolutionary laws, expensive reforms, or public relief. Anyone could solve his personal problem in his own bedroom. The State needed to contribute nothing beyond legalizing contraceptive methods, and even that was not absolutely essential, for there were ways of greatly reducing the chances of conception without mechanical or chemical devices.

The Mathematics of Conception

The best-tried 'natural' method of avoiding pregnancy seemed to be temporary abstention from sexual intercourse, but not by following Malthus's recommendation to live in celibacy for most of one's life and to marry only when the sex-impulse was weakening. It was enough, on the alternative theory, if a woman carefully noted when her menstruation periods occurred, and abstained from intercourse during a certain stage between them, because conception occurred only during a relatively short phase. This method was very old: one of the most important gynaecologists of antiquity, the Greek physician Soranus of Ephesus, who lived in Rome at the beginning of the second century A.D., knew and described it; but, like so many things known to the Greeks and Romans, it had become forgotten and had to be rediscovered in later centuries. Malthus does not seem to have known of it, or he might possibly have recommended it, for it did not at all conflict with his moral principles.

Particularly important was the fact that the Catholic Church, which strictly condemned all artificial and forcible means of preventing pregnancy, sanctioned this method. A regular consultation had taken place on the subject in the 1760s. In answer to a question from a French doctor, the Cardinal-Archbishop of Rheims, certainly acting in agreement with the Vatican, had expressly approved the procedure in a diocesan letter. In Germany it was recommended by Dr. Capellmann, an eminent representative of Catholic pastoral medicine, after whom it was known as the 'Capellmann rule'.

There was, however, much disagreement concerning when the fertilization of the ovum took place, and how long before that a woman had to observe sexual abstinence. Most of the specialists believed that the rate of conception was highest immediately after menstruation. This also seemed obvious to laymen; menstruation loosened up the female sexual organs, thus facilitating conception.

Capellmann was particularly cautious in his estimate of the time during which conception could take place, and advised married couples who wanted to have no more children to abstain from sexual intercourse for a fortnight, counting from the beginning of the previous menstruation and, for safety's sake, also during the three or four days preceding the next. That meant, after all, abstention from coitus during seventeen or eighteen days of the normal menstrual cycle of twenty-eight—a fairly hard thing to ask of most young people. Furthermore, specialists of repute maintained that Capellmann's rule was at variance with the physiological facts: the disposition to conceive was strongest between the twelfth and seventeenth days after the beginning of the preceding menstruation.

Later investigations pushed the date still farther forward. The new calculations counted back. Ogino worked out that the 'critical' time for conception was from the sixteenth to the twelfth day before the date on which the next menstruation was due. For safety's sake, however, women wishing to avoid conception were to abstain from intercourse for three days before that, the three days being the spermatozoa's life-period after coitus. They must therefore practise a rule of abstinence from the nineteenth to the twelfth day before the beginning of each period, and then they would be safe. Dr. Knaus, another distinguished specialist, came to a very similar conclusion on the basis of quite different calculations, and declared even more categorically that conception took place only on five days in a normal menstrual cycle, viz. between the eighteenth and the fourteenth days before the date on which the next menstruation was normally to be expected.

For a while the Ogino and Knaus rule enjoyed a certain authority among both doctors and laymen; then it, in its turn, proved to be extremely unreliable.[185] American doctors now take yet another basis of calculation, and reckon that the critical period for fertilization is that from the eighth to the fourteenth day after menstruation, while between the fourteenth and the twenty-fourth day, i.e. in the last ten or eleven days before menstruation, conception is unlikely to occur.[186]

As we see, the mathematics of conception still has its mysteries and its uncertainties, even for women who keep very careful diaries of their menstruation periods. For the great majority of women of the people, however, sums like this always seemed too subtle for the natural processes of sex-life. Simple people demanded simple rules of thumb, even if they were wrong. The simplest of all such rules was the belief, general among women, that they could not conceive so long as they were still suckling a child. Although this assumption was proved countless times to be erroneous, or at least highly uncertain, it remained firm-rooted, especially in rural districts. When Malthus's theories were in fashion, a French doctor proposed that the State should make it obligatory on all women to suckle their children for three years; there would then be no more over-population.[187]

This supposed method of avoiding conception lost further credit with the growth of female labour in factories and offices which made it impossible for a mother to give the breast. But even mathematically it was fallacious as a means of limiting families. Assuming that every woman suckled each of her children eighteen months, and that no conception occurred during this period, she could still bring ten children into the world if she married at twenty.

The only effective preventive method, requiring no external treatment, no apparatus and no medicaments, thus remained the *coitus interruptus*, as doctors had called it since the days of William Goodwell; more accurately, emission of the semen outside the woman's genitals. In France, where this practice was already very prevalent in the nineteenth century, especially in country districts, it was also known as *onanisme conjugal*. It is a trick by which the understanding outwits nature, but those who practise it do so at the cost of part of their pleasure. The *coitus interruptus* formerly stood in very bad repute among neurologists, who thought that it might lead to frigidity in the woman and severe neuroses in both partners. Today most doctors do not regard it as so harmful, but it is admitted not to be the ideal method of avoiding pregnancy.

Men under Lock and Key

As the sex-instinct proved so difficult to hold in check, various attempts were made to proceed against it by external compulsion. In the later Middle Ages, as we have already mentioned, jealous husbands used to put chastity girdles on their wives, lock them and take the key with them when they went away. Now, however, when the problem was how to limit the number of children, even that would have been useless, seeing that men were no less addicted to sexual indulgence than women. If Malthus's warnings were to be heeded, then, logically, men also must be put under lock and key.

In the 1820s, in fact, a certain Dr. Weinhold of Halle an der Saale, a man as learned as he was conscientious, proposed solving the population problem in the Malthusian sense by this method. Being a kindly man, he did not at once suggest castrating men; it would be enough to solder them up until a certain age in such fashion as to make it impossible for them to practise sexual intercourse. This required an operation, but one which, in his view, was harmless; he had himself carried it out with success on juvenile onanists. It was, in fact, the operation widely practised among the primitive peoples of Malaya and also well known in ancient Rome—infibulation. Weinhold wrote:

The operation itself is easy and almost entirely painless, as are the soldering and affixing of the metal seal. . . . The foreskin is drawn forward and gently compressed between a pair of perforated metal plates, so that when a hollow needle containing a core of lead wire is stuck through it, this is hardly felt. When the wire has been drawn through, it is bent, so that it cannot press on the adjacent parts; both the two ends are now brought together and soldered together with a small soldering-club. As soon as the knot, which is about the size of a lentil, has cooled off, a solid object is held against it; a small metal seal is pressed on it and this is afterwards kept in safety. This makes it quite impossible to open the infibulation and afterwards secretly close it again without the seal, without this being discovered at the next inspection.[188]

The primary purpose of the soldering was 'to prevent the act of generation before marriage' and it was to be effected on such persons 'as demonstrably do not possess the means to maintain and bring up extra-maritally begotten issue until the age of legal independence. It would be left for life on persons who never reached a position in which they were able to maintain and provide for a family.'

Neither the State of Prussia, nor the government of any other land, could steel itself to accept this proposal, and the population problem thus remained unsolved. The Neo-Malthusians tried milder ways of averting the undesired consequences of the sex instinct. In particular, they recommended the use of the *condom*. This was no invention of theirs. Here, again, the Romans had been before them: the device is mentioned in Antonius Liberalis's *Metamorphoses*. The first exact description, however, is one by the great Italian doctor Gabriel Fallopius, who probably rediscovered it. In his treatise on syphilis[189] he recommends the use of a linen bag, steeped in a certain medicament and put on over the male member, as a safeguard against infection. For some centuries

thereafter, the device was still used, as it is at times today, chiefly
as a safeguard against venereal diseases. Technically, however, it
had been greatly perfected. In France it was manufactured of the
finest membrane from the coecum of young sheep; these 'French
bladders' were exported all over the world.

Towards the end of the nineteenth century the animal substance was replaced by rubber, which at first involved a technical
retrogression, for the new appliance was thicker and broke more
easily. The demand had become so great, however, that a mass-
produced article was necessary, for the device was used not only
as a protection against syphilis and gonorrhoea, but also to avert
marital and extra-marital pregnancies.

Preventive Technique for Women

The counterparts of the condom are the various methods of
preventing the entry of the spermatozoa into the womb, and
thence into the ovaries, where fertilization takes place, by stopping
up the entrance in the woman. These are nearly all inventions of
the nineteenth century. The pessary method was first suggested
by a Berlin doctor, F. M. Wilde, in 1838, as a way of avoiding
pregnancies, but it was a considerable time before any apparatus
of this sort was devised which was at all certain and not too
uncomfortable. The real paternity of the occlusive pessary is
usually ascribed to a doctor of Flensburg named Mensinga, who
described a new model for closing the vagina in his *Facultative
Sterility*, written in 1881. Being rather nervous, he first published
this under a pseudonym, C. Hasse, but his invention came just
at the right moment, when Neo-Malthusianism was carrying all
before it outside Germany. Mensinga soon became famous, and
his name remained a general term for occlusive pessaries in the
Anglo-Saxon countries.

Some time later, an English chemist named Rendell added to
the contraceptive devices a vaginal suppository of his own
manufacture, consisting of a small pellet of cocoa-butter and
quinine, which women were to introduce into the vagina before
coitus. The inventor declared that this would prevent conception.

Although the effect of these tablets was uncertain, they re-opened a branch of preventive technique which had already been familiar to the ancient Egyptians: that of anti-conceptive chemistry. One discovery followed another, in quick succession, of products alleged to immobilize and kill the spermatozoa with absolute certainty. It was a regular battle against spermatozoa: tablets, salves, fluids, powders, harmless and dangerous, partially effective and totally ineffective, were sold to women across and under the counter, or at the street door. This method had no great effect, except that some preparations produced inflammation, or some apparatus, clumsily handled, injured the mucous membrane.

Much more effective, not perhaps in individual cases but as a mass practice, were douches after sexual intercourse. This method, again, was known to the ancient Romans but only re-introduced in the nineteenth century—by that same American doctor, Charles Knowlton, whose book stirred up so much dust in England. Knowlton recommended douches of a fairly strong acid solution, but it was found afterwards that mild disinfectants and even plain water were almost as good, since the effect resulted less from the chemical substances than from the mechanical ablution. The irrigators in particular, which many countries issued to women at health centres, proved to be an anti-conceptive method of the first order, and many authorities ascribe the chief part in the recession of the birthrate to this, the most harmless and hygienically indispensable apparatus of all.[190]

In towns, at least, after their experiences of the many quackeries of earlier centuries, women had almost stopped taking internal medicines to prevent pregnancy. But the use of drugs (most of them dangerous) to induce miscarriages was still all too common. Recently, however, doctors in America have been experimenting again—apparently with some success—in internal prophylactics.

In 1821 the English philosopher John Stuart Mill, a convinced Malthusian, declared: 'the great practical problem is thus to find out how to limit the number of births'. A century later the problem had still not been solved completely, but the progress made was such that the number of undesired conceptions had diminished enormously. Except in the case of physiological obstacles in either party, pregnancy had become a volitional act; it was no longer an automatic consequence of sexual intercourse. The sex-instinct and the reproductive instinct had been separated as they had not been since the days of the Roman Empire.

Without any essential change in the law, a sex-revolution had taken place, the consequences of which thenceforward left their stamp on both public and private life. The fall in the birthrate which set in in France in the 1840s, in England in the 1880s, and in the other civilized countries of the West at the beginning of the present century, became as real a bogy as the swift growth of the population in Malthus's day. The transition from the big family in which the undertaker and the midwife were regular visitors, to the small one with two or three children, took place from one generation to the next. It was a radical change in ways of living, particularly for women, who now ceased to be child-bearing machines. They were able to take an interest in public and also in domestic affairs for which they had previously had no time. They were no longer dependent upon servants, and many were able to practise a profession even after marriage. The real emancipation of women began in the bedroom and the bathroom, with the rationalization of sex-life.

17

EROS ASTRAY

No one knows how many sexual anomalies there are, but it is improbable that the number varies greatly from one generation to another. Yet at the turn of the nineteenth to twentieth centuries it might have been thought that the world had suddenly become filled with perverts. Sadists and masochists, fetishists and narcissists, male and female homosexuals, nymphomaniacs and satyrs, sodomites and necrophiles, and every other possible variant from the normal, apparently infested not only the cesspools of the great cities but also respectable country towns, schools and clubs, the highest circles of society, and the proletariat.

Where did they come from? Today we can confidently say: in most cases from the imagination. A few sensational individual cases had attracted public attention to sexual freaks; the smell of the illicit which hovered around them tempted other completely normal people to copy them, and thus the impression was created that every second man or woman was sexually abnormal. Few ages have been so keenly interested in matters of sex, and few, too, so misled by their own discoveries. To outward appearance, it was an age of perverts; in reality, one of suffering for those whose dispositions differed at all from the normal.

Yet, unlike the preceding generation, it was not a prudish age. It was considered *chic* to know everything and to speak about everything. The man-about-town ideal of the period had, however, produced another kind of intolerance which turned against any form of unfashionable conduct, including chastity. If a young girl tried to keep the *prima nox* for her husband and did not allow him at least to anticipate it, people suspected something wrong in her sexual make-up.

These changes certainly did not come out of the blue. They were a reaction to the hide-and-seek which the preceding generation had played with sex. The younger generation revolted against being treated like children; the women, above all, insisted on the new style of living. The emancipated woman of 1900 was no blue-stocking and no suffragette fighting for equal political rights for women and forgetting as she did so that she was a woman. She was emphatically sexual, but self-confident and proud of her sex. She was convinced that man was in no way her superior, but was only exploiting privileges acquired in the dawn of history by brute force and guile. The days of these privileges were clearly numbered. Women sat in university lecture rooms and in laboratories, played games, rode bicycles, even fenced, and won extraordinary successes in every field which they entered.

Many of them had already made themselves financially independent through their own efforts and talents and no longer needed to be kept by their parents, or as some man's wife or mistress. This gave them the fullest title to lead whatever sex-life they pleased. The licence which ensued differed in essential respects from that of earlier ages. It was unromantic and realistic, but not commercial in the same measure as in the eighteenth century. A woman was no longer a mere object to be bought or hired by a man.

The strong individualist tendency which this gave to sex-life was, however, in contradiction to the democratic ideas of the age. Previously, men or women whose birth or talents set them apart, had been allowed to ignore the general code of conduct in their sex-lives also. Now they were expected to conform to the general restrictions of the law, like other people. The great, however, were obviously disinclined to do this. The result was the sex-conflicts and sex-scandals which gave these decades the stamp of a particularly vicious and decadent age.

The Bullets of Mayerling

The most sensational cases were those that occurred in the

Habsburg monarchy. That a monarch nearly sixty years of age and no longer greatly interested in sex should, with the full consent and, it was even said, on the initiative of the Empress, have a liaison with an actress from the Court theatre some twenty years his junior, was itself hard to reconcile with the title 'Apostolic Majesty' officially borne by the Austrian Emperor. But the manner of living of the heir to the throne, the Archduke Rudolf, evoked criticism from the most loyal monarchists. Rudolf was married to a Belgian princess who had presented him with a daughter, but so far with no male heir to the throne. He sought consolation for this dynastic misfortune in the arms of other women.

His love-affairs changed more rapidly than the weather. An official procuress provided for him, as she did for the other archdukes of the House of Habsburg. A well-known Viennese cocotte, Mitzi Kaspar, was among his intimates, but he also often bestowed his favours on ladies of the Court. With one of them, Princess Aglaia von Auersperg, something went wrong. Her brother complained to the Emperor and demanded satisfaction from the man who had sullied the family honour. The Emperor agreed in principle, but a regular duel with the Crown Prince was, of course, impossible. It would not be understood; moreover, it would be quite impossible to hush it up. The parties agreed to settle the affair on more discreet lines—by an 'American duel'. The duellists would not exchange bullets, but draw them. The one who drew the white bullet had won; he who drew the black bullet must leave the world within six months. Fate proved just; Prince Auersperg drew the white bullet, and the Crown Prince was left with the black.

At first Rudolf went on with his life as though nothing had happened, but as the day approached on which his period of grace would expire, he increasingly lost his nerve and his balance. He spun political intrigues, and his nights grew wilder than ever. To soothe him and distract his thoughts, the Empress's niece, Countess Larisch-Wallersee, introduced to him a girl of seventeen, Baroness Mary Vetsera. She was not of so great a house as the

Princess Auersperg and not particularly beautiful, but, despite her youth, not without experience in the arts of love, possessed of a peculiar oriental charm (her mother came from Smyrna), and extremely submissive.

The little Baroness was smuggled again and again through a secret door into the Hofburg. For a few days His Highness's spirits seemed brighter, but then his fits of depression came back. In his more lucid hours he made desperate endeavours to escape from his fatal undertaking. Behind his father's back, he asked the Pope to annul his marriage with Princess Stephanie; then he would perhaps be able to marry Princess Auersperg morganatically and go on living. The Vatican did not answer him. One day the Crown Prince found his own letter, together with a negative decision from the Pope, in the hand of his father, who was furious at this move.

Meanwhile a much more wicked decision had been maturing in Rudolf's mind. He was prepared to pay his debt of honour and to execute on himself the sentence of the black bullet. But he would not go to his death alone: he wanted to take a woman with him. Someone must share death with him. This idea came to obsess him. He asked the various women with whom even now he was passing his tortured nights to die with him; but they thought the wild suggestion was a silly joke and refused it, laughingly. Only little Baroness Vetsera agreed.

On the morning of 30 January 1889 the valet at the hunting lodge of Mayerling got no answer when he knocked on Rudolf's bedroom door. When the door was broken open, the thirty-year-old heir to the Austrian crown, the only son of the Emperor Franz Josef, was found lying in bed, his skull shattered. Mary Vetsera, also lifeless, lay beside him. The autopsy proved that Rudolf had first shot his lover, then himself. The people and the world were not, however, allowed to learn of the crime committed by so eminent a person. The only immediate thought of the Imperial family, the government and the police, was to hush up the scandal. Mary Vetsera's corpse was dressed in travelling clothes, put in a cab, driven by night to a neighbouring village graveyard, and there secretly interred. Thus 'the blot on the scutcheon' was wiped off.

There remained the difficult task of drawing a suitable veil over the Crown Prince's death. The first version given out was that he had died of heart failure; the next spoke of a shooting accident. It was only when the whole world knew that Rudolf had committed suicide that so much was officially admitted—but nothing more. That before dying he had killed a woman, remained an official secret of State so long as the monarchy existed. Franz Josef did penance after his own fashion: he had Schloss Mayerling partly demolished, and a Carmelite convent built on its site. A chapel now stands on the exact spot where the death-bed had been.

These are the facts of the tragedy of Mayerling, as disclosed by recently discovered records of the police.[191] It was formerly suspected that some political motive lay behind Rudolf's suicide, but today there can be no doubt that from its inception to its lurid end it was a drama of sex, one of the most complex and most monstrous that the world has ever witnessed. The story of the black and white bullets on which the heir to a great Empire staked his life sounds so incredible that even Alexandre Dumas would have hesitated to invent it. But for all its operatic-romantic form it was simply one of those duels with which sex battles were customarily settled in the nineteenth century.

From the point of view of sex-psychology, the final act of the drama of Mayerling is more interesting. To all appearances it was one of the many love-tragedies in which two human beings who feel themselves inseparably bound to one another die together. Even where—as is usually the case—the man kills the woman before turning the revolver on himself, it is, psychologically speaking, a double suicide—an excess of monogamy, like the Indian suttee. But that was not the case here. Rudolf and Mary Vetsera were in no way inseparably bound to one another. For her it was undoubtedly a supreme romantic love experience, and Rudolf was the fairy prince, the man for whom the beloved must make heroic self-sacrifice. For him, however, Mary Vetsera was only one of many. He had actually spent the night before his last with his mistress Mitzi Kaspar.

It may be that Rudolf was trying to overcome his own fear of suicide by the sacrifice of a woman. If he killed a woman he would have no recourse other than flight into death—although there have been cases enough in which precisely then the killer's courage failed him. But the Austrian Crown Prince was not a coward. Nothing suggests that he lacked the courage to end his own life. It is much more likely that the compulsive idea of coupling murder with suicide, of making a woman die with him, was a flare-up of sadistic impulses, a revenge for the trap into which his sex-life had led him. Women were to blame—he did not of course blame himself that he must die—then a woman should die with him and make his own dying easier.

The Discovery of Masochism

To make it possible for the suicide to receive Christian burial, the doctors who conducted the autopsy on Rudolf's body diagnosed pathological changes in Rudolf's bones which indicated the possibility of mental unbalance. Yet science had not then, nor has it today, reached the stage of being able to diagnose from a corpse whether he took his life in a fit of insanity. But it was known, even then, that there were certain sexual predispositions and aberrations which did not go with diagnosable anatomical malformations and symptoms. Precisely in Austria this was familiar knowledge.

A few years before the tragedy of Mayerling, an Austrian psychiatrist had for the first time submitted the whole field of sexual pathology to a thorough analysis. This was not Sigmund Freud, who at that time was occupied with quite different questions. The founder of the modern doctrine of sexual derangements and perversions was a police doctor, Richard von Krafft-Ebing. He was a native of Mannheim, but practised for many years, first in Graz then in Vienna, which he found a particularly rich field for his observations on sexual pathology. He systematized and classified the various anomalies of sex-life, producing plausible explanations for some, and thus created a new branch of knowledge.

Krafft-Ebing had the courage to regard a genuine disposition to perversity as a sickness and not, as was then usual, a vice. He was, however, a highly moral man and in his moral zeal he committed the error—a strange one for a psychologist—of describing all the details of pathological sexual behaviour in a distinctly un-Ciceronian Latin. The devotees of pornographic literature consequently equipped themselves with dictionaries and made straight for the Latin passages. Krafft-Ebing's heavy scientific work thus became uncommonly popular, and by 1902, when its author died, it had gone into twelve editions,[192] and since has been further reprinted a number of times.

Krafft-Ebing's special claim to fame is that for the first time he clearly defined the nature of masochism, for which he also invented the name, now universally in use. The theme was, indeed, a particularly familiar one in Graz, where Krafft-Ebing wrote his *Psychopathia Sexualis*. From 1870 onward an Austrian, Ritter Leopold von Sacher-Masoch, had been producing novels and short stories, each depicting in some fresh variant a type of man who satisfied his sexual needs by making a woman inflict pain on him. Sacher-Masoch himself was such a man, so Krafft-Ebing felt justified in calling this form of perversion after the notorious writer, even in his lifetime. When attacked for this, he replied that Sacher-Masoch was a sick man and sickness was no disgrace. Sacher-Masoch thus achieved the same world fame as the Marquis de Sade, whose exploits and literary works gave birth—in his case only after his death—to the use of the word 'sadism' to describe sexual pleasure derived from the sufferings of others. Sadism and masochism are twins, and mutually complementary, and the two men who bequeathed them their names had in fact many features in common.

Like de Sade, Sacher-Masoch came of an old and noble family. He traced his ancestry back to a Spanish hidalgo, Don Mathias Sacher, who fought in the Emperor Charles's army at Mühlberg in 1547, was wounded, and finally settled in Bohemia. The

Spaniard's descendants became high officials in Austria. Leopold's father was a powerful and greatly-feared man, first Director of Police in Lemberg, where his son was born in 1836, then Stadt-hauptmann of Prague, and finally Chief of Police in Graz.

His mother's qualities, too, were not such as to support any hereditary weakness. Her father, Professor von Masoch, Rector of the Univerity of Lemberg, was a doctor who had done valuable work in the field of public health. As von Masoch had no sons, the Emperor gave his son-in-law permission to use both names, hyphenated; and thus this blameless scholar became the involuntary ancestor of masochism.

Furs and Whips

Leopold von Sacher-Masoch was an extremely gifted child, and his father's and grandfather's positions smoothed his way in life. At twenty he was already a history tutor at Graz University. Besides his academic distinction, he early won a name as an author of comedies and historical novels. Privately, he led the life of a provincial Don Juan, had a liaison with the wife of a doctor, who finally, to his grief, went off with another man; but he consoled himself with actresses and other admirers of his writings. Everything thus seemed in good order, in this respect as in others.

When, however, Sacher-Masoch reached his early thirties something changed in him. He sought and found women stronger than himself, and his greatest pleasure lay in submitting himself absolutely to them. He laid himself at their feet like a dog and made them maltreat and humiliate him; the more violent they were, the greater his pleasure. Communicative as he was all his life, he soon gave literary expression to these feelings. In his *Das Vermächtnis Kains* (Cain's Heritage), a collection of short stories published in 1870, he wallows in descriptions of cruel women and abject men. Here and there he moralizes a little, but it is evident that this relationship between woman and man answered his own sexual needs.

The most famous of these stories is 'Venus in Furs'. Wanda, the brutal, masterful woman, lures her adorer Severin into a trap, has him tied up and then steps in front of him, whip in hand. Thereafter furs and whips became the regular properties of all masochistic literature. The whip is the instrument of lust; the fur is the man's fetish. But while in Sacher-Masoch's earlier stories the sadistic element—the woman's brutality—is still the strongest, his later stories are dominated by the passive, purely masochistic element: the sexual pleasure, rising to the orgasm, in the physical pain which his lover inflicts on the man by beating him with rods, and by whipping and tortures of every kind. Here is a sample from his story 'Under the Whip':[193]

In a holy night of love he lay at her feet and besought her in supreme ecstasy: 'Maltreat me, so that I may endure my happiness, be cruel to me, give me kicks and kisses.'

The beautiful woman bent on her adorer a strange look from her green eyes, icy and devouring, then she went across the room, stepped slowly into a splendid loose coat of red satin, richly trimmed with princely ermine, and took from her dressing table a whip, a long thong attached to a short handle, with which she was wont to punish her great mastiff.

'You want it,' she said, 'then I will whip you.'

'Whip me,' cried her lover, still on his knees, 'I implore you.'

The Baroness (most of Sacher-Masoch's stories are set in aristocratic circles) suggests tying up her lover, but he rejects this proposal indignantly, for it would look as though being whipped by her brought him no satisfaction. The Baroness then tells him that whipping him gives her no pleasure, since she loves him too much. 'But I should like,' she adds, 'to whip a man whom I did not love: that would be a pleasure.' In spite of this difference of taste the lovers have themselves photographed for a keepsake, she reclining on a sofa, with fur and whip, he at her feet.

Most of Sacher-Masoch's productions are no better than this. As literature they are far inferior to the novels of the Marquis de Sade, who possessed a certain imagination and narrative gift. In his Austrian counterpart the story always centres on the inevitable whipping scene; the rest is flat, unimaginative society trash. For all that, during his lifetime Sacher-Masoch was counted a great writer and pioneer of psychology. The *Biographical Lexicon of the Austrian Empire*, published in 1874, when he was not yet forty years old, devotes seven pages to him, and when he celebrated his twenty-fifth anniversary as an author, those who sent their congratulations included Ibsen, Björnson, Victor Hugo, Zola, Alphonse Daudet, Pasteur, Gounod, Rubinstein and many other leading men of literature, art and science from all over Europe.[194] He is still the idol of men afflicted by the same perversion as his, and even today in the personal columns of the press a 'Severin' occasionally advertises for a 'Wanda' (an allusion to the chief characters of *Venus in Furs*).

Verlaine and Rimbaud

Sacher-Masoch reflected, in a measure, the general feminine aspect of the age, but had yet something typically Eastern about him. His sexual images came from a world in which human relationships are a matter of ordering and obeying, a world ruled by police sabres and the knout, in which the victim of a thrashing respectfully kisses the hand which inflicts it. In the West, a homosexual undertone mingles not infrequently in the literature of the *Décadence*; its two most important representatives, Paul Verlaine and Oscar Wilde, were notorious homosexuals.

Verlaine, the grand master of the French *Décadence*, was sexually a monstrosity. Homosexual and heterosexual leanings alternated in him, but the former obviously affected him the more deeply. He was irritable and choleric with both men and women. Syphilis disfigured his body, absinthe ravaged his brain, he deliberately debased himself and sank into dependence on prostitutes who robbed and exploited him. When fame came to him and all Europe hailed him as one of the greatest poets of the century, he was no longer able to pull himself together.

Of well-to-do parentage, the son of an officer, Verlaine had so many distressing proclivities that he cannot justly be called a victim of homosexuality, though it was this that caused his first and severest shock. He made the acquaintance of a young poet, congenial to him, named Arthur Rimbaud; the friendship developed into a paederastic relationship. Historians of literature still debate which corrupted the other; many believe that both were already beyond corrupting. The happiness for which Verlaine deserted his wife was short-lived. The two friends attacked each other with knives, and then Verlaine shot at Rimbaud and paid for it with two years in a Belgian prison.

This was the only one of Verlaine's sexual affairs in which intellectual interests were a factor. His second friendship with a male (apart from casual adventures) was with a simple nineteen-year-old peasant boy. His third homosexual period was a vicious existence passed in the country with male prostitutes whom he fetched from Paris. Then his money ran out, and without money it was still easier for such a repulsive and degraded bohemian to make female acquaintances than to attach young men to himself. His sexual life ended as it had begun, heterosexually; nevertheless, the homosexual episodes remain an integral part both of his life and of his work.

The Tragedy of Oscar Wilde

The graph of Oscar Wilde's life coincides with Verlaine's only in its last phase of sordid poverty in cheap Paris hotels. Up to that point it ran straighter: a gradual rise, some years of glory, then a sudden fall, through a homosexual friendship. Up to the autumn of 1894, when Wilde was already about forty, nothing was known, or at least admitted, in England of his abnormal proclivities. It was a theme which was taboo in good society, although by this time many things were openly discussed which had been banned as 'shocking' in the first decades of the Victorian Age. Oscar Wilde was an extravagant, cynical dandy, not taken seriously, but his private life appeared to be unexceptionable. He had contracted a good middle-class marriage and was the father of two children, whom he worshipped. Neither was there anything in his poems or his essays to hint at his secret desires.

Wilde had, indeed, written (in French) a play on the perversion of Salome, and when Sarah Bernhardt proposed to perform in it on the London stage the Lord Chamberlain refused a licence.

Messalina. Drawing by Aubrey Beardsley.

The incident was forgotten, however, in the great success subsequently achieved by Wilde with his comedies; it was only recalled when, two years later, an English version of *Salome* appeared in book form, with provocative illustrations by Aubrey Beardsley, though Oscar Wilde was not directly responsible for its publication. A young English poet of aristocratic family, Lord Alfred Douglas, had made the translation. This seemed to indicate that Wilde himself wished to have nothing more to do with the reprobated work.

Thus, even literary circles in London were astonished when

rumours began to circulate, towards the end of 1894, that Lord Alfred Douglas was something more than a translator to Wilde. The accusation originated with Lord Alfred's father, the Marquess of Queensberry. Wilde happened to be abroad, travelling in North Africa. In Algiers he met a young French writer, André Gide, who never made any secret of his homosexual inclinations. The two spoke openly of the danger threatening Wilde in London. Gide warned the older man: 'But if you go back, what will happen? Do you know what a risk you are running?' Wilde, epigrammatic and self-assured as always, answered: 'It is best never to know. . . . I must go on as far as possible.'[196]

On his return he sued the Marquess of Queensberry for slander, and lost his case. Police were waiting outside the court to arrest him. He was tried and sentenced to two years' imprisonment for unnatural vice—or, as English law puts it, 'gross indecency'. This sentence did not destroy Wilde's creative ability: in prison he wrote De Profundis and The Ballad of Reading Gaol. Afterwards he led a nomadic, outlawed life on the Continent until his death in 1900. In England his plays, to which the London public had flocked before his trial, vanished from the theatre-bills, his books from the shop-windows. Society had passed a moral death sentence on him.[197]

The sentence on Wilde had far-reaching general consequences. It hit the entire English decadent movement. Publishers, authors, and artists became nervous. The most talented of them, Beardsley, who had ventured farthest, both in his pen-and-ink drawings and in his novel Under the Hill, crept ruefully and repentantly back to the fold; his last wish, expressed as he lay dying of tuberculosis, was that 'all obscene drawings' which he had ever produced should be destroyed. Meanwhile, the law operated with extreme severity. Even such a work as Havelock Ellis's The Psychology of Sex, the most important contribution to the subject since Krafft-Ebing, was banned.

Imperial Urnings

Charges of homosexuality were also a favourite method of

publicly attacking and overthrowing influential men, especially in the Germany of William II. The percentage of homosexuals to the total population at the turn of the century may have been no higher there than in previous ages, but their behaviour and their influence certainly made them more conspicuous. Foreigners pointed the finger at them. The French called homosexuality *le vice allemand*, the German vice. The German legislation against homosexuality was severe, but it was usually applied only in cases which involved seduction of youth or produced a real public scandal, and almost exclusively against little people.

Nevertheless, rumours circulated increasingly that men of abnormal habits were occupying high positions in the army and the civil service, and, above all, in diplomacy. Was this a sound reason for dismissing and perhaps prosecuting them, even though their record might be entirely satisfactory in other respects? The majority thought not. Liberal circles, especially, regarded such action as an unwarrantable interference in private life. In other respects Imperial Germany was no haven of liberty; it was regarded as some compensation if it was more liberal and magnanimous than many other countries in matters of sex.

Opinion, however, swung round when *Die Zukunft*, a respected Berlin periodical, declared that there existed at the Imperial Court a clique of homosexuals who were cutting off the monarch from his proper and responsible advisers and leading him into disastrous decisions, or—more dangerous still in the long run—into a policy of indecision. A point never rightly cleared up was how the Emperor came to be influenced so strongly by homosexuals, for there was no doubt whatever that William II was himself sexually normal. Nevertheless, a small group of *urnings*, as homosexuals were then called, wormed their way into the Emperor's confidence. They hedged him about, and formed a secondary government—or even the actual government, for the Emperor listened to them far more readily than he did to his own ministers.

In this acute form the question of homosexuality took on another aspect. No one was able or willing to tolerate a Court clique of perverts. The man to open the Emperor's eyes and break the power of this dangerous breed would, it was thought, be performing a great patriotic service. Maximilian Harden, the publisher of *Die Zukunft*, who with remarkable personal courage undertook this campaign, provided his readers with a second important argument against homosexuals. It was not to be supposed that there were only a few of them, the handful of malefactors at the Court. The real danger was that the *urnings* hung together everywhere, inside and outside Germany. They formed an international fraternity, and, for that reason alone, treason was always a serious possibility wherever homosexuals were. Diplomats with homosexual tendencies were therefore particularly dangerous.

In Harden's polished language, the *catamites*—another synonym for *urnings*—formed 'a comradeship which is stronger than that of the monastic orders and of freemasonry, which holds closer and throws a bond across all the walls of creed, State and class, which unites the most remote, the most foreign, in a fraternal league of offence and defence. Men of this breed are to be found everywhere, at Courts, in high positions in armies and navies, in the editorial offices of great newspapers, at tradesmen's and teachers' desks, even on the Bench. All rally together against the common enemy. Many of them look down on normal men as beings of another kind, insufficiently "differentiated".'[198]

Very similar words had been heard two hundred years earlier, when homosexual courtiers had founded a fraternity at Louis XIV's Versailles. Now, similar attempts were being made. In 1901 a certain Count Günther von der Schulenburg sent a circular to a select number of sympathizers which began with the words: 'I beg you to permit a person of equal rank and similar tastes to yourself to express in the following pages his ideas about a union of noble *urnings*.' The primary purpose of this curious league of noblemen was to be social, but it was also to be a brotherhood in arms, watching the interests of titled homosexuals. For this purpose members were required to pay a modest annual subscription; nothing more. The appeal ends: 'Without support from noble-minded *urnings* I can do nothing.'

This sounds more farcical than dangerous to the State. But, Harden argued, Count von der Schulenburg was himself only a secondary figure in this circle. It was the chief actors that must be exposed. The most influential of them all, not because he was himself very important, but because he stood closest to the Emperor, was Prince Philip zu Eulenburg und Hertefeld, member of the Herrenhaus, sometime Prussian Minister in Bavaria and German Ambassador in Vienna. He no longer had an official position, but was entirely at home at the Court. He accompanied the Emperor on all his long journeys; had his ear and enjoyed his complete confidence. He was the man Harden was chiefly after.

The Eulenburg Case

Harden had first been told of Eulenburg's peculiar proclivities by Bismarck, immediately after the latter's dismissal. That, however, was now a long time ago. Moreover, Bismarck's allusions had been phrased in too general terms. Harden was able to advance to the attack only after Privy Councillor von Holstein, for decades the *éminence grise* of the Foreign Ministry and now just dismissed, passed him more concrete material. Even then the enterprise was still uncertain, since homosexuals do not habitually operate in the open. It seemed fairly certain that Prince Eulenburg's tastes were abnormal, but that he was a practising homosexual—and only that would bring him within reach of the law—was hard to prove.

Harden accordingly opened his campaign with extreme caution. The first articles which he published in *Die Zukunft* against the Court camarilla, in 1906, were made up of allusions so obscure as to remain unintelligible to the ordinary reader. The initiated, however, would soon see who was meant; perhaps also the objects of the allusions, and the Emperor, might draw the necessary conclusions. The Court, however, made no move. Then Harden grew more explicit and mentioned names. This forced Eulenburg to sue him.

It was a similar situation to the Oscar Wilde case, but at first it went differently. Eulenburg denied all the charges on oath, and the court decided that the evidence submitted by Harden was insufficient to prove his case. A Berlin court sentenced Harden to four months' imprisonment for libel. This did not, however, end the matter. Harden followed up on a secondary line: attacks made on him by another newspaper gave him the opportunity of reopening the case, this time before a magistrate's court in Munich. A lucky chance came to his aid. After the trial in Berlin a milkman from Upper Bavaria had come spontaneously to Harden's counsel and blabbed: 'He made camarilla with me.'

The misunderstanding over the word 'camarilla', which the milkman believed to be a term out of the dictionary of sex-life, proved the key to the problem. The witness could speak openly, for he could no longer be penalized, even if he had taken any part in the 'camarilla'—it had all happened far too long ago. His story was that when he was a boy of nineteen, and working on a boat on the Starnberger See, a 'fine gentleman', who was none other than Philip Eulenburg, had made overtures to him, and eventually got what he wanted. Eulenburg had been a generous friend. He had given this young sailor 1,500 marks—more than his wages for a whole year—invited him to his castle and treated him sumptuously. A second witness was found, a fisherman from the Starnberger See, who had had exactly similar experiences.

This appeared to prove that Eulenburg had committed perjury. The law was, in fact, set in motion against him, but he was too sick to appear before the court, and thus escaped judicial punishment. But that did not matter; morally, he had been condemned, and could no longer play the councillor at Court. Harden had achieved his purpose; the camarilla vanished. It is not our purpose here to consider whether William II was better advised after he had dismissed the *urnings* from his entourage, than before. But it is certain that the Eulenburg affair contributed not a little to discrediting the monarchy and the rule of the nobility in Germany, and thus opened the way to another form of State.

Even greater were the effects on the population at large. The homosexuality trials (besides the Eulenburg trials there were others which ended inconclusively—revolving round Count

Kuno von Moltke, Adjutant to the Emperor and Governor of Berlin) were the talk of the country for years. Millions of people who had formerly possessed scarcely any inkling of the subject were now peering into every detail of homosexual relationships. Para. 175 of the German Penal Code, which contained the provisions against unnatural vice between men (similar conduct between women was not punishable) became a catchword: people used to ask, anxiously or humorously, whether their neighbours were '175-ers'.

Magnus Hirschfeld, the Berlin sexologist, probably the most distinguished authority in this field, became one of the most popular figures in Germany. Hirschfeld coined the phrase 'the third sex' to express all forms and nuances of homosexuality, including 'sexual intermediary stages'. This technical expression, too, soon became familiar to all. Magnus Hirschfeld maintained that members of the 'third sex' should be protected by law, not outlawed and persecuted as criminals, but his frequent appearances as an expert witness earned him, rather, the public reputation of a ferreter out and revealer of forbidden sex-relationships. The ferreting mania of the day was caricatured in the Munich humorous paper, *Simplizissimus*. The Weimar Poets' Monument represents Goethe and Schiller standing hand in hand: the cartoon shows Goethe cautiously withdrawing his hand and saying to Schiller: 'Fritz, let go! Here comes Magnus Hirschfeld!'

On the whole, the prosecutions and debates on the question of homosexuality strengthened the normal man's repugnance towards sexual outsiders. The demarcation-line against the third sex grew clearer. Anyone who was known to have committed in any way and at any time a homosexual offence was socially boycotted—with the result that the sexual minority were welded into a still closer clan. There were, however, many normal persons on whom the discussions about homosexuality produced a different effect. Curiosity and sensationalism inclined them, also, towards the aberrations of the third sex. These *débutants* and pseudo-*urnings* imitated the true homosexuals in speech, movements, and manners, and thus further strengthened the impression that the world, and Germany in particular, was rife with sexual anomalies and that the age was really one of perversion.

Lust of the Eye

Paris kept its reputation, even in these years, as the citadel-in-chief of heterosexual love. Social life, after a slight recession in the first years of the Republic, had again become splendid, luxurious, and extravagant, and more international than ever. It was not without justice that the years round 1900 were later called *la belle époque*; it was truly a *belle époque*—for those who could pay for what Paris offered.

In this city of glitter and luxury, woman reigned unchallenged. People came to Paris from all parts of the world to admire, conquer, and buy beautiful and elegant women. He who lacked the talent to conquer and the inclination or the money to buy, could at least feast his eyes to the full. This branch of eroticism, too, was most skilfully organized and commercialized.

Among those who do not practice normal coitus, sexual-pathology distinguishes a visual type, the so-called *voyeurs* who derive their chief satisfaction from seeing naked individuals of the opposite sex and staring at their sexual organs or even watching the coitus of others. It is only in extreme cases that this could be called perversion, since pleasure in the sight of the naked body is common even among normal persons. The lust of the eye is the first stage of sexual pleasure. In certain cases, however, it is also the last stage, because the love-action, for one reason or another, goes no farther. Either accompanied by onanism or pollution, or without them, it becomes a substitute for the normal final act. Often a *voyeur* does not even get a sight of a living woman: he contents himself with a representation. It is thus a double substitution. This substitutive eroticism is, however, no peculiarity of the abnormal. A soldier in an outlying post who pins up a photograph of a naked woman on the wall is not made a perverse *voyeur* thereby, any more than an impotent old man, to whom seeing is the only thing left him, is necessarily a pervert.

This field is very wide and full of nuances; the wishes are

manifold. The tourist industry of Paris took this fact into account and was at pains to show every man what he desired, within the limits set by his taste and his purse—from pornographic photographs to nude revues in the music halls, from strip-tease acts on the vaudeville stage to exquisite private shows for genuine *voyeurs*. Automatic machines were installed for the benefit of poorer people, who through them could view a series of photographs of a woman undressing, showing each successive motion. Other pleasures were at the disposal of well-to-do clients. There were luxury brothels in which two daughters of the house displayed variations of sexual intercourse between man and woman, with the help of repulsive appliances of leather. The establishments had agreed on a sort of mystical system of numbers, which recalled that of ancient India; there were thirty-two postures, no more and no less. Tourists still more curious were taken by guides to quiet parks outside Paris, or into houses where they could get close-up views of loving couples in their intimate embraces.

Only a small circle of *voyeurs*, however, found enjoyment in such peculiar pleasures. The average tourist was satisfied with what he saw on the stage. This was, at first, not much. While the words of the revues and cabarets were lewder than today, the dresses on the stage were more decent. It was thought daring if dancers or chorus-girls let something of their breasts be seen. The high-point of exhibitionism was the can-can in the Moulin Rouge or the Tabarin, in which the dancers revealed something of their natural charms above their long stockings. As then danced, however, it was more of an acrobatic turn than a sexual stimulant.

The first time that a woman appeared on the stage completely nude was at the Folies-Bergère in 1912. She was only visible for one moment.[199] A scandal was feared, but the public soon got used to this erotic enrichment of the theatre, and after the First World War naked women figured in the programme of every Parisian revue. Even in London the appearance of naked women on the stage was permitted on condition that they did not move. So long as they stood still, like statues, it was art—so the English specialists decided; it was only the movement of the naked body that might induce immoral thoughts in the spectator. In France, on the contrary, it was held that the sight of beautiful naked women moving their limbs gently, was a completely aesthetic one which could not offend the modesty of a man of normal tastes. The thousands of visitors from all countries who flocked to see the Paris nude revues seemed to endorse the French view of aesthetics.

18

VICTORIES OF KNOWLEDGE

THE period of which the pathological side has been considered in the preceding chapter was a great epoch of sex-research and sex-medicine in the widest sense. It did not, indeed, discover how to abolish, or even modify to any important extent, sexual anomalies due to genuine predisposition; but other maladies, physical and mental, which derived directly or indirectly from sex-life, yielded far more readily to new medical knowledge. It was, indeed, necessary first to clear away old superstitions and acquire new knowledge. Revolutionary progress in this respect was made in the last decades of the nineteenth century and the first of the twentieth.

The most important of the discoveries and therapeutic innovations were in the field of venereal disease. It is difficult to imagine today what those scourges meant to the world of fifty to a hundred years ago. In big cities the figures relating to new infections were rising disastrously. In Copenhagen, for example, 416 new cases of *lues* (syphilis) per 100,000 inhabitants were recorded every year from 1875 to 1885, and 500 new cases of *ulcus molle* (soft chancre), some of which were probably incipient cases of syphilis, for the diagnosis was still not easy. That meant that in the course of a generation roughly one person in three, men and women, contracted one of these diseases.[200]

It was much the same in other great cities. An official census of venereal disease carried through in Prussia in 1900 showed that in Berlin, in that single year, about 10,000 persons were undergoing medical treatment for gonorrhoea and over 6,000 for syphilis. In the view of the most competent experts, however, these figures were far too low. Blaschko, one of the leading experts in the field, reckoned that in Berlin and Hamburg 37 per cent. of all males contracted syphilis between their fifteenth and fiftieth years, and every male, on an average, contracted gonorrhoea more than once.

The Victims of Venereal Disease

Even if these estimates were, perhaps, somewhat exaggerated, it was beyond doubt that a very high proportion of the male population—and, of course, also many women—contracted some venereal disease in the course of their lives. In small towns and country districts the danger of infection was less: on the other hand, sufferers there were even less ready to submit to treatment, partly out of sheer laziness, partly because they were unreasonably ashamed to face the doctor. The number of cases which were treated quite inadequately, or not at all, was enormous. This resulted in severe after-effects, which had no apparent connection with sex-life but yet, in reality, derived from venereal infection.

The most conspicuous phenomenon was the steady increase in nervous and mental diseases of syphilitic origin: it was a common sight in the streets to see men walking with a peculiar strut, putting their feet involuntarily too far forward because they had lost control over their motor-nerves. This was a sure sign of the terrible disease known to doctors as *tabes dorsualis* and to laymen as spinal consumption. It was a late stage of syphilis, and sufferers from it ended infallibly in hospital, or, like Heinrich Heine, who was one of them, on a 'mattress grave'. Even more common was creeping paralysis, commonly known as softening of the brain, again a consequence of *lues*, which led irremediably to idiocy. It struck down some of the most outstanding minds: its victims in the 1890s included Guy de Maupassant and Friedrich Nietzsche. Hugo Wolf, the composer, who died in 1903, was another, as Donizetti had been half a century earlier.

No less devastating were the after-effects of gonorrhoea. Although rarely fatal, they produced prolonged and often irremediable internal complaints, especially in women. An American doctor of German origin, Emil Noeggerath, published a paper maintaining gonorrhoea to be the chief cause of sterile marriages. As it was usually the husband who infected his wife, and on their wedding night, he used the term 'honeymoon-gonorrhoea'. His colleagues were outraged at this blasphemy. Unfortunately, however, he, not they, was on the right track. Later investigations proved that in 20-30 per cent. of the cases where a marriage proved sterile, or produced only one child, gonorrhoea was responsible (Noeggerath, had indeed, put the figure at 90 per cent.).

The world stood helpless and inactive while venereal disease spread wider and wider. In most countries such diseases were regarded as a disgrace and best not mentioned. When Ibsen treated the problem of inherited syphilis on the stage, in *Ghosts*, both the aesthetes and the moralists were disgusted. Incest could be discussed in high tragedy—Sophocles himself had set the precedent —but *lues* was taboo.

The public health authorities thought that they had done all they could and needed to do when they imposed further regulations on prostitution. The old debates were revived: whether to allow brothels or forbid them, and how to get street-walkers to submit to regular medical inspection. Yet it had long been obvious that measures like this made little real difference. Berlin, where brothels had been abolished since 1844, was as heavily infected as Paris. Marseilles, with its brothel-quarter, was just as bad as Hamburg, in which street-prostitution predominated.

The problem of venereal diseases could not be solved from this angle alone. They had long ceased to be a prostitutes' speciality and had become real mass diseases. Rich and poor, married and unmarried, men and women of all professions and all age-groups suffered from them. Every country contained many tens of thousands of persons suffering from these diseases in their acute, highly infectious stages, as well as hundreds of thousands of advanced syphilitics and sufferers from chronic gonorrhoea. Even if professional prostitution had been destroyed root and branch, this would not have freed the world of venereal diseases. To control them, medical science had to produce new and more effective weapons.

Albert Neisser's Discovery of the Gonococcus

The first successful blow delivered was against gonorrhoea. Here, until the 1870s, science was still groping in complete darkness. The tragic error made by doctors in the Renaissance period, who believed gonorrhoea to be no independent disease but only an initial stage of syphilis, had maintained itself stubbornly, though it was now sometimes questioned. Since the beginning of the century some investigations, designed to prove it false, had been conducted experimentally, especially in France. In 1812 Jean François Hernandez, a doctor attached to a Toulon prison, had for the first time infected one person with gonorrhoea from another for experimental purposes. The victims were condemned criminals, with whom he could do what he liked. Hernandez's method was primitive and drastic enough. He introduced the discharge from persons suffering from gonorrhoea into the urethra of his human guinea-pigs, who then promptly contracted gonorrhoea but showed no symptoms of syphilis. The process was unnatural in this respect, that the gonorrhoea was transferred from man to man. Normally a man contracts it from a woman, or vice versa; it is only between Lesbians, or where hygienic conditions are exceptionally bad, that occasional non-heterosexual infection is possible.

Doctors and medical students repeated the Toulon experiment on their own bodies, infecting themselves with gonorrhoea from women. In the zeal of the moment, patients in hospitals were even sometimes used for these experiments without their knowledge or consent. The results were always the same, but were still not absolutely conclusive, since it happened occasionally that a person artificially infected had been suffering from syphilis, unknown to himself or the doctors, so that symptoms both of syphilis and of gonorrhoea appeared after the injection. Many doctors therefore, for safety's sake, followed the age-old practice of giving sufferers from gonorrhoea the mercury treatment for syphilis, neglecting the local treatment until the acute gonorrhoea became chronic.

The definitive proof that gonorrhoea was a separate disease was produced by a young man of only twenty-four, an assistant at the Breslau University clinic. This young man, Albert Neisser by name, was the first to apply Robert Koch's colour-technique to the investigation of venereal diseases. He smeared discharge from a gonorrhoea patient on a slide, dried it, dyed it with a violet methylic stain and placed it under a high-powered microscope. Then the riddle was suddenly solved. In the discharge were round bodies, split down the centre, like tiny coffee-beans. Nothing like this had ever been seen in any other disease. These were obviously the micro-organisms which produced gonorrhoea. Neisser was modest enough not to talk immediately of cause and effect. In the brief report on his discovery published by him in 1879 he only said that this form of micrococcus was characteristic of gonorrhoea. It was only after his observations had been confirmed in hundreds of clinics and laboratories and there could be no more doubt that he had discovered the cause of gonorrhoea, that he gave the microbe the name, now universally used in medicine, of gonococcus.

Neisser's discovery was one of the first importance. Not only had it definitively settled the old controversy over the relationship between gonorrhoea and syphilis, but there was now a certain method of ascertaining whether the sickness was healed, at any rate in the case of males. If repeated examination showed a patient to possess no more gonococci, the doctor could with a clear conscience give him leave to resume sexual intercourse, without danger to his partner.

Microscopic diagnosis remained more difficult in the case of women, since gonococci often remained latent in the female sexual organs after all external symptoms of the disease had disappeared. The commonest case was when an apparently healthy woman was delivered of a child which came into the world with blenorrhoea, a suppurating infection of the eyes—a dreadful disease which resulted in total blindness. Neisser's discovery proved beyond doubt that blenorrhoea was a genuine gonorrhoeic infection, produced by the same microbes as gonorrhoea in the sex-organs. It had thus to be attacked by the same methods.

After long experimentation, a Leipzig gynaecologist named Credé succeeded in 1884 in discovering a simple and effective remedy: all that was necessary was to drip a little solution of nitrate of silver into the eyes of every newborn child (whether gonorrhoea was suspected in the mother, or not) immediately after the severance of the umbilical cord; this saved the infant's eyesight. The success of Credé's prophylactic method was striking. Wherever it was strictly carried through, blenorrhoea in newborn infants disappeared. Many homes for blind persons could be closed, for until then most of their inmates had been persons who had contracted their blindness at birth or before it, through infection from their mothers. At the beginning of the twentieth century Germany still contained 6,000 sufferers from blenorrhoea blindness, but they gradually died out, and new cases were rarer and rarer. If any case of blindness deriving from gonorrhoea in the parents still occurred, it was due to ignorance or negligence on the part of the midwife.

Another half-century was to pass before any further decisive advance took place in the treatment of gonorrhoea in adults. Then the use of sulphonamide and, above all, the introduction of penicillin, discovered in 1929 by the Scottish bacteriologist, Alexander Fleming,[201] and of other antibiotics, made it possible for doctors to banish acute gonorrhoea in a very short period, often with a single injection, and speedy and complete cures were effected even in chronic cases. The effects on public health were not so radical, however, as the therapeutic advances might have led the world to expect. There were still thousands of sufferers from gonorrhoea who failed to submit themselves to treatment, or did so too late, and infected thousands more. Again, the fear of venereal disease diminished rapidly, and extra-marital intercourse increased accordingly, this in its turn leading to more infections.

Ehrlich-Hata 606

The fight against syphilis proved much more difficult. Up to the beginning of the twentieth century, medicine had, in practice, made no advance for three hundred years. Gradually, it is true, the after-effects of syphilis had been recognized and palliatives discovered for one or other induced disease, but the scourge itself still baffled the profession. He who had once contracted the infection had always to count with the possibility that twenty or thirty years later he might be attacked by paralysis, become an idiot, succumb to a disease of the aorta, or in some other way perish of the after-effects of syphilis. The redeeming factor in relation to sex-life was that syphilis in its tertiary stage, i.e. from about the fourth year, is usually less easily transmissible. 'Tertiary' syphilitics, even if they had not submitted themselves to any treatment, were less infectious to their fellow-beings; elderly prostitutes were therefore in this respect less dangerous than young ones. Before the disease had advanced to this stage, however, a single syphilitic could infest countless healthy persons.

It was patent that, except in very rare cases, syphilis was transmitted through direct contact; but what occasioned the infection was not known. Since Pasteur and Koch had shown the way, the germs of dozens of sicknesses had been discovered, but the most powerful microscopes and the most expert methods of staining had failed to trace the cause of syphilis. Many bacteriologists believed that it must be one of those ultra-microscopic bodies afterwards termed viruses. Then, however, light once more came suddenly—through darkness. Unlike other germs, that of syphilis could not be detected in the light. The microscope had to be darkened to see it. The first man to whom this remarkable idea occurred was an East Prussian zoologist named Fritz Schaudinn.

Schaudinn was not a doctor, and his credit therefore stood low in the profession; the great Robert Koch disliked him. He was a solitary who did not kill his microbes before examining them, nor stain them. What good could come of such methods? Yet under Schaudinn's eye, a new world was born in the microscopic field of darkness. The bodies of syphilitics were found to contain tenuous, pale, coiled microbes, shaped like the turns of a corkscrew (hence Schaudinn's name for them—*spirochaeta pallida*). They were found only in sufferers from syphilis, so that it was highly probable that they produced *lues*, through transmission from one person to the other at coitus. After Schaudinn had published his great discovery in 1905[202] he was appointed to the Institute of Tropical Hygiene in Hamburg. He died there, only a few months later, at the age of thirty-five, of experiments with the amoebae of dysentery, with which he had injected himself.

Fundamental as Schaudinn's discovery of the syphilis spirochaetae was, it had less therapeutic importance than the discovery of the gonococcus, since spirochaeta were not found in all patients, or at all stages of the disease. An advance of great practical value was made when, in 1906, the Berlin bacteriologist August von Wassermann worked out a method of blood-testing which made it often possible to decide in doubtful cases whether syphilis was present or not. If the Wassermann reaction is positive, it is certain proof of the presence of the disease; a negative reaction is, however, not absolute certain proof of the contrary. In spite of this limitation, 'the Wassermann', as doctors call it for short, has afforded important indications in innumerable cases and has often averted infection.

But improved diagnosis did not carry things much farther forward. What was needed were new, more effective treatments. In this field, too, the great advance came from Germany. Paul Ehrlich was even more individual and unorthodox in his methods of work than Schaudinn. His teachers thought he would never make a chemist, and failed him in his examination; yet, while still a young man, he made such epoch-making discoveries in the field of chemotherapy that even his opponents had to defer to him. He was somewhat of a scientific speculator, and sometimes drew too far-reaching general conclusions from his observations. He never, however, remained content with theorizing. He experimented indefatigably, trying out chemical combinations which to others appeared meaningless. He believed it was necessary to 'play' in the laboratory—i.e. to leave the imagination to have free play. He himself called his own work 'play-chemistry', a word often scornfully used against him by his critics.

Nevertheless, in 1909 (by which time he was fifty-five years old and head of an experimental institute in Frankfurt-am-Main) he succeeded, with the help of this play-chemistry, in discovering a cure for syphilis which has since freed millions from their sufferings and prolonged their lives. This was salvarsan. It was not at all the outcome of idle playing about, but the result of a long series of experiments with the derivatives of arsenic. Ehrlich used to keep careful records of his work, and this was precisely the 606th experiment which he had made along these lines. As a Japanese assistant named Sahachiro Hata had been helping him, he gave the preparation the laboratory number (which quickly came into general use) of Ehrlich-Hata 606.

The successes achieved with salvarsan were astonishing. I myself still remember how Albert Neisser, who had since become Director of the University Clinic for Venereal and Skin Diseases in Berlin, a confirmed sceptic, showed his pupils an athlete on whose chest were tattooed the words 'Love, Suffer, Forget'. 'Look here, gentlemen,' said Neisser, 'that was this patient's motto, and it has come true; love—that was love; suffer—that was *lues*; forget—that is salvarsan.'

Then, as with every new medicine, there came the disappointments. The technique of using salvarsan was very complicated, and grave accidents happened before doctors had mastered it. Ehrlich, however, had not rested on his laurels. He had made some three hundred further experiments, and at the 914th he discovered a substance which was less dangerous and also easily dissoluble; this he called neo-salvarsan. In this form the preparation was used throughout the whole world.

It was soon certain, beyond any doubt, that it was possible to remove the symptoms of the disease in its first stages and greatly to diminish the danger of infection. The great question remained, however: were the patients really cured, or had they to expect the later, often fatal, after-effects of syphilis? Only time could show. The answer proved unexpectedly favourable. Tabes vanished almost completely, and both paralysis, the scourge of the nine-teenth century, and also the other organic diseases of syphilitic origin, became much less common. New cases were still counted in their tens of thousands, but even they became fewer year by year with the diminution of the risk of infection. In Germany there were still 215,000 fresh cases of *lues* in 1919; only 75,000 in 1927, and barely 43,000 in 1934.[202] In the course of fifteen years the number of new infections had thus fallen by 80 per cent. Since that year the scourge has been still further reduced by anti-biotics, which have been used with effect in this field also; and there is a good prospect that one day this worst plague of sex-life will become, in civilized countries, a mere memory, as leprosy is today.

The Sex-life of the Child

Just as doctors were beginning to conquer venereal disease, the world learnt that there were other illnesses—this time, of psychic character—very closely connected with sex-life. This disconcerting discovery was made in Vienna, the metropolis of sex-research, but not by one of the great figures whose names alone carried weight everywhere, but by a specialist in nervous disorders whose name was quite unknown outside a very small circle of his colleagues: Sigmund Freud.

Freud's thesis sounded absurd enough: he maintained that some of the commonest nervous diseases, especially hysteria and the obsessional neuroses, were to be traced to the patient's having suffered a *trauma*, or mental shock, in earliest childhood. This was usually the result of the child's erotic impulses having been thwarted and then repressed or otherwise prevented from achieving their aims. The incident had since been forgotten, but lived and worked on in the unconscious, and led to the formation of morbid notions and inhibitions which might even induce physical paralysis. The doctor's business was to recall to the patient's memory the original incident and the accompanying effect; the patient would then be liberated from his complex, and often completely cured.

That there are nervous disorders which have their roots in the unconscious and can be removed by a catharsis—an unloading and discharge of mental distress—had long been known, although in earlier days it had been poets and priests, rather than doctors, who had occupied themselves with the phenomenon. But that the true cause of the mischief should lie in a sexual experience of childhood seemed quite incredible. Even admitting the hypothesis that childhood impressions might produce morbid symptoms twenty or thirty years later—as the germs of syphilis might produce paralysis—how could it be supposed that those impressions were sexual in character? Sexual life clearly only began with puberty. Before that the sexual organs of boys and girls were too undeveloped to fulfil any sort of function. But without the physical preconditions no mental effects could be produced. This was common ground among doctors of all schools. Only a fool could doubt it.

Freud did not allow these objections to dissuade him. He investigated other fields of the mind, of healthy people as well as sick. He got his patients to tell him their dreams, analysed his own, and found sexual ideas figuring in all of them. Even while men slept, sex was awake. The sexual instinct, it was true, disguised itself in peculiar ways. It expressed itself in a language of symbols which had to be learnt before a dream could be properly interpreted.

It was the same case in the almost totally unexplored field of slips in everyday life—slips of the tongue and the pen, forgetting or mixing up names and things. Sex was always at the bottom of them, playing its strange, undetected game. Often its behaviour was quite harmless, but often very malicious, like the medieval devil of sex. It harassed men, and women even more, and if they repressed it, kicked up a row inside them in the most extraordinary ways, and confused their spirits.

When Freud was not far short of fifty he determined to make a vigorous attack on this disturber of the peace, but not by trying to cast it out, like a medieval devil. The sexual instinct was part of human nature. But it had to be exposed, so to speak, and taken where it did most damage: in childhood. In 1905 Freud published his *Three Essays on the Theory of Sexuality*, these constituting, as he afterwards himself emphasized, no complete theory of sex, but 'containing only what psychoanalysis is compelled to accept, or able to confirm'. Nevertheless, the book is still fundamental for Freud's doctrine.

Sigmund Freud was no unworldly academic scholar. He knew very well what were the problems on which public interest was then focused, and up to a point he shaped his work accordingly. The very title of the first of the three essays touched on a subject which at the time was of topical interest: 'The Sexual Aberrations.' It is true that Freud had little new to say on perversion among adults; but this was for him only a pretext to lead on to the real theme which interested him, perversion in children.

But is it possible to speak of perversion in children at all? The idea of perversion supposes by definition an exception from the rule, a small minority. In matters of sex mankind is extremely democratic: the majority decides. The dispositions and the behaviour of the majority are normal, the divergences therefrom are abnormal. If most human beings were homosexual, homosexuality would be the normal, and heterosexuals the abnormal, even though the function of reproduction still fell on them. In this respect there is no other criterion but the majority principle. But according to Freud, everybody has perverse leanings. If seduced by adults or by other children, children can even become 'polymorphously perverse',[204] i.e. they are capable of every kind of perversion. As a rule, however, human beings in their childhood go, sexually speaking, through a certain development with clearly demarcated stages, each more or less corresponding to some form of adult perversion.

Freud describes this process in his second essay, which bears the challenging title of 'Infantile Sexuality' and forms the kernel of his theory. Infantile sexuality is perhaps his greatest discovery, or, as some think, his greatest invention. In any case, the idea was absolutely new, even allowing that a doctor or a pedagogue before him may have spoken of sexuality, or even of sexual activity, in a child. For previous observers such manifestations of active sex-propensity were signs of dangerous precocity or regrettable degeneration, or simply vice, from which the child must be forcibly weaned. Freud, on the contrary, regards them as completely normal.

Every human being is born with a sex-impulse (called by Freud 'libido'), a need, the satisfaction of which, like the stilling of hunger, is accompanied by certain pleasurable sensations. Germs of sexual activity exist even in newborn infants. They go on developing for a while, then they are suppressed, until the child's sex-life manifests itself clearly in about its third or fourth year. This 'flowering time' of infantile sexuality, which usually lasts till the fifth year of life, is followed by another period of latency, lasting till puberty. Even the periods of relative sexual quiescence are, however, by no means unimportant for the sexual development and the later mental life. It is during them that the prime causes of severe mental conflicts and defects often occur.

While the sex-life of adults is chiefly concentrated on the region of the genitals, in sucklings and very young children it is physically more diffused, but yet attached mainly to 'erogenous' zones, i.e. to certain parts of the body which the child obviously likes having touched or moved. Even sucklings enjoy playing with their external genitals, little boys with the penis, little girls with the clitoris—an occupation which Freud regards as masturbation. A second phase of infantile masturbation begins in about the fourth year of life; a third is the familiar onanism of the age of puberty.

This preoccupation with the genitals is, however, only one of the forms of infantile sex-life, and by no means the most characteristic. Two other erogenous zones appear to afford a child much more pleasure still: the mouth and the anus. Freud accordingly distinguishes an 'oral' phase, in which the mouth, particularly the lips and the tongue, take over the role of a sex-organ, and the somewhat later 'anal' phase, in which the libido is satisfied by anal activity; more precisely, by stimulation of the erogenous mucous membrane of the intestine.

Oral eroticism in its earliest stages includes the reception of food, sucking the mother's or nurse's breast or even the rubber teat of the milk-bottle. Hunger and libido are not yet distinguished and both are directed towards the same object. The suckling flings itself on the breast which nurtures it as though it would devour it. It wants, so to speak, to incorporate its sex-object in itself, for which reason Freud gave the oral sexual pleasure the somewhat forceful epithet 'cannibalistic'. Later, however, the need for nourishment becomes completely distinct from the pleasure in sucking—the sucking of any object, the thumb being a favourite one. The sucking of a finger, according to Freud, is a sexual process.

The 'anal' phase bears even more clearly features found among adult perverts, not only paederasts, but also sadists. Freud therefore calls the second pre-genital phase 'that of the sadistic-anal organization'. Children forcibly hold back their stools; everything connected with excrement gives them pleasure; they soil themselves, they retain their excrement as though it were some object belonging to them, of which they have power to dispose. But masochistic elements, also, appear: many children wet the anal parts, although this produces a painful irritation.

The Oedipus Complex

Even this does not exhaust the repertoire of infantile sexuality. In every child there is a sexual explorer. Its thirst for knowledge becomes particularly lively if it gets a brother or a sister. It wants to know whence and how this new thing has come, and sometimes conceives the most remarkable anatomical ideas. But it is equally interested to know whether the newborn infant is made the same way as itself. It is particularly concerned with the question of the genitals. A little boy expects the younger child to have a penis, like itself, and when the child is a girl he regards her lack of a penis as a defect for which he can find no natural explanation. Some act of violence must have been done, and this frightens him. So, according to Freud, there arise 'castration complexes', which may later lead to serious mental derangements. Girls appear to be less surprised at their brothers being made differently from themselves. At the most, the sister is envious of the little boy who possesses a member lacking in herself.

If not the child's own brothers and sisters, then other children furnish the answer to the question of the genitals and the associated problem of sex-differences. Children are at once *voyeurs* and exhibitionists. They want to see and to show what they have. Boys, in particular, show off with their genitals. Freud speaks of a 'phallic phase'—and this sexual pride sometimes leads to morbid narcissism and to other sexual aberrations and neuroses. Perversion and neurosis are in Freud's mind closely connected. Both are survivals of infantile sexuality. If one or other of the sexual activities peculiar to childhood becomes 'fixated' and overpowerful, perversions arise; if, however, the inclination to such activities is not genuinely overcome but only repressed, often by punishment or threats of it, the desire is transmuted into mental inhibitions of apparently quite a different nature, and thus neuroses arise. 'The neurosis,' says Freud in a famous sentence, 'is, so to speak, the negative of the perversion.'

The child's sex-life, except for the sucking at the breast of the mother or the nurse, is 'auto-erotic'; it satisfies itself on its own body. This does not mean, however, that it feels no sexual emotions, whether of inclination or aversion, towards other persons. It has long been known that heterosexual, and also homosexual, leanings towards other children are felt long before puberty. Precisely the social circles which attached most importance to good upbringing and were very severe on eroticism in young people, used to stimulate child-eroticism by 'bride and bridegroom' masquerades in public processions, at weddings of adults and on other occasions—always on the assumption that these were innocent child's play and had nothing to do with sexuality.

Freud taught that the sexual impulse towards other persons also arises in earliest childhood, being at first directed towards the persons nearest the child—its parents and brothers and sisters, but also nurses, nurse-maids, servants, governesses, etc. According to him, there was no such thing as a perfect, a-sexual love, towards one's family. Particularly the child's love for its parents assumes in many cases a typically erotic character. The same groupings, moreover, always appear. The commonest and most clearly-marked is the Oedipus Complex, the love of the son for the mother, combined with jealousy of the father and of brothers to whom the mother shows attachment. The analogous complex in a girl—called, by a similar allusion to Greek mythology, the Electra Complex—occurs when a daughter is erotically attached to her father; she tries to take her mother's place and to keep her away from her husband; she even wants 'her father to present her with a child, to bear him a child'.[205]

The sexual phantasies of children are not markedly monogamous. Even while the son is engaged in the spirit in an incestuous relationship with his mother, and the daughter with her father, they make up to one another. If a brother has several sisters, he usually picks out one of them and makes her his favourite sister, behaving towards her as erotically as any lover; similarly, if a girl has several brothers, she usually concentrates her affections on one, her favourite brother, with the corresponding feelings of jealousy if some other of her sisters has chosen the same brother to be her secret lover. It may be surprising to read that in Freud's kindergarten, in which homosexual tendencies are so rife, erotic relationships inside the family are directed towards the opposite sex. Even so, however, there remains the anomaly of twofold incest. If Freud is to be believed, every apparently normal family is a hotbed of the most perverse passions.

Freud's Opponents and His Pupils

It is not surprising that Freud's theory of sex should have been very widely regarded as the abortion of a morbid brain. What, compared with this, was the Marquis de Sade, or Sacher-Masoch? They had depicted a few monsters, a few obvious perverts, but had always stressed that the great majority of human beings led entirely different lives. Freud, however, turned the exception into the rule. All children were little monsters, or at any rate, so predisposed. Mothers, fathers, teachers rose in their wrath. Where were the proofs of so appalling an assertion?

The evidence submitted by Freud to the public was in fact somewhat meagre: a few interesting observations on the lives of children, references to processes which had perhaps been regarded too uncritically, or just as naughtiness, like the obstinacy in the 'anal-sadistic' phase; plus a few detailed case-histories of persons who had been cross-questioned on their sex-lives and family relationships in a way not previously used in medical practice. Very nearly all of what Freud regarded as arguments was simply an interpretation—a very daring one, at that—of generally familiar facts. He had arrived at his idea of infantile sexuality by two methods: first, by drawing very vague analogies between the pleasurable sensations which children elicit from their own bodies, and perverse sexual acts of adults; and secondly, by interpreting the feelings of children towards their parents as a sort of eunuch-love or eunuch-hate, the sexual manifestations of the impotent.

Nothing had been proved beyond the possibility of doubt. One could believe it or not. Most doctors did not believe it. When, at the Hamburg Psychiatric Congress of 1910, a speaker in the general discussion raised the subject of Freud's theories, the chairman, Wilhelm Weygandt, stopped him, saying: 'That is no subject for a scientific congress; it is a matter for the police.' Ten years after that, when there were already many specialist practitioners of psychoanalysis and Freud had been given a Chair at the University of Vienna, he was still completely ignored by the psychiatric clinic of Berlin University, and it was the same with most other European universities. Even his books made their way only gradually, although they were written in a crystal-clear style, without any of Krafft-Ebing's learned obscurity. In four years not all the thousand copies of the first printing of the *Three Essays on the Theory of Sexuality* had been sold. Freud was regarded not merely as a charlatan, but as a scoundrel who had libelled childish innocence and besmirched pure childish love.

There were, however, special reasons why the great majority of scholars were so antagonistic to Freud, who had, after all, been lecturing at Vienna University since 1885. This was the time at which the supreme ambition of psychologists and psychiatrists was to establish the relationship between body and mind. Every mental process had to have its counterpart in the brain or the nervous system. It seemed especially important to unearth the physical roots of phenomena connected with sex-life. Could there be a psychology without a physiology of sex, without an anatomy of sex?

To this Freud answered, in tones of increasing acerbity, that psychoanalysts could not wait until branches of knowledge dealing with the physical world came to its help. It had to operate with purely psychological conceptions and 'keep itself clear of assumptions of anatomical, chemical or physiological nature alien to itself'.[206] These words, coming from a man who himself had started as a physiologist and brain anatomist, sounded derisive. Nor was the terminology created by Freud to make his ideas more easily intelligible to his pupils, and to spread his teachings, calculated to win him friends among his conservative colleagues. Sometimes he used literary paraphrases, e.g. the metaphor of the Oedipus Complex, but more often coarse, blunt expressions which caused offence.

The chief objection raised against his theory was, however, that it exaggerated the sex-element. Critics talked of the 'pansexualism' of psychoanalysis, which was alleged to try to explain everything by a sex-motive. Freud was able to rejoin that he recognized the 'ego-instinct' as well as the libido, and contrasted them as life and death instincts. Nevertheless, there was something in the objection that Freud was suffering, if not from pansexualism, at least from sex-mania; that he was a sort of sexual *voyeur*, only concerned with finding and observing sexual processes. His over-valuation of the libido was also one of the main reasons why his most important pupils soon parted company with him.

The Viennese psychologist Alfred Adler saw the strongest force not in sex but in the will to power, which is often the outcome of an inferiority complex. In Freud this motive force, too, is ultimately sexual, but it plays only a secondary part inside the 'anal-sadistic phase' and in the narcissistic tendencies arising out of the 'castration complex'. For Adler, eroticism is only a form of the will to conquer and rule; even the yielding of self is only an indirect way to attain domination over another human being. Adler also doubts the reality and sincerity of childhood sexual recollections: 'The neurotic does not suffer from reminiscences—he manufactures them.'[207] Mental disorders, he maintained, did not derive from the obscurity of the past, but from a purpose often still sleeping in the unconscious. The need of self-assertion was the essential factor. Where the difference of opinion was so great, collaboration with Freud was of course impossible, and Adler went his own way.

Soon after this—in 1913—another of Freud's earliest disciples, the Swiss psychoanalyst C. G. Jung, also forsook his master. Jung still retained the expression libido, but gave it a totally different sense. Jung's libido is the sum of the mental energy, which can embrace all possible forces and impulses, not least those collective moral, religious and magical ideas which live in a people (a conception which elicited from Freud the comment that he himself was a dualist, in that he recognized sex-instincts and ego-instincts, but that Jung was a monist).[208] Jung does not deny the existence of a sexual element in mental life, but he has so de-sexualized the conception of the libido as to leave practically nothing Freudian in it. More recently, he has turned more and more to spiritualistic studies, a fact which, the trend of the age being what it is, has substantially increased the number of his adherents. He was, however, one of the first to apply psychoanalytic methods in the treatment of severe mental disorders, particularly schizophrenia.

The latest Austrian school, although standing nearer to Freud on points of detail, has tried to get on without any concept of the libido.[209] The word 'psychoanalysis', too, is being replaced in its country of origin (in which, incidentally, it never enjoyed wide circulation) by another expression, also occasionally used by Freud, 'depth-psychology'. This means a Freudianism freed from all objectionable elements—house-trained, as it were—blended with some Adler and Jung.

Freud's doctrine, in its original form, is, however, by no means dead. A considerable part of it has now been adopted by medical teaching; in a text-book[210] by that very psychiatrist who pronounced sentence of outlawry on Freud in 1910, Freud is one of the authors most frequently quoted. His influence in England, and above all in America, is still much greater than on the continent of Europe. It extends far beyond medicine and psychology. No doctrine born of natural science, since Darwin's day, has evoked such echoes in intellectual life, in literature, in education, even in day-to-day speech, as Freud's sexual theory. Even this, indeed, is no evidence for the truth of the Oedipus Complex or for the hypothesis of castration-anxiety.

It remains, however, Freud's undeniable achievement to have been the first to establish a self-contained system of healthy and morbid sex-life. Even though individual stones in the edifice may crumble, the structure as a whole stands fast, thanks to the genius of a great, unflinching thinker.

19

THE EMANCIPATION OF WOMAN

For a hundred years sex had influenced politics, but politics had not greatly influenced sex. By now, however, plenty of sexual problems had accumulated which only political decisions could solve. The issue of the First World War gave the opportunity. Four great empires: the German Reich, the Austro-Hungarian Monarchy, Czarist Russia, and the Ottoman Empire —had collapsed; from the Rhine to the Tigris the world was in open revolt. Many new States came into being and even the older ones gave themselves new constitutions; everyone wanted to build up a new life on new foundations. A natural concomitant was thorough revision of the legislation on sex-life.

The victorious States were naturally less convinced of the necessity for radical change, but even in them the readiness for reform was there. The common denominator which dominated the debates on sex in both camps was the word 'freedom'; the specific objective was the emancipation of women from all restrictions and disadvantages attaching to them from earlier ages. It is true that each country understood this in its own way; yet an underlying tendency of markedly liberal character was perceptible in every country, independently of forms of State and economic systems.

After 1918, complete equality for women in public and professional life seemed justified by the experiences of the war. Militarily, indeed, the First World War had been fought entirely by men, apart from small auxiliary formations and the part taken by women in partisan and revolutionary fighting. But behind the Front, women had 'played a man's part' in innumerable occupations into which they had not been admitted in time of peace.

This of itself gave them a claim to complete political equality. In all Eastern countries, and most Western, they were given both the active and passive franchise; religious and conservative circles which had previously opposed this now saw that women, of nature or of tradition, incline to conservative views, and became the most zealous champions of votes for women; but even the parties of the Left, which stood to lose by it, supported it on principle.

Simultaneously with the parliamentary vote, women conquered the professions and public positions previously closed to them—women were appointed to high administrative positions. At last it was recognized that the word 'statesman' was out of date, and that it was not only among crowned heads that real 'stateswomen' of political and administrative ability were to be found. The Anglo-Saxon countries were the first to draw the logical deduction and to appoint women to ministerial office. After some resistance, women were also admitted to a profession which they had till then been allowed to practise only in the drawing-room or the bedroom—that of diplomacy. The result showed that even without gold-laced uniforms, women carried out their jobs as Ambassadors and Ministers just as well, or just as badly, as men. The strongest resistance was to admitting women to the Bench, since it was doubted whether they would be objective; but at least they were everywhere allowed on assessors' panels and juries—a point of considerable importance especially in sex-cases; women are usually severer than men.

Taken by and large, the battle for the constitutional emancipation of women was over by the end of the 1920s. Women had gained least in the land of women, France, which opened the doors of its legislature to them only after the Second World War. But, taken all in all, the change has been very swift. According to an Unesco report, there were in 1955 only fifteen countries in which women were excluded from the franchise; the only two such European States were Switzerland and Liechtenstein. A few decades had brought woman more political gains than thousands of years before that.

Meanwhile, what has thus been solved is only part of the problem, and not, perhaps, its most important part. The limitations under which women suffer in marriage and family life, in respect of pre-marital sexual intercourse, in decisions relating to conception and birth, are of deeper importance for their lives. Here the question is not simply one of equal rights with men, but of women's entire sex-rights. What is permitted to them, what forbidden? Not everything can be regulated by law. Even if the State removed every ban, this would be no guarantee of absolute freedom. Custom, religion, economic and social restraints would continue to play an enormous role in all questions relating to sex. But law and justice still mark off the limits which the individual knows that he is bound to observe—even when he transgresses them.

Turkey Unveiled

There were two countries in which, during the First World War and immediately after it, the sex-laws were altered in a way so radical as to justify calling the changes a true sexual revolution. These were Russia and Turkey. In both, State and Church had previously been closely interlinked, and the sex-law of the day was based almost entirely on the old ecclesiastical law. In both a sharp dividing line was now drawn between Church and State: sex-law became the State law. But the parallel only holds good up to this point; beyond it, the objects and methods of the sexual revolutions were entirely different.

Today we know that the sexual revolution in Turkey was the more radical, the more lasting, and the more far-reaching in its effects. It was, indeed, also the less original. It amounted, in essence, to Turkey's adopting the marriage and family law of the Western world. On paper, the process was accomplished very simply by the decision of the Turkish National Assembly, on 20 April 1926, to bring in a new civil code which was, trivial modifications apart, simply a copy of what was at the time the most recent and most modern of the Western civil codes, that of Switzerland. As early as 1918, and increasingly thereafter, when

Mustafa Kemal had become absolute dictator of the new Turkey, the government introduced a great series of reforms designed to abolish polygamy and other masculine privileges. It was only the civil code of 1926, however, which declared monogamy the sole admissible form of marriage. Even the well-to-do classes—and in practice they alone were affected—accepted the prohibition of polygamy remarkably quickly and easily.

With the thousand-year-old marriage law of the Koran there disappeared also the outward signs of the old régime. Men had to put off the fez, and women the veil. The *yashmak*, the slit veil worn by Turkish ladies of quality, had, indeed, been only a frail armour against masculine lust. It left revealed precisely those parts of the face hidden by the Venetian mask, the eyes and the upper half of the nose. Moreover, it was woven of such thin white material as to leave every curve visible. Twenty years earlier, however, under Abdul Hamid, it would still have gone ill with any woman who exposed her mouth to the sight of strange men in the street. This unveiling law, too—not a permission, but an order, disobedience of which was punishable—was carried through very quickly and energetically. By the summer of 1926 no veiled woman was to be seen in a Turkish town; it was only in the country districts that a woman sometimes, out of habit, drew her kerchief over her face if a man approached her.

In the West the unveiling of the Turkish women was looked at chiefly in its picturesque aspect. What did it matter if Turkey modernized itself in externals? The area left to the new Turkey contained a bare fourteen million inhabitants, and outside were 250 million Mohammedans who held strictly to the old customs and the old marriage law. In Syria, Iraq, and Egypt no Mohammedan woman showed herself out of doors unveiled; in Persia, the women were wrapped in thick black veils, like shades of the underworld. Yet the Turkish example infected those countries also. One after the other emancipated its women from the medieval compulsion to hide themselves. Other régimes were not so radical as that of Mustafa Kemal. It was a social revolution from above. The ladies of the ruling classes and of the Courts put aside the veil, showed themselves in public in deep *décolletées*, travelled blithely to Europe to enjoy themselves there. The women of the people began by being shocked; then they imitated the example of their social superiors, so far as their means allowed, and began to Westernize their own clothes.

The sport movement and the militarization of women, especially in Egypt, set the seal on the breach with tradition. Young Mohammedan girls paraded through the streets in shorts. Men got used to the sight, and no longer felt an erotic thrill at the sight of a woman's bare thigh. The sexual over-excitability of the East turned out to be a mere habit which did not stand up to the changing times. In the course of half a generation male sex, too, had become Westernized.

Relics enough of the old order, of course, lived on. To this day the great majority of Mohammedan women live in complete economic dependence on men and this alone makes for a sex hierarchy which is only slightly mitigated by the man's sexual subordination. But the tendency of the development is unmistakable. Polygamous marriage still exists in North Africa and Arabia, but it is dying out in the countries of the Middle East. In this respect, too, what Mustafa Kemal introduced was not only a national revolution but also an international one.

Marriage in Soviet Russia

While Westernization was an end for the Turkish sex-revolution, for the Russian it was only a starting-point. In December 1917, only a few weeks after the victory of the Bolsheviks, the new government issued a law abolishing church marriage—until then the sole legal form—and replacing it by civil registration. At the same time divorce was introduced, also effected by simple notification to a registrar, conditional only on the consent of both parties. If only one party wanted the divorce and the other not, the courts had to decide. It was a great revolutionary act, closely modelled on the French legislation of 1792, but still only a provisional solution. Did it conform to the principles on which the new socialist State was to be built up? Opinion among the men of the new régime differed widely on this point.

In fact, when the Russian Revolution broke out, the Marxists possessed no uniform doctrine on sex-life. They were only agreed on the thesis that marriage in bourgeois society had been corrupted by capitalist influences and that abolition of private property would simultaneously sweep away the exploitation and humiliation of women by marriages for money, by domestic slavery, and by prostitution. The aim, in so far as a clear aim existed, was to separate economic life and sex. Sex-life was to be de-economicized, and thus made again pure and natural, no longer distorted as it had been for so many thousands of years by male greed and tyranny.

This was certainly a lofty and noble intention, but hardly sufficient foundation for a new order of sex-life. Above all, the question arose, how had nature created men? Were they fundamentally monogamous, or polygamously inclined? Was the family a natural community, or only a product of specific economic systems?

Karl Marx, himself a virtuous husband and father, had not troubled greatly over these questions. The only authoritative answer to them was contained in a few sentences in a late work by Friedrich Engels. In his *Origin of the Family*, published at the age of sixty-four, Engels had declared himself a fervent adherent of monogamy, boldly proclaiming: 'Since sexual love is of its nature exclusive—although this exclusiveness is today only completely realized in women—so marriage founded on sexual love is of its nature monogamous.' Engels was convinced that, in the socialist State of the future, men too would very soon become monogamous. 'If, now, the economic considerations which make women tolerate this habitual infidelity of men—anxiety for their own livelihood, and still more, for the future of their children—if these disappear, then all experience shows that the effects of the equality thus achieved by women will be far more to make men truly monogamous than to make women polyandrous.'[211]

Even Engels did not, indeed, believe that love lasted for ever in the heart of every married man or woman. 'If only the marriage founded on love is moral, only that in which love lasts remains moral.' Consequently, the emergency exit of divorce must be allowed, not after adultery has been committed, but to prevent the commission of it. Things are not to be made too difficult for married couples, and they are to be spared 'wading through the unnecessary filth of a divorce case'.

In essentials, the legislation of the Russian Revolution followed these principles. By no means all the revolutionaries, however, agreed with them. Although the leading men of the Revolution were in no way libertines, many of them thought that Engels had rated man's monogamist instinct too high and that he had been too much influenced by the ideas of the bourgeois-romantic ideal marriage. Other and still weightier objections came from the economic doctrinaires. Even if the State were in the future to take material charge of the children (and for the present, that was out of the question), was there not a danger that monogamy would help the old family egotism to survive, and was this compatible with a collectivized economic system?

These questions were argued for several years. The casting vote was finally given by Lenin, who came down decisively in favour of the preservation of the family on a basis of monogamous marriage. After Lenin's death in 1924, however, the opposition reasserted itself. The progress of industrialization and of collectivization worked in the same direction; millions of marriages had broken up because the husband or the wife had found work in another town, often in a far-distant province. Married couples were parted for life and contracted new sexual relationships without first divorcing the previous partner. Concubinage flourished, fostered by the housing shortage. The institution of wedlock was on the way to dissolving itself.

The marriage legislation of 1927 encouraged this process by further facilitating divorce. Free sexual cohabitation was put on the same level as marriage. A husband who was living with another woman no longer needed to ask his wife's consent to a divorce, or to plead for it before the courts—a simple notification to the registrar (*ZAGS*) sufficed. A little later the wife received a notification that she was divorced. It was the same thing when the wife contracted a new partnership without her husband's knowledge. The registry office looked after the whole matter. This was the period of the famous 'divorce postcards'. Formally, monogamy still existed in the Soviet Union, but in practice this was only a legalization of free love and often only a cover for promiscuity and even prostitution.

The very numerous abuses, and love and family tragedies, which resulted from this system led to a popular reaction. But the most important point of all was that these short-term marriages did not bring the State as many children as the Kremlin wished. Economic conditions had improved and the foreign political situation had grown more threatening. The State needed workers and soldiers, and was anxious that the new generation should be large. Marriage for life seemed, after all, the best means of ensuring this. In 1936 a new law was enacted, completely reversing the tendency of the previous legislation. Registry offices could only register a divorce if both parties consented. The divorce was entered on the documents of the parties concerned, and—the biggest deterrent of all—a progressive tax was imposed on divorces. The first cost fifty roubles, the second 150, the third and all subsequent divorces, 300 each. That was a sum which few workers could get together.

In July 1944, towards the end of the Second World War, divorce was made more difficult still. The procedure was assimilated to that of Western countries. A person wishing for a divorce had first to apply to the People's Court; the court tried to reconcile the parties, and only if this proved impossible was the divorce pronounced. At the same time the fees were raised, up to 2,000 roubles for habitual divorcers, so that only people earning large incomes, such as engineers, writers, or high civil servants could afford the luxury of several divorces. Even they preferred not to approach the courts too often, for divorce had now a bad name. The hallmark of a good Soviet citizen, from this date on, was a good, solid married life.

State-controlled Abortion

In the subsidiary fields, sex-policy ran parallel to the development of marriage law. What most surprised and interested other countries was the Soviet Union's legalization of abortion. Marxists of every shade had always branded abortion as a product of unhealthy economic systems. Now, however, in the first modern State to hoist the flag of Socialism, it was precisely the women who insisted on being allowed to interrupt an unwanted pregnancy. It is true that conditions were extremely hard and that the motive of most women was undoubtedly fear that they would be unable to bring up a child. Yet there were many who saw in the matter a touchstone for the emancipation of women. A régime which had promised women total freedom could not forbid them to decide for themselves whether or not they wanted to bear a child.

The government consulted the doctors. Some were against, others thought that putting abortion under State control was still better than exposing women to the perils of secret illegal operations. This argument won the day, and 18 November 1920 saw the issue of a decree which forms a landmark in sexual history. For the first time since antiquity a great country authorized abortion, on condition that it was induced by a doctor in a public hospital. The official explanation given was that the previous secret operations had produced blood-poisoning in 50 per cent. of the cases and death in 4 per cent. The new law was not, therefore, as a few Western observers believed, a recognition of 'a woman's right to her own body', but simply a public-health measure.

Its practical effects were limited, at least in the first period, by the fact that so soon after the Civil War and the war with Poland, Russia did not possess nearly enough hospital beds to accommodate all the women who wanted not to have children.

The decree remained in force for sixteen years. Only in 1936, simultaneously with the tightening up of the divorce law, was abortion again made illegal out of considerations of population policy. Important exceptions were that it was permitted where continued pregnancy constituted a serious threat to the life or health of the mother; or where serious transmissible disease was present in either parent. Doctors contravening the law rendered themselves liable to one to two years' imprisonment. The penalties incurred by the woman, on the other hand, were made milder: public admonition for the first offence and a fine if it was repeated.

The new tendencies after the death of Stalin were reflected, *inter alia*, in Soviet sex-legislation. A decree of 17 August 1954 abolished the legal responsibility of a pregnant woman for an abortion, and on 23 November 1955 the Presidium of the Supreme Soviet resolved on the complete abolition of the ban on abortion. The official preamble, however, again emphasized that the purpose of the government of the U.S.S.R. was not to encourage abortion but, on the contrary, to promote maternity. The measures which had been taken to achieve this purpose and 'to awaken conscience and the desire for culture in women' made it possible to dispense with the ban on abortion.

Even under this new dispensation, however, operation was only legal in a public clinic properly equipped for the purpose. Doctors or midwives who undertook secret abortions risked ten years in prison. It is clear that the authorities expected the new system to produce more favourable results also in the field of population-policy than the old, under which the birthrate had been sinking rapidly.

The Battle over Birth Compulsion

No country except the Soviet Union allows women a general legal right to interrupt pregnancy. Abortion is considered a serious offence, and in many countries punished by prison sentences of barbarous severity. To assist in or to connive at it is also punishable. From the moment that a woman has conceived, she ceases to be a free agent; she must bear the fruit. This is the law as it stands.

Even immediately after the First World War, however, voices

demanding reform were raised in the West. The opponents of the ban on abortion talked of 'birth compulsion'; its advocates, of an elementary law of nature. Yet even if birth compulsion were a law of nature, it was a fact that millions of women all over the world broke it every year. Since abortions had to be induced privately, the exact figure was not obtainable, but to judge from the miscarriages and other indications which came to the doctors' eyes, it must have been extremely high, and it was rising steadily. The fall in the birth-rate which had set in since the turn of the century in almost all Western countries was by no means due exclusively to the use of contraceptive devices and methods, but in very large measure to interruption of pregnancy. All specialists agreed on that.

Abortion was most widespread in the United States. American doctors believed that in many towns the number of abortions was almost as high as that of births. In Europe, France led the way. Estimates for Paris as early as 1910 went as high as 100,000. But Imperial Germany was now not far behind France in this respect. Ernst Bumm, Director of the Berlin University Clinic for Women, calculated that nine-tenths of all miscarriages were artificially induced, and that the annual figure for abortions in Germany reached 300,000: other experts said 500,000.[212]

By comparison with the total number of abortions, the number of cases brought before the courts was infinitesimal. The highest figure of sentences in Germany in one year was 977, in 1912. Even that accounted for only two or three per thousand abortions, since in many cases several people were sentenced. It was mostly the botched cases that got into court. Women taken to hospital with an infection or some other complication were brought thence to court and heavily punished. The great majority of cases escaped punishment. In other countries the discrepancy between the letter of the law and its application was equally flagrant.

Opponents and supporters of the ban on abortion alike asked themselves whether, in these circumstances, there was any point in retaining so ineffectual a law. The demand for a change in existing legislation became general, but opinions differed on the nature and on the direction of the reform proposed. Some jurists of repute advocated legalizing abortion in the first months of pregnancy, when the operation is relatively safe; but the biological objection was raised that the embryonic life is there from the moment of fertilization of the ovum.

There was equally little support for a proposal to make abortion legal in principle for any woman who had already brought up several children. Elaborate calculations showed that, taking sterile marriages and the demographic factors into account, it would be enough if, in each fruitful marriage, an average of three children were reared to the completion of the fifth year of life; the population would then not only not diminish, but actually show a slight excess of births over deaths. A woman who had done her duty to the State to this extent should then be left to decide for herself whether she wanted to bring more children into the world. Although this suggested rule was unexceptionable from the demographic point of view, the moralists objected to the idea of degrading motherhood to a quantitative duty. Neither did the social criterion of allowing women in straitened economic circumstances to interrupt their pregnancies find grace in the eyes of legislators. A judge might take it into account when deciding what sentence to pass in an individual case, but the law could not make abortion a privilege of the poorer classes, which since time immemorable had always been the biggest contributors to the population.

The only point on which there was general agreement was in the benevolent though often incorrect assumption that in cases of abortion the woman was the victim and the persons helping her the real criminals. The legislation of several countries was altered accordingly. France led the way in 1923, with a law which differentiated the various penalties particularly sharply: the authors of the abortion and their accomplices were liable to penal servitude, while the woman risked only simple imprisonment, or, in mitigating circumstances, a fine. The reform of the relevant paragraph 218 of the German penal code, which was voted in 1926 after debates which had dragged on for years, worked in the same direction. The heavy sentences of penal servitude which had previously been the penalty for abortion were changed into terms of imprisonment, except for professional abortionists, and the woman might get off with as little as one day in prison.

On the whole, the penal system of the Weimar Republic confined itself to proceedings against doctors and, above all, against midwives who fattened on the fears and difficulties of pregnant women. Under Hitler, birth compulsion was made a State slogan. The old sentences of penal servitude were re-introduced and ruthlessly enforced. The women, too, were most severely punished and publicly proscribed for their failure to present their Führer with soldiers.

It is only quite recently that attempts have been made in some countries to find a more humane and reasonable solution to the problem. It is assuredly not by chance that the lead has been taken by small States which have no ambition to engage in power politics. Neutral Switzerland has introduced an innovation for which doctors in other countries have been vainly fighting for decades: the so-called medical 'indication'. Abortion is permitted if the continuation of the pregnancy would endanger the woman's life or affect her health severely. Before sanctioning it, however, the doctor in charge of the case must get the further approval of an official specialist consultant. In Austria too, where the law still threatens a woman who destroys the life in her womb with anything up to five years' imprisonment, this system is applied in practice.

Sweden allows weighty social reasons, the same medical test, and also a eugenic test, if there is a grave danger of hereditary taint. Finland permits the interruption of pregnancy on the same grounds. The laws of the Nordic States on abortion thus resemble the Russian law of 1936. Most Western countries, however, still today treat the interruption of pregnancy, for whatever reason or in whatever circumstances, as a crime, notwithstanding that hundreds and thousands of women commit it daily. So variously do views even of peoples belonging to the same cultural world regard one of the cardinal questions of sex-life.

Birth Control

Naturally, those persons who, for whatever reason—individualistic, health, social, or economic—have advocated the limitation of births, have always thought contraceptive methods to be the desirable way of reaching this goal. In the United States a nursing sister named Margaret Sanger gave the Neo-Malthusian movement fresh impetus in 1914 by inventing an infectious slogan, 'birth control'. She was herself one of a family with a number of children, she had known poverty and sickness in her home, and she had lost her mother early. But even if these may have been the reasons which impelled her, while still a young woman, to take up the cudgels for 'voluntary motherhood', in her propaganda the social point of view was soon outshadowed by the individualist. Married people, and in particular women, should decide for themselves whether or not they wanted to have children. Birth control was no affair of the State, but the individual's private concern. Women must be helped to exercise this control. In particular, she maintained, poor women desirous of avoiding families must be effectively advised and assisted.

Since Mrs. Sanger carried on her recruiting campaign suffragette-fashion, by vigorous demonstrations, including street processions, she was arrested several times, but never sentenced, and the organization founded by her, the Birth Control League, acquired a wide membership. In nearly every large town of North America 'advice centres' (their number gradually grew to six hundred) were set up, in which women could receive advice both on how to obtain the blessings of motherhood and on how to avert them. In England two hundred such family-planning clinics were established. The Anglo-Saxon system of public advisory centres also took root in the Scandinavian countries. The State facilitated their work. Chemists were bound to stock and sell contraceptives and medical students had to learn how to handle them.

In other European countries the sale of contraceptives, and even instruction on the subject, encountered many difficulties. The severest legislation was that enacted in France in 1920, when the decline in the birth-rate, after the losses suffered in the First World War, was thought particularly menacing. Efforts to secure repeal of this law and to procure the introduction of birth control, in all forms into France have recently again met with very strong opposition, not only from clerical and conservative circles, but also from the Communists, whose spokesman, Maurice Thorez, and his wife, Jeannette Vermeersch, have spoken out very sharply against the 'anarchistic methods of Neo-Malthusianism'.[212a]

The birth-control movement has met with great success in recent years in the densely-populated countries of Asia, if not among the populations, at least among the governments. India, in particular, looks to the limitation of births to reduce the growth of its population—five million a year—and to make a better standard of living possible. At first a female pupil of Gandhi's who was in charge of the Ministry of Health tried to make headway without artificial help, by appealing for continence and application of the Ogino-Knaus rule, asking married people to abstain from intercourse except in the period when the woman was incapable of conceiving. To enable the women, most of whom were illiterate, to work out their menstrual calendars, the authorities distributed chains of green and black beads, green for the 'safe' days on which coitus brought no dangers, black for days on which conception might occur. But even with this help the arithmetic of conception proved difficult. Some women regarded the chains as fetishes which always safeguarded them against conceiving, others adorned their cows with them, instead of working out the calculations.

After this experiment had broken down, Nehru's government tried a more rational approach and had the latest American methods tried out. These, too, were difficult to apply to the inexperienced Indian women, and the best way seemed after all to open public advice centres and give the women individual help. In 1956 a great State organization was founded at a cost of ten million dollars, providing for the establishment of two to three thousand clinics for family planning on the Anglo-American model.

Pakistan, Singapore, Thailand, and Japan have also set up State-supported birth-control clinics in which women receive free advice and are, if it seems necessary, supplied with contraceptives. Japan expressly permits midwives and nursing sisters to give women advice on the avoidance of conception, and the government has educational films on contraception shown. The swiftly falling birthrate shows that this propaganda is having its effect. Even Communist China appears to have decided, after long debate, to follow a policy of limitation of births.

Voluntary and Imposed Sterilization

Compared with the frequency of sterile marriages, artificially induced sterility is of little importance, but no longer so rare as not to require a mention. The sterilization of women by surgical methods requires a major operation, and if only for that reason very few women are willing to undergo it. But soon after the discovery of Röntgen rays it was observed that the formation both of semen and of ova could be prevented by application of the rays. In women, in particular, it is possible to produce sterility, temporary or permanent according to the treatment. At first it was almost exclusively well-to-do women who availed themselves of this discovery, but in time sterilization by X-ray treatment spread to others also. In Sweden, in 1954, 1,768 women had themselves sterilized, but only seventy-nine men. A Swiss doctor has written a report[213] on 187 women of the proletariat who submitted voluntarily to this treatment because they did not want any *proles*, or issue; thus does the meaning of the word change.

If voluntary sterilization were taken as the criterion, it would be necessary to conclude that the paternal instinct is more strongly developed than the maternal. Although the methods employed by surgery today consist of relatively harmless minor operations which have nothing in common with the old castration, with its complete removal of the glands, yet very few men take this step.

Most that do so are married men who already have children and wish to spare their wives further pregnancies. There is no doubt that what holds men back is not only dislike of the thought of never again being able to beget children but, even more, fear that the operation—ligature of the spermal ducts—may rob them of the ability to practise intercourse and turn them into physical and mental eunuchs. Some specialists maintain that this is not usually the case and that a man's ability to perform coitus can be dissociated from ability to beget issue, and can be retained even if the latter power is deliberately destroyed.

Such experience as we possess in this field comes—apart from war casualties—chiefly from criminals or feeble-minded persons who have been forcibly sterilized in America since the end of the nineteenth century. At first the old method of castration, which affects the entire organism, was used. Thus in 1898, in a lunatic asylum in the State of Kansas, forty-eight young men were castrated to prevent them from bringing idiot children into the world. In 1909 California made the castration of lunatics compulsory. In the interval, however, a prison doctor in Jeffersonville, Indiana, one H. O. Sharp, had discovered vasectomy, which consists of excising a sector of the spermal duct; and this operation is now practised very widely to sterilize habitual criminals, especially sexual offenders.

Except in Hitlerite Germany, which saw in it a weapon against 'race pollution', Europe has been slower to accept compulsory sterilization, not only on grounds of humanity, but also because we realize that our knowledge of heredity is still too small to justify investing the State with such powers.

Rejuvenation and Change of Sex

The efforts to regulate sex-life as desired, with the help of the art and science of medicine, have evoked great expectations in other directions also. Man's old dream of renewing his youth by mysterious ablutions, medicaments, or operations—an Egyptian papyrus of the seventeenth century B.C. deals with the problem—seemed to have been realized when, on 1 June 1889, the famous

French physiologist Brown-Séquard presented himself to the Paris *Société de Biologie*, claiming to have made himself twenty years younger. Before that, Brown-Séquard, who was then seventy-two, had seemed thoroughly senile, both physically and in all other respects. Suddenly he appeared looking like a man of fifty, and told his colleagues with delight that he had also recovered his virility, all by injecting himself with scrotal extract.

The doctors present shook their heads sceptically; they thought that poor Brown-Séquard had now succumbed to erotic-senile delusions. In fact, the methods of rejuvenation by which he had effected this miraculous cure on himself had no effect worth mentioning on other old men. The experiment did, however, open up an entire new field of biological knowledge: the doctrine of hormones. Not only the reproductive glands, the scrotum, and the ovaries, but also other organs of the body produce and discharge by inner secretion certain bodies, the hormones, which exercise a decisive influence on the working of the sexual system. Some hormones stimulate, others inhibit it. In 1915 Marañon, in Spain, showed that the woman's menopause, in particular, when menstruation and the ability to conceive cease, is produced by changes in the inner secretions, in which not only the ovaries but also other glands, the thyroid, the suprarenal, and above all the hypophysic, play a part.

In the next decades Allen and Corner in America, Butenandt in Germany, and others threw considerable light on the chemical composition of the sex-hormones: it even proved possible to manufacture some of these synthetically. Innumerable experiments were made with hormones and some of these led to remarkable results. In 1930 Migliavacca showed that scrotal extract also affects the female organism, small doses stimulating the working of the ovaries and larger ones inhibiting it. It was later shown that the effect was exercised indirectly, via the hypophyse. But women can get rid of disorders of the ovaries without the help of men. They themselves normally produce 'male' hormones (androgenes),[215] which are presumably the origin of masculine characteristics, including sometimes a respectable beard, which some elderly women acquire.

There exist today a great number of hormone preparations for reducing and—which are more in demand—for stimulating activity in men and women, for mitigating the difficulties of change of life, and sometimes even for postponing the climacteric by some years. When, in 1910, Karin Michaelis wrote her *The Dangerous Age*, describing women's spiritual difficulties at the approach of the change of life, she, or her heroine, ought to have been told to consult a competent doctor; many of their inhibitions and anxieties could easily have been removed. What many women so greatly hope for—to see their child-bearing age substantially prolonged and the physical changes attendant on the climacteric banished—has, however, not yet been achieved.

Nor have the operating methods which made the Austrian physiologist, Eugen Steinach, and the Russian Serge Voronoff (who practised in France) such sensational figures in the 1920s, succeeded in turning old men into young men. It proved possible in isolated cases to restore the generative power or to arrest the onset of impotence, but success was too doubtful and the cost too high for the treatment to take firm root. The rejuvenation operation has remained a somewhat dubious privilege of rich people. In spite of the progress which has been made, it cannot be said that the physical intensity or the duration of sex-life has been markedly extended since the discovery of hormones.

Even greater hopes were attached to experiments aiming at influencing the differentiation of the sexes and possibly inducing a transformation of the sexual organs and functions by artificial means. In this field, also, Steinach was one of the pioneers. No less an authority than Sigmund Freud[217] confirmed that Steinach, in one of his experiments, had succeeded in turning a male into a female and a female into a male, 'the psychosexual behaviour of the animal changing in accordance with the somatic sex-characteristics, and simultaneously with the alteration in them'.

These experiments have since been repeated with improved technique and extended, in Europe, America, and Japan. Very extensive sex-changes have been induced in frogs, birds, mice, rabbits, and many other creatures by removal or transplantation of glands and by hormone injections. Experiments of this kind have recently been made—with little success, it is true—on monkeys (by Dantschakoff in 1950) and even on the human embryo (by Davis and Potter in 1948). After each successful experiment the public became convinced that it would soon be possible to have a boy or a girl at choice, and that an adult dissatisfied with his or her own sex would be able to change it.

In fact, the instances occasionally reported in the papers, of men changing into women and vice versa, relate exclusively to physically abnormal persons—sexual intermediates—whose sexual character has been developed more strongly, in one direction or the other, by hormone treatment or by operation. We are still a long way from genuinely changing the sex of a normal person, and also from determining at will or artificially changing the sex of a human embryo. There is much to support the hypothesis that the predisposition of the embryo is bisexual. We know roughly how the differentiation takes place, and it seems probable that hormones play a large part in this, but how to influence decisively the differentiation is still one of the unsolved riddles of science. If the riddle were once solved and men could decide freely how many boys and how many girls should be born, the consequences would far exceed those of any sex-revolution hitherto known to history.

20

THE END OF AN ILLUSION

THE sex-life of mankind is no one-way street. In all ages there have been counter-currents, criss-crossings, traffic accidents; and legislators attempting to force everything to go in one direction have always come to grief. Men who have tried to regulate sex-life on a basis of strict monogamy have not been able to prevent a traffic springing up on by-roads where quite different rules operate.

This old experience has now again proved true in America. Only a generation ago the sex-habits of the United States seemed entirely different from those of European countries. It was true that each big contingent of immigrants brought with it from its country of origins its own habits in respect of marital fidelity, pre-marital sexual intercourse, and prostitution. Life in the Southern States, particularly in New Orleans, where relics of the French settlement still survived, was somewhat laxer than in the north; in States with a large Italian population the birth-rate was higher than in the areas of Germanic immigration. Even in sexual respects, however, the American 'melting pot' produced its unificatory effect. The puritanical spirit of the English colonists determined the State code of morals and forced all other tendencies to submit to it.

The last step towards standardization of sexual morality was taken in 1887, when the Mormons were forbidden to practise polygamy. Thereafter there existed no State, no sect, no association entitled to depart publicly from the ruling norms of sex-life. Most legislation on sex was, indeed, still enacted by the States, not by the Federal government, and thus showed greater variations than that of European countries, but the differences in law were outweighed by the strong social pressure which extended over the whole country. Sexual laxity incurred a stigma against which neither physical charm nor wit availed. American literature produced no poisonous flowers from Baudelaire's garden, American painting no notable tributes to sex. No American Fragonard, Manet, or Toulouse-Lautrec endangered morality. Amateurs of the nude had to smuggle it in from Europe or otherwise acquire it under the rose.

There were, of course, always men and women who offended against the written or unwritten laws of sexual morality, but they were outlaws, deserving no mercy. In no other country did the sex-element play so small a part in business, and above all in politics, as in the United States. The history of America is as poor in great sex-scandals as it is rich in great financial ones. Never, either in domestic or in foreign politics, has an American statesman been dominated by some seductive woman. Of the thirty-four Presidents of the U.S.A., only one—James Buchanan —was unmarried, and there has not been one case of petticoat government. Washington seemed proof against the sex-demon.

War Eroticism

Yet even in that model land of chastity and marital fidelity, which looked like Victorian England fossilized, sex began to rear its head when four million men were called to the colours in the First World War. The war showed Americans that there were other husbands and other wives besides their own, and ended with 300,000 divorces. The golden rain of the 'twenties led to a commercialization of love such as America had not previously seen, and the distress of the 1930s fostered secret prostitution beyond any that Europe had known. Yet the veil of puritanical prudery was still intact. It was rent asunder in the Second World War, when trained psychologists taught the military authorities that it was not possible to put sex in cold storage for the duration of a long campaign. Never since Napoleon's expedition to Egypt had an army's sexual needs been so scientifically catered for. The place of real sex-life was to be filled by a stage-sexualism, by pretty actresses and film-stars, erotic songs and mildly-spiced gags.

On the whole, this eroticism through the eye and the ear worked fairly well during the war. Sexual excesses were rare, homosexuality not widespread, and morale excellent. It was, nevertheless, an abandonment of the principles on which sex-education had hitherto been based. The soldiers' attention was not distracted from sex. On the contrary, it was fed to them; the 'sex-bombs' of Broadway and Hollywood took the place of monogamy. After these had been officially held up to millions of men for four years as a mirror of sex-life, they could hardly be expected from the day of their demobilization to look for love-happiness only to the domestic hearth.

Whereas in Europe the privations of the first post-war years led to more sobriety in sex-life, in America the sexual hunger so long dammed up, and artificially whipped up, led to a state of high tension reminiscent of Europe in 1900. America entered, so to speak, on an age of sexual exploration.

Affairs with prostitutes, which had formerly been hushed up or minimized, now became sensational scandals. Hordes of American students raided women's colleges and carried back the girls' underwear as trophies of the chase, if only as substitutes for other prizes. The stage and light literature were dominated by sexual themes—and that precisely at a time when French drama and literature, which for centuries had concerned itself almost entirely with the tragic or amusing conflicts of sex-life, was beginning to draw its subject-matter increasingly from other fields. America, which had formerly imported its means of sexual excitement, now became the exporter-in-chief of eroticism. American 'sex appeal', a new version of 'It' or the 'certain something' launched in the 1920s by the English novelist, Elinor Glyn, conquered the world via the film.

Kinsey's Revelations

The appetites of his fellow-countrymen were still further whetted by the two books written by the American zoologist, Kinsey, on sex-behaviour in the male and female specimens of the genus *homo*.[218] Never before in America had a strictly scientific work awakened so lively an interest in the widest circles. Of the second volume, which dealt with women, 200,000 copies were ordered before publication, and that although Kinsey did not make things easy for the curious reader. His reports consisted essentially of a dry accumulation of statistical tables based on an extensive inquiry into the sex-life of 5,300 men and about 6,000 women. Contrary to the indication of the title, this was not a survey of the genus *homo* in all its species, but only of the North American variety, and only of white men and white women, at that. Kinsey left the negro population of the United States aside, not out of any racial prejudice, but in order not to break up the inquiry and complicate its results still further.

For all their limitations, Kinsey's reports were among the most informative books on sex-life ever written, and fully deserved the reception accorded to them in America. The Americans discovered to their surprise that 86 per cent. of the men under thirty questioned by Kinsey and his assistants, and nearly half the women, had had pre-marital intercourse. Even more astonishing was the fact that 97 per cent. of the men had indulged in some form of sexual activity forbidden by the law; 70 per cent. had had intercourse with prostitutes, and 40 per cent. of the married men had been unfaithful to their wives. Another sensational feature was the frequency of perversion. Although the inquiry, unlike those of Krafft-Ebing and Freud, was conducted among apparently normal average people, not among morbid cases and notorious perverts, 37 per cent. of the men and 19 per cent. of the women admitted to having had physical relationships of a homosexual character at some period in their lives, and one in every six American farmhands practised sodomy, i.e. sexual intercourse with animals.

The publication of the Kinsey reports spelled for the Americans the end of a great illusion. Kinsey, the professional entomologist, had opened their eyes to what was going on behind the façade of morality with its assumption of sexually abstinent men and unapproachable women. Suddenly they became aware that their severe laws against procuration and prostitution, against seduction and unnatural vice, had been no more effective than the numerous public and private institutions for advising candidates for marriage, furthering married happiness, and preserving sexual morality.

Kinsey was, indeed, no Columbus. In the 1920s and 1930s various American sex-investigators had undertaken similar inquiries—on a far more modest scale, it is true, and with a less perfect technique. The results, however, had not been very disturbing. An inquiry made by K. B. Davis,[219] in the 'twenties, had shown only 7 per cent. among over 2,000 women as having had sexual relations before marriage. In the next decade the virtue of American women had looked less immaculate, but this had probably been due to the economic crisis, during which many things got out of hand. By then, one out of every four women entering the bridal bed was no more a virgin. According to Terman[221] no fewer than two-thirds of all newly-married persons born after 1909 had eaten of the tree of knowledge before their bridal night, but the majority of them had only had intercourse with their future spouses, an offence against the moral law but, after all, no mortal sin. Terman's gloomy prophecy that if things went on so, by 1955 no single American girl would be a virgin at marriage seemed all the less justified since the number of young women on which it was based was quite inadequate.

Even intercourse between engaged couples was less common in America than in Europe. At the beginning of the century a statistician from Saxony had conducted a very odd inquiry into the subject, using a method which was certainly more convincing than the American. He had compared the dates of birth of the first children of a marriage with the dates of their parents' weddings, and had calculated that in the kingdom of Saxony two out of every three first children of agricultural and industrial workers were born in or before the seventh month of wedlock and therefore conceived before marriage; the figure of children owing their existence to pre-marital coitus was 41 per cent. for civil servants, 30 per cent. for lawyers and doctors, and 15 per cent. even for clergymen, teachers and officers.²²² In England in 1938 the number of children conceived before their parents' marriage but legitimized by it was twice that of illegitimate births.²²³

American figures from the pre-war period for other fields of sex-life were also by no means alarming. Homosexual relationships were relatively frequent among juveniles but, since Freud had taught teachers that this was a normal transition phase, this was not taken too seriously. The heterosexual activity of Americans was not very great, probably below that of Europeans. By one of Terman's calculations, even men in the twenties did not reach the figure of twice a week recommended by Luther to married couples. This was not due to lack of virility, however, but because young Americans saved their strength for work and sport. Even if less austere in their outlook on sex than the Pilgrim Fathers, they were still moderate and disciplined by comparison with men of their age in Europe.

The principle in Russia during the first twenty years of the Soviet régime and, up to a point, today also, was to control economic life but to leave sex-life as free as was compatible with the interests of the State. The official principle in America is the exact opposite: free economic activity, regulated sex-life. He who desires sexual intercourse shall first be solemnly united in marriage with his partner. The registrar's consent is, strictly, sufficient, but the blessing of the Church is desirable, if only on social grounds.

State and Church in America make entry into the married state extremely easy. They are available on call, night and day. The longest time that it takes to obtain a marriage licence is five days; many States have no waiting period at all. The cost is minute. The whole system is directed towards ensuring that American citizens, male and female, shall not copulate secretly, but only after obtaining official sanction. If they neglect to do this, they are not always punished, but the State has done what it could to make extra-marital intercourse difficult. The mantraps of the law are set outside every hotel-door behind which an unsanctioned couple has crept. In New York a lapse may cost some years in prison.

The Divorce-mills of Nevada

Nevertheless, American legislation is in many respects more indulgent than European. It does not require a married couple to embitter their lives if they no longer want to remain together. The United States has the most liberal divorce law of any Western country, and possessed it even before the Soviet Union set up a new record. Of the forty-eight Federal States, all except three recognize 'cruelty' as ground for divorce. This does not mean that a husband has to beat his wife, or she to sling vitriol in his eyes, before an American judge will pronounce a divorce. 'Mental' cruelty is also recognized as an offence making marriage impossible. If the husband of a film-star takes too much, or too little, interest in her successes, that can be regarded as sufficient ground for divorce.

Not all States, it is true, are so lax. The strictest divorce law is that of New York, which lies nearest to Europe and thus has the largest heritage of European prejudices. In the State of New York adultery is the sole ground for divorce. If a married couple have not committed adultery and yet want to dissolve their marriage, they must at least pretend to an adultery; many agencies will help them to do so. If, however, they have the money and the time they need not resort to this *pons asinorum*; they need only change their domicile for a short period.

In the 1920s it was customary for well-to-do Americans who were in a great hurry to go for their divorces to Yucatan in the south of Mexico. Practised lawyers enabled them to buy themselves free from the yoke of marriage without so much as disembarking from the ship. When the American authorities withdrew recognition from this Mexican express procedure, this important branch of industry, like others, established itself on Federal territory. The little State of Nevada, in the west of the Rocky Mountains, took advantage of the confused situation and opened its doors hospitably to those who, from all parts of the

United States, were in need of help. Six weeks' residence in the State of Nevada is enough to get a divorce there, whereas most other States require a residence of one to two years.

It proved to be a brilliant idea. The attractive little mountain resort of Reno soon became a divorce centre for all America. Its primacy has recently been challenged by the neighbouring and still more elegant town of Las Vegas, but the industry is such a flourishing one that there are certainly enough customers for both. One goes to Reno or to Las Vegas as though for a cure at a watering-place; in six weeks one is rid of one's complaint and can begin a new life. For this, again, Nevada offers the best facilities. No need there even to undergo a blood-test before marrying, as is required by most American States. Nevada possesses not only the most famous divorce-mills of the world, but also a marriage-market of the very first order. In 1953 52,000 marriages were concluded there, whereas the whole State possessed only 6,000 single women of marriageable age. Naturally there has been considerable unfavourable criticism of the Nevada divorce industry and for a time it looked as though Reno would suffer the fate of Yucatan. In 1942, however, the Supreme Court admitted the validity of the Nevada divorce law.

This decision was one of great importance, especially for the orderly sex-life of Hollywood, whose inhabitants are among Nevada's regular visitors. While the leading figures of the film world are thus experienced experts on divorce in their private lives, they can make no use of their knowledge on the screen, it being *de facto* forbidden to a film producer to treat the subject of divorce. In the theatre and literature of the United States, too, the problem of divorce occupies a place far inferior to that which it holds in real life. Paradoxically the word divorce is taboo—in the leading divorce country of the Western world.

The fear that public discussion of divorce might stimulate interest in it and undermine still further the solidity of marriage affects even the statistics. The United States—the country with the best financial and economic statistics, the most advanced techniques of investigation for discovering the facts of the most complex social phenomena, the most secret emotions and the most intimate processes of sex—does not know how many marriages are dissolved annually within its frontiers. Washington, at any rate, professes not to know, since not all the Federal States publish regular divorce statistics and some of the most important issue no figures on the subject. The estimates for the whole Union are therefore very vague and contradictory.

According to official estimates[224] the total number of divorces since 1949 has been approximately 400,000 a year, following a post-war peak which reached 610,000. In North America, as everywhere, there were exceptionally many marriages and divorces in the first years after the war; shipwrecked marriages were liquidated and new ones contracted, extremely fast, by returning soldiers. The proportion between marriages and divorces has, however, remained approximately constant since the end of the war at about 4 : 1. In 1930 it was 6 : 1, in 1910 only 12 : 1, and in 1890 actually 18 : 1. The very strong and continuous rise of the divorce rate is thus beyond question.

It is harder to say how many marriages end in divorce, for if four times as many marriages take place in one year as divorces, this does not necessarily mean that every fourth marriage is dissolved. Some of the marriages dissolved today were contracted many years ago. But even if one takes as a basis of calculation marriages contracted during the last ten years, the proportion is still about 4 : 1.

The Art of Gold-digging

Life in America is thus increasingly moving towards a condition which may be described as one of successive polygamy. A marriage is contracted for life, but the State admits a sort of right of revocation if difficulties arise. In the transition period from the first to the second marriage, or from the second to the third, there often occurs a bigamous condition, in which the husband or wife entertains sexual relations with his or her future partner before divorcing the predecessor. This is presumably one explanation for the relatively large number of cases of adultery recorded by Kinsey.

The rise in the divorce rate is no specifically American phenomenon. Divorce is on the up-grade also in Europe. In England, where the number of divorces was very low before 1939, it increased more than fourfold after the war; in several other countries it doubled.[225] There is, however, an essential difference in the economic position. In Europe divorce is seldom economically profitable for the woman. In America the alimonies fixed by the courts, or the sums agreed between the parties without legal intervention, are so high as to leave a divorced woman economically independent, and sometimes very well-off indeed.

Divorce has thus ceased to be the threat to the wife which it was in the days of the old repudiation, when at best she could take out of the marriage what she had brought into it, and has become an instrument of security and even a source of livelihood. To marry a rich man and divorce him quickly has become a career, and many specialists practise this art with real virtuosity. It is a sexual form of 'gold-digging', which became so fashionable in the 1920s, the period of the great prosperity, as to be endowed with a special name. The 'gold-diggers' did not always go for marriage. The threat of a little scandal often sufficed to extort a sum which took the place of a wedding-ring. As divorce got easier, however, marriage, followed by divorce, proved on the whole the more profitable course.

These short-term marriages may be compared with the connections of the nineteenth-century women of the *demi-monde*, whose associations with rich men also usually lasted for several years and, chronologically, amounted to a sort of successive polygamy. It is, however, not quite the same thing. For the 'gold-digger' who pulls off a marriage with a rich man thereby acquires a position in society which remains permanently denied to the *demi-mondaine*. Unless she commits some extraordinary *gaffe*, she remains a member of society from her marriage onward and keeps this status even after her divorce. A materially successful *divorcée* thus corresponds rather to a rich widow of earlier times.

For completeness' sake it should be remarked that sexual gold-digging on the highest level is not exclusively a woman's profession in America; Caribbean diplomats, Caucasian princes and celebrities in other spheres practise it with success. In certain circles of the upper ten thousand the special ambition of rich women seems to be to have been married for some time to one of these gentlemen—the desire for a title is no longer the principal motive, as it used to be at the beginning of our century. There are some tennis or other champions who have wedded successively four or five of the most coveted dollar-princesses.

The Sexual Principle of Marriage

Important as economic factors may be in the increase of divorce, in many cases they yet play no role, or only a secondary one. Kinsey tried to establish what were the purely sexual causes which often led to estrangement between spouses even in the early years of their married life, and finally to divorce. The problem is no new one: it had been exhaustively discussed in the previous generation, on the appearance of Vandevelde's widely read book *Ideal Marriage*. Kinsey, like Vandevelde, concludes that married couples often lack the most primitive physiological and anatomical knowledge, this ignorance marring sexual intercourse, especially for the woman. Many women achieved orgastic excitement more easily by onanism or even by homosexual practices than through normal coitus.

This evidence of Kinsey's was tantamount to giving American women a special testimonial, in the shape of an acquittal from the reproach of frigidity often levied against them. Kinsey believes only 10 per cent. of American women to be truly frigid, i.e. incapable of the orgasm. The other, very frequent cases of apparent frigidity are due to unpreparedness on the woman's part or clumsiness and egotism on the man's. This thesis of Kinsey's has, however, been particularly sharply contested by American critics of his reports; and the observations of European gynaecologists and psychiatrists also fail to bear it out. Many specialists believe that 60 per cent. of all women are more or less frigid, and submit only unwillingly to sexual intercourse, either in order to have children, or to prevent their husbands from seeking satisfaction outside the marriage bed.

Kinsey regards pre-nuptial sexual intercourse as a means of sexual selection and sexual training. But for it there would certainly be more unhappy marriages and divorces. Women who have had sexual experience before marriage are in no respect worse wives, less attached to their children and their husbands. No marriage market, however well organized, no advice centre, no National Marriage Guidance Council (as now exists in England) can take the place of pre-nuptial experience. Knowledge is power. In the bridal night of old, the man alone possessed knowledge, however muddied the springs whence he had drunk it. Today, half of all American women, and at least two-thirds of all European,[226] have been deflowered before marriage. The bridal night has lost its mystique for both parties. Others besides the romantics may deplore this, but it undoubtedly has its good side. The dread of the unknown, the inhibitions centring round 'deflowering to order', which often led to physical disorders (*vaginism*) are gone; women who enter on marriage with knowledge behind them are partners from the first, sexually as otherwise, and not subjects. What has been realized here is a part of the emancipation of women, and not the least important part.

With the spread of pre-nuptial intercourse, marriage has more and more lost the monopolistic position which the State had designed for it. Although the change since the beginning of the century looks striking, especially in the Anglo-Saxon countries, its extent should not be over-estimated. The very fact that illegitimate births numbered 10 per cent. of all births in most countries and 20 per cent. in some, and that on top of that a high proportion of the first children of all marriages had been conceived before wedlock, proves that the preservation of virginity up to marriage had often been no more than a pious aspiration.

Legislation and the administration of justice have long taken this fact into account. The principle accepted in antiquity and the Middle Ages that a marriage was invalid if the wedding-night showed the bride to have been deflowered previously, has been dropped almost everywhere. Even if the bride or her relatives assure the bridegroom that he is getting a pure virgin to wife, and this turns out not to be the case, the disappointed husband can no longer send his bride back to his father-in-law. He must accept the fact that he has been fooled, and make the best of it. In America it is only the State of Maryland that admits unchastity in the woman before marriage as ground for divorce.

It is different if the woman is already with child by another man when she marries and her husband is unaware of it. A number of the States of the Union and several European countries regard this as a serious fraud which justifies annulment or dissolution of the marriage. It is not everywhere, however, that a husband is protected against his wife's laying cuckoo's eggs in his nest. The French *Code Civile* contains to this day the much-derided sentence: *L'enfant conçu pendant le mariage a pour père le mari* ('the father of the child conceived in wedlock is the husband'). If, the adultery being notorious, the husband wishes to repudiate paternity, a special procedure is necessary: divorce alone does not free him. In most countries the wife is better protected against the husband's bringing back fruit from other orchards. Many countries make it illegal to adopt a husband's extra-marital children, even with the wife's consent.

On all these points the legal position varies from country to country. There is no question on which so many differences of opinion exist, as on how to keep people monogamous. Only on one point are all legislations agreed today: that marriage is a sexual partnership and not an institution for reproduction. Reproduction is desirable, but not a condition, whereas sexual cohabitation is a spouse's duty. A husband or wife refusing or physically unable to fulfil this duty gives his or her partner the right to contest the validity of the marriage or to insist on divorce. Whether the sexual union results in issue is left to fate or to the will of the parties. In any case, childlessness does not give either party the right to have the marriage dissolved.

The sexual character of marriage is probably most sharply

expressed in the English law. A marriage only becomes definitely valid after it has been physically consummated by the sexual act between the partners. If either partner refuses to perform this, or if the husband is impotent, it can be annulled. It is regarded as consummated, however, if the sexual act has been performed with the use of contraceptive methods, and thus without the intention of producing children. A decision of the House of Lords in 1947 expressly confirmed this.

It took centuries before the sexual principle finally prevailed in law over the reproductive principle. Princes whose marriages had proved sterile pressed Rome again and again to get their marriages annulled under canonical law, and when divorce was legalized in Protestant countries the question arose all over again among commoners. Was it not to degrade marriage to make of it a mere sexual partnership without considering whether it really served reproduction or not? Why should men and women who genuinely wished to have children be prevented from doing so by being forcibly kept together when years of marriage had shown that no children could be born of their union? Would it not be better to give them the chance of having children in another marriage?

Objections such as this to the sexual principle in marriage have been raised in our own century. The English philosopher Bertrand Russell has suggested that marriage should not be legally binding until the wife's first pregnancy.[228] Russell would, indeed, allow also a second form of marriage: a companionate marriage for persons unwilling or unable to have children. The American Judge Lindsey[229] has made a similar suggestion. He proposed that deliberately childless companionate marriages should be dissoluble at the wish of both parties, no further grounds for divorce being required, and no alimony payable. These proposals evoked such indignation in America that Lindsey was dismissed from his position of magistrate in a juvenile court. Russell, too, was obliged to give up his Chair of philosophy in New York.

In France radical reform of marriage law had been under debate even before the First World War. The spokesmen of the

Radicals, the writers Paul and Victor Margueritte and Léon Blum were primarily concerned to break down the rigid barrier between legitimate wedlock and the socially outlawed free-love unions. Léon Blum's book on marriage[230] was a red rag to the conservative moralists, and the worst was expected from this 'subversive' man. But when, thirty years later, Blum became Prime Minister, he had his hands so full with inflation and banking reform that he had no time for reforming the law on sex. On the whole these various attempts to bring the legal forms governing sex-life into closer touch with reality have seldom got beyond paper. It has been found easier to ignore the old Tables of the Law than to change them. The increased addiction of women to pre-marital sexual intercourse and the growing fashion for early marriages in bourgeois circles, especially among students, somewhat reduced the scope for professional and near-professional prostitution, but not to the extent of eliminating the problem. Its most faithful clientele has always been drawn from elderly married men, not from sex-hungry beginners.

To protect female honour from the stigma of organized prostitution, and also to protect the prostitutes themselves from exploitation, France and Belgium abolished brothels by law after the war—which did not, indeed, end the practice of exhibiting women for sale in brightly lit windows, like any goods, in special streets of Antwerp, as of Hamburg and other sea-ports. In Japan, too, the closing of houses of ill-fame was enacted in 1956, but two years' grace was allowed to enable the geishas to find other work. Communist China, following the Russian example, has adopted more radical methods and has established special reform institutes for prostitutes—a system already common in the Middle Ages. In France missionaries have tried to accustom prostitutes to a different life by getting them placed in families;[231] but in this field, too, there has been no important change in the law.

Artificial Insemination

It is only from the physiological side that a problem has arisen which even the old sexual law cannot simply evade: that of artificial insemination. For thousands of years all marriage law has been based on the assumption that coitus is necessary for the reproduction of the human race. For some decades past, however, it has been known that this assumption is not scientifically correct —a woman can conceive, carry and bring into the world a completely normal child just as easily if she has received the male semen in the form of an injection given by a doctor. No embrace of two human beings, no mutual contact of genitals, no sexual excitement are necessary for the fertilization of the ovum. It is sad, but true; Nature is not so romantic as poets—and not they alone—have hitherto assumed. It is not even necessary that the man giving the semen should exert his sexual imagination. It is completely indifferent for the further course of things whether the semen was retained in a contraceptive at coitus, whether it was derived from onanism, or whether a few drops were taken from the man, in a purely mechanical fashion, by massaging the prostate.

The technique of the injection, too, is simple. The one requirement is strict cleanliness. The doctor carrying out the operation may confine himself to introducing the semen into the vagina, as in coitus, or, if practised enough, he may inject the semen directly into the uterus through the outer opening of the womb.

In America, which has most experience in this field, fifty injections are usually required, these being usually given in the critical half-way period between two menstruations, when the likelihood of conception is greatest. The operation is, of course, suspended as soon as menstruation ceases, or if chemical tests show that pregnancy has begun; failing this, the injections are repeated the next month. In about 25 per cent. of all cases conception is said to result after the very first injection. The results are therefore more favourable than with natural copulation. This agrees with the results obtained by the artificial insemination of animals.

So much for the physiological part. That is, however, only one aspect of the problem. Not less important is the question under what circumstances a woman should resort to this method and, above all, who should be the donor of the semen. It is clear that in most cases only women who are unable to achieve conception by natural means will resort to artificial insemination. Often a woman may be physically incapable of sexual intercourse, but capable of conception. In such cases the husband will provide the semen, as in cases when husband and wife are separated for a long period but wish to have a child. This situation often arises in time of war; in the Second World War many soldiers in the American army sent their semen by air to be injected into their wives.

In peace-time such long-distance insemination will rarely be necessary. The typical case is rather when a marriage has been unfruitful owing to the husband's sterility, but both parties want a child and the wife, in particular, presses for one. The sterility may not necessarily make the husband incapable of sexual intercourse. In any case, the only solution, in such a case, is 'hetero-insemination', in which another man donates the semen and the woman lets it be injected into her body without physical contact with the strange man, and with her husband's consent.

American doctors have already drawn up certain rules defining what men can be used as semen-donors. The choice naturally falls on those who are physically and mentally healthy, morally unexceptionable, and free from any hereditary taint: if possible, men who have already produced healthy offspring. For greater safety's sake, they are not taken too young; if possible, not under thirty-five years of age. Too little is yet known of the laws of heredity to ensure that the selection is absolutely safe, but the risk is in any case no greater than that inevitably run by any woman in choosing her husband.

Yet even a doctor's certificate that all conditions for a successful artificial insemination have been fulfilled does not end the matter. The Catholic Church has already several times occupied itself with the problem: Pius XI in an Encyclical in 1930, Pius XII in 1949, and in May 1956 at an international congress on fertility and sterility. Especially on the last-named occasion the Pope most strongly condemned artificial insemination of human beings, even if effected with the husband's semen. A marriage contract does not give married people the right to have a child, but only to 'natural acts' able and calculated to produce a new living creature. The Church equates hetero-insemination with adultery. Some lay authorities have taken the same view. The husband's consent is not decisive for determining whether adultery has taken place. The question is particularly delicate in America, where most States regard adultery as a criminal offence punishable with prison.

None the less, hetero-insemination has been operated in thousands of cases, and is still on the increase both in America and in Europe. Usually the choice of the donor is left to the doctor, husband and wife not knowing and not wishing to know who is the father of 'their' child. The donor, also, does not know who has received his semen. It is a new form of anonymous paternity, and one which, if any leakage occurred, might give rise to complex legal questions, and also to emotional attachments and conflicts. Many couples, however, accept these drawbacks and risks, because they say that a child conceived with their knowledge and of their will is still nearer to them than an adopted child, which they would otherwise probably have taken.

Surplus Women

Artificial insemination is a solution which does not affect only childless couples. It may also appeal to widows and unmarried women who want a child, but cannot find a suitable husband. Anonymous insemination without the sexual act may, in particular, be the way out for spinsters approaching the climacteric with no prospect of marriage and reluctant to submit physically to any man. Many grave psychic disorders might be averted by this means.

The problem of the childless ageing woman is the more acute because everywhere in the West (in India the reverse is still the case) there are more women than men. In Germany the difference is particularly large: in the German Federal Republic the female population in 1955 was three million, or 12 per cent., larger than the male. In Britain the surplus of women is two million. This disproportion is only partly due to war losses. The surplus of women is increasing steadily even in countries which suffered no male losses in the war, or only relatively slight ones. The reason is that, although more boys are born than girls (the average figure is 104 : 100), women, on the average, live longer.

In the United States about 100,000 more boys than girls are born each year, but the male deaths outnumber the female by 200,000. The growth of the female population thus exceeds that of the male by about 100,000 a year. It is probable that this development will not go on for ever, or the United States would gradually become a country of women, and men would have grown so few that it would be necessary to revert to the Mormons' polygamy or to introduce obligatory artificial insemination to keep the stock from dying out. But it has already gone so far that while, in 1954, the surplus of women in the total population was only one million, it was $2\frac{1}{2}$ millions in the age-groups 18+.

The shortage of males is thus already perceptible in all fields, and this may be one of the chief causes of the large increase in extra-marital sexual activity among women. For women who get husbands late, sexual intercourse in early life is pre-marital, but for millions of others it remains the only way of escaping sexual loneliness. The growth of divorce may also be explicable in part by the surplus of women; the supply of women is so great as to tempt husbands to change wives more often. Divorced wives have thus much less chance of marrying again; in the United States the number of women divorced and not remarried is 30 per cent. larger than that of men in the same situation.

One may twist and turn this problem as one will, but monogamous marriage can only work where the numbers of men and women of marriageable age are approximately equal. As soon as one gets a surplus of women of 10 per cent. or more, as is the case in many countries today, the trend towards polygamy inevitably grows stronger; and since most women are too proud to content themselves with the position of second wife, unless for substantial material reward, polygamy goes over into promiscuity. We will not maintain that the demographic position is the only, or even the chief cause of this tendency, but it has certainly contributed to it.

Sex-instinct and Reproduction

The sex-instinct and the reproductive instinct are the two motive forces of sexual life, but their mutual interactions are far more complex than used to be supposed. Neither of them is constant, or unaffected by influences of moral standards, religion, economic circumstance, State authority, taste in beauty, sport, love of adventure, or desire for self-assertion. Within certain limits, the reproductive instinct is easier to regulate, stimulate, or damp down than the sex-instinct. Precisely in the last decades it has been shown that it is relatively easy to bring a birth-rate up by 20, 30, or even 50 per cent. No compulsion is necessary; prosperity, as in America, or the provision of extensive material advantages for large families, as in France, have the same effect. Quick successes in this field are possible today, because movements of population are cushioned by extensively practised limitation of births. What we call a rise in the birth-rate is only a reduction of birth control; it has nothing whatever to do with the sexual instinct.

Were it desired to utilize to the full the reproductive potential of women—that of men is in practice unlimited—the figures of births could be raised, not merely by 20 or 30 per cent., but by 300 per cent. or more. This would, however, lead to a big reduction in standards of living and to a complete revolution in public and private life. Woman would sink back to the zoological level of an animal mother, exclusively occupied with reproduction. No one wants that. The only difference is that some people say it, while others shrink from admitting it and cling to the fiction that the sex-instinct exists only to ensure reproduction.

Yet there cannot be the slightest doubt that the sex-instinct in mankind is an independent instinct which technical development alone is making increasingly independent of the reproductive

instinct. The use of contraceptive methods and artificial insemination would already make it possible today to separate the two
completely; people could have all the sexual intercourse they
wanted without getting children, and have as many children as
they wanted without sexual intercourse. The generative act can
be separated completely from the sexual act.

It is improbable that this complete separation will be carried
through in the near future; but the trend is already moving from
the subordination to the co-ordination of the two instincts. For
centuries sex-life laboured under the nightmare that a night of
love might result in an unwanted child, and the reproductive
instinct lived in constant dread of frustration or betrayal through
the sex-instinct of the partner in wedlock. If it gradually becomes
possible to dispel these fears, that will certainly be no cause for
regret. It will be all the easier to keep the sex-instinct and the
reproductive instinct within the limits appropriate to individual
and social needs without sacrificing either the one or the other.

REFERENCES

1. N. I. Berrill, *Vie sexuelle des animaux et des plantes*. French translation of *Sex and the Nature of Things* (Paris 1954), p. 254.
2. N. Tinbergen, *The Origin and Evolution of Courtship and Threat Display in Evolution as a Process*, edited by Julian Huxley, A. C. Hardy and E. B. Ford (London 1954), pp. 235ff.
3. E. Piette, 'La station de Brassempouy et les statuettes humaines de la période glyptique', *L'Anthropologie*, VI (1895).
4. J. Szombathy, 'Die Aurignacschichten im Löss von Willendorf'. *Korrespondenzblatt der Deutschen Gesellschaft für Anthropologie, Ethnographie und Vorgeschichte*. XI Jahrgang, No. 9/12 Sept.-Dec. 1909.
5. Marcellin Boule et Henry V. Vallois, *Les Hommes fossiles* (4th ed., Paris 1952), pp. 337-338.
6. Salomon Reinach, 'L'art et la magie', *L'Anthropologie* (1903).
7. J. G. Frazer, *The Golden Bough* (London 1923-1927).
8. C. F. C. Hawkes, *The Prehistoric Foundation of Europe to the Mycenean Age* (London 1940), p. 39.
9. George Goury, *Origine et Évolution de l'Homme*, Vol. I, *Époque Paléolithique* (2nd ed., Paris 1948), p. 277.
10. I. F. Lafitau, *Mœurs des sauvages américains, comparées avec les mœurs des premiers temps* (1724).
11. L. H. Morgan, *The League of the Iroquois* (Rochester 1851).
12. L. H. Morgan, *Ancient Society* (1877; 2nd ed., Chicago 1910).
13. Friedrich Engels, *Der Ursprung der Familie, des Privateigentums und des Staates* (Zürich 1884).
14. August Bebel, *Die Frau in der Vergangenheit, Gegenwart und Zukunft* (Zürich 1883).
—— *Die Frau und der Sozialismus* (25th ed., Stuttgart 1895).
15. E. A. Westermarck, *History of Human Marriage* (London 1891), pp. 61ff.
16. Georgene H. Seward, *Sex and the Social Order* (Penguin Books, 1954), p. 80.
17. B. Malinowski, 'Kinship', *Man* (London 1930), p. 21.
18. *Histoire générale des Civilisations*, ed. Maurice Crouzet, Vol. 1, André Aymard and Jeannine Auboyer, *L'Orient et la Grèce antique* (Paris 1953), p. 581.
19. A. Moret, *Le Nil et la Civilisation Egyptienne* (Paris 1926), p. 329.
20. W. M. Flinders Petrie, *Social Life in Ancient Egypt* (London 1923), p. 319.

21. Adolf Erman, *Die Literatur der Aegypter* (Leipzig 1923), pp. 303ff.
22. L. Delaporte, *La Mésopotamie. Les Civilisations babylonienne et assyrienne* (Paris 1925), p. 95.
23. Herodotus, *Histories*, I, 199.
24. I. Plessis, *Étude sur les textes concernant Ishtar-Astarté* (Paris 1921), p. 250.
25. A. Parrot, *La tour de Babel* (Neuchâtel 1953).
26. Sir Frederick Kenyon, *The Bible and Archaeology* (London 1940), pp. 122ff.
27. *Genesis* 38: 8-10.
28. *Leviticus* 18 and 20.
29. Adolphe Lods, *Israel des origines au milieu du VIII siècle* (Paris 1932), p. 227.
30. *Time* (New York, 5 April 1954), p. 96.
31. *Atharva Veda*, 18, 3, 1.
32. R. W. Frazer, 'Sati' in *Encyclopaedia of Religion and Ethics* (London 1920), Vol. XI, p. 207.
33. P. Masson-Oursel, H. de Willman-Grabowska, Philipp Stern, *L'Inde antique et la civilisation indienne* (Paris 1933), p. 84. Edward Thompson, *Suttee* (London 1928).
34. C. R. Majumdar, H. C. Raychandhuri, Kalinkar Datta, *An Advanced History of India*, Part I: *Ancient India* (London 1949), p. 197.
35. M. Rostovtzeff, *History of the Ancient World* (Oxford 1927), Vol. 1, p. 287.
36. George Thompson, *Studies in Ancient Greek Society. The Prehistoric Aegean* (London 1948).
37. Homer, *Odyssey*, XI, 489. Hesiod, *Works and Days*, 376, 405.
38. Gustave Glotz, *Histoire grecque* (Paris 1938), Vol. I, p. 368.
39. L. Beauchet, *Histoire du droit privé de la république athénienne* (Paris 1897), Vol. I, pp. 398ff., Vol. III, pp. 465ff.
39a. Ugo Enrico Paoli, *Die Frau im alten Hellas* (Bern 1955), p. 73.
39b. Sir Arthur Pickard-Cambridge, *The Dramatic Festivals of Athens* (Oxford 1953), pp. 268-270.
40. Plato, *Republic*, Book V.
41. Plato, *Laws*, Book VIII.
42. Aristotle, *Natural History*, IX, 1. *Politics*, I, 2.
43. Erik Nordenskiöld, *The History of Biology* (New York 1928), pp. 41-43.
44. Plutarch, *Pericles*, 24.
45. O. Navarra, 'Mérétrices' in the *Dictionnaire des Antiquités grecques et romaines*, ed. Ch. Daremberg and Edm. Saglio (Paris 1904), Vol. III, pp. 1823-1938.
46. Strabo, VIII, 6, 20.
47. Plato, *Symposium*, XVI.
48. Ulrich von Wilamowitz-Moellendorf, *Platon* (Berlin 1919), Vol. I, 44, Werner Jaeger, *Paideia* (New York 1945), Vol. III: *The Conflict of Cultural Ideals in the Age of Plato*.

49. Hans Neumann, *Sittenspiegel* (Salzburg 1952), p. 57.

50. Cicero, *De Inventione*, I, 24, 55.

51. Ettore Pais, *Histoire romaine des origines à l'achèvement de la conquête* (Paris 1940), pp. 86ff.

52. Ludwig Friedländer, *Darstellungen aus der Sittengeschichte Roms* (10th Ed., Leipzig 1921-1926), Vol. I, pp. 267ff.

53. Plutarch, *Cato min.*, 25.

54. Justinian, *Institutiones, de adoptione* I, Tit. XI, para. 9.

55. Publius Ovidius Naso, *Amores*, 4th Elegy.

56. Martin Schanz, *Geschichte der römischen Literatur* (4th ed., München 1935), 2nd part, pp. 207ff.

57. Oscar Forel, *L'accord des sexes* (Paris 1953), p. 274.

58. Tacitus, *Annales*, XV, 44.

59. Marcel Simon, *Les premiers chrétiens* (Paris 1952), p. 19.

60. *St. Matthew* 19: 3-12.

61. *Mischna, Gittin*, IX, 10.

62. Ettore Pais, *Histoire Romaine*, p. 81.—Pauly's *Real-Enzyklopädie der classischen Altertumswissenschaft*, Art. '*Matrimonium*' (Stuttgart 1930), 28th half vol., pp. 2270, 2271.

63. *St. Mark* 10: 11.

64. *St. Luke* 16: 18.

65. *I Corinthians* 7: 10, 11.

66. Declaration by the Archbishop of Canterbury, 11 December 1954.

67. James Hastings, *A Dictionary of the Bible*, Art. '*Marriage*' (Edinburgh 1900), Vol. III, pp. 292ff.

68. *Ephesians*, 5: 22-24.

69. *St. Matthew* 21: 32.

70. *Gospel according to St. Luke* 7: 37.

71. R. P. Sanson, *Marie-Madeleine, celle qui a beaucoup aimé* (Paris 1934), pp. 74, 84.

72. *I Corinthians* 7: 1.

73. Adolf von Harnack, *Lehrbuch der Dogmengeschichte* (5th ed., Tübingen 1931), Vol. III, p. 262.

74. Adolf von Harnack, *op. cit.*, Vol. II, p. 12.

75. Eugène Albertini, *L'Empire Romain* (Paris 1936), p. 36.

76. *Koran*, Sura IV, 15.

77. *Koran*, Sura XXIV, 13.

78. *Koran*, Sura XXIV, 4.

79. *Koran*, Sura IV, 34.

80. *Koran*, Sura VI, 152.

81. Arthur Jeffery, 'Family Life in Islam' in *The Family: Its Function and Destiny*, ed. Ruth Nanda Anshen (New York 1949), p. 48.

82. Mohammed Marmaduke Pickthall, *The Meaning of the Glorious Koran* (New York 1954), pp. 405-406.

83. *Koran*, Sura IV, 3.

84. *Koran*, Sura IV, 171; Sura V, 73.

85. J. Oestrup, 'Alf laila wa-laila' in M.Th. Houtsma and others, *Encyclopédie de l'Islam* (Leiden-Paris 1913) Vol. I, pp. 255-259.

86. *Les mille et une nuits, contes arabes*, 12 vols. (Paris 1704-1717).

87. *Der duftende Garten des Scheich Netzaui:* Neuman, *Sittenspiegel* (Salzburg 1952), p. 30.

88. I Timothy 3: 1-5.

89. Abelard und Héloïse, *Briefwechsel* (Leipzig, n.d.), p. 78.

90. *ibid.*, p. 100.

91. *ibid.*, p. 118.

92. Oscar Forel, *L'Accord des Sexes* (Paris 1953) pp. 87-88.

93. O. Cartellieri, *La Cour des ducs de Bourgogne* (Paris 1946).

94. Henry Charles Lea, *History of the Inquisition of the Middle Ages* (New York 1888), Vol. III, pp. 492-549.—W. G. Soldan and U. Heppo, *Geschichte der Hexenprozesse* (3rd ed., Stuttgart 1912), 2 vols.

95. Heinrich Edw. Jacob, *Sechtausend Jahre Brot* (Hamburg 1954), p. 152.

96. Augustin Flèche, *L'Europe Occidentale de 888 à 1125* (Paris 1930), p. 649.

97. Joseph Bédier, Alfred Jeauroy and F. Picaret, 'Histoire des Lettres' in G. Hanotaux', *Histoire de la Nation Française*, Vol. XII (Paris 1952), p. 136.

98. Marcelin Defourneaux, *La vie quotidienne au temps de Jeanne d'Arc* (Paris 1952), p. 136.

99. Robert Briffault, *The Mothers* (London 1927), Vol. III, p. 216.

100. George F. Fort, *History of Medical Economy during the Middle Ages* (1883), pp. 336-347.—Victor Robinson, *The Story of Medicine* (New York 1943), pp. 213-215.

101. *Le Livre du chevalier de la Tour Landry pour l'enseignement de ses filles* (late fourteenth century, reissued by A. Montaignon, Paris 1854).

102. P. G. Dublin, *La vie de l'Arétin* (Paris 1937), p. 46.

103. Ulrich Thieme and Fred P. Willis, *Allgemeines Lexikon der bildenden Künstler* (Leipzig 1921), Vol. XIV, pp. 215-219.

104. *Les Sonnets luxurieux de Me. Pierre Arétin traduits en français et illustrés d'après les compositions de Jules Romain* (Paris 1947).

105. Vesalius, *De humani corporis fabrica libri septem* (Basle 1543).

106. Manni, *Istoria del Decamerone* (Florence 1742).

107. Arturo Castiglione, *Storia della Medicina* (Verona 1948), Vol. I, pp. 396-397.

108. Ivan Bloch, *Der Ursprung der Syphilis* (Jena 1911).

109. Karl Sudhoff, *Der Ursprung der Syphilis* (Leipzig 1913).

110. *Earliest Printed Literature on Syphilis*, ed. Karl Sudhoff. *Monumenta medica*, Vol. III (Florence 1925).

111. Victor Robinson, *The Story of Medicine* (New York 1943), p. 274.

112. Ovid, *Metamorphoses*, VI, 145-312.

113. Philipp Melanchthon, *Loci communes rerum theologicarum* (1521).

114. H. Hauser and A. Renaudet, *Les débuts de l'Age moderne* (Paris 1946), p. 363.

115. Ernest Lavisse and Alfred Rambaud, *Les guerres de Religion* (2nd ed., Paris 1905), p. 17.

116. André Michel, *Histoire de l'Art* (Paris 1913), Vol. V, part 2, pp. 513ff.

117. Marcel Brion, *Michel-Ange* (Paris 1939), p. 324.

118. A. Farinelli, *Don Giovanni. Note critiche* (Turin 1896).

119. *Mémoires de Messire Pierre de Bourdeille, seigneur de Brantôme, contenant les vies des dames illustres de France de son temps* (Leiden 1665).

120. Brantôme, *Vies des dames galantes. Discours premier sur les dames qui font l'amour et leurs maris cocus*, ed. René-Louis Doyon (Paris n.d.) pp. 157-168.

121. René Descartes, *Les traités de l'homme et de la formation du foetus* (Amsterdam 1680).

122. Emilie Guyénot, *Les sciences de la vie aux XVII. et XVIII. siècles* (Paris 1941), p. 212.

123. Marcello Malpighi, *De formatione pulli in ovo* (1669).

124. R. de Graaf, *De mulierum organis generationi interventibus tractatus novus* (1672).

125. *Observationes D. Anthonii Lewenhoeck de natis e semine genitali animalculis.* Royal Society, Philos. Transactions, No. 143 (London 1678).

126. Louis Gallien, *La sexualité* (Paris 1951), p. 15.

127. Victor Robinson, *The Story of Medicine* (New York 1943), pp. 307-308.

128. N. Brian Chaninov, *Histoire de la Russie* (Paris 1948), p. 243.

129. Edmond Rossier, *Profils de Reines* (Lausanne n.d.) pp. 166-167.

130. Robert Pignarre, *Histoire du Théâtre* (Paris 1946), p. 27.

131. Franz Haböck, *Die Kastraten und ihre Gesangskunst* (Berlin-Leipzig 1927), pp. 481-482.

132. Georg August Griesinger, *Biographische Notizen über Joseph Haydn* (Leipzig 1810; re-issued by Franz Grasberger, Vienna 1954), p. 10.

133. Joseph Gregor, *Kulturgeschichte des Balletts* (Vienna 1944), p. 201.

134. *Mémoires complètes et authentiques du duc de Saint-Simon*, ed. M. Chebruel (Paris 1878), Vol. XIII, p. 59.

135. G. Rattray Taylor, *Sex in History* (London 1953) p. 189.

136. *Chronologie de la Régence et du Règne de Louis XV* (1718-1765) *ou Journal de Barbier, avocat au Parlement de Paris* (Paris 1885), 1st series, p. 468.

137. Roland Mousmer et Ernest Labrousse, *Le XVIII siècle* (*Histoire Générale des Civilisations*, Paris 1953), pp. 165-166.

138. J. Lucas-Dubreton, *Le Don Juan de Venise Casanova* (Paris 1955), p. 121.

139. John Langdon-Davies, *A Short History of Woman* (London 1938), p. 228.

140. Sophocles, *Oedipus Tyrannus*, 935-936.

141. Victor Margueritte, *Jean-Jacques et l'amour* (Paris 1926), p. 252.

142. *Bulletin de la Société de Médicine*, XIX, 2-3 (Paris, April 1925). Jean Guéhenno, *Jean Jacques* (Paris, 1948), Vol. 1, pp. 249 and 319-322.

143. Pierre de Vaissière, *Lettres d'aristocrates. La Révolution racontée par des correspondances privées* (Paris 1907), p. 166

144. Jules Bertaut, *Les Parisiens sous la Révolution* (Paris 1953), pp. 229-230.

145. Jean Robiquet, *La vie quotidienne au temps de la Révolution* (Paris 1950), p. 75.

146. August von Kotzebue, *Meine Flucht nach Paris im Winter 1790. Ausgewählte prosaische Schriften* (Vienna 1824), Vol. IX.

147. Jules Bertuat, *Madame Tallien* (Paris 1954), p. 44.

148. Henri D'Almeras, *Le Marquis de Sade—l'homme et l'écrivain* (Paris 1906), p. 222.

149. Jean Robiquet, *La vie quotidienne au temps de Napoléon* (Paris 1954), pp. 224-235.

150. Raoul Auernheimer, *Metternich—Staatsmann und Kavalier* (Vienna 1947), pp. 154-155.

151. Viktor Bibl, *Metternich* (4th ed., Leipzig and Vienna 1941), pp. 145-146.

152. Josef Schrank, *Die Prostitution in Wien in historischer, administrativer und hygienischer Beziehung* (Vienna 1886), Vol. 1, p. 242.

153. D. Melzner, *Findlinge* (Leipzig 1846).

154. Maurice Paléologue, *Talleyrand, Metternich, Chateaubriand* (Paris 1925).

155. Johann Peter Eckermann, *Gespräche mit Goethe* (2 April 1829).

156. Stendhal, *De l'amour* (Paris 1822).

157. George Sand, *Lélia* (Paris 1833), Vol. II, pp. 25-28.

158. André Maurois, *Lélia ou la vie de George Sand* (Paris 1952), p. 176.

159. Hans Ostwald, *Kultur-und Sittengeschichte Berlins* (2nd ed., Berlin n.d.), p. 197.

160. Heinrich Ed. Jacob, *Johann Strauss, Vater und Sohn* (Hamburg 1953), p. 25.

161. Ant. J. Gross-Hoffinger, *Die Schicksale der Frau und die Prostitution* (Leipzig 1847), pp. 136-143.

162. Ostwald, *Kultur-und Sittengeschichte Berlins*, p. 618.

163. S. E. Turner, *A History of Courtesy* (London 1954), pp. 164-166.

164. G. Rattray Taylor, *Sex in History* (London 1953), p. 216.

165. Pisanus Fraxi, *Index Librorum Prohibitorum* (London 1877).

166. R. S. Reade, *Registrum Librorum Eroticorum* (London 1936).

167. Simone-André Maurois, *Miss Howard* (Paris 1956).

168. Octave Aubry, *Napoléon III* (Paris 1929), p. 173.

169. Paul Guériot, *Napoléon III* (Paris 1933), Vol. I, p. 200.

170. Gustave Lanson, *Histoire de la Littérature française* (11th ed., Paris 1909), p. 1070.

171. Alexander Dumas *fils*, 'Le Demi-Monde', préface, in *Théâtre* (Paris 1909), Vol. II, pp. 12-14.

172. Emile de Senne, *Madame de Païva, étude de psychologie et d'histoire* (Paris 1911). Frédéric Loliée, *La Païva* (Paris 1920).

173. Victor Champier, 'L'Hôtel Païva'. *Extrait de la Revue des Arts Décoratifs* (Bordeaux 1902).

174. *An Essay on the Principle of Population* (London 1798).

175. Thomas Robert Malthus, *An Essay on the Principle of Population; or a View of its Past and Present Effects on Human Happiness* (London 1803), p. 505.

176. *Handwörterbuch der Staatswissenschaften* (3rd ed., Jena 1908), Vol. III, pp. 602-604.

177. Frank H. Hankins, 'Birth Control' in *Encyclopaedia of the Social Sciences* (New York 1948), Vol. I, pp. 559-565.

178. Charles Knowlton, *The Fruits of Philosophy, or the Private Companion of Young Married People* (first published anonymously, New York 1832; Boston 1833).

179. E.g., into German as *Elemente der Gesellschaftswissenschaft* (1872).

180. Francis Galton, *Hereditary genius, its law and consequences* (1869).

181. Gustav Schmoller, 'Einige Bemerkungen über die zunehmende Verschuldung des deutschen Grundbesitzes und die Möglichkeit, ihr entgegenzuwirken'. *Landwirschaftliche Jahrbücher* (Berlin 1882), Vol. XI, p. 622.

182. Richard Lewinsohn, 'Die Stellung der deutschen Sozialdemokratie zur Bevölkerungsfrage.' *Jahrbuch für Gesetzgebung, Verwaltung und Rechtspflege* (Berlin 1922), 46 Jahrg., Heft 3/4.

183. Alfred Grotjahn, *Soziale Pathologie* (Berlin 1923), p. 490.

184. C. Capellmann, *Fakultative Sterilität ohne Verletzung des Sittengesetzes* (14th thousand, Aachen 1897).

185. Koenig, 'Périodes et fertilité'. *Revue médicale de la Suisse romande*. 42 Jahrg. (1944), No. 2.

186. Anton J. Carlson and Victor Johnson, *The Machinery of the Body* (4th ed., Chicago 1953), pp. 548-549.

187. London, *La solution du problème de la population et la subsistance* (Paris 1842).

188. Weinhold, *Von der Übervölkerung in Mitteleuropa und deren Folgen auf die Staaten und ihre Zivilisation* (Halle 1827), pp. 32ff.

189. Gabriel Fallopius, *De morbo gallico liber absolutissimus*, Cap. 69: *De preservatione e carie gallica* (1564).

190. Alfred Grotjahn, *Geburtenrückgang und Geburtenregelung im Lichte der individuellen und sozialen Hygiene* (Berlin 1914).

191. *Die Wochen-Presse* (Vienna 1955), 10 Jahrg., No. 35ff. There are a number of other versions of the affair.

192. R. von Krafft-Ebing, *Psychopathia sexualis* (1886; 12th ed., Stuttgart 1902).

193. Sacher-Masoch, *Die Messalinen Wiens. Geschichten aus der guten Gesellschaft* (Leipzig 1873), pp. 126ff.

194. Carl Felix Schlichtegroll, *Sacher-Masoch und der Masochismus* (Dresden 1901), p. 114.

195. Antoine Adam, *Verlaine, l'homme et l'oeuvre* (Paris 1953), p. 24.

196. Holbrook Jackson, *The Eighteen Nineties* (Penguin Books, 1939), p. 72.

197. Vyvian Holland, *Son of Oscar Wilde* (London 1955).

198. Maximilian Harden, 'Fürst Eulenburg', in *Prozesse, Köpfe, Dritter Teil* (Berlin 1913), pp. 182-183.

199. Jacques Chastenet, *La Belle Époque* (Paris 1951), p. 51.

200. A. Blaschke, 'Verbreitung der Geschlechtskrankheiten', *Vortragsbericht, Medizinische Reform*, 1910, Nos. 4 and 5.

200a. Helene Bettelheim-Gabillon, *Die genialen Syphilitiker* (Berlin 1926).

201. Sir Alexander Fleming, *Penicillin. Its Practical Application* (London 1946).

202. Archiv des Kaiserlichen Gesundheitsamtes (Berlin 1905), Vol. 22, p. 527.

203. Erwin Marcusson, *Sozialhygiene* (Leipzig 1954), p. 169.

204. Sigmund Freud, 'Drei Abhandlungen zur Sexualtheorie', in *Gesammelte Schriften* (Leipzig-Vienna-Zürich 1924), Vol. V, p. 65.

205. Sigmund Freud, 'Der Untergang des Oedipuskomplexes' (1924), *Gesammelte Schriften* Vol. V, p. 429

206. Sigmund Freud, 'Vorlesungen zur Einführung in die Psychoanalyse' (1916-17). *Gesammelte Schriften*, Vol. VII, p. 14.

207. Alfred Adler, *Ueber den nervösen Charakter* (Wiesbaden 1912), p. 55.

208. Sigmund Freud, 'Jenseits des Lustprinzips'. *Gesammelte Schriften*, Vol. VI, p. 245.

209. Peter R. Hofstätter, *Einführung in die Tiefenpsychologie* (Vienna 1948), p. 8.

210. W. Weygandt und H. W. Gruhle, *Lehrbuch der Nerven-und Geisteskrankheiten* (2nd ed., Hall a.d.S. 1952).

211. Friedrich Engels, *Der Ursprung der Familie, des Privateigentums und des Staates* (1884; 5th ed., Berlin 1952), pp. 81-82.

212. Richard Lewinsohn, 'Frauenkrankheiten und Gebärtätigkeit' in A. Grotjahn, *Soziale Pathologie* (3rd ed., Berlin 1923), pp. 188-189.

212a. *Le Monde* (Paris), 16th May 1956.

213. 'Praxis', *Revue Suisse de médicine*, 1952, No. 47.

214. Paul Guilly, *L'Age critique* (Paris 1953), p. 6.

215. S. Topfer, 'Männliche Sexualhormone in der Frauenheilkunde', *Wiener Medizinische Wochenschrift* (1955), 105 Jahrg., Nos. 38-39.

216. Eugen Steinach, *Verjüngung durch experimentelle Neubelebung der alternden Pubertätsdrüsen* (Berlin 1920).

217. Sigmund Freud, *Gesammelte Schriften*, Vol. V, pp. 90-91.

218. Alfred C. Kinsey and others, *Sexual Behavior in the Human Male* (Philadelphia 1948); *Sexual Behavior in the Human Female* (Philadelphia 1953).

219. K. B. Davis, *Factors in the Sex Life of 2200 Women* (New York 1929).

220. C. Landis, A. T. Landis and M. M. Bolles, *Sex in Development* (New York 1950).

221. L. M. Terman, *Psychological Factors in Marital Happiness* (New York 1938), p. 321.

222. *Zeitschrift des Kgl. Sächsischen Landesamts.* 59 Jahrg. (1914), p. 173.

223. E. S. Turner, *A History of Courting* (London 1954), p. 262.

224. Statistical Abstract of the United States 1954 (Washington 1954), pp. 61, 63, 84.

225. United Nations, *Demographic Yearbook 1953* (New York), pp. 273-283.

226. Ludwig von Friedeburg, 'Die Umfrage in der Intimsphäre.' *Beiträge zur Sexualforschung* 1953, Heft 4. L. R. England, 'Little Kinsey, an Outline of Sex Attitude in Britain.' *Public Opinion Quarterly* 1949, No. 13. Helmut Schelsky, *Soziologie der Sexualität* (Hamburg 1955), pp. 54-55.

227. *Code civil*, Art. 312.

228. Bertrand Russell, *Marriage and Morals* (London 1929).

229. Ben B. Lindsey and Wainwright Evans, *The Companionate Marriage* (New York 1927).

230. Léon Blum, *Du Mariage* (Paris 1907).

231. A. M. Talvas, 'Le reclassement des victimes de la prostitution', *Revue de l'Action Populaire* (Paris), January 1956.

INDEX

ABELARD, PETER, 125-8
Abortion, 20, 45, 47, 84, 196, 378-81
Adler, Alfred, 367
Adultery. *See* Infidelity
Agrippina, Julia, 80-1
Alexander VI, Pope, 134, 173, 179
Amazons, 39-41
America. *See* United States of America
Anglicus, Gilbertus: *Compendium Medicinae*, 196
Animals, sex-life of, 1-2
Aquinas, Thomas, 196
Arabian Nights. *See:* Thousand and One Nights
Aretino, Pietro, 156-9, 185-6: *Dialogue between Magdalene and Julia*, 158; *Humanita di Cristo*, 158; *Ragionamenti*, 157-8; *Sonnetti lussuriosi*, 155-7, 158
Art: prehistoric, 3-4, 6, 7, 9; French, 300ff.; Greek, 42-3, 151; Renaissance, 44, 151-7, 185-8; Roman, 71-2
Artificial insemination, 108, 404-6
Augustus, Emperor, 76-9
Austria, 4-6, 147-8, 268ff., 284-5, 312-13, 330ff.

BABYLON, 19-20, 23-9
Bachofen, Johann Jakob, 12, 14: *Das Mutterrecht*, 12
Baer, Karl Ernst von, 202
Balzac, Honoré de: *Physiologie du Mariage*, 276-7
Barberina, La (*née* Barbara Campanini), 220
Baudelaire, Pierre Charles, 302
Beardsley, Aubrey, 339, 340
Beaumarchais, Pierre Augustus Caron de, 240-2: *Le Mariage de Figaro*, 241-2
Bebel, August, 14
Benedict VII, Pope, 124
Besant, Annie, 317-19
Belgium, 403
Bible, the, 30, 31, 32, 292
Birds, sex-life of, 2
Birth control. *See* Contraception
Boccaccio, Giovanni: *Decameron*, 162-3, 184, 188
Borgia, Cesare, 165, 166, 179
Lucrezia, 165-6
Rodrigo, 165
Botticelli, Sandro: *Venus Anadyomene*, 152-3
Boucher, François, 225
Brantôme, Pierre de Bourdeilles, Seigneur de: *Memoires et Vies des dames galantes*, 191

Bride inspection, 281ff.
Brothels: abolition of, 287, 403; in France, 287, 347, 403; in Greece, 55-7; in the Middle Ages, 145-50; Temple, 27; and Venereal diseases, 351; in Victorian England, 292. *See also* Prostitution
Byron, Lord, 273

CABARUS, THERESIA. *See: Notre Dame de Thermidor*
Calvin, Jean, 175
Carpeaux, Jean-Baptiste: *La Danse*, 301-2
Casanova, Giovanni, 228-9
Castrati, 216-17
Castration, 216-17, 384-5
Catherine I of Russia, 210-11
Catherine II of Russia, 213-14
Cave drawings, 9
Celibacy, 99-101, 122-5, 172ff., 184
Chastity girdles, 142-4
Children, sex-life of, 294, 358ff.
Chopin, Frédéric, 280-1
Christianity, 83ff., 122ff.
Circumcision, 31-3
Claudius, Emperor, 80-1
Cleopatra, 20-2
Clement VII, Pope, 156-7, 180, 181, 185
Clothes: and art, 186-7; *directoire*, 252-3; under Louis XV, 225-7; under Philip IV, 193-4; in prehistoric times, 7, 11; and prostitutes, 148, 150; in 1790, 242; and the theatre, 217; Victorian, 293
Contraception, 84-5, 314ff., 382-4, 408
Council of Trent, 182-4
Counter-Reformation, 172ff.
Cour d'Amour, 141
Courbet, Gustave, 300
Cranach, Lucas, the Elder, 154, 175
Credé, Karl, 354

DARWIN, CHARLES, 315-16: *Origin o Species*, 12, 315
d'Agoult, Countess Marie, 281, 304
Deborah, 31
Demi-monde, 302ff.
Depth-psychology, 368
Divorce: adultery and, 89-90, 245, 268 395, 401; in Babylon, 24-5; childlessness and, 24, 90-1, 177, 401, 402; Christian, 88ff., 177ff.; in England, 178ff., 289, 398, 402; in France, 245-6, 254, 267-8, 401, 402-3; grounds for, today, 395, 401ff.; Henry VIII and, 179-82; Lutheran, 177-8; Mohammed's law of, 106, 107; Mosaic law of, 87-8; in